LIBERALISM PROPER AND PROPER LIBERALISM

BY THE SAME AUTHOR

ÜBER FORMULIERUNG DER MENSCHENRECHTE (1956)

THE FEDERALIST: A CLASSIC ON FEDERALISM AND FREE GOVERNMENT (1960)

IN DEFENSE OF PROPERTY (1963)

MAGNA CARTA AND PROPERTY (1965)

AMERICA'S POLITICAL DILEMMA: FROM LIMITED TO UNLIMITED DEMOCRACY (1968)

YOUTH, UNIVERSITY, AND DEMOCRACY (1970)

BEDEUTUNGSWANDEL DER MENSCHENRECHTE (1972)

TWO CONCEPTS OF THE RULE OF LAW (1973)

DEUTSCHLAND, WO BIST DU? SUCHENDE GEDANKEN AUS WASHINGTON (1980)

KANT UND DER RECHTSSTAAT (1982)

ESSAYS ON THE AMERICAN CONSTITUTION: A COMMEMORATIVE VOLUME IN HONOR OF ALPHEUS T. MASON (ED.) (1964)

LIBERALISM PROPER AND PROPER LIBERALISM

GOTTFRIED DIETZE

The Johns Hopkins University Press
Baltimore and London

Printed in the United States of America

The Johns Hopkins University Press, Baltimore, Maryland 21218
The Johns Hopkins Press Ltd., London

Library of Congress Cataloging in Publication Data
Dietze, Gottfried.
Liberalism proper and proper liberalism.
Includes index.
1. Liberalism. 2. Democracy. I. Title.
JC571.D53 1985 320.5′12 84-7847
ISBN 0-8018-3220-9

FOR

ALPHEUS THOMAS MASON

McCORMICK PROFESSOR OF JURISPRUDENCE,

STUDENT OF FREE GOVERNMENT, TEACHER, FRIEND

CONTENTS

PREFACE

Liberalism proper is not necessarily proper liberalism. Given the uncertainties and numerous interpretations of freedom and propriety, the following reflections on liberty and order examine what classic liberals considered proper during the formative period of the liberal movement which in the New World witnessed the founding of the United States of America. This analysis should further our understanding of liberalism at a time when the use and abuse of liberal ideas, ideals, and ideologies and the complexities of liberal trends suggest that by virtue of its very open-endedness and open-mindedness, liberalism requires some limitation or direction from standards beyond itself, such as morality and propriety.

Heeding Burckhardt's warning of translations and Santayana's of subjectivity, I have tried to analyze systematically the thoughts of Montesquieu, Adam Smith, Kant, and Jefferson. What impressed me is their sense of balance. These advocates of freedom recognized the need for order and believed in free government under the rule of law as an ethical minimum. The analysis of their thoughts is complemented by an evaluation of modern liberal democracy, which to many people has become characterized by an Orwellian environment. Perhaps the measured liberalism of the men here examined, which on the whole was shared by America's Founding Fathers, can help to solve some of the problems of democratic liberalism.

Washington, 1984

LIBERALISM PROPER AND PROPER LIBERALISM

INTRODUCTION

Liberty without restriction—and only unqualified liberty is liberty unqualified—implies the ability to do good or evil.[1] Similarly, unqualified liberalism, or liberalism proper, can result in what is good or bad. Since evil has little appeal, liberals have ordinarily claimed to favor a proper liberalism, as distinguished from liberalism proper. The historical movement known as liberalism, conceived as a polemic against monarchical despotism, began with the Reformation and climaxed in the nineteenth century. Its representatives in different places and times have had different aims. We speak, for instance, of English, French, and German liberalism, of liberalism in the seventeenth century, in the eighteenth. However, they all usually maintained that they favored the proper kind of liberalism. This prompts the question as to what a proper liberalism is.

It has been assumed that liberalism according to law must be proper because law is an enforceable minimum of propriety. However, if law does not constitute a maximum of propriety, the liberalism it provides cannot be totally proper. In view of this, the present study, after remarks on liberalism and the rule of law, examines what Montesquieu, Smith, Kant, and Jefferson consid-

1. Friedrich Wilhelm Schelling's study on the nature of human freedom shows that freedom is the ability to do good and evil. "Philosophische Untersuchungen über das Wesen der menschlichen Freyheit und die damit zusammenhängenden Gegenstände," in *F. W. Schelling's philosophische Schriften* (Landshut, 1809), vol. 1. Schelling thus goes beyond the opinion of Descartes, who held that liberty exists so that good may be done.

ered a proper liberalism. If we find that they agree on certain salient principles, we might get closer to knowing what it is.

Representatives of the eighteenth century were chosen for a variety of reasons. In the period in which the movement known as liberalism has existed, that century occupies a central position. Liberalism can be said to have been advanced by Luther from a religious point of view and to have been given its first major defense with respect to politics by Locke. It reached its peak in the era that stretches from the Manchester School to the human rights declarations and legislations of our day. The eighteenth century is thus right in the middle between the centuries that prepared the advancement of liberalism and those that witnessed its general recognition. It may well reflect classic liberalism.

Marx, observing the Manchester School at close range, accused it of being excessive. Similar accusations have been made by the open enemies of liberalism ever since. However, liberalism today is also criticized by its friends for having become too permissive. Therefore, it seems to be advisable to be reminded of liberal thought prior to the time it developed into Manchester capitalism and into license. Liberal thought of the eighteenth century is likely to be more mature than that of preceding centuries because the authors representing it had the benefit of earlier discussions, notably the writings of Locke. Theories mature. Just as de Tocqueville's and Bryce's classics on American government came forth in the century after the founding of the United States and the writing of early theoretical defenses of American constitutionalism, there is a good probability that classic treatises on modern liberalism appeared after it was established in the Glorious Revolution and commented upon by the defender of that revolution.

Liberalism was described as the vital center, standing between national socialism and communism.[2] It could well be that the vital center of liberalism itself is that described by authors representing the century that is in the middle of the liberal era. Modern liberal scholars, whatever their differences of opinion may be, agreed on the importance of the eighteenth century. Becker, who during the New Deal considered liberalism the doctrine that rationalized the emancipation of the individual from class, corporate, or governmental restraint, wrote that it comes to us from the eighteenth century.[3] Writing after the New Deal and known for his antipathy to that program, Hayek considered himself a liberal in the sense of the eighteenth century and made the point that the word "liberal" appears for the first time in the writing of Adam Smith.[4]

The eighteenth century was one of transition and rich in that important aspect of liberalism—innovation. In *Reflections on History,* Jacob Burckhardt emphasized the creativity of crises. A period of transition is one of crisis. Certainly the old, being challenged, is in a critical state. But so is the new

2. Arthur M. Schlesinger, Jr., *The Vital Center* (Boston, 1949).
3. Carl L. Becker, *Everyman His Own Historian* (New York, 1935), 92.
4. F. A. Hayek, *The Constitution of Liberty* (Chicago, 1960), 408, 530.

because it is open to doubt whether it will succeed and last. And new ideas there were plenty in the eighteenth century.

In the English Revolution, the argument of the parliamentary party was similar to that used by the barons at Runnymede. The king was accused of acting in excess of the powers he had under traditional law. Significantly Sir Edward Coke, who told James I, the defender of the divine right of kings, that the king was ruled by the law, had revived Magna Carta. The Glorious Revolution reduced the possibility of arbitrary rules and regulations on the grounds of a customary law believed to reflect the laws of nature and of God. Basically, the English Revolution was a seventeenth-century version of the *diffidatio* of 1215. It merely defended constant and universal principles of the law. From that point of view, there was little revolutionary about it.

By contrast, Montesquieu considered law to be something relative, as is obvious from the first sentence of his major work. This idea was considered revolutionary and shocking. He seemed to be inclined to establish right by the fact, whereas previously one had been used to reconciling the facts of human experience with truths already revealed. The French aristocrat ushered in modern legislation, which was given additional stimulus by the American and French revolutions.

The liberalization of lawmaking was complemented by other liberalizations. Adam Smith suggested free enterprise. Thomas Jefferson helped to bring about the independence of the New World from the old. He favored a complete freedom from monarchy, as did the French revolutionaries. Rousseau suggested the transition from a contractual to an organic theory of the state, from the age of reason to that of romanticism, from traditional to modern education. His admirer Kant liberated philosophy from old fetters. In France, the *ancien régime* was abolished. It can be added that many another *ancien régime* was shed in the eighteenth century all over the occident. Concerned with the social sciences, with law, economics, government, and philosophy, the examples just given are especially relevant to the liberal movement.

Social innovations are risky. While there can be no progress without change, change does not necessarily bring about progress. Often, it makes things worse. One should never be too optimistic. The Lisbon earthquake in the middle of the eighteenth century, in the year Montesquieu died, brought home that idea. It did not seem to square with the heavenly city of the eighteenth century philosophers, characterized by a desire for change.[5] The beautiful capital of a country known for its tolerance, a center of the exploration of the globe, looking toward the Atlantic and America, lay in ruins that buried thousands. Many of those who believed in the inevitable advancement of the human race by virtue of human reason and human rights, despaired and saw in the natural disaster a punishment for the optimism of their age.

5. Carl L. Becker, *The Heavenly City of the Eighteenth-Century Philosophers* (New Haven, 1932).

The freeing of legislation from the law, of philosophy from metaphysics, the liberation of the businessman from restrictions of egoistic activities, of children from their educators, of the New World from the Old, could well amount to liberal intoxication. Liberalism could lead to license and even result in despotism. For instance, the transfer of power from a monarch to a legislature was defensible if monarchy was left intact as a symbol of authority, a reigning center attenuating liberal democratic disturbances. It could be dangerous once the monarchical form was discarded and replaced by formless pluralistic masses or, as Rousseau would have it, by a formidable general will which could turn out to be a veritable *forme diable.* Free enterprise could result in laissez faire, laissez passer, bringing about not only cut-throat competition and the unfair elimination of the honest competitor by the slick operator, but general license. Complemented by a liberated legislation and an abolition of educational restrictions, it could be an acceptance of the dictum, *chacun à son goût,* the egalitarian version of the monarchical *tel est Notre plaisir.* It could result in anarchy or, in case of acquiescence in the belief *la majorité à son goût,* in a majoritarian despotism more oppressive than the tyranny of the monarch in the age of absolutism who, after all, knew that he was outnumbered by the majority. Or, if a demagogic leader would sway the majority, laissez faire, laissez passer could bring about one man's rule of terror. One is prompted to ask where liberalism could lead to if human beings were not as good as Rousseau, reputed for his absolutist proclivities, thought; if freedom would not be used to do good, but to do good and evil or evil rather than good?[6]

Given these risks, the question arises whether the great liberal representatives of the century that stressed political science as a means of finding the right relationship between the right kind of freedom and the right kind of police, a century which was called one of morality,[7] provided for safeguards against liberal excesses. Montesquieu, Smith, Kant, and Jefferson, citizens of four nations, did. Considering positive law a mere ethical minimum changeable at the whim of legislators, they urged strong limitations upon human behavior not only through positive laws, but also through higher law and morals. Men of measure and not of *hubris,* they favored a sound balance between a responsible freedom of the individual and a responsible role of the government. They appreciated liberty, but opposed anarchy. They made it clear that human behavior ought to be restricted by law and morals, that government, while constituting a threat to freedom, is necessary for the well-being of society and the individuals composing it.

An analysis of the political thought of Montesquieu, Smith, Kant, and Jefferson will be followed by a last chapter showing that the ideas of these

6. Martin Heidegger, *Schellings Abhandlung über das Wesen der menschlichen Freiheit (1809)* (Tübingen, 1971), shows that Schelling's treatise deals for the better part with evil.

7. Carl Schmitt, "Das Zeitalter der Naturalisierungen und Entpolitisierungen" (1929), in *Der Begriff des Politischen* (Berlin, 1963), 80 ff.

authors are relevant to our time. Those who today emphasize the freedom of the individual from the government often tend to forget that the government has important functions to fulfill. Those promoting government action often tend to forget the dangers of big government. The followers of Montesquieu, Smith, Kant, and Jefferson are likely to believe in the golden mean of free government and for the sake of human rights will fight a police oppressing people and favor one helping mankind. The term "free government" was often used during the American Revolution.[8] The ideas behind it in a large measure derive from the political philosophy of John Locke. For the reasons stated, this study concentrates on liberal representatives of the eighteenth century and thus does not devote a separate chapter to that seminal thinker whose political thought has been amply and ably discussed in recent years elsewhere.[9] It has also been covered by my previous writing. Locke's importance for liberalism will, it is hoped, be evident throughout this work.

8. Cf. Gottfried Dietze, *The Federalist: A Classic on Federalism and Free Government* (Baltimore, 1960), esp. 69, 117–18, 148, 268.

9. Cf. John Dunn, *The Political Thought of John Locke* (Cambridge, 1969); J. W. Gough, *John Locke's Political Philosophy,* 2nd ed. (Oxford, 1973); Raymond Polin, *La politique morale de John Locke* (Paris, 1960); M. Seliger, *The Liberal Politics of John Locke* (London, 1968).

CHAPTER I

LIBERALISM AND THE RULE OF LAW

Liberalism

Liberalism can have a variety of meanings. It is related to liberty or freedom,[1] concepts that in their literal meaning include the freedom to be left alone by, to help, to hurt every thing, every person, and God. This wide freedom is possible only if human beings are with their kind. Otherwise, they cannot be left alone by and act for or against others. We thus deal here with the freedom of the individual in society.

Withdrawal within, or emigration from, a group is often due to the search for more freedom and demonstrates that freedom does not fully exist there. It hardly can do so because freedom has not yet been defined. Ever-growing

1. The words *freedom* and *liberty* will be used interchangeably in this study. Thirty years ago, I drew a distinction between them (*Über Formulierung der Menschenrechte* [Berlin, 1956], 47). My sojourn in the United States and the generally observed use of these terms made me tend to agree with Friedrich August Hayek, *The Constitution of Liberty* (Chicago, 1960), 421n1: "There does not seem to exist any accepted distinction in meaning between the words 'freedom' and 'liberty'." A distinction probably does exist, however, even though it may not be generally accepted. This is admitted by Hayek when he writes that he has a personal preference for freedom but that "it seems that 'liberty' lends itself less to abuse." Obviously, the interchangeable use of "freedom" and "liberty" is in a large measure a matter of convenience. This points to the probability that both terms will be interpreted and used by individuals as they see fit. The resulting great mass of definitions indicates the problem of whether or not freedom and liberty can be defined, leaving open the possibility of abuses or, since in the last analysis an abuse of liberty from a purely liberal point of view is not possible, of improper, unethical uses of liberty.

discoveries of new aspects of freedom, referred to as liberties,[2] as well as never-ending and seemingly vain attempts to discover what liberty as a general comprehensive concept is,[3] indicate that liberty defies definition, that freedom is by definition without bounds. As the opposite of restrictions of any type, liberty can range from the freedom from being hurt in the least to that of hurting others to the utmost. Liberty can be at the root of the best and the worst. It can exist *ad gloriam* and *ad nauseam*.

Restrictions of liberty from the Greek *isonomia* to modern categorical imperatives confirm liberty's basically unlimited nature. Intrinsically, freedom is what Kant called wild freedom. The philosopher thus clearly recognized the unlimited nature of freedom, although he stressed that the freedom under moral law was the true freedom. If liberty is taken at face value, then a restricted liberty is a contradiction in terms. Kant's contemporary, Patrick Henry, is reputed to have said "give me liberty, or give me death!" While these words, uttered when independence from England was being discussed, may have meant just that particular type of liberty, they may also oppose the truth of boundless liberty to death as the moment of truth, spoken as they were by a firebrand of the American Revolution. At any rate, they could well hover over

2. Cf. Georg Jellinek, *Die Erklärung der Menschen- und Bürgerrechte* (1895; 3rd ed., ed. Walter Jellinek, Leipzig, 1919); Dietze, *Über Formulierung der Menschenrechte,* esp. 36 ff.; Hayek, *Constitution of Liberty,* entitles the first chapter "Liberty and Liberties."

3. Immanuel Kant wrote: "Denn die Unerforschlichkeit der Idee der Freiheit schneidet aller positiven Darstellung den Weg ab." *Kritik der Urteilskraft* (1790; Königlich Preussische Akademie der Wissenschaften, ed., *Kant's Werke,* Berlin, 1907–12), 5:275. Abraham Lincoln stated: "The world has never had a good definition of the word liberty, and the American people, just now, are much in want of one. We all declare for liberty; but in using the same *word,* we do not all mean the same *thing.* With some the word liberty may mean for each man to do as he pleases with himself, and the product of his labor; while with others the same word may mean for some men to do as they please with other men, and the product of other men's labor. Here are two, not only different but incompatable [*sic*] things, called by the same name liberty. And it follows that each of the things is, by respective parties, called by two different and incompatable names—liberty and tyranny." Address at Sanitary Fair, Baltimore, Maryland, Apr. 18, 1864, in Roy P. Basler, ed., *The Collected Works of Abraham Lincoln* (New Brunswick, N.J., 1953), 7:301–2. If both emancipators and slaveowners maintain that they stand for liberty, liberty can mean about everything. The situation has not changed to this day, when we are literally inundated with different concepts of freedom. Hayek, *Constitution of Liberty,* 421n2, bewails the philosophers' curious definitions of freedom. Admitting "a very acute semantic analysis of the term 'freedom'" in Maurice Cranston, *Freedom: A New Analysis* (New York, 1953), he considers it of limited value. Cranston's book had a third edition in 1967. After old analyses of freedom, readers obviously appreciated his new analysis, perhaps considering the new the true, perhaps not asking whether the new deviated from the true. Comp. Carl L. Becker, *New Liberties for Old* (New Haven, 1941). Hayek, *Constitution of Liberty,* draws attention to "a more ambitious survey of the various meanings" of freedom in Mortimer Adler, *The Idea of Freedom: A Dialectical Examination of the Conceptions of Freedom* (New York, 1958), and "an even more comprehensive work by H. Ofstad, announced for publication by Oslo University Press." However, he does not assert that these authors succeed in defining freedom. In view of Hayek's admission that freedom so far has not been satisfactorily defined, his *Constitution of Liberty* is from the very outset meant to show his own evaluation of liberty.

America as a confession to freedom unlimited, as Barry Goldwater's statement that "extremism in the pursuit of liberty is no vice" shows. The reaction to this statement indicates that the danger resulting from unlimited liberty was recognized.[4] It does not change the fact that on its face, liberty can spawn, and even go beyond, good and evil.

Similarly, there seem to be no limits to liberal behavior. According to Webster's Dictionary, an archaic use of *liberal* is "free from restraint, unchecked, licentious."[5] This may well indicate the original meaning of *liberal.* The word does not imply any restrictions whatsoever. *Des Menschen Wille ist sein Himmelreich:* "Man feels like Heaven if he has his way." This saying could be considered the liberal credo. Under liberal doctrines man is his own boss, his own sovereign, free to be good, bad, beautiful, ugly, moral, immoral, egoistic, altruistic, loving, cruel, diligent, lazy, law-abiding, law-infringing, tolerant, intolerant.[6] He may act properly and improperly. It does not matter whether he gets away with it or not. What matters is that he has his way. *Il suffit qu'il veut.*

The liberal may ignore, negate, and destroy accepted values. When Max Weber favored value-free research he did so for the sake of finding the truth, a value he considered beyond doubt.[7] By contrast, liberals may liberally reject the truth, mocking Kant's assertion that lying is the worst of evils. In using freedom, the liberal may abuse it. One can take issue with the Roman belief that property rights include the *ius abutendi* by pointing out that the word *proprietas* implies a proper use of property. No inherent limitations can be found in the word *libertas.* The liberal is the negator and creator of values *par excellence.* In rejecting values, he does not necessarily act out of a desire for

4. Moses C. Tyler, *Patrick Henry* (Boston, 1898), 145, referring to Henry's speech of Mar. 23, 1775. The critical reaction to Goldwater's statement in his acceptance speech at the 1964 Republican Convention may have been because it was quoted without the words following, "moderation in the pursuit of justice is no virtue," indicative of Goldwater's recognition of the dangers of anarchy and the need for law and order, i.e., restrictions of unlimited freedom.

5. Paul Robert, *Dictionnaire alphabetique et analogique de la langue française* (Paris, 1963), defines *liberté* "(Au sens large) Etat de ce qui ne subit pas de contrainte—possibilité, pouvoir d'agir sans contrainte. V. License (vieilli)—prendre des libertés: ne pas se gêner en prendre à son aise, se montrer d'une familiarité inconveniente—irrévérence—Des libertés insolentes, offensantes—Prendre des libertés avec une femme." Nicolò Tommaseo/Bernardo Bellini, *Dizionario della lingua italiana* (Torino, 1929): *Liberale* is "Uomo che ama la libertà, que ne ha i sentimenti e i principii." According to the *Diccionario de la lengua española* (Real Academia Española, 19th ed. [Madrid, 1970]), *libertad* is "Facultad natural que tiene el hombre de obrar de una manera o de otra, y de no obrar, por lo que es responsable de sus actos—prerogartiva, privilegio, licencia—desenfrenada contravención a las leyes y buenas costumbres."

6. One is inclined to consider an intolerant liberal a contradiction in terms and liberals intolerant toward those who do not share their views, pseudo-liberals. On the other hand, if the liberal is free to be and to do everything he wishes, he must be free to be intolerant and to act in a way that appears intolerant to others. For tolerance is something subjective; there is no known objective standard of tolerance. If a liberal acts in a way that is considered intolerant by others, he need not think that he is intolerant. In its strict semantic meaning, liberalism permits the assertion and rejection of all values.

7. Max Weber, *Wissenschaft als Beruf* (Munich, 1919).

value-freeness, for the negation of a value often will be due to an assertion of another value, or countervalue. The liberal may be arbitrary, moody, and whimsical. Praised for doing something worthy, he may become spiteful and do the very opposite in order to invite criticism. The liberal may favor the worthless or the worthy. He may act under the principle of value-freeness or under that of value-appreciation. What he is doing can be *wertfrei, wertlos, wertvoll.*

Liberalistic is a higher, intensified dimension of liberal. Just as the national becomes intensified through the nationalist and nationalistic and the social through the socialist and socialistic, liberal becomes intensified by the liberalistic. The absence of a word *liberalist* suggests that what is liberal hardly can wait to become liberalistic, as if it wanted to outdo what is national and social. It shows that the liberal is less bridled than the national or the social: Whereas the road from the national to the nationalistic goes via the nationalist, and that from the social to the socialistic via the socialist, the road from the liberal goes straight to the liberalistic.

Liberalism may, but does not necessarily, indicate liberalistic force and perhaps aggressiveness in the way nationalism and socialism demonstrate aggression. Aiming at the exultation of a nation or a class, nationalism and socialism have specific forceful directions. By contrast, liberal exultations of freedom are not tied to particular directions and are not aggressive by definition. Nationalists and socialists march on straight, one-way roads. The liberal scene is like the confusion of a big square in which individuals and groups mill about as they please, free at any time to stand still and be left alone, to move and turn in any direction. Liberalism probably is the most permissive of "isms," for it can be anarchism. A great liberal's statement that anarchy is worse than despotism, does not alter this fact.[8]

It is its permissiveness that makes liberalism alluring. People may question the advisability of promoting a nation or a class; few will entertain doubts about promoting liberty. While liberalism can bring about the greatest negation of good and the greatest creation of evil, it will be cherished because it also can be at the beginning of the negation of the greatest evil and the creation of the greatest good. People often will claim their evil behavior to be good and cherish freedom because it entitles them to do evil. If an ideal grows with the improbability of becoming realized, then the ideal of liberalism, unlimited as it is, may be the greatest of ideals. Liberalism may be fraught with danger: the greater the ideal, the greater the appeal. What shines, blinds. Liberalism may be the most formidable incentive to do good as well as the seducer to commit evil, basic to the negation and creation of civilization.

As an ideal, liberalism is a singular concept. People may have different ideas on what it is and thus conceive of different liberal ideals. Their subjective

8. Wilhelm Röpke to Pierre F. Goodrich in a letter of Aug. 18, 1952: "Lord Acton certainly did not mean to deny that, if there is something worse than despotism, it is anarchy, i.e., the absence of power."

views do not alter the fact that objectively, there is just one ideal of liberalism. It is perhaps this comprehensive oneness that gives liberalism a strength and appeal approaching that of the one God.

Liberalism also can mean something real. As such, it constitutes a partial realization of the ideal, since an ideal, as long as it is not totally known, will always be larger than realizations of some of its aspects. It has, for instance, been said that liberalism here on earth is tantamount to laissez faire in the wide sense of Foigny,[9] as distinct from the narrower economic laissez faire. However, the term *laissez faire* rather than *allons faire* implies that it is permitted, even decreed, by the government. Actually, while laissez faire can benefit from governmental policy, it can, in the sense of *allons faire,* exist without governmental sanction. A liberal may act liberally simply because it pleases him, according to the principle *tel est mon plaisir.* He may claim prerogatives once reserved for absolute monarchs for he is a little king all by himself. Liberalism does not indicate a grant by some outside power. The liberal can act according to his heart's desire, with or without inhibitions, with or without a conscience. Just as he may fight opportunism wholeheartedly, the liberal may be highly opportunistic. The *Weltanschauung* of liberalism (I refrain from speaking of the religion of liberalism because liberalism implies the freedom to deny God even though it permits the fanaticism of religious zealots), can spawn proper and improper actions.[10]

While wide interpretations of real liberalism are possible, the term *liberalism* has been used in narrower senses. It has been applied to specific periods in the history of nations and civilizations and connected with concrete aspects of liberty under particular governments. However, the wider meaning of liberalism, plainly following from that term, must be kept in mind because it lurks in the background of all specific liberalisms.

Hobhouse dates the beginning of "Liberalism" from the protests against the authoritarian order of modern states during the era of absolutism. For Laski, European liberalism rose from the Reformation to the French Revolution. Ruggiero begins his history of European liberalism with a discussion of the eighteenth century.[11] The nineteenth century has been called the liberal

9. Gabriel de Foigny, *Les aventures de Jacques Sadeur dans la decouverte et le voiage de la terre Australe* (Paris, 1705). Cf. Geoffroy Atkinson, *The Extraordinary Voyage in French Literature before 1700* (New York, 1920); *Les relations de voyages du XVIIe siècle à l'évolution des idées* (Paris, 1924); Gilbert Chinard, *L'Amérique et la rêve exotique dans la littérature française au XVIIe et au VIIIe siècle* (Paris, 1913).

10. Rousseau is said to have assumed that in spite of impulse and spontaneity in the truly free individual who has thrown off the shackles of traditional civilization, action flows without interruption in a certain beneficial direction. See Claes G. Ryn, *Democracy and the Ethical Life* (Baton Rouge, La., 1978), 132.

11. L. T. Hobhouse, *Liberalism* (1911; Galaxy ed., New York, 1964), 14; Harold J. Laski, *The Rise of European Liberalism* (1936; Unwin Books ed., New York, 1962), 11; Guido de Ruggiero, *The History of European Liberalism,* trans. R. G. Collingwood (1927; Beacon ed., Boston, 1959). Cf. Cranston, *Freedom,* 47–48.

century, extended at times from the French Revolution to World War I. Some observers have said that the era of liberalism is over.[12] Others have maintained that we now live in the heyday of liberalism.[13] To ascertain the liberal era becomes even more difficult when different societies are said to have experienced liberalism at different times and their respective liberal periods are dated differently.[14]

Similarly, the essence of liberalism has been judged in a variety of ways. Speaking of "the ambiguity of liberalism," Cranston discusses English, French, German, and American liberalism,[15] pointing out their differences. Authors have even viewed liberalism within particular nations differently. Mason spoke of "liberal variations" in the United States, and such variations can be noticed in other societies.[16] In addition, writers have distinguished major types of liberalism: a liberalism emphasizing the freedom of the individual from the government, one stressing popular participation in government, a liberalism protected by customary law, one created by legislation.[17]

With all these interpretations, one is faced by a veritable labyrinth of liberalisms. This is not surprising. If, according to liberal doctrine, people can do as they please, certainly liberal authors are free to pick their kind of liber-

12. This opinion is prevalent among Marxists and fascists. Convinced that the liberal era is over, they no longer consider liberalism a serious competitor and compete with each other. The decline of liberalism has also been admitted by others. See, for instance, John H. Hallowell, *The Decline of Liberalism as an Ideology* (Berkeley, 1943). Joseph A. Schumpeter, *Capitalism, Socialism, and Democracy* (New York, 1942), considers the decline of that aspect of liberalism, capitalism, inevitable because it will destroy itself.

13. Ludwig Erhard's social market economy (*Soziale Marktwirtschaft*) for the Federal Republic of Germany, imitated by other nations, as well as decisions by the Supreme Court under Chief Justice Warren, bringing about modern permissiveness, are indications of this opinion. F. A. Hayek, *The Road to Serfdom* (Chicago, 1944, 1970), ends with the words: "The guiding principle that a policy of freedom for the individual is the only true progressive policy remains as true today as it was in the nineteenth century."

14. Laski, *Rise of European Liberalism,* 22, describes the great diversity of the liberal movement in various places and times. Ruggiero, *History of European Liberalism,* under the heading "English Liberalism" uses the following subtitles: "Radicalism," "The Economists," "Religious Development," "The Manchester School," "The Conservative Reaction," "The Development of Liberalism," "Crisis and Reconstruction," 93 ff. As to France, he distinguishes the liberalism of the Second Empire from that of the Third Republic, 196 ff.; the subtitles of his discussion of German liberalism are "Romanticism," "Hegel," "The Age of Frederic William IV," "The Juridical Conception of the State," "Social Liberalism," "Political Liberalism" (211 ff). Cranston, *Freedom,* 53 ff., 58 ff., 65 ff., 70 ff., also points to the various interpretations of liberalism in England, France, Germany, and the United States.

15. Cranston, *Freedom,* 45 ff.; Ruggiero, *History of European Liberalism,* 93 ff.

16. Alpheus T. Mason, *Free Government in the Making* (New York, 1949), chap. 16. The title of this book indicates the changing nature of free government. Cranston, *Freedom,* 77, writes that "the name 'liberal' has been . . . captured and exploited in the United States itself by people whose political views are at variance with what was once understood as liberalism, exploited, that is, by various sections of the ideological Left."

17. Cf. Georg Jellinek, *System der subjektiven öffentlichen Rechte* (Freiburg i. Br., 1892).

alism, and their opinions often will differ from those of their critics. According to Laski, "liberalism has been, in the last four centuries, the outstanding doctrine of Western Civilization." However, writing that his book on the rise of European liberalism is just a sketch, he adds: "The more I have worked at it, the more clearly I have come to understand how much more research is necessary, for example in the relation between law and economic development, or between the social composition of legislatures and their statutes, or again, between the idea of toleration and the economic effects of persecution, before any really full account of the liberal idea can be written."[18] Ever since these lines were written additional problems have arisen, complicating matters further. Small surprise that so far not even a complete understanding of liberalism as a historical reality has come about.

The great variety of interpretations raises the question of the proper kind of liberalism. Property has "proper" on its face and often has been used interchangeably with propriety. Liberalism cannot be considered proper by definition. Is there a distinction between liberalism proper and proper liberalism?

At its face value, liberalism permits acting as one sees fit. A concept without qualifications and references to values other than freedom, liberalism proper does not prescribe any kind of ethical behavior. Liberalism proper can be proper and improper, and because it permits freely desiring everything and acting accordingly, all liberal desires and actions must be in tune with it. It is another question whether these actions are proper from the point of view of propriety. No doubt many of their advocates thought they were. Although liberals can do what is improper as much as what is proper, they usually will prefer the latter. The success of liberal movements is in large measure due to the fact that they were believed to be proper. However, human evaluations of liberal actions, especially those interested, are based upon subjective judgments. The question is whether such actions can be considered proper from an objective point of view.

This difficult question can be answered with "perhaps" at best. If liberalism proper permits improper as well as proper behavior, manifestations of its specific aspects can be improper or proper. Although the propriety of liberalisms ought to be judged from their respective environments, environments do

18. Laski, *Rise of European Liberalism,* 5. Cranston, *Freedom,* 47–48, writes: "To write about liberalism in more than a domestic context one must write about *liberalisms.* Historians who have failed to acknowledge this have had inevitably to fall back, often without realizing what they were doing, on stipulative definition. The universal liberalism they have analysed is 'liberalism' as defined by them, not 'liberalism' as variously understood by other people." Cranston then proceeds to give examples that underscore this opinion.

not necessarily make liberal behavior proper. Such behavior, while in accordance with liberalism proper, is not always of propriety. Liberalism proper is not bound by values other than liberty. It may even be used to destroy freedom.[19] Concrete liberal movements, much as they may correspond to liberalism proper, may be interpreted differently from the point of view of propriety and subject to a variety of evaluations.

To the abundance of specific manifestations of liberalism proper is thus added one of opinions on whether these liberalisms are proper from the point of view of propriety. In order to find out what can make liberalism proper a proper liberalism, we look for proper restrictions upon liberalism. However, these restrictions must not curtail liberalism to the degree of endangering it. It must not be forgotten that liberalism as the opposite of restriction is basically without limitations. If liberalism is to exist, limiting it in accordance with propriety must be measureful so as not to jeopardize it. A proper liberalism is still a liberalism.

Liberalism can be made proper, but never be totally replaced by propriety. Much as liberalism may be at the root of proper achievements and contain strong elements and potentials of propriety, it does not equal propriety and does not necessarily imply proper action, just as propriety does not necessarily imply the progress characteristic of liberalism. Furthermore, replacing liberalism by propriety would not do much tangible good, since propriety without legal sanction is not enforceable. We look for less than the maximum of propriety to make liberalism proper at least to a certain degree a proper liberalism, making sure that it will not be reduced so much as to become jeopardized. We turn to what has been called an ethical minimum, the law.[20] Because of its propriety, the rule of law often has been invoked for the promotion of liberal movements. Therefore, it can probably insure a certain propriety of liberal behavior and aid in making liberalism proper a proper liberalism.

19. At first sight, the statement that liberalism may be used to destroy freedom sounds about as strange as Rousseau's assertion that man can be forced to be free, made in book 2, chap. 33, of the *Social Contract.* But an individual may use his freedom to destroy his life, liberty, and property. The Roman *ius abutendi* was a truly liberal right. Unrestricted freedom cannot only be used to hurt oneself, so that under the principle *volenti non fit iniuria* it does not really inflict an injustice. It also may be used to hurt others, as is indicated by cut-throat competition. If a legislature is not bound by constitutional provisions to protect the freedom of the individual, it is free to destroy that freedom by means of laws. This occurred in the Weimar Republic due to reservations in favor of the lawmaker (*Gesetzesvorbehalte*) in provisions protecting human rights. Having learned from that experience, the Bonn Basic Law binds the legislature, as well as the power amending the Basic Law, to honor these rights in articles 1, 19, 79. It also prohibits the abuse of constitutionally guaranteed rights in article 18.

20. Georg Jellinek, *Die sozialethische Bedeutung von Recht, Unrecht und Strafe,* 2nd ed. (Berlin, 1908), 45.

The Rule of Law

Rules have their exceptions and laws their gaps. In our human existence, we trust and doubt what rules and laws prescribe. The rule of law, considered an embodiment of clarity, is often shrouded in mystery. It can rule and fall, succeed and fail, at any time.

The rule of law has been discussed for ages, and yet we are still not sure about its exact meaning. As we have become captivated by its *vinculum iuris,* we have remained uncertain as to whether it is *vinculum* rather *ius,* or *ius* rather than *vinculum.* We wonder whether it promises freedom or constraint. The rule of law seems to be unknowable. This is hardly surprising in view of the fact that law itself has defied definition.[21] Much as we may approach the discovery of the rule of law, we seem to be unable to find out what it really is. The rule of law is a *vinculum iuris* not only because it constitutes restrictions upon human action, but also because of our uncertainty about what it should be, what it is, and what it will be. Confidence and doubt are the steady companions of the law. They are present before lawmaking and after, before adjudication and after, before the execution of the laws and after. While they are perhaps proof of the existence of an absolute justice which in our human frailty we can only surmise, our constant awareness of injustices often makes us not only confide in, but also cast doubt upon and despair of the law. The rule of law, credited

21. William Seagle, *The History of Law* (New York, 1946), begins his introduction with a quotation from Sheppard's Touchstone: "THE SUBJECT *matter of law is somewhat transcendent, and too high for ordinary capacities. . . .*" On page 4, he quotes various definitions of the law: Demosthenes: "That is law, which all men ought to obey for many reasons, and especially because every law is an invention and gift of the Gods, a resolution of wise men, a corrective of errors intentional and unintentional, a compact of the whole state, according to which all men who belong to the state ought to live." Cicero: "Law is the highest reason implanted in nature, which prescribes those things which ought to be done, and forbids the contrary." Hooker: "A Law is properly that which Reason in such sort defineth to be good that it must be done." Grotius: "A rule of moral action obliging to that which is right." Blackstone: "A rule of civil conduct prescribed by the supreme power in the state, commanding what is right, and prohibiting what is wrong." Jhering: "The sum of the rules of constraint which obtain in a state." Tolstoi: "Rules established by men who have control of organized power and which are enforced against the recalcitrant by the lash, prison, and even murder." In "More about the Nature of Law," in Max Radin ed., *Legal Essays in Tribute to C. K. McMurray* (Berkeley, 1935), 513, Dean Pound begins: "From the beginning the question, What is Law?—the problem of the nature of law—has been a battle ground of jurisprudence. More than one important book of jurisprudence is wholly occupied with this question. But in recent times there has been a growing impatience with it and disinclination to engage in the kind of argument which it involves. Bluntschli compared it to Pilate's question, 'What is truth?'; and many who propound it today, like Pilate, wait not for an answer." In view of all this, it is not surprising that jurists maintained that a definition of the law is impossible. See Thurman W. Arnold, *The Symbols of Government* (New Haven, 1935), 36; Jerome Frank, *Law and the Modern Mind* (New York, 1930), 42. Karl N. Llewellyn argues that a definition need be neither true nor false since it is simply a tool. "A Realistic Jurisprudence—The Next Step," *Columbia Law Review* 30 (1930): 431 ff. Cf. Seagle, *History of Law,* 5 ff. Seagle's chapter on administrative law starts under the subtitle "The Law Nobody Knows" (326).

with supplying certainty, also is a generator of doubt. This doubt is in no way decreased by the many varieties in which the rule of law can exist.

The rule of law can mean different things from a quantitative point of view. It can be the rule of the totality of all norms as well as that of any particular part of it, be it a smaller sum of laws or a legal code or any one of their particular provisions. For example, the rule of law in a given society can be the totality of all the laws of that society, be they the laws of nature, "higher,"[22] customary, codified, public, private, constitutional, or ordinary laws. It also can mean each one of these kinds of laws or any one of their various subdivisions, codes, or any one of their particular provisions. A rule of law can thus appear as a concrete order and a labyrinth of its composites.

It is hard to tell whether a plurality of norms led to a single concept of the rule of law, or whether the latter spawned the former. A supposition has been in favor of the first alternative in the case of customary law, and in favor of the second alternative in the case of codified law. However, as the experience of the *ius dicere* has shown, each one of a plurality of customs might have come into existence as much as a formalization of one generally accepted code of behavior, just as such a code might have come into being as an accumulation of various specific customs.[23] Similarly, codifiers probably were as much influenced by existing laws and customs as by the desire of creating new law. The work of legislative chambers and constitutional conventions bears testimony to this belief.

It has been asserted that the sum total of laws is superior to its components.[24] For instance, if we consider a constitution and discard the possibility of superior and inferior constitutional norms,[25] the question arises whether the constitution as a whole is more important than its particular provisions. The

22. Edward S. Corwin, "The 'Higher Law' Background of American Constitutional Law," *Harvard Law Review* 42 (1929):149 ff.

23. On law as a formative force, see Carl J. Friedrich, *Constitutional Government and Democracy,* rev. ed. (Boston, 1950), 15 ff. The question as to what came first, code or custom, will perhaps never be answered. Customs develop as a result of codes, just as codes are transmutations of customs into written norms. For a famous debate on the pros and cons of customary and codified law, see A. F. J. Thibaut, *Über die Nothwendigkeit eines allgemeinen bürgerlichen Rechts für Deutschland* (Heidelberg, 1814), and the answer by Friedrich Karl von Savigny, *Vom Beruf unserer Zeit für Gesetzgebung und Rechtswissenschaft* (Heidelberg, 1814), and "Stimmen für und wider neue Gesetzbücher," *Zeitschrift für geschichtliche Rechtswissenschaft,* 3, no. 1 (1816). Cf. Carl Schmitt, *Die Lage der europäischen Rechtswissenschaft* (Tübingen, 1950).

24. Lincoln felt he had the right to suspend the provision on habeas corpus of the U.S. Constitution in order to save the whole Constitution. "Are all the laws, *but one,* to go unexecuted, and the government itself go to pieces, lest that one be violated?" he asked in his special message to Congress of July 4, 1861. *Works,* 4:430. On Apr. 4, 1864, he wrote A. G. Hodges "that measures, otherwise unconstitutional, might become lawful, by becoming indispensable to the preservation of the constitution, through the preservation of the nation." *Works,* 7:281.

25. Cf. Dietze, "Unconstitutional Constitutional Norms? Constitutional Development in Postwar Germany," *Virginia Law Review* 42 (1956):1 ff.

same pertains to other kinds of law, showing additional difficulties of ascertaining the meaning of the rule of law. These difficulites are further increased by the fact that the rule of law can mean different things from the qualitative point of view.

It can be understood as the rule of the law of nature and anything contradicting it denounced as unnatural, false, and perverted. Every matter, plant, animal, and human being is under that rule. It determines everything and everybody, revealing itself in specific laws of nature, some of which have been discovered. The finding that there are exceptions may only prove the rule.[26] The closer we come to know the law of nature by discovering specific aspects, the more these exceptions may be those parts of the law of nature which the human mind had been unable to see. Our "mastery" of nature probably is based upon the knowledge of, and obedience to, certain laws of nature, just as demonstrations of the might of nature, such as accidents and disasters, may be due to our failure to know other laws of nature and to take precautions against them. The natural, not necessarily ascertainable, rule of law seems to be inevitable, inescapable.[27] On the surface, it appears to be value-free. Factors such as the condition of dead matter, the course of the planets, the fall of a stone, the growth and withering of plants, the life and death of animals and human beings all indicate nature's indifference to happiness and suffering. However, the law of nature may well be of value by giving people the desire and the capacity to formulate their own values, an important one of which, providing for peace and order among human beings, is the human rule of law.

Discerned by individuals, the human rule of law is subjective and relative. Different societies have different rules of law. In contrast to the one and probably unchangeable law of nature, there have existed various changing human rules of law revealing themselves in a variety of categories, such as administrative regulations, legislative statutes, customary law, and "higher" law, as proposed by men. Each one of these aspects of the human rule of law, may, but need not, approach "the law of nature and of nature's God."[28] This applies especially to natural and "higher" law, as distinguished from the law of nature. Natural law philosophers have maintained that natural law approaches the law of nature to a greater extent than other kinds of human law. However, the great variety of natural law philosophies brought forth by evaluating and often calculating men, and the admission that natural law has a changing

26. See Werner Heisenberg, *Wandlungen in den Grundlagen der Naturwissenschaften,* 9th ed. (Stuttgart, 1959); William C. Price and Seymour S. Chissick, eds., *The Uncertainty Principle and Foundations of Quantum Mechanics* (New York, 1977).

27. See Carl Bergbohm, *Jurisprudenz und Rechtswissenschaft* (Leipzig, 1892); Heinrich Rommen, *Die ewige Wiederkehr des Naturrechts,* 2nd ed. (Munich, 1947); Edgar Bodenheimer, *Jurisprudence,* rev. ed. (Cambridge, Mass., 1974), 134 ff.

28. On these words of the Declaration of Independence, see Carl L. Becker, *The Declaration of Independence* (New York, 1922), 23 ff.

content,[29] demonstrates the vainness of human attempts to completely discover the law of nature. If such different concepts as divine right, popular sovereignty, conservatism, liberalism, communism, fascism are defended on grounds of natural law, it becomes evident that natural law theories may stand on weak ground and do not necessarily constitute an ethical maximum. Yet, some of them may come close to the objective truth of the law of nature. But so may laws that are denounced by natural law philosophers, be they in the form of customary law, statute law, or administrative regulations. Although as we move from natural and customary law to statutes and administrative rules and regulations the risk of human arbitrariness increases. This takes us to the distinction between arbitrary and nonarbitrary human law.

The rule of law can derive from the arbitrary pleasure of rulers. *Quod principi placuit legis habet vigorem.* It can be the particular law that is made or interpreted or executed at any particular moment by those in power in a monarchy, aristocracy, or democracy. The government is not limited by any law and may act arbitrarily. It is the law. *La loi c'est moi.* This kind of rule of law can be more temporary than the existing government, for it need not last as long as that government which can change the law at its pleasure.

The arbitrary rule of law can be anything from a quantitative as well as qualitative point of view. It can be a maximum or minimum of rule with a maximum or minimum of law. It can be the worst or best rule of the worst or best law. The distinction between much and little, evil and good is irrelevant. All that matters is that some rule of law exists by virtue of the moment's rulers. Its purpose is often to secure the existence of the present government. It is designed to achieve the order necessary for such more or less temporary existence. Order is its value, and it is determined by the temporary values of the ruler. The fact that the *summum ius* may turn out to be the *summa iniuria* does not question the existence of the arbitrary rule of law, because concepts such as *ius* and *iniuria* do not necessarily enter into it. Rule simply means government, dominance, *imperium, dominium* as prescribed by the momentary ruler: Its "ruly" aspects disappears behind its "ruling" one. Law has the meaning of its French root, *loi* as distinguished from *droit.*[30] It is derived from *lex* which, as opposed to *ius,* is a law made by men at their momentary pleasure according to good or bad judgments and desires. By standards of justice, it may be right or wrong. The meaning of the rule of law in this sense is perhaps conveyed by the

29. Cf. Rudolf Stammler, *Die Lehre von dem richtigen Rechte* (Berlin, 1902), and *The Theory of Justice,* trans. Isaac Husik (New York, 1925).

30. It may be asked whether *law* derived from *loi,* as distinguished from *droit,* originally was viewed with contempt and later lost its bad connotation by the absorption of imported *loi* into English customs. The resilience of the common law vis-à-vis imported law is described in Roscoe Pound, *The Spirit of the Common Law* (Boston, 1921).

term *Herrschaft des Gesetzes, Herrschaft* being any kind of rule,[31] and *Gesetz,* as distinguished from *Recht,* being any kind of law set by men, right or wrong, and constantly subject to revision by them.

The arbitrary rule of law is thus a rule of those who momentarily hold power. Human as it is, it is not necessarily humane. It can be endowed with all the nobility of the human being, but can also be inflicted with human frailty. It may reflect the greatness and baseness, wisdom and folly, reason and passion of those who determine it. It may degenerate from the highest to the lowest or rise from the lowest to the highest in no time. The exit of one ruler and the arrival of another can bring about a complete turnover, as can any action of an incumbent ruler. The rule of law thus appears as a fleeting yet powerful force. It exists by virtue of the human will, an arbitrary will that may have all the attributes of a calm or tempest, of measure and *hybris.* It may be in or out of tune with the laws of nature. Depending upon the values injected into it by individuals, the arbitrary human rule of law may reflect the inevitability and certainty, the trueness and perfection of those laws. However, being independent of them, it may also be uncertain, false, imperfect, and filled with the questionable values of mortals. Its *vinculum iuris* may amount to *ius* rather than *vinculum* or to *vinculum* rather than *ius.* Experience has shown the latter to be more likely. As a consequence, the history of the arbitrary human rule of law is, on the whole, one of the ruthless making and enforcement of that rule. As those subject to arbitrary law tend to harbor doubts about it, those decreeing it tend to enforce it ruthlessly, as if they wanted to dispel doubts concerning its quality as *ius.*

It is not surprising that advocates of the arbitrary rule of law often favored absolute rulers, or were favored by them. Defenses of arbitrary rule have existed since antiquity, consider Kreon in Sophocles' *Antigone.* They can be found during the struggle for constitutional government, a struggle that turned around the question of whether the ruler ought to be under law. For James I, the true law of monarchies was one made by kings, and by kings alone. "The kings were the authors and makers of the Lawes, and not the Lawes of the kings," and "the Kings revealed will [is] in his law."[32] Half a century later, Hobbes wrote that there "is annexed to sovereignty, the whole power of

31. *Herrschaft* can mean a noble, dignified rule, with emphasis on the noble and dignified, in the sense of what a dignified man, a *Herr,* does, *schafft.* However, the word has increasingly lost the connotation of *noblesse. Grimms Wörterbuch* states under the word *Herrschaft* "Die erfolgte begriffliche Anlehnung des Wortes an *herr dominus,* die sich auch äusserlich in der seit dem 16. Jahrhundert allgemein gewordenen Schreibung *herrschaft* kundgibt, lässt den Accent der Bedeutung weniger auf Vornehmheit, als auf das Gebieten fallen." Perhaps *Herrschaft,* in distinction to *Regierung,* even has the meaning of emotional rather than rational rule. "'Die Frau soll herrschen und der Mann regieren, denn die Neigung herrscht und der Verstand regiert,' sagt Kang."

32. *The True Law of Free Monarchies* (written in 1598), "Speech in the Star Chamber," June 20, 1616, in *The Political Works of James I,* ed. Charles H. McIlwain (New York, 1918, 1965), 62 ff., 333 ff.

prescribing the rules, whereby every man may know what goods he may enjoy, and what actions he may do. . . . These rules of propriety, or *meum* and *tuum*, and of *good, evil, lawful,* and *unlawful* in the actions of subjects, are the civil laws. . . ." He considered it an "error" to maintain "that in a well-ordered commonwealth, not men should govern, but the laws."[33] His contemporary Filmer put it more bluntly, stating that "every power of making Laws must be Arbitrary; for to make a Law according to Law, is *contradictio in adjecto.*"[34] Without doubt the rule of law was one of men; it could be any rule of any law. Law was nothing but a species of command that could have any content and could be addressed to any particular individual or all the subjects, just as the sovereign saw fit.[35]

In the nineteenth century, John Austin, whose affinity to Hobbes has often been stressed and who has been considered the founder of legal positivism, wrote: "Every positive law or every law simply and strictly so called, is set by a sovereign person, or a sovereign body of persons, to a member or members of the independent political society wherein that person or body is sovereign or supreme."[36] The sovereign is not restricted by any legal limitations, whether imposed by higher principles or by his own laws. Law is separated from ethics and not oriented toward higher justice. It is "a rule laid down for the guidance of an intelligent being by an intelligent being having power over him." It is a "command,"[37] the command of the sovereign. That command may be as unruly and unfair as can be. According to Austin, this would not affect the quality of law as law: the most despotic rule of law would still be a rule of law.

The latter point was made explicit by the founder of the Pure Theory of Law, Hans Kelsen. The *Rechtsstaat* is for him a state of law not because the state is under law, but because it sets law. It exists irrespective of the arbitrariness of its content and exercise. We are reminded of the writings of the defenders of royal absolutism when we read in Kelsen's discussion of monarchy: "Entirely senseless is the assertion that under despotism there exists no

33. Thomas Hobbes, *Leviathan,* ed. Michael Oakshott (Oxford, 1960), 117, 448.

34. Robert Filmer, *The Anarchy of a Limited or Mixed Monarchy* (1648), preface.

35. Cf. statements such as *tel est Notre plaisir, l'Etat c'est moi, Honi soit qui mal y pense: Dieu et mon droit.*

36. John Austin, *Lectures on Jurisprudence,* ed. Robert Campbell, 5th ed. (London, 1885), 1:84. He continues: "Or (changing the phrase) it is set by a monarch, or sovereign number, to a person or persons in a state of subjection to its author." On page 172, Austin writes: "The *science of jurisprudence* . . . is concerned with positive laws, or with laws strictly so called, as considered without regard to their goodness or badness."

37. Ibid., 86. On page 178, we read: "Laws properly so called are a species of *commands.* But, being a command, every law properly so called flows from a *determinate* source, or emanates from a *determinate* author . . . whenever a *command* is expressed or intimated, one party signifies a wish that another shall do or forbear: and the latter is obnoxious to an evil which the former intends to inflict in case the wish be disregarded. . . . Every sanction properly so called is an eventual evil *annexed to a command.* . . . Every duty properly so called supposes a *command* by which it is created. . . . And duty properly so called is obnoxiousness to evils of the kind."

order of law (*Rechtsordnung*), but only the arbitrary government of the despot."[38] To Kelsen, the rule of law in a democracy may be as despotic as that in a monarchy without the least jeopardy to its quality as a rule of law. There is no such thing as a wrong rule of law: "A wrong of the state must under all circumstances be a contradiction in terms."[39] The similarity of this statement made by one who believed in social democracy, to that made by Filmer, who advocated absolute hereditary monarchy, is striking yet not surprising. Opinions that the power of making laws must be arbitrary and that to make a law according to law is a contradiction in terms, fit in well with the idea that laws made by a sovereign, arbitrary as they may be, cannot be wrong.

Since the adherents of the arbitrary rule of law look at that rule merely from a formal point of view, they can afford to liberally confess to the greatest variety of values. They can believe in good or bad laws, in monarchical or popular government, and so on. Whatever their beliefs, the arbitrary rule of law permits the accommodation of all their claims. That rule simply constitutes the temporary legal order. Under it, the dignity of a human being can be as irrelevant as the dignity of an animal or of matter probably explaining why the arbitrary concept of the rule of law usually aided regimes that disregarded human dignity. The *vinculum iuris* degenerated into a *vinculum tyrannidis*. The spirit of the laws which could be something noble, by being deprived of its nobility, became something like Montesquieu's "Mr. Law." Like Rousseau's Legislator, it could be as despotic in a multitude as in the person of one.

Aside from an arbitrary rule of men, there has been a human rule of law designed to prevent arbitrary government. Kreon's concept of the rule of law was challenged by Antigone. Hobbes denounced Aristotle's concept of the rule of law. Austin and Kelsen reacted to nonarbitrary concepts of the rule of law. The fact that advocates of the arbitrary rule of men have taken issue with a rule of law as distinguished from that of men, indicates the existence of a nonarbitrary rule of law.[40]

38. Hans Kelsen, *Allgemeine Staatslehre* (Berlin, 1925), 335–36.

39. Hans Kelsen, *Hauptprobleme der Staatsrechtslehre* (Vienna, 1923), 249. It is recognized that Kelsen made this statement from a merely logical point of view as a representative of the positivist Pure Theory of Law. Nevertheless, the statement was dangerous in so far as, on the face of it, it sanctioned the worst and most oppressive laws.

40. This was even expressed by Rudolf von Jhering, *Law as a Means to an End,* trans. I. Husik (Boston, 1913), 315: "Exclusive domination of the law is synonymous with the resignation, on the part of society, of the free use of its hands. Society would give herself up with bound hands to rigid necessity, standing helpless in the presence of all circumstances and requirements of life which were not provided for in the law, or for which the latter was found to be inadequate. We derive from this maxim that the State must not limit its own power of spontaneous self-activity by law any more than is absolutely necessary—rather too little in this direction than too much. It is a wrong belief that the interest of the security of right and of political freedom requires the greatest possible limitation of the government by the law. This is based upon the strange notion that force is an evil which must be combated to the utmost. But in reality it is a good, in which, however, as in every

Ideas on the nonarbitrary human rule of law have been advanced from early times in different civilizations under different circumstances in different ways. Whereas in these ideas the rule of law is distinguished from that of men, the meanings attributed to it are of a great variety. It can be above rulers and limit them: *Non sub homine sed sub (deo et) lege.*[41] It can be the mass of law accumulated over the ages in order to restrain those in power. It puts obligations upon the government, be it monarchic, aristocratic, or democratic emphasizing that those in power are limited by law and cannot be arbitrary. Under the traditional rule of law, the government is the servant of the law, even though not necessarily its first servant, as Frederick the Great would have it. The rule of law usually will have existed before a particular government came into being and will survive such a government.

Although it precludes the arbitrariness of momentary rulers, the nonarbitrary rule of law in many respects is similar to its arbitrary counterpart. It can be anything from a quantitative and qualitative point of view. It can be a maximum or minimum of rule with a maximum or minimum of law. It can be the worst or best rule of the worst or best law. The distinction between much and little, evil and good is irrelevant. All that matters is that some rule of law exists that constrains the government. The nonarbitrary rule of law secures society from governments through an order determined by the more or less lasting values of past and present generations. The fact that the *summum ius* may turn out to be a *summa iniuria* does not question the existence of the nonarbitrary rule of law because concepts such as *ius* and *iniuria* do not necessarily enter into it. *Rule* means government, dominance, *imperium, dominium* only insofar as it is one of a law to which both rulers and ruled owe obedience, a law that has come into existence in the past as well as the present according to men's good or bad judgments, a law in which "ruling" aspects disappear behind "ruly" ones. By standards of justice, that law may be right or wrong. The meaning of the rule of law in this sense is perhaps conveyed by the German term *Herrschaft des Rechts,* if we understand *Herrschaft* to mean a rule that is not arbitrary and under *Recht,* what has come about not only by the whim of a momentary government, but by the sanction of the ages.

Although made by men, the nonarbitrary rule of law prevents a sheer rule of those in power. This does not necessarily make it humane. It is, after all, a rule of law made by human beings. It can be endowed with all the nobility of humanity, but also be inflicted with all its frailty. It may reflect the greatness

---

good, it is necessary, in order to make possible its wholesome use, to take the possibility of its abuse into the bargain." With respect to communism, cf. Boris Mirkine-Guetzéwitch, *Die rechtstheoretischen Grundlagen des Sowjetstaates* (Leipzig and Vienna, 1929), 117. As to Italy, see "Quelques aspects de la crise du droit public an Italie," *Revue internationale de la théorie du droit* 6 (1931–32):2 ff. For Germany, cf. Carl Schmitt, "Was bedeutet der Streit um den 'Rechtsstaat'?" *Zeitschrift für die gesamte Staatswissenschaft* 95 (1935):189 ff.; "Der Führer schützt das Recht," *Deutsche Juristen-Zeitung* 39 (1934):945 ff.

41. Henry Bracton, *De legibus et consuetudinibus angliae,* folio 5.

and baseness, wisdom and folly, reason and passion, of those who have determined it in past and present. It may have degenerated from the highest to the lowest or risen from the lowest to the highest in the course of time. Neither the exit of one ruler, the arrival of another, nor the action of any incumbent ruler is supposed to bring about its complete turnover. The nonarbitrary rule of law thus appears as a powerful, not fleeting phenomenon which exists by virtue of the human will in past and present, a will that may have all the attributes of calm or tempest, measure and *hubris*. It may be in or out of tune with the law of nature. Depending upon the values injected into it by men in times past and present, the nonarbitrary rule of law may reflect the inevitability and certainty, the trueness and perfection of the law of nature. However, being as independent of that law as that law is independent of men, it may also be evitable, uncertain, false, imperfect, and filled with the questionable values of mortals. Its *vinculum iuris* may amount to *ius* rather than *vinculum,* and vice versa.

The history of the nonarbitrary rule of law on the whole is one that demonstrates humanity's love of freedom and justice. As "rule of law," it has been distinguished from its arbitrary counterpart, referred to as the "rule of men." In the following, the phrase "rule of law" will be used in the sense of the nonarbitrary rule of law.

The rule of law has been characteristic of Western civilization.[42] In

42. The importance of law in the doctrines of Han Fei Tsŭ and other legalists in ancient China is discussed in Fung Yu-Lan, *A History of Chinese Philosophy,* trans. Derk Bodde (Peiping, 1937; Princeton, 1952). Quoting from the Kuan-tsû, the author writes: "The intelligent ruler unifies measures and weights, sets up different standards, and steadfastly maintains them. Therefore his decrees are promulgated and the people follow them. Laws are the models for the empire and the representative standards for all affairs. . . . Therefore the government of the intelligent ruler carries out punishments according to the law. Hence when crimes are punished according to law, the people will go to their death, without resentment, and when meritorious deeds are measured according to law, the people will accept their rewards without being under a sense of obligation. This is the merit of achievement by means of law. Hence the chapter, 'The Meaning of Laws' (chap. 46), says: 'When a state is governed by law, things will simply be done in their regular course.'

"The intelligent ruler bases his regulations on laws and standards, and therefore his multitude of ministers govern squarely and uprightly, without daring to be wicked. The people know that the ruler conducts affairs according to law, and so when the officials have law for what they enforce, the people obey them, and when they lack law, the people stop (obeying them). By means of law the people can check the officials, and superiors can conduct business together. Therefore false and deceiving men do not gain the opportunity of deceiving their superiors, jealous men have no chance to use their destructive minds; flatterers are unable to display their wiles; and even a thousand *li* away no one dares to usurp or to commit evil. Therefore the chapter, 'The Meaning of Laws,' says: 'When there are regulations based on laws and standards, there cannot be any craftiness based on deception'." (1:321).

Whether this rule of law implies that the ruler himself is under law is dubious. Cf. 312: "The great political tendency of the time was a movement from feudal rule toward a government by rulers possessing absolute power; from government by customary morality (*li*), and by individuals, to government by law." See, however, chap. 27 of the *Han-fei-tsŭ:* "Disregarding laws and methods (*shu*), and relying upon his mind for government, even Yao could not put one state in order" (321).

Greece, Solon is credited with having said that the best government was where the subjects obeyed their prince and the prince, the laws.[43] *Isonomia,* implying the rule of law, was contrasted to the arbitrary rule of tyrants. With the advent of democracy, it became distinguished from men's arbitrary rule in a democracy. Herodotus preferred *isonomia* to *demokratia,* and Plato contrasts the two.[44] By the end of the fourth century it was stressed that "in a democracy the laws should be masters."[45] Aristotle said that the law ought to be supreme, that "it is more proper that the law should govern than any of the citizens." Rulers "should be appointed only guardians and servants of the law," and "the laws should be the rulers." He condemned a government in which "the people govern and not the law," in which "everything is determined by majority vote and not by law."[46]

In Rome, the idea of the rule of law can be recognized in the Twelve Tables, which prohibited the making of statutes "contrary to the law."[47] Later, Livy spoke to the "empire of laws more mighty than that of men" (*imperia legum potentiora quam hominum*).[48] Cicero wanted legislation to be governed by law, the *leges legum.* Believing in a true law, he stressed the "sacred obligation not to attempt to legislate in contradiction to this law; nor may it be derogated from nor abrogated. Indeed by neither the Senate nor the people can we be released from this law."[49] This suggestion was generally followed by the "Roman practice to incorporate in statutes a saving clause to the effect that it was no purpose of the enactment to abrogate what was sacrosanct or *jus.*"[50] Cicero left no doubt that the judges were bound by true law and were nothing but the mouth of that law. Both Seneca and Tacitus, much as they differed in their general points of view, believed in a rule of law that was above rulers. The Justinian Code mentions the duty of the emperor to acknowledge that he was bound by law.[51]

The idea of a rule of law was also evident in the Middle Ages. The Church fathers maintained that emperors were under law.[52] Chlotar II issued an edict

43. See Hayek, *Constitution of Liberty,* 164–165, esp. 460n19.

44. Herodotus considered isonomy rather than democracy the "most beautiful of all names of a political order." *Histories,* iii. 80; cf. also iii. 142 and v. 37; Plato, *Republic,* viii. 557 bc, 559 d, 561 e.

45. Hyperides, *In Defence of Euxenippus,* xxi. 5, in J. O. Burtt, ed., *Minor Attic Orators* (Loeb Classical Library), 2:468.

46. Aristotle, *Politics,* 1287 a, 1292 a, as quoted by Hayek, *Constitution of Liberty,* 165, from the translation by W. Ellis in the Everyman edition.

47. See S. P. Scott, ed., *The Civil Law* (Cincinnati, 1932), 1:73.

48. Titus Livius, *Ab urbe condita,* 2, 1.1.

49. Quoted in Corwin, " 'Higher Law' Background," 157. The reference to *leges legum* can be found on 160.

50. Ibid., 159, with reference to Brissonius (Barnabé Brisson), *De formulis et solennibus populi Romani Verbis* (Leipzig, 1754).

51. See Corwin, " 'Higher Law' Background," 159 ff.

52. R. W. and A. J. Carlyle, *A History of Mediaeval Political Theory in the West* (New York, n.d.), 1:163 f.

binding the king's *missi* to folk law.[53] The rule of law was recognized in Aragon.[54] In the tenth century Emperor Conrad II decreed that "no man shall be deprived of his fief, . . . but by the laws of the Empire."[55] John of Salisbury took issue with the doctrine that the ruler is *legibus solutus,* for "he may not lawfully have any will of his own apart from that which the law or equity enjoins." He distinguished "a tyrant" as "one who oppressed the people by rulership based upon force" from "a prince" as "one who rules in accordance with the laws." For him, the very title *rex* is derived from doing what is right (*recte*), that is, in accordance with law.[56] Charlemagne's grandsons announced at Mersen: "We will not condemn or dishonor or oppress anyone contrary to the law and to justice."[57] In Magna Carta, which stated what the king could not do under the law of the land, John acknowledged the supremacy of the law.[58] The same was done seven years later, upon request from the barons of Hungary, by Andrew II in the *Bulla Aurea,* or Golden Bull. The rule of law was recognized by Bracton, the outstanding authority on English law during the thirteenth century.[59] It was also respected in the practice of the English courts and "through the old cases runs a red thread of 'fundamental law' which neither the king nor his Parliament can touch."[60] Similar theories and practices based upon the acknowledgment of the rule of law existed on the continent.[61]

Sir Edward Coke, who has been considered "constitutionally a medievalist rather than a modern,"[62] played an important role in the recognition of the rule of law at the beginning of the modern age. An admirer of Magna Carta, he revived the awareness of the significance of that document. His belief in the rule of law is evident in several stages of his career. It was demonstrated in Dr. Bonhams's case when he decided that "the common law will controul acts of parliament, and sometimes adjudge them to be utterly void."[63] He was backed in this attitude by public opinion. In the same year the Petition of Grievances, a

53. R. Schroeder and E. Künssberg, *Lehrbuch der deutschen Rechtsgeschichte,* 7th ed. (Berlin, 1932), 712.

54. William S. Holdsworth, *A History of English Law,* 3rd ed. (London, 1945, 1966), 4:168.

55. Seagle, *History of Law,* 224.

56. *The Statesman's Book of John of Salisbury,* ed. John Dickinson (1927, New York, 1963), 7, 335. On 335, we also read: "The prince fights for the laws and the liberty of the people; the tyrant thinks nothing done unless he brings the laws to nought and reduces the people to slavery."

57. See John Dickinson, *Administrative Justice and the Supremacy of Law in the United States* (Cambridge, Mass., 1927), 80.

58. Clause 39. Comp. Dietze, *Magna Carta and Property* (Charlottesville, 1965), 38 ff.

59. Henry Bracton, *De legibus et consuetudinibus angliae* (London, 1569).

60. Dickinson, *Administrative Justice,* 81.

61. Otto von Gierke, *Political Theories of the Middle Ages,* trans. Frederic W. Maitland (1900; Cambridge, Mass., 1922), 75–76, 85; *Johannes Althusius,* 2nd ed. (Breslau, 1902), 142, 264 ff.

62. Charles H. McIlwain, *Constitutionalism Ancient and Modern* (Ithaca, N.Y., 1940), 89.

63. Quoted in Seagle, *History of Law,* 216. Cf. T. F. T. Plucknett, "Bonham's Case and Judicial Review," *Harvard Law Review* 40 (1926):30 ff.; Louis Boudin, "Lord Coke and the American Doctrine of Judicial Power," *New York University Law Review* 6 (1928–29):223 ff.

plea of the House of Commons provoked by royal regulations, stated that among the rights of Englishmen "there is none which they have accounted more dear and precious than this, to be guided and governed by the certain rule of law, . . . and not by any uncertain and arbitrary form of government."[64] In the following decade, Coke asserted the superiority of the rule of law over that of men when he countered James's argument that the king controls the law, maintaining that the king was controlled by the law.[65] During the discussion occasioned by the Statute of Monopolies of 1624, he stressed that Magna Carta as a document embodying the rule of law was as valid in his time as it had been in 1215. "Magna Carta," he said, "is such a Fellow, that he will have no sovereign."[66] For Coke, the rule of law was above that of one man, such as the king. The abolition in 1641 of the Star Chamber, "a court of politicians enforcing a policy, not a court of judges administering the law,"[67] was symbolic for the victory of the rule of law over the king. Pamphlets of the period stressed that the law should be king: *Lex, Rex.*[68]

The sovereignty of the law was not only stressed vis-à-vis the rule of one, but also vis-à-vis that of many. This idea was advanced by royalists and Roundheads. "They had no intention of substituting for a king *legibus solutus* a Parliament equally *legibus solutum.*"[69] Much as he was a champion of parliamentary power, Coke himself emphasized that Parliament ought to be under the rule of law, warning them "to leave all causes to be measured by the golden and straight mete-wand of the law, and not to the incertain and crooked cord of discretion."[70] Cromwell agreed with him, denouncing the drift during the

64. Great Britain, Public Record Office, *Calendar of State Papers,* Domestic Series, July 7, 1610.

65. See Pound, *Spirit of the Common Law;* Seagle, *History of Law,* 214 ff.

66. Charles H. McIlwain, *The High Court of Parliament and its Supremacy: An Historical Essay on the Boundaries between Legislation and Adjudication in England* (New Haven, 1910), 83. In a Proeme to *The Second Part of the Institutes of the Laws of England* (London, 1809), we read: "The highest and most binding laws are the statutes which are established by parliament; and by authority of that highest court it is enacted (only to shew their tender care of *Magna Charta,* and *Charta de Foresta*) that if any statute be made contrary to the great charter, or the charter of the forest, that shall be holden for none: by which words all former statutes made against either of those charters are now repealed."

67. Frederic W. Maitland, *The Constitutional History of England* (Cambridge, 1908, 1961), 263.

68. [Samuel Rutherford], *Lex, Rex: The Law and the Prince* (London, 1644).

69. Hugh H. L. Bellot, "The Rule of Law," *Quarterly Review* 246 (1926):346. Charles I told his subjects: "For the People. And truly I desire their Liberty and Freedom, as much as any Body whomsoever; but I must tell you, That their Liberty and their Freedom, consists in having of Government; those Laws, by which their Life and their Goods, may be most their own. It is not for having share in Government (Sir) that is nothing pertaining to them. A Subject and a Soveraign, are clean different things; and therefore, untill they do that, I mean, That you do put the People in that Liberty as I say, certainly they will never enjoy themselves." *Speech Made upon the Scaffold at Whitehall-Gate, immediately before his Execution* on Jan. 30, 1649 (London, 1649), 9–10.

70. Sir Edward Coke, *The Fourth Part of the Institutes of the Laws of England* (London, 1809), 41.

Long Parliament toward arbitrariness and away from the rule of law. His *Instrument of Government* of 1653 was designed to secure that rule.[71] Cromwell said in 1654: "In every government there must be somewhat fundamental . . . , somewhat like a *Magna Charta,* that should be standing and be unalterable. . . . Of what assurance is a *Law* . . . if it lie in one or the same Legislature to *un*law it again?[72] Two years later, James Harrington published *Oceana* describing a utopia meant to be Cromwell's England. In that book occurs the famous passage that "an Art whereby a Civil Society of men is instituted and preserved upon the foundation of common right or interest, or (to follow *Aristotle* and *Livy*) it is the Empire of Lawes and not of Men."[73] Shortly before the Restoration, the principle of the government of laws as distinguished from that of Parliament was expressed in a *Declaration of Parliament Assembled at Westminster,* according to which "the people should be governed by the laws, and that justice be administered by such only as are accountable for mal-administration."[74]

With the Glorious Revolution, the recognition of the rule of law within the framework of English government became official. John Locke, the major defender of that revolution, left no doubt about the value of that rule. Opposed to the proposition that the individual is "subject to the inconstant, uncertain, unknown, arbitrary will of another man," he favored "a standing rule to live by, common to every one of that society, and made by the legislative power erected in it." Even the legislature "cannot assume to itself a power to rule by extemporary arbitrary decrees, but is bound to dispense justice and decide the rights of the subject by promulgated standing law." It has no absolute arbitrary power.[75] Similarly, executive and judicial officials are bound by the law.[76]

71. See Friedrich, *Constitutional Government and Democracy,* 133–134. Cromwell's skepticism toward legislative omnipotence was seen by Jean Louis de Lolme, *The Constitution of England or an Account of the English Government,* 4th ed. (London, 1784), 431.

72. He continues: "It will be like a rope of sand; it will give no security; for the same men may unbuild what they have built." Speech of Sept. 12, 1654, in S. C. Lomas, ed., *The Letters and Speeches of Oliver Cromwell* (New York, 1904), 2:382.

73. James Harrington, *The Commonwealth of Oceana* (London, 1656), 2.

74. Francis D. Wormuth, *The Origins of Modern Constitutionalism* (New York, 1949), 71. We also read "that all proceedings touching the lives, liberties and estates of all the free people of this commonwealth, shall be according to the laws of the land, and that the Parliament will not meddle with ordinary administration, or the executive part of the law: it being the principal care of this, as it hath been of all former Parliaments, to provide for the freedom of the people against arbitrariness in government."

75. John Locke, *The Second Treatise of Government,* 3rd ed. by J. W. Gough (Oxford, 1966), 13 (sec. 22), 69–70 (secs. 136, 137). For Locke, "The reason why men enter into society is the preservation of their property; and the end why they choose and authorize a legislative is that there may be laws made, and rules set, as guards and fences to the properties of all the members of the society, to limit the power and moderate the dominion of every part and member of the society." Ibid., 110 (sec. 222).

76. See ibid., 73 ff. (secs. 143 ff.)

Recognition of the rule of law is evident in later years.[77] It could be seen when the Act of Settlement of 1701 provided for the tenure of judges;[78] when five years later the arbitrary action of the legislature was denounced on occasion of the passage of the last bill of attainder;[79] when the doctrine *nullum crimen, nulla poena sine lege poenalis* was restated in the House of Commons at a time Dr. Johnson was reporting the debates;[80] when Lord Camden in the Wilkes case stated that public policy, reflecting as it was the will of men, is not an argument in a court of law.[81]

The arrival of parliamentary supremacy did not seriously jeopardize the general recognition of the rule of law. Its principle underlies Blackstone's *Commentaries on the Laws of England.* While stressing the supremacy of Parliament, these commentaries leave no doubt that the men in Parliament are bound by the rule of law. It was above all the rule of law that impressed the outstanding foreign observer of England during the eighteenth century, Montesquieu. His *De l'Esprit des Lois,* which is full of admiration for English institutions, clearly distinguishes the rule of laws from the will of the prince. The other great observer of the English constitution, de Lolme, advanced similar ideas.[82] By that time, the rule of law had taken such a firm hold upon the English that for Hume, the essence of the history of England was the evolution from a "government of will to a government of law."[83]

The idea of the rule of law also found recognition in America. As a matter of fact, it existed in a purer and less vulnerable form in the colonies than in the motherland. While in theory Parliament was under the rule of law, in practice it

77. See Hayek, *Constitution of Liberty,* 171 ff.

78. "As the result of all these consequences of the independence of the courts, the doctrine of the rule or supremacy of the law was established in its modern form, and became perhaps the most distinctive, and certainly the most salutary, of all the characteristics of English constitutional law." Holdsworth, *A History of English Law* (London, 1938), 10:647.

79. See Thomas B. Macaulay, *The History of England from the Accession of James the Second* (Everyman's Library ed., New York, 1953), 4:272 ff.

80. "That where there is no law there is no transgression, is a maxim not only established by universal consent, but in itself evident and undeniable; and it is, Sir, surely no less certain that where there is no transgression there can be no punishment." Speech of Mr. Campbell on Nov. 26, 1740. *The Works of Samuel Johnson* (London, 1787), 13:22.

81. Hayek, *Constitution of Liberty,* 172.

82. De Lolme, *Constitution of England,* esp. the following passages: "Such is the *greatness* and uninterrupted *prevalence* of the law . . . , such is in short the continuity of omnipotence, of resistless superiority, it exhibits, that the extent of its effects at length ceases to be a subject of observation to the Public. Nor are great or wealthy Men to seek for redress or satisfaction of any kind, by any other means than such as are open to all: even the Sovereign has bound himself to resort to no other: and experience has shewn that he may without danger, trust the protection of his person, and of the places of his residence, to the slow and litigious assistance of the law." (443–44) "The law doctrine we have above described, and its being strictly regarded by the High governing authority, I take to be the most characteristic circumstance in the English Government, and the most pointed proof that can be given of the true freedom which is the consequence of its frame" (456). See also xiii, 314–18, 344, 361–62, 375–78, 423, 435–42, 451, 454–55, 471, 482–85.

83. Friedrich Meinecke, *Die Entstehung des Historismus* (Berlin, 1936), 1:234.

could not be forced to be because it was the supreme legislature and the highest court. And whereas parliamentary government became generally accepted by the English, it was not popular with the colonists, as their struggle with Parliament demonstrated. While the English came to accept the Blackstonian version of the rule of law, which in theory put Parliament under that rule, the colonists continued to believe in the Cokeian version of the rule of law, under which that rule was even less vulnerable from the legislature because the courts constituted a practical, and not just theoretical, check upon Parliament. It has been said that the "political life of the colonists branched from that of England in the seventeenth century, when in England the legal view of politics was strongest—when questions of state were approached from a dominantly legalistic angle."[84] This is not surprising in view of "the fact that the colonial governments derived their powers from legal instruments, such as charters and deeds, and questions of politics were thus inevitably questions of the law of *ultra vires* as well." In distinction to England where Parliament, with its legislative and judicial supremacies, could not well be convicted of acting *contra legem legi* in the Ciceronian sense, in America the British Parliament was blamed for doing just that, for having infringed upon the rule of law as it existed in the common law and in colonial charters and deeds. In colonial America, political thinking retained the legalistic turn which in England disappeared as parliamentary supremacy became established.

In their struggle with the mother country, the colonists accused Parliament of having substituted their own rule for that of the law.[85] The Declaration of Independence accuses the king of the same misbehavior. After independence had been declared, the constitutions adopted by the newly independent states favored "a government of laws, not of men."[86] The Constitution of the United States was established to secure the rule of law over that of men.[87] This is obvious in the classic commentary to that Constitution, *The Federalist*.[88] No

84. Dickinson, *Administrative Justice,* 95. See also Abbott L. Lowell, *The Government of England,* new ed. (New York, 1912), 2:472, 481; Barrett Wendell, *Liberty, Union, Democracy* (New York, 1906), chap. 1.

85. See Charles H. McIlwain, *The American Revolution, a Constitutional Interpretation* (New York, 1923).

86. Constitution of Massachusetts of 1780, Part I, Art. 30. The idea pervades other state constitutions. Cf. especially the constitutions of Connecticut (1776), par. 2–4; Delaware (1776), Art. 25; Georgia (1777), preamble; Maryland (1776), 3, 7, 15, 21, 42; Massachusetts (1780), preamble, Part I, Art. 10, 11, 12, 14, 20, 22, 24; New Hampshire (1784), 14, 15, 19, 23, 29, 35, 38; New Jersey (1776), 21, 22; New York (1777), which quotes the whole Declaration of Independence, 3; North Carolina (1776), 5, 12, 24, 44; Pennsylvania (1776), Declaration of Rights, 9; South Carolina (1778), 42; Vermont (1777), chap. 1, 16; Virginia (1776), Bill of Rights, secs. 5, 7, 8.

87. See Dietze, *America's Political Dilemma* (Baltimore, 1968), 8–9, 12, 15, 33, 142, 146–50, 155, 272; Hayek, *Constitution of Liberty,* 176 ff. Hayek's index, while mentioning under "Rule of Law" the English, French, German and Prussian versions, makes no reference to the American rule of law.

88. Esp. in essay 78, where Hamilton advocates tenure for judges during good behavior: "In a monarchy it is an excellent barrier to the despotism of the prince; in a republic it is a no less

doubt was left by Chief Justice Marshall when in the decision that officially established national judicial review for the sake of the rule of law, he wrote: "The Government of the United States has been emphatically termed a government of laws, and not of men."[89] Similar statements were made by others in following generations.[90] As one author put it, the framers of the American Constitution "were concerned not to make America safe for democracy, but to make democracy safe for America. From Lord Chief Justice Coke to the Supreme Court of the United States is a long way, but a clear one. The controlling rule of law which the seventeenth century set above King or Parliament, which the Puritans exalted in matter both civil and ecclesiastical, which the philosophers saw as the governing principle of the universe, which the colonists invoked against the absolutism of Parliament, this was now made the essential principle of [American] federalism."[91]

Recognition of the rule of law was also evident in modern continental nations. The spreading of that concept was in large measure due to the writings of Montesquieu.[92] Rousseau considered it "the great problem in politics . . . to find a form of government which places the law above men," something he compared to "squaring the circle in geometry."[93]

In France, the struggle between the Parlement of Paris—a royal court in many respects comparable to the English "high court of Parliament"[94]—shows that an awareness of the value of the rule of law existed under the *ancien régime.* The controversy between Louis XIV and the Comte d'Ormesson, the president of the Parlement, was similar to that between James I and Lord Coke on that Sunday morning conference in which Coke, speaking for the judges, spoke up to the king.[95] D'Ormesson refused to register a royal ordinance

excellent barrier to the encroachments and oppressions of the representative body. And it is the best expedient which can be devised in any government, to secure a steady, upright, and impartial administration of the laws." For Hamilton, the tenure of judges was "conformable to the most approved of the State constitutions [Massachusetts], and among the rest, to that of this State [New York]." "The courts must declare the sense of the law; and if they should be disposed to exercise WILL instead of JUDGMENT, the consequence would equally be the substitution of their pleasure to that of the legislative body."

89. *Marbury* v. *Madison,* 5 U.S. (1 Cranch), 137, 163 (1803). In *Osborn* v. *Bank of United States,* Marshall stated: "Judicial power, as contradistinguished from the power of laws, has no existence. Courts are the mere instruments of the law, and can will nothing. 22 U.S. (9 Wheaton) 739, 866 (1824).

90. See, e.g., Justice Brown in *Holden* v. *Hardy,* 169 U.S. 366, 389 (1898); Justice Lamar in *Simon* v. *Southern Ry.,* 236 U.S. 115, 122 (1915).

91. R. A. Humphreys, "The Rule of Law and the American Revolution," *Law Quarterly Review* 53 (1937):98.

92. Walter Jellinek, *Verwaltungsrecht,* 2nd ed. (Berlin, 1929), 6–7.

93. "Lettre à Mirabeau," *Oeuvres* (Paris, 1826), p. 1620. Comp. Hans Nef, "Jean Jacques Rousseau und die Idee des Rechtsstaates," *Schweizer Beiträge zur allgemeinen Geschichte* 5 (1947):167 ff.

94. See McIlwain, *The High Court of Parliament and its Supremacy.* Chapter 1 of Coke's *Fourth Part of the Institutes* has the title "Of the high and most honourable Court of Parliament."

95. The story is recounted in Pound, *Spirit of the Common Law,* 60–61.

which the Parlement regarded as contrary to the law of the land, whereupon the king forced his will upon the Parlement, dismissing the comte from his office and banishing him.[96] In France, the friends of the rule of law were not as immediately successful as they were in England. The will of the king prevailed, and the Parlement was eliminated as an effective advocate of the rule of law. The *ancien régime* became characterized by the arbitrary rule of the monarch. Louis XIV's phrase, *L'Etat c'est moi,* meant *la loi c'est moi* as well as *le droit c'est moi.*[97]

In view of the absence of the rule of law under the *ancien régime,* the French Revolution was considered as much of a victory of the rule of law as the English and American revolutions had been. It was referred to as "the coming to power of the law."[98] About a century after it occurred, the outstanding British exponent of the rule of law wrote: "The Bastille was the outward and visible sign of lawless power. Its fall was felt, and felt truly, to herald in for the rest of Europe that rule of law which already existed in England."[99] Article 16 of the Declaration of the Rights of Man and Citizen indicates belief in the rule of law when it stresses the importance of the constitution as supreme law. Similar confessions to the rule of law can be found in constitutions made during the revolution.[100] Lafayette, back from America, appealed to the "reign of law" against the "reign of the clubs."[101] Later de Tocqueville stated that

96. Seagle, *History of Law,* 224–25.

97. *Dieu et mon droit* implied that any law (*loi*) the king made was right (*droit*) by definition because he ruled by divine right. At the time of Louis XIV, the law, according to Schmitt, *Die Lage der europäischen Rechtswissenschaft,* 25, was unproblematical because it was not yet divided into legitimate and legal law, hence there did not exist a difference between *loi* and *droit.* Things seem to have changed with Blackstone, of whom Corwin, "'The Higher Law' Background," p. 405, writes: "Nor is Blackstone's appeal to men of all parties difficult to understand. Eloquent, suave, undismayed in the presence of the palpable contradictions in his pages, adept in simulating new points in view without unnecessarily disturbing old ones, he is the very exemplar and model of legalistic and judicial obscurantisicism."

98. J. Michelet, *Histoire de la révolution française* (Paris, 1847), 1:xxiii. See also F. Mignet, *Histoire de la révolution française* (Paris, 1824), at the beginning. Commenting on Michelet, Jean Ray, "La Révolution Française et la pensée juridique: l'idée du règne de la loi," *Revue philosophique de la France et de l'étranger* 128 (1939):364, writes: "Il lui semble, pourtant, que le changement fut moins profond qu'on ne l'a cru, parce que la loi aurait simplement pris la place du roi dans une conception persistante d'un ordre imposé par la force." Ray's article tries to show that during the era of the French Revolution "l'idée de loi s'est imprégnée d'une signification et d'une force neuves, qui ont retenti sur les principales institutions de notre temps."

99. Albert V. Dicey, *Introduction to the Study of the Law of the Constitution* (1885, 8th ed., London, 1915), 188.

100. Under the constitution of 1791, the civic oath was: "Je jure d'être fidèle à la Nation, à la Loi et au Roi." The king would swear to be "fidèle à la Nation et à la Loi." In a speech of Nov. 14, 1791, d'Isnard stated: "Mon Dieu, c'est la loi; je n'en ai pas d'autre." François Victor Alphonse Aulard, *Histoire politique de la Révolution Française. Origines et développement de la démocratie et de la république (1789–1804)* (Paris, 1901), 395. According to Hayek, *Constitution of Liberty,* 194, "the early efforts at constitution-making are full of painstaking and often pedantic endeavors to spell out the basic conceptions of a government of law."

101. Quoted Hayek, *Constitution of Liberty,* 195.

when he saw a right and a faculty given to any power to do whatever it chooses, whether people or king, democracy or aristocracy, whether exercised under a monarchy or under a republic, then there is the germ of tyranny, and, for his part, he would look for another system of laws under which to live.[102]

The rule of law was also acknowledged on the other side of the Rhine. As a matter of fact, it was probably in Germany where it found its most systematic and juristic elaboration.[103] The term *Herrschaft des Gesetzes* can mean something noble and did so in the first half of the nineteenth century, when it did not so much imply the rule of law in the sense of *Gesetz,* but rather the rule of law in the sense of *Recht.* It was at that time but another term for *Herrschaft des Rechts*—rule of right, state of right, right state, or *Rechtsstaat.*[104]

Although the German movement for the rule of law started under Frederick the Great, it gained momentum only after his death. Enlightened as the rule of Voltaire's friend may have been, it was still a despotism that did not totally discard the arbitrary concept of the rule of law.[105] The rule of law was a product of liberalism rather than enlightened despotism. While Kant promoted the trend toward the rule of law in Germany, English and American influences ought not to be overlooked. "It is probably no accident that the beginning of the theoretical movement that led to the development of the ideal of the *Rechtsstaat* came from Hannover, which, through its kings, had had more contact with England than the rest of Germany. During the latter part of the eighteenth century there appeared here a group of distinguished political theorists who built on the English Whig tradition; among them E. Brandes, A. W. Rehberg, and later F. C. Dahlmann were the most important in spreading English constitutional ideas in Germany."[106] Furthermore, it is not without significance that Robert von Mohl, probably the staunchest advocate of the *Rechtsstaat,*[107] was strongly influenced by American constitutionalism with which he became first acquainted on a sojourn in Paris and of which he remained a student for the rest of his life.[108] That liberal's appreciation of the *Rechtsstaat* was matched by his conservative contemporary, Friedrich Julius Stahl, whose well-known definition of the *Rechtsstaat* starts out with the words:

102. *Democracy in America,* ed. Phillips Bradley (New York, 1945), 1:260.

103. Hayek, *Constitution of Liberty,* 196 ff.

104. See Dietze, *Two Concepts of the Rule of Law* (Indianapolis, 1973), esp. 9 ff.

105. For the case of the miller Arnold, in which Frederick imprisoned judges, see Walter Jellinek, *Verwaltungsrecht,* 80 ff.; for that of the miller of Sanssouci, showing confidence in the rule of law under that king, see Hayek, *Constitution of Liberty,* 481n16.

106. Hayek, *Constitution of Liberty,* 482n26.

107. See Dietze, "Robert von Mohl, Germany's de Tocqueville," in Dietze, ed., *Essays on the American Constitution: A Commemorative Volume in Honor of Alpheus T. Mason* (Englewood Cliffs, N.J., 1964), 187 ff., and *Two Concepts of the Rule of Law,* 18 ff.

108. Mohl's review of Joseph Story's *Commentaries on the Constitution of the United States,* "Nordamerikanisches Staatsrecht," *Kritische Zeitschrift für Rechtswissenschaft und Gesetzgebung des Auslandes* 7 (1835):1 ff., impressed so favorably that it was translated in *American Jurist* 14 (1835):330 ff., and 15 (1836):1 ff.

"The state must be a Rechtsstaat."[109] The English influence upon the development of the *Rechtsstaat* is also evident in the fact that its outstanding advocate in the second half of the century, von Gneist, was an authority on the English constitution.[110]

The rule of law exists in a large measure by virtue of its past acceptance. It can consist of good and bad laws and can have come about under any form of government. Human dignity is irrelevant only insofar as traditional law makes it irrelevant; it is relevant if that law makes it relevant. A man may be worth nothing if that law says he is worth nothing; he may be worth a lot if it says he is. The latter usually has been the case, and the rule of law has aided people in their struggle for rights. To them that rule was not so much a vacuum that could be filled with any values a government might believe in, but a demonstration of the time-honored dignity of man, which had to be respected. However, this does not mean that the values read into the rule of law, while considered protective of human dignity, could not be of the most varied kind. Nor does it imply that the rule of law could not stand for a great many things. The rule of law has been understood in different ways in different places and times and by different names: government of law, government of laws, reign of law, reign of laws, justice under law, justice under laws, the supremacy of law, the supremacy of laws, the "absolute" reign of law.[111] Whereas the use of various names could indicate that the rule of law has been evaluated differently by different people, it does not necessarily do so. What one author refers to as rule or government may well be referred to by another as supremacy or reign. What some call absolute rule may be nothing but what others simply call rule. Similarly, people may speak of law (singular) or laws (plural) and mean the same thing.[112] Various terms may, but need not, have various meanings, and different meanings can be discerned irrespective of the terminology used. The rule of law can mean the rule primarily of natural, or customary, or legislative, or written, or unwritten law. It can imply different enforcements of the law.

Even nations with similar institutions can believe in many concepts of the rule of law because of different conceptions of law. In England, the fight for the rule of law at the time Magna Carta was signed and then revived four centuries later was chiefly based upon the desire to have the common law rule. While

109. Friedrich Julius Stahl, *Die Philosophie des Rechts,* vol. 2: *Rechts- und Staatslehre,* part 2 (1837, 5th ed., Tübingen and Leipzig, 1878), 352.

110. Rudolf von Gneist, *Der Rechtsstaat* (Berlin, 1872); *Der Rechtsstaat und die Verwaltungsgerichte in Deutschland* (Berlin, 1879), also wrote *Das heutige englische Verfassungs- und Verwaltungsrecht,* 2 vols. (Berlin, 1857–60); *Das englische Verwaltungsrecht* (Berlin, 1867); *Das englische Verwaltungsrecht der Gegenwart in Vergleichung mit den deutschen Verwaltungssystemen,* 3rd ed., 2 vols. (Berlin, 1883–84).

111. Seagle, *History of Law,* gives chap. 15 the title "The Rule of Law," and chap. 19, "The Absolute Reign of Law," 209 ff., 299 ff.

112. Thus Chief Justice Marshall termed the government of the United States "a government of laws, and not of men," while the inscription on the building of the United States Supreme Court is "equal justice under law."

natural law was considered important,[113] it was deemed relevant only because for generations it had been recognized and commonly accepted. The "cult" of the rule of law was above all one of a common law believed to contain natural law, not one of natural law as such. When in his controversy with James I, Coke emphasized the superiority of the artificial reason of the law over natural reason, he had in mind the artificial reason of the down-to-earth, time-honored common law, the accumulation of legal opinions over the ages.[114] In the struggle between Parliament and the king, the former mainly favored the rule of the common law.[115] Once Parliament had been victorious, it was primarily the mouthpiece of the common law. Blackstone's statement, made after the Glorious Revolution, that Parliament was bound by the law of nature, ought not to be interpreted to mean that he considered the law of nature superior to the common law. For him, the common law was a reflection of natural law.[116] Being the transmutation of vague natural law into something tangible, it had a greater binding value and could constitute more of a rule of law than could natural law.[117] His reminding Parliament that they were bound by natural law was probably just his way of telling them that they were bound by the common law as it had come down to them through acceptances by the English people of natural law.[118] It was a warning lest Parliament discard the common law because the latter had a large natural law ingredient.

113. Bracton's statement, *non sub homine sed sub Deo et lege* could be interpreted to mean that customary law, having been honored for ages, must be natural and enjoy the blessings of God.

114. Cf. Pound, *Spirit of the Common Law,* 60–61; Seagle, *History of Law,* 215.

115. See Charles H. McIlwain, "The English Common Law, Barrier Against Absolutism," *American Historical Review* 49 (1943):23 ff.

116. William Blackstone, *Commentaries on the Laws of England,* ed. Thomas M. Cooley (Chicago, 1899), book 1, Introduction, sec. 2, has the subtitle, "Human law must not contravene nature." We read: "This law of nature, being coeval with mankind, and dictated by God himself, is of course superior in obligation to any other. It is binding over all the globe, in all countries, and at all times: no human laws are of any validity, if contrary to this; and such of them as are valid derive all their force, and all their authority, mediately or immediately, from this original" (41).

117. The *Commentaries* are primarily discussing the enforceable laws of England. Blackstone's emphasis on the need for enforceable and enforced laws is especially evident in remarks on the enormous power of Parliament in the second chapter of book 1.

118. After a student publication, *The Absolute Rights of British Subjects,* he discusses rights in chap. 1 of book 1 of the *Commentaries,* under the heading, "Of the Absolute Rights of Individuals." Under a subtitle, "Charters of liberty," he writes that "the great charter of liberties," according to Coke "was for the most part declaratory of the principal grounds of the fundamental laws of England. Afterwards by the statute called *confirmatio cartarum* . . . , the great charter is directed to be allowed as the common law;" He mentions the "*petition of right,*" the "*habeas corpus* act" and the "*bill of rights,*" which was enacted by an act of parliament, recognizing "'all and singular the rights and liberties asserted and claimed in the said declaration to be the true, ancient, and indubitable rights of the people of this kingdom.' Lastly, these liberties were again asserted at the commencement of the present century, in the *act of settlement* . . . whereby the crown was limited to his present majesty's illustrious house: and some new provisions were added . . . for better securing our religion, laws, and liberties; which the statute declares to be 'the birthright of the people of England' according to the ancient doctrine of the common law" (127–128).

The American concept of the rule of law can be considered a result of Blackstone's warning. The Declaration of Independence, speaking of the rights of men rather than Englishmen, emphasized the form of his thinking without doing away with its substance. While showing an awareness of the value of the common law, Americans put greater emphasis upon natural law than did the English. Americans had felt the kind of oppression Blackstone feared when he warned Parliament to abide by natural law. Because of their experience, they were more skeptical toward legislatures than were the English. They were aware that Parliament might not abide by the common law and thus deprive people of their rights or replace the common law, customarily impregnated with natural law, by a law bare of natural law; they feared that the natural reason of the members of Parliament might deprive the common law of its artificial reason, which was oriented toward natural law. All these fears had come true, Americans thought, when acts of Parliament deprived them of their rights.

Americans questioned whether legislatures would obey the common law. In view of men's perpetual temptation to replace the rule of law by that of men, they suspected that legislatures might be inclined to overemphasize the human law ingredient of the common law and to discard its natural law ingredient. As a result, Americans, while continuing to believe in the common law tradition, came to stress the "higher," as distinguished from the "common," law background of the rule of law.[119] They felt that the common law, being closer to the rule of men than natural law, might more easily lose its grip upon the legislators than natural law. Consequently, they saw to it that the natural law background of their constitution was more formally acknowledged than it was in England. They adopted a written constitution, leaving no doubt that it reflected natural as well as common law and was superior to acts of the legislature. The adoption of judicial review resulted from this thinking,[120] but it would be wrong to consider the American Constitution a rigid transmutation of natural law into positive law. Americans did not discard their heritage. Their Constitution remained a common-law constitution insofar as the judges interpret it.[121] It remained a constitution of precedent. Natural law was more emphasized and formalized under the American conception of the rule of law than under its English counterpart, but its common law content was not neglected. In the United States, as in England, the ordinary courts of justice became the guardians of the rule of law. The greater formal acknowledgment of natural, "higher" law in the United States explains why unlike English courts, American courts have the right to test legislative acts for their compatibility with the Constitution. Therefore, the rule of law for the English implies more of a legislative rule than it does for Americans.

119. Cf. Corwin, "'Higher Law' Background."

120. Cf. Edward S. Corwin, *The Doctrine of Judicial Review* (Princeton, 1914).

121. See Dietze, *America's Political Dilemma,* esp. 8–9, 12, 15, 33, 142, 146 ff., 155, 272.

The concepts of the rule of law differ in nations with similar heritages, so it will hardly surprise that they do so in countries with different traditions. France is a case in point. Here the rule of law (*règne de la loi, règle de droit*) means more or less the rule of legislation. In contrast to England and the United States, the idea of the rule of law was hardly recognized under the *ancien régime*. Jean Bodin, the exponent of sovereignty who favored *droit gouvernement,*[122] left no doubt that the king could not be restricted by anyone, that he had "a perpetual, humanly unlimited, and unconditional right to make, interpret, and execute law."[123] On the other hand, the sovereign was bound not only by natural law but also by certain constitutional laws, the *leges imperii.*[124] After Bodin, the latter aspect became less and less recognized; soon the will of the king was law: *Rex, lex.*[125] Customary law did not prevent this evolution, but rather went along with it. Therefore, the "arrival of the law" in the French Revolution meant not so much the revival of customary law, but the arrival of legislative fiat. The major achievement of the French Revolution was the transfer of power from the executive to the legislature or, as an authority on the rule of law in France remarked, the substitution of the *roi* by the *loi.*[126] Unlike the English Parliament, the French legislature did not show much respect for customary law. On the contrary, it reacted against that law and saw its main function in creating new law. The rule of law thus became tantamount to that of legislation, of the codes adopted under Napoleon I and thereafter.[127] "I do not know civil law, I only teach the Napoleonic Code," said Bugnet. Demolombe complemented him: "My principle, my belief is this: the texts before everything!"[128] In England, Blackstone had warned Parliament that they were under the law of nature. In the United States, the legislature was actually limited by the higher law as it was embodied in the Constitution. In France, natural law lost its awe and became a tool. The French parliament acted as if it was convinced that it was so reasonable that everything it enacted—constitutions as well as other laws—was sanctioned by natural law, a law to which lip service was paid frequently.[129] No sharp line was drawn between the sup-

122. Jean Bodin, *Les six livres de la republique* (Lyon, 1579), 1: "REPUBLIQUE est vn droit gouuernement de plusieurs mesnages, & de ce qui leur est commun, auec puissance souueraine." So begins chap. 1 of book 1 under the title: "Quelle est la fin principale de la Republique bien ordonné."

123. George Sabine, *A History of Political Theory,* 3rd ed. (New York, 1964), 407.

124. Ibid., 409.

125. Cf. James I, *The Trew Law of Free Monarchies* (London, 1598).

126. Cf. Ray, "La Révolution française," 364 ff. See also Maxime Leroy, *La loi. Essay sur la théorie de l'autorité dans la démocratie* (Paris, 1908), 79, referring to Michelet's "l'avènement de la loi."

127. Cf. Dietze, *In Defense of Property* (Chicago, 1963), 71–72, 111, 132, 149–50, 156–57.

128. Quoted by Georges Ripert, *Le régime démocratique et le droit civil moderne,* 2nd ed. (Paris, 1948), 45–46.

129. See Dietze, *In Defense of Property,* 149 f.; Georges Ripert, *La règle morale dans les obligations civiles,* 3rd ed. (Paris, 1935), 15; Julien Bonnecase, *La notion de droit en France au XIX*[e] *siècle* (Paris, 1919), 48.

posedly perfect written constitution and other laws that were considered just as perfect, because all of them were made by the same body, the legislature. There was no rationale for judicial review. Judges were prohibited from testing laws for their compatibility with the constitution and from filling gaps in the law.[130] In the French Revolution, the "enthronement of the law" was accompanied by a degradation of the jurists whose pitiful lot under Napoleon, the very man who has been compared to Justinian and boasted about his work of codification, often has been decried.[131] Whereas in England and America the possibility to contest administrative acts in the ordinary courts was considered a guaranty for the individual's enjoyment of the rule of law, in France there were established administrative courts. It was asserted that these courts were as good, if not better, guaranties of the rule of law, as were ordinary courts,[132] a thought that was obnoxious to the Anglo-Saxons.[133]

A still different conception of the rule of law prevailed in Germany. While the Germans were influenced by the French Revolution, the fact that the ideas of that revolution were in large measure imposed upon Germany by conquering French armies, made the Germans suspicious of French ideas.[134] The rejection by French revolutionaries of the past and their claim to be rational were viewed with skepticism and counterbalanced by the notions of *Volksgeist,*[135] which became reflected in the German idea of the rule of law, an idea influenced by the English concept in which respect before the common law ranked high. When Thibaut, impressed by the Napoleonic codes, suggested the codification of German law, he immediately drew criticism from Savigny, who maintained that codification was risky even at a time which, unlike his own, abounded in great jurists, and he showed the shortcomings of modern codifications, warning against leaving the safe ground of customary law.[136] The *Rechtsstaat* was conceived to be similar to the English rule of law. Its *Recht* was primarily *gemeines Recht.* Significantly, the term *Gesetzesstaat* was seldom used.[137] *Rechtsstaat* meant a state (or rule) of law in which the *Recht,* something which for generations had commonly been considered to be right, something which reflected natural law as sanctioned and accepted by the *Volk,* prevailed. Respect for legislation was not thereby excluded. However, legisla-

130. Law of Aug. 14–24, 1790, Arts. 10, 11; constitution of Sept. 3, 1791, Tit. III, ch. 5, art. 3; constitution of 5 Fructidor, Year III, art. 203; Code Pénal, art. 127.

131. Paul Koschaker, *Europa und das römische Recht,* 2nd ed. (Munich, 1953), 135–36; Carl J. Friedrich, "The Ideological and Philosophical Background," in Bernard Schwartz, ed., *The Code Napoleon and the Common Law World* (New York, 1956), 7–8; Schmitt, *Lage der europäischen Rechtswissenschaft,* 31.

132. Gneist, *Der Rechtsstaat und die Verwaltungsgerichte in Deutschland.*

133. See Dicey, *Law of the Constitution,* esp. 198–99.

134. Cf. Savigny, "Vom Beruf unserer Zeit."

135. See Sabine, *History of Political Theory,* 628 ff.

136. See Thibaut, *Über die Notwendigkeit;* Savigny, *Vom Beruf unserer Zeit.*

137. One used, however, the term *Herrschaft des Gesetzes* in lieu of *Rechtsstaat.* See Hayek, *Constitution of Liberty,* 484n35.

tion did not constitute the better part of *Recht*.[138] Whereas the Germans accepted the substance of the English rule of law, they did not follow the English example of guaranteeing that rule exclusively through ordinary courts, but moved toward French practice by establishing administrative courts.[139]

The rule of law as conceived under the original concept of the *Rechtsstaat,* increasingly became a *Herrschaft des Gesetzes,*[140] a rule of legislative fiat. Gradually, the French idea that the legislatures could do no wrong was accepted.[141] Toward the end of the nineteenth century, Germany experienced a wave of codification similar to that in France under Napoleon I.[142] The *Rechtsstaat* developed into a *Gesetzesstaat.*[143] During the Weimar Republic, the fight of *Recht* against *Gesetze* was discussed.[144] After the Hitler regime had produced its own version of the rule of law, a resurrection of the original concept of the *Rechtsstaat* was attempted. Judicial review was introduced.[145]

In France, where the idea of legislative supremacy had been strongly advocated from the beginning of the Revolution and became generally accepted during the following generations, the increase of legislation from the nineteenth to the twentieth century was not considered incompatible with the rule of law.[146] The fact that the collapse of the Third Republic occurred when Hitler's armies invaded France, made Frenchmen believe that the traditional concept of the rule of law as it derived from legislative supremacy was beyond reproach. Whereas the Germans, in an attempt to resurrect the original *Rechtsstaat,* undertook a thorough reevaluation of natural law and democracy, such a re-

138. It must be remembered that Germany was under the *gemeine Recht* until some time after unification in 1871.

139. The main proponent of this trend was von Gneist, whose significance was stated in an anonymous pamphlet, *Herr Professor Gneist oder der Retter der Gesellschaft durch den Rechtsstaat* (Berlin, 1873). Cf. Eduard Lasker, *Zur Verfassungsgeschichte Preussens* (Leipzig, 1874); Fritz Fleiner, *Institutionen des deutschen Verwaltungsrechts,* 8th ed. (Tübingen, 1928).

140. Now in the sense of the rule of legislative acts. The change in the meaning of *Herrschaft des Gesetzes* from a rule of law in which the *gemeine Recht* and customary law predominated to one in which modern legislation constituted the better part was natural in view of increased legislation and offers an example of the mutation of a concept.

141. Cf. Hermann von Kirchmann, *Die Wertlosigkeit der Jurisprudenz als Wissenschaft* (Berlin, 1848; Stuttgart, 1938), 37: "Die Juristen sind durch das positive Gesetz zu Würmern geworden, die nur von dem faulen Holz leben; von dem gesunden sich abwendend, ist es nur das Kranke, in dem sie nisten und weben . . . drei berichtigende Worte des Gesetzgebers und ganze Bibliotheken werden zu Makulatur."

142. Legal codes that were formulated and introduced from the unification of Germany on were: Bürgerliches Gesetzbuch (BGB), Strafgesetzbuch (StGB), Handelsgesetzbuch (HGB), Zivilprozessordnung (ZPO), Strafprozessordnung (StPO), among others.

143. See Dietze, *Two Concepts of the Rule of Law,* 33 ff.

144. Marschall von Bieberstein, *Vom Kampf des Rechtes gegen die Gesetze* (Stuttgart, 1927).

145. See Dietze, *Two Concepts of the Rule of Law,* 36–37. See Dietze, "Judicial Review in Europe," *Michigan Law Review* 55 (1957):551 ff.

146. See however Fernand Auburtin, *Une législation qui tue* (Paris, 1922).

evaluation was not obvious in France.[147] The constitution of the Fourth Republic was basically a replica of that of the Third Republic, but brought about such changes as a mild form of judicial review.[148] The constitution of the Fifth Republic went further, restricting legislative supremacy.[149] The *règne de la loi* in today's France is not the same as the original one, although it goes by the same name.

Similar observations can be made with respect to the rule of law in the United States, the development of which was on the whole different from that in continental nations. In Europe judicial review emerged as a guaranty of the rule of law largely because it was believed to have been useful in the United States. It declined in the country of its origin.[150] Just as it was said in the thirties that judicial review is the most characteristic feature of American government,[151] it can be stated today that its fading with respect to national laws has been characteristic of that government ever since. In America, where natural and common law became formalized in a Constitution so that they might constitute an effective check upon the democratic political branches of government, these branches seem to win out over the Constitution. Legislation has so enormously increased that it has been asked whether the United States is still a common law country.[152] Furthermore, legislation also has become qualitatively stronger insofar as the supremacy of the Constitution over legislation has been less recognized. Much as it has been active in striking down state laws after World War II, the Supreme Court since 1937 has been reluctant to declare acts of Congress unconstitutional.[153] In the United States, the rule of law is approaching the type originally conceived by the English. The Constitution is about to become a mere moral check upon Congress, the kind of check Blackstone had in mind when he wrote that Parliament was under the law of nature. Yet, in spite of this shift, the government of the United States is still considered a rule of law.[154] The fact that in the twentieth century the guardianship of the law has become increasingly exercised by quasijudicial bodies of administrative agencies and the legislature in lieu of the ordinary courts[155] is not considered

147. See Dietze, "Natural Law in the Modern European Constitutions," *Natural Law Forum* 1 (1956):77, 87 ff.

148. Cf. Michel Debré, *La république et ses problèmes* (Paris, 1952). See Dietze, "Judicial Review in Europe," 558–59.

149. Title VII of the Constitution (Art. 56–63).

150. See Dietze, "America and Europe—Decline and Emergence of Judicial Review," *Virginia Law Review* 44 (1958):1233 ff.

151. Edward S. Corwin, "Judicial Review," *Encyclopedia of the Social Sciences* 8:457.

152. Cf. H. R. Hahlo, "Here Lies the Common Law: Rest in Peace," *Modern Law Review* 30 (1967):241 ff.

153. See Dietze, *America's Political Dilemma,* 152 ff.

154. Cf. Arthur E. Sutherland, ed., *Government Under Law* (Cambridge, Mass., 1956).

155. Cf. Dwight Waldo, *The Administrative State: A Study of the Political Theory of American Public Administration* (New York: 1948); Dickinson, *Administrative Justice and the Supremacy of Law in the United States.*

incompatible with the traditional reputation of American government as one of laws, not men.

The rule of law has perhaps undergone the least change in England. In that nation, where recourse to the ordinary courts was considered the criterion of the rule of law, no administrative courts were established. Also, there existed a reluctance to establish quasijudicial legislative or administrative bodies.[156] Nevertheless, in the most conservative of the nations here discussed, the rule of law is not quite the same today as it was when first established. Coke's opinion that the power of parliament is so absolute that it cannot be confined within any bounds[157] and Blackstone's words that Parliament "hath sovereign and uncontrollable authority in the making, confirming, enlarging, restraining, abrogating, repealing, reviving, and expounding of laws, concerning matters of all possible denominations," that it was "the place where that absolute despotic power which must in all governments reside somewhere, is entrusted by the constitution of these kingdoms,"[158] were not taken as a sign for parliamentary license. After all, Blackstone had stated limitations of the power of Parliament. Acknowledging these limitations, Parliament, active as it may have been since the days of Blackstone and de Lolme, refrained from doing many things they could have done. Even Bentham's and Austin's theories of legislative supremacy did not change this fact. Parliamentary practice, and the constitutional limitations from which it resulted, were recognized as late as the twentieth century by such diverse commentators as Dicey, a *laissez-faire* liberal, and Laski, a leader of the Labour Party.[159] Still, because of the activities of Parliament, the rule of law changed. The common law in large measure was superseded by acts of Parliament and by rules and regulations made by administrative agencies under the authority of legislation. Acts of Parliament, reflecting an increasing exercise of parliamentary policy-making, have been complemented by a growing number of rules and regulations which demonstrate the growth of administrative discretion. The "absolute despotic power" of Parliament, which Blackstone mentioned but did not complain of because he felt that Parliament would heed his warning to abide by natural law and not be despotic, spawned "the new despotism" of administrative agencies of which Lord Chief Justice Hewart complained. And yet, the official doctrine is still that England is a nation with the rule of law.[160] The dilemma of that rule in England is evident in Jennings's *The Law and the Constitution.* While that modern commentary admits that "there are many things, as Dicey and Laski

156. Even Dicey later became more convinced that administrative courts were not as bad as he originally believed they were. "*Droit Administratif* in Modern French Law," *Law Quarterly Review* 17 (1901):302 ff.

157. Coke 4 Inst. 36.

158. Blackstone, *Commentaries,* book 1, chap. 2, III.

159. Cf. Harold J. Laski, *Parliamentary Government in England* (New York, 1938).

160. Lord Gordon Hewart of Bury, *The New Despotism* (London, 1929).

both point out, which Parliament cannot do,"[161] it states: "In England, the administration has powers limited by legislation, but the powers of the legislature are not limited at all. There is still, it may be argued, a rule of law, but the law is that the law may at any moment be changed." For Jennings, "the rule of law is apt to be rather an unruly horse."[162]

It is not surprising that various types of the rule of law would exist in various nations, given the fact that each nation has its own legal system. However, even within particular nations the rule of law has been understood to mean different things at different times, and some nations introduced a kind of rule of law when that kind was discarded elsewhere.[163]

Dicey's exposition of the rule of law "proved to be so acceptable that until recently it was generally assumed that the rule of law and Dicey's exposition of it were the same."[164] However, Jennings sees the rule of law as it has existed in the English liberal tradition in a different way. While he admits that "Dicey honestly tried (in *The Law of the Constitution,* not in his polemical works) to analyse," he asserts that "like most, he saw the Constitution through his own spectacles, and his vision was not exact."[165] According to Jennings's view of

161. Ivor Jennings, *The Law and the Constitution,* 5th ed. (London, 1959, 1961), 148.

162. Ibid., 57, 60.

163. Harry W. Jones, "The Rule of Law and the Welfare State," *Columbia Law Review* 58 (1958):145, writes that "it is difficult to find any common understanding among American lawyers, judges, and scholars as to the meaning, the essential attributes, of the rule of law."

164. Jennings, *The Law and the Constitution,* 53–54. Dicey, *Law of the Constitution,* 198–199, states: "That 'rule of law,' then, which forms a fundamental principle of the constitution, has three meanings, or may be regarded from three different points of view.

"It means, in the first place, the absolute supremacy or predominance of regular law as opposed to the influence of arbitrary power, and excludes the existence of arbitrariness, of prerogative, or even of wide discretionary authority on the part of the government. Englishmen are ruled by the law, and by the law alone; a man may with us be punished for a breach of law, but he can be punished for nothing else.

"It means, again, equality before the law, or the equal subjection of all classes to the ordinary law of the land administered by the ordinary Law Courts; the 'rule of law' in this sense excludes the idea of any exemption of officials or others from the duty of obedience to the law which governs other citizens or from the jurisdiction of the ordinary tribunals; there can be with us nothing really corresponding to the 'administrative law' (*droit administratif*) or the 'administrative tribunals' (*tribunaux administratifs*) of France. The notion which lies at the bottom of the 'administrative law' known to foreign countries is, that affairs or disputes in which the government or its servants are concerned are beyond the sphere of the civil Courts and must be dealt with by special and more or less official bodies. This idea is utterly unknown to the law of England, and indeed is fundamentally inconsistent with our traditions and customs.

"The 'rule of law,' lastly, may be used as a formula for expressing the fact that with us the law of the constitution, the rules which in foreign countries naturally form part of a constitutional code, are not the source but the consequence of the rights of individuals, as defined and enforced by the Courts; that, in short, the principles of private law have with us been by the action of the Courts and Parliament so extended as to determine the position of the Crown and of its servants; thus the constitution is the result of the ordinary law of the land."

165. Jennings, *Law and the Constitution,* 316.

the liberal interpretation of the rule of law in England, it "is not enough to say with Dicey that 'Englishmen are ruled by the law, and by the law alone' or, in other words, that the powers of the Crown and its servants are derived from the law. . . ." The doctrine of the rule of law "involves some considerable limitation on the powers of every political authority, except possibly (for this is open to dispute) those of a representative legislature. Indeed it contains . . . something more, though it is not capable of precise definition. It is an attitude, an expression of liberal and democratic principles, in themselves vague when it is sought to analyse them, but clear enough in their results. There are many facets to free government, and it is easier to recognise it than define it. It is clear, however, that it involves the notion that all governmental powers, save those of the representative legislature, shall be distributed and determined by reasonably precise laws." Most states have sought to attain the rule of law "by written constitutions, for such a constitution is fundamental law which limits by express rules the powers of the various governing bodies and thus substitutes constitutional government (in large part a synonym for the rule of law) for absolutism."[166] From the aforesaid it appears doubtful whether Jennings provided a more exact definition of the rule of law than did Dicey.

Similar differences of opinion concerning the rule of law can be discerned in the United States at any particular time. For instance, in the 1920s, Holcombe, discussing "the reign of law," and Dickinson, discussing "the supremacy of law" (and both dealing with the same subject matter in spite of the different terminology), wrote at some length about Dicey's ideas. And whereas their remarks make evident that they firmly believed in the rule of law, their statements reveal differences of opinion as to the meaning of that rule and as to the chances of its survival and adaptation in the face of growing administrative and public law.[167] The picture has not changed a generation later. Uncertainty as to what the rule of law actually constitutes was evident in a conference on occasion of the bicentennial of John Marshall, who, it will be remembered, considered the government of the United States one of laws, and not of men.[168] In that conference, devoted to a discussion of "government under law," different advocates of the rule of law advanced quite different opinions as to what they understood that rule to be.[169]

166. Ibid., 47, 48–49.

167. Arthur N. Holcombe, *The Foundations of the Modern Commonwealth* (New York, 1923), 436–79.

168. *Marbury* v. *Madison,* 5 U.S. (1 Cranch), 137, 163 (1803).

169. Justice Frankfurter stated: "The confining limits within which courts thus move in expounding law is not the most important reason for a conception of government under law far transcending merely law that is enforced in the courts. The day has long gone by when Austin's notions exhaust the content of law. Law is not set above the government. It defines its orbit. But government is not law except insofar as law infuses government. This is not wordplaying. Also indispensable to government is ample scope for individual insight and imaginative origination by those entrusted with the public interest. If society is not to remain stagnant, there is need of action

The dilemma of the absence of a generally accepted definition of the rule of law was stated by Jones: "Some explanation is imperative . . . as to the sense in which that elusive phrase, 'the rule of law,' is . . . used. . . . It is difficult to define the term, even as understood in the United States. The term itself is not common coin in American legal theory; we are more likely to say 'supremacy of law,' 'government under law' or (less accurately, I think) 'government of laws and not of men.' The one nugget of agreement discernible in the American writings is the idea, with which I devoutly agree, that state power is the great antagonist against which the rule of law must forever be addressed. The notion of an imposed or self-accepted constraint on governmental power may not exhaust the concept of the rule of law, but there is substantial agreement in American thought that the rule of law's great purpose is protection of the individual against state power-holders. Beyond this, it is difficult to find any common understanding among American lawyers, judges, and scholars as to the meaning, the essential attributes, of the rule of law. When an American writes or speaks on our general topic, he usually begins with a confident assumption that everybody knows what the rule of law is and then devotes the rest of his time to a bold and eloquent statement in favor of it."[170]

A French jurist favoring the rule of law will usually act a little differently. Instead of assuming that everybody knows what the rule of law is, he will try to state his own concept of that rule and say why the concepts of others are wrong. Needless to say, this kind of procedure is as unlikely to produce any common understanding of the rule of law as the procedure of American jurists. The desire of French jurists to be absolutely right in their definitions and formulations makes agreement among them probably more difficult to achieve than among their American counterparts. The likelihood of a greater disagreement among the French is probably enhanced by the fact that they tend to disagree on various points on which Americans tend to agree. For instance, Americans

---

beyond uniformities found recurring in instances which sustain a generalization and demand its application. But law is not a code of fettering restraints, a litany of prohibitions and permissions. It is an enveloping and permeating habituation of behavior, reflecting the counsels of reason on the part of those entrusted with power in reconciling the pressures of conflicting interests. Once we conceive of 'the rule of law' as embracing the whole range of presuppositions on which government is conducted and not as a technical doctrine of judicial authority, the relevant question is not, has it been achieved, but, is it conscientiously and systematically pursued." "John Marshall and the Judicial Function," in Arthur E. Sutherland, ed., *Government under Law,* 27–28. On the other hand, Judge Charles E. Wyzanski, Jr., stated in the same conference: "Indeed all that one seems able to spell out of the rule of law concept, when looked at universally, is first, that the state recognizes a presumption that an individual has the right to have his person or property free from interference by any officer of the government unless that officer can justify his interference by reference to a general law, and second, that the state provides some machinery for the vindication of that right before an independent tribunal in all cases where a crime is charged, and sometimes in other cases involving serious interferences with persons or their property. To go beyond this is to indulge in readily disproved fictions." "Constitutionalism: Limitation and Affirmation," ibid., 482.

170. Jones, "The Rule of Law and the Welfare State," 144–145.

generally agree that the rule of law is protected only if there exists judicial review over legislative as well as administrative acts; the French are divided as to whether judicial review ought to include legislation.[171] For some the rule of law is equivalent to a rule of the constitution; for others it is equivalent to the rule of the ordinary law which they suppose to be automatically in conformity with the constitution. Both legitimists and legalists pose as adherents of the rule of law.[172] Furthermore, whereas Americans generally agree that the rule of law is best protected by the ordinary courts, Frenchmen feel that it should be protected by administrative courts as well.[173]

If we add that, to the French, law can mean both *droit* and *loi,* it is understandable why in France there is a greater variety of concepts of the rule of law than in the United States. This has brought forth a number of terms, all of which more or less convey the meaning of the rule of law, such as "sovereignty of law," "judicial review," "judicial supremacy," "legality," "reign of legality," "sovereignty of the law," "reign of law under the highest and the most subtle aspects of legality."[174] During World War I, Hauriou discussed the *règne de la loi, empire de la loi, suprematie de la loi,* and made it clear that the *loi* of France was above its *droit.*[175] Shortly thereafter his contemporary Duguit, another advocate of the rule of law, dealt with the *règle de droit, régime de droit,* and indicated that *loi* was under, or at least not above, *droit.*[176] Similar differences of expression and opinion are evident in the writings of other French advocates of the rule of law. Hauriou and Duguit also discussed, re-

171. See Dietze, "Judicial Review in Europe," esp. 542 ff., 551 ff. Cf. Jeanne Lemasurier, *La constitution de 1946 et le contrôle juridictionnel du législateur* (Paris, 1954).

172. Hamilton's distinction in Federalist no. 78 between a superior constitution and inferior acts of Congress was felt not to apply to France where the ordinary lawmaker was also the constitution-maker and where the power of amending the constitution was usually vested in the legislature.

173. Cf. B. Schwartz, *French Administrative Law and the Common Law World* (New York, 1954).

174. See Dietze, "Judicial Review in Europe," esp. 541 ff., 555 ff.

175. Maurice Hauriou, *Principes de droit public,* 2nd ed. (Paris, 1916), 219 ff. In the beginning of that book, x–xi, we read: "La loi écrite, qui devient la base du régime juridique de l'Etat, comporte une stabilité des situations très différente de la stabilité coutumière, en ce sens qu'elle se concilie avec une plus grande dose de mobilité et, par suite, avec une plus grande somme de libertés communes, car la liberté ne va point sans une certaine possibilité de changement. En effet, la loi écrite, bien qu'établie en principe à toujours, peut être modifiée par une décision delibérée du gouvernement en employant une procédure relativement rapide. . . . la Révolution de 1789, ce n'est pas autre chose que l'avènement absolu de la loi écrite et la destruction systématique des institutions coutumières. Il en est résulté un état perpétuellement révolutionnaire, parce que la mobilité de la loi écrite n'étant plus équilibrée par la stabilité de certaines institutions coutumières, les forces de changement se sont trouvées plus puissantes que les forces de stabilité."

176. Léon Duguit, *Le droit social, le droit individuel et la transformation de l'Etat,* 3rd ed. (Paris, 1922), 7, 10. Cf. that author's *Les transformations générales du droit privé depuis le Code Napoléon* (1912; 2nd ed., Paris, 1920), 6 ff., 12 ff., 24 ff., 29, 176; *Les transformations du droit public* (Paris, 1913).

spectively, *l'état de droit* and *l'Etat de droit,* having in mind the same thing.[177] Their discussions, however, reveal different conceptions of the subject matter. Admitting that if one tries to find a precise definition of the *état de droit,* he is hindered by difficulties which so far have not been resolved in an entirely satisfactory fashion, Hauriou arrived at a definition at which Duguit would have taken exception. It is probably no exaggeration to maintain that there were perhaps no two French authors who at any time agreed on what the *état de droit* resp. *Etat de droit* meant, or, for that matter, who agreed as to the meaning of the rule of law and the various names that have been used for it in French.

The situation is similar in Germany. Different conceptions of the rule of law are evident in the fact that the rule of law was identified with both the *Rechtsstaat* and the *Gesetzesstaat,* and that each one of these terms was understood differently by different people at any particular time.[178] We mentioned above the conceptions of the *Rechtsstaat* during the first half of the nineteenth century in the writings of the liberal Mohl and the conservative Stahl. Later on, Mohl modified his ideas. In 1866 he published a third, "considerably revised" edition of his *Die Polizei-Wissenshaft nach den Grundsätzen des Rechtsstaates.* It shows essential changes in the fundamental beliefs of the author.[179] Unlike the first edition of 1832, which considered the *Rechtsstaat* something negative and based upon the idea that the freedom of the citizen is the supreme principle, the third edition indicates a more positive role of the state and omits saying that the freedom of the individual comes first.[180] Other advocates of the *Rechtsstaat,* writing at about the same time, would generally agree with Mohl's new position and pay their respects to Stahl.[181] Still, they were not in absolute agreement with Mohl, Stahl, or, for that matter with each other. Bähr, von Stein, Gneist—they all had their own ideas about the *Rechtsstaat.* The dispute over the meaning of the German variation of the rule of law became a characteristic feature of juristic discussion in following periods, as the rich literature before and after World War I demonstrates.[182] In 1935 Schmitt could write on

177. See Hauriou, *Principes de droit public,* 17 ff., 219 ff. These sections have the titles, "L'Etat de droit" and "La règne de la loi," respectively. On page 17, Hauriou writes of "La notion de l'état de droit ou de l'Etat soumis au régime du droit." Cf. Léon Duguit, *Traité de droit constitutionnel* (Paris, 1911), 2:1 ff.

178. Otto Bähr, *Der Rechtsstaat: Eine publicistische Skizze* (Cassel, 1864) favored a more "justicialist" Rechtsstaat (leaving the control of administrative acts and actions to the ordinary court) than Gneist, who favored administrative courts. And whereas Gneist emphasized, as did Lorenz von Stein, *Die Verwaltungslehre,* 2nd ed. (Stuttgart, 1869), a national Rechtsstaat, Johann Jacoby put the idea of liberalism over that of nationalism in his speech of Aug. 23, 1866, in the Prussian legislature. *Stenographische Berichte* 1 (1866):73.

179. See Dietze, *Two Concepts of the Rule of Law,* 23–24.

180. See Robert von Mohl, *Die Polizei-Wissenschaft nach den Grundsätzen des Rechtsstaates* (Tübingen, 1832), 1:7; 3rd ed. (1866), 1:12–13, 15–16.

181. See Dietze, *Two Concepts of the Rule of Law,* 25 ff.

182. Walter Jellinek, *Verwaltungsrecht,* 83 ff., could well discuss "today's Rechtsstaat."

"the dispute over the *Rechtsstaat,*" discussing the meaning of the *Rechtsstaat* for the Third Reich and the question of its survival under, and adaptation to, the Hitler regime as well as the general disagreement concerning the *Rechtsstaat* prior to 1933. This disagreement was reflected in the fact that there "could be a Christian and an anti-Christian, a liberal, a national, and an antinational *Rechtsstaat,*"[183] a "liberal, bourgeois, social, national and finally national-socialist *Rechtsstaat,*"[184] and different versions of the latter.[185] The Bonn Basic Law provides in articles 20 and 28 for the "social *Rechtsstaat,*" the interpretation of which is disputed.[186]

In conclusion it may be said that the possibilities for variations of the rule of law seem to be inexhaustible. That rule appears to be something infinite and indefinite in spite of the fact that concrete notions of it defy neither description nor precision. The many varieties of the rule of law are not surprising in view of that rule's similarity to its arbitrary counterpart, which may be anything from a quantitative and qualitative point of view.

Although in distinction to the rule of men, which basically exists by virtue of momentary government and thus is something temporary, the rule of law basically exists vis-à-vis such government and constitutes a limitation upon it, it may still be temporary insofar as the government may alter it in a way that is compatible with the rule of law, that rule being nothing but an agglomeration of previous alterations of the law. Because of its viability the rule of law cannot absolutely prohibit being amended. It will always be within the discretion of governments to bring about such changes, and this discretion implies a certain degree of arbitrariness. Thus even the rule of law can to a certain degree be arbitrary. Although a temporary government will generally respect the rule of law, it will, in the last analysis, determine what that rule actually is.

The arbitrary behavior of governments is not out of tune with the character of the rule of law. Being the mass of law that has been accepted over the ages, that rule, irrespective of how much it may constitute a limitation upon those in power, is, after all, something that has been made by those who held power. It constitutes a rule discovered or made by men, and by men alone, no matter how much its discovery or making may have been influenced by metaphysical considerations or the law of nature. And although people, having discovered or made the law, will usually have been guided by law already known to them, they will, when changing law, act according to their desires and pleasures, i.e., more or less arbitrarily. The rule of law is thus an accumulation of human

183. Schmitt, "Was bedeutet der Streit um den 'Rechtsstaat'?".

184. Ernst Forsthoff, "Begriff und Wesen des sozialen Rechtsstaates," *Veröffentlichungen der Vereinigung der Deutschen Staatsrechtslehrer* 12 (1954):15.

185. Heinrich Lange, *Vom Gesetzesstaat zum Rechtsstaat* (Tübingen, 1934); Hans Frank, "Der deutsche Rechtsstaat Adolf Hitlers," *Deutsches Recht* 4 (1934):120 ff.

186. See Dietze, *Two Concepts of the Rule of Law,* 37 ff.

actions that are not necessarily nonarbitrary, much as they have been hampered by a basic respect for existing law. However, since it is less of an accumulation of mere arbitrariness, but more of an exertion of power impeded by respect for existing law, the rule of law, unlike that of men, is likely to be quantitatively and qualitatively good rather than bad because men in the long run tend to accept what is good rather than what is bad. Probability thus speaks for an ethical superiority of the rule of law over that of men. Still, probability is no certainty. From a mere formal point of view, the rule of law may be close, and even inferior, to its arbitrary counterpart. For the latter may be the best as well as worst rule of the best as well as the worst law.

Aside from being liable to coming close to the rule of men, the rule of law can vary a great deal even if it does not approach the rule of men. It was shown that within nations there may exist many conceptions of the rule of law. This is due to an abundance of factors: government by one, a few, the many; federal or unitary structures; concentration or separation of powers; the prevalence of civil or common law; of written or unwritten constitutions; the recognition or nonrecognition of constitutions as superior law; judicial review ranging from the review of administrative acts to that of constitutional norms; the prevalence of private or public law; ordinary and administrative courts. If, in addition, we consider that these factors exist in many variations, the possibilities of combinations seem inexhaustible and the possible notions of the rule of law, indeterminable. If, furthermore, we take into account that within each particular nation there exists different concepts of the rule of law at any given time, showing great varieties of emphases and that the rule of law actually is realized only when a specific decision is rendered in a specific case, then we arrive at the result that within any legal order the rule of law is always susceptible to change. Until the juristic moment of truth, the verdict and its execution, the shadow of uncertainty veils what presumably is the certainty of the rule of law.

If interpretations of the rule of law differ within various countries, it is not surprising that they differ from nation to nation. The English, Americans, French, Germans, and others—they all have had their own ideas on the rule of law, although the same principles may coexist in different countries.

In view of these enormous variations in the rule of law, it is difficult to define that rule. This does not mean that a correct definition is impossible. The adoption of the rule of law in more and more societies brought about improved variations of it. Nations could use the experience of other nations. Known patterns of the rule of law could be compared, and refined concepts resulted from such comparison. Continuing experience with the rule of law may have brought us closer to the discovery of its perfect type. But so many perfections of the rule of law might be suggested that confusion as to what a perfect rule of law is may grow.[187]

187. In Germany, the liberal *Rechtsstaat* was followed by a national, social, national-social, and national-socialist one. Proponents of the later concepts of the *Rechtsstaat* were of the opinion that

The Rule of Law and Liberalism

The rule of law has been instrumental in the inception and establishment of the historic movement called liberalism. It was invoked in various countries against rules of men considered arbitrary and detrimental to the rights of the individual. However, the fact that liberal movements were directed against oppressors does not mean that liberals favored anarchy. The enjoyment of human rights implies not only the absence of curtailments by the public power, but the security of those rights from others. It means restrictions of the government as well as governmental protection of individuals according to the law. A necessary minimum of governmental control of individual freedom is matched by a maximal governmental protection of individuals from other individuals, and the scarcity of laws, rules, and regulations is balanced by the strictness of their enforcement. The rule of law is enforceable toward government and citizens alike. Although it has been emphasized that the rule of law secures freedom from arbitrary government, one should recall that the rule of law still is, as Harrington put it, an empire of laws, an *imperium* to strictly enforce the laws. *Droit gouvernement,* much as it must be just, is still a government; the *Rechtsstaat* is still a state, much as it is supposed not to be arbitrary.

Although characterized by the basic feature of the protection of the individual from the government and fellow-citizens, the rule of law can stand for a great variety of principles, as far as its material content is concerned, given its many interpretations liberally supplied in various times and places by lawmakers, lawbreakers, and commentators.[188] Consequently, it can be rather *prinzipienlos,* unprincipled, turning out to be rather unruly. This raises the problem of the feasibility of law as a proper restraint upon liberalism, itself unruly by definition.

The question as to whether or not something unruly can restrain something unruly need not be answered in the negative. Unruliness does not necessarily carry with it the inability to rule or restrain, even though a ruly ruler usually will be better than an unruly one, which seems to be a contradiction in terms. Furthermore, certain things, unruly as they are, are ruling and restraining by definition. Law, a body of norms prescribing and proscribing human behavior, is one of them. Restriction is the essence of the law. Therefore, law is a restraint

these concepts constituted improvements of their predecessors. Thus the Third Reich was considered a better *Rechtsstaat* than that under previous regimes, as is indicated in the title of Lange's book. The most cruel regime Germany ever experienced was thus elevated to its most rightful one! The great variety of meanings of *Rechtsstaat* and the resulting confusion and problems is described by Carl Schmitt in *Verfassungslehre* (Munich and Leipzig, 1928), esp. 35–36, 125 ff., 138 ff., 200 ff.

188. The term "rule of law" became best known through its use by Dicey, *Law of the Constitution.* His formal concept of the rule of law, in tune with his idea that Parliament was omnipotent, provoked an attack by Bellot, "The Rule of Law." Schmitt, "Der Führer schützt das Recht," denounced the Rechtsstaat for aiding criminals by replacing the principle *nullum crimen sine poena* by that of *nulla poena sine lege.*

upon liberalism under all circumstances, for what by definition restrains must curtail what by definition is unlimited. Legal restraint is rather effective. In contrast to ethics and morals, law can be enforced, certainly vis-à-vis individuals, much as the possibility of its enforcement against governments is disputed although not necessarily deniable, especially when the sovereign is the people and the government its agent. While despotism can be, and has been successfully fought with appeals to the rule of law, that rule, as enforced by governments including liberal ones, can restrain liberalism, excessive and anarchical as it may be.

The idea that laws are checks upon liberalism presupposes that law stands above liberal behavior, that its norms are unbending to liberal desires. It is conceivable that there are norms which have weathered time and constitute some kind of permanent restraint upon liberalism. Even laws that have been created on the spur of the moment and are more or less fleeting can restrain liberal behavior. After all, they are laws. However, given the fact that laws are not static, they do not permanently check liberal behavior. No matter how old fundamental and superior laws may be and how static they may appear, they mirror changing values and practices. Even that example of a rigid constitution, the Constitution of the United States, has been brought into line with modern times.[189] Fundamental laws that could not be formally amended to suit new conditions have been adjusted informally through interpretation and mutation. The flexibility of the law is even greater in the case of ordinary laws, rules, regulations, and decrees as they have been produced and overproduced by legislative and administrative bodies and agencies. In ages of legislation and administration, the norms prescribing and proscribing human action have been more and more liberally changed. The liberal era became one of legislation and is becoming one of administration. Legislation and administration as well as fast-changing laws, rules, regulations, and decrees are aspects of modern liberalism, all constituting what is called the rule of law. Given this fact, it is doubtful whether that rule, changeable as it is, can be an effective restraint upon liberalism. It will even be asserted that the rule of law has become a reflection of liberalism, including liberalism at its worst. Can the rule of law improve liberalism?

An affirmative answer to the question whether law can make liberalism proper a proper liberalism is encouraged not so much by having recourse to the rule of law proper, but by applying the proper rule of law. If law changes with the views of men, it can change liberally from good to evil and from bad to worse, depending upon the propriety or impropriety of human behavior to which there are no limits under the doctrine of liberalism. To find proper legal restraints upon human action, we must look for proper law, which probably

189. To Chief Justice Marshall the American Constitution was "intended to endure for ages to come, and, consequently, to be adapted to the various crises of human affairs." *McCulloch* v. *Maryland,* 17 U.S. (4 Wheat.) 316, 415 (1819).

existed when law came into existence. For if the speculation that law was originally concerned with the transfer of property is correct, then law must properly have seen to the protection of property, which was considered proper.

The thought that law originally served the proper protection of something proper like property is supported by the fact that property rights generally are considered the oldest of human rights.[190] Since rights are hardly conceivable without their effective protection and since such a protection exists by virtue of the law, the oldest law must have protected property rights. As a matter of fact, legal history reveals a preponderant concern with property from early times. That concern has remained evident. Property rights figure prominently in Roman law, defined broadly as *ius utendi, fruendi, abutendi,* indicating their propriety. Property rights are basic to the common law. The course on property is, together with that on contract, required reading for all students. Property occupies the highest rank in the philosophy of John Locke, the defender of the English Revolution and the philosopher of the American Revolution. The American Constitution, in a large measure, was adopted to protect property rights.[191] The French Revolution may have been the great divide of French history and destroyed most things of the *ancien régime,* but property rights survived it and the Napoleonic Code was called a code of property.[192] Property rights also rank high in that other great codification of the nineteenth century, the Civil Code of Germany (*Bürgerliches Gesetzbuch*).

The connection of property with propriety is evident also in language, that good indicator of the people's values. In the West, where liberalism as a historical movement came about and where the majority of liberal governments can be found, property has been given an ethical connotation. In English, another word for property is *goods,* in French, *biens,* in German, *Gut,* in Spanish, *bienes.* For a long time the English used the word *propriety* for *property.* In Latin nations, the same word is used for propriety and property.[193]

Given this connection, a proper rule of law, conducive to proper liberalism, may well be one providing for a far-reaching protection of property. But then, opinions on what constitutes such a protection may differ from nation to nation as well as within nations. Therefore, even a proper rule of law may still be unruly and prevent the discovery of proper liberalism. Furthermore, property, while on the face something proper, might be used improperly. People may take issue with the Roman idea that property implies a right to abuse. Much as property may be the most proper of rights, much as it may be used interchangeably with *propriety,* it is not identical to propriety. Consequently, laws favoring

190. Carl J. Friedrich, *Man and His Government* (New York, 1963), 358.

191. Cf. Charles A. Beard, *An Economic Interpretation of the Constitution* (New York, 1913); Robert E. Brown, *Charles Beard and the Constitution* (Princeton, 1956); Forrest McDonald, *We, the People* (Chicago, 1958).

192. Barthélemy Terrat, "Du régime de la propriété dans le Code Civil," in *Le Code civil, 1804–1904; livre du centenaire,* Société d'Etudes Législatives (Paris, 1904), 1:327 ff.

193. See Dietze, *In Defense of Property,* 9 ff.

property rights probably can be considered a proper minimum rather than maximum.

Propriety being greater than a minimum or part of propriety, something more than proper law appears to be necessary to make liberalism proper a proper liberalism, namely, a propriety transcending that required by the laws, one going beyond simply obeying the laws and their proprietary minimum, one urging a better and more proper behavior than that prescribed by proper laws. This implies limitations of human actions that go beyond those enforceable through the laws. It implies autolimitation, prompted by a person's conscience. While it limits liberalism more than do proper laws, it does, under the principle *volenti non fit iniuria,* not hurt. By restraining himself freely according to his desire to act properly and thus being truly humane, the human being can have the feeling of perfect freedom. Liberalism may thus be more proper than provided for by proper law. On the other hand, people are not likely to agree to a behavior that is more proper than that prescribed by proper laws. Their judgments on propriety will vary and further increase the difficulty of determining proper liberalism.

In view of past failures to provide satisfactory definitions of liberty and liberalism and the obvious difficulty of defining these concepts, it seems advisable to confine this study to examining how they were seen by great liberals in various nations. Should these men be in basic agreement in spite of their different backgrounds, major tenets of liberalism can perhaps be discovered. Since we are interested not only in liberalism proper but in proper liberalism, we choose authors from what has been considered a period of moralism, the eighteenth century,[194] and shall examine the thoughts of Montesquieu, Smith, Kant, and Jefferson. Selecting them is advisable for another reason: they fought an uphill battle and thus probably were more convinced of their ideas than liberals writing in liberal establishments. The seriousness of convictions can usually be measured by the willingness to suffer for them. Montesquieu lived under the *ancien régime,* Smith during mercantilism, and Kant in absolutist Prussia. Jefferson experienced trade restrictions and other aspects of absolutism. Furthermore, liberal thought probably was more mature in their age than earlier because it benefitted from the wisdom of preceding centuries which, drawing from the renaissance of older ideas, witnessed a growing awareness of liberty within the political order.[195]

194. Carl Schmitt, "Das Zeitalter der Neutralisierungen und Entspannungen," (1929), in *Der Begriff des Politischen* (1932; Berlin, 1963), 82 ff.

195. See Laski, *The Rise of European Liberalism.* That work shows well that between the Reformation and the French Revolution liberals never lost sight of the need for order in society. In the first two chapters alone, dealing with the rise of liberalism in the sixteenth and seventeenth centuries, the word "order" recurs frequently (12, 15, 31, 35, 37, 40, 41, 43, 44, 47, 52, 69, 71, 74, 77, 78, 87, 88, 92, 95, 96). The idea of order is also obvious on 29, 32, 33, 73, 75, 93, 100, 101).

This awareness was the natural result of new discoveries in all walks of life, aided by the revival of learning. They made the old world of the Middle Ages crumble, for discovery is the herald of freedom. They were made on a large scale, pointing to newer and freer worlds. Cosmological advances liberated men from old concepts of the universe, from beliefs that often were imposed by the authorities. Geographical exploits freed people from traditional ideas about the nature of the earth, its culture and population, bringing reports from foreign lands and showing that there were ways of life other than those one was accustomed to and expected to be content with. The rediscovery of biblical truths led to freedom from dictated papal dogmas. There was an appreciation of the emerging national state, freeing individuals from restricting feudal relationships. Thus the end of the *respublica Christiana* resulted in the division of an all-embracing church as well as an all-embracing empire, spawning numerous religious sects and sovereign states. This development made people aware of an increasing number of beliefs, concepts, and ways of life. It whetted their appetite for freedom of choice.

To the new discoveries mentioned were added those in science and technology, the invention of invention, and, last but not least, innovations in the field of economics leading to free enterprise. The breakdown of feudalism brought about a redefinition of human relations. By the end of the fifteenth century, the spirit of capitalism[196] had gained a hold over the minds. Medieval moral rules concerning the acquisition of wealth were considered constraints interfering unduly with individual activity.

The growing assertions of liberty did not imply a desire for anarchy. Luther and Calvin protested against papal power, not against the authority of the state. Luther denounced the Peasants Revolt and the *Bilderstürmer* in unmistakable terms and favored a strong principality to ensure the success of the Reformation. Similarly, Calvin advocated the strict political order of Geneva. As to capitalism and its economic freedom, it was felt during the sixteenth century that it would best succeed within the legal frameworks provided by sovereign states. The successful pursuit of economic freedom was believed to be most secure where the government was strong enough to protect it. It has been asserted that liberalism came about in well-organized national states.[197] Be this as it may, it certainly was furthered in England and Holland, countries which had their national unity established early. It was secure in Italian states as long as they were not troubled by internal dissension. It was safer in the France of Colbert than it had been when centrifugal forces threatened the unity of that

196. Cf. Max Weber, "Die protestantische Ethik und der 'Geist' des Kapitalismus," *Archiv für Sozialwissenschaft und Sozialpolitik* 20 (1905):1 ff.; 21 (1905):1 ff. Laski, *The Rise of European Liberalism,* p. 12, writes: "With the triumph of the new order in the nineteenth century, the church had given birth to the state as an institutional arbiter of human destiny. The claims of birth had been succeeded by the claims of property. The invention of invention had made change, instead of stability, the supreme characteristic of the social scene."

197. See Laski, *The Rise of European Liberalism,* 22.

nation. It was delayed in Germany because of religious wars that prevented legal orders in which liberty would be secure.

Much as those favoring free enterprise criticized and evaded medieval rules and regulations, the spirit of enterprise, bringing about a new scale of things in risk-taking and the accumulation of capital, welcomed the states with their guarantees of internal peace. At times it did so to the point of accepting mercantilism, a policy of governmental regulation of economic life which has been called "the first step taken by the emerging secular state on the road to the full achievement of liberalism." But while in the beginning state aid for enterpreneurs in the form of regulations was welcome, interventionism as an established policy was attacked by the liberal forces once they were sufficiently established. This could be expected: the liberal is a fighter for freedom. He will admit governmental regulations if they serve his emancipation, but resent them if they are considered obstructive to his activities.[198] The House of Commons told James I as early as 1604 that "all free subjects are born inheritable to the free exercise of their industry."[199] Regulation of the economy was considered acceptable as long as it produced the internal order necessary for individual enterprise.[200]

Once the bourgeoisie as the standard-bearer of liberalism was sufficiently entrenched, it wanted the regulatory power of the monarch transferred to its representatives who would decrease governmental restrictions with respect to economic and other rights of the individual. This was the gist of the struggle between the English Parliament and the king. The Whig challenge to the divine right of kings ended in 1688 with a victory of the liberal forces. Resenting the absolute state as an obstacle to the full use of man's abilities, the Whigs were far from desiring the abolition of the state's legal order, which was believed to be indispensable for liberalism. They merely wanted to replace absolute monarchy by a constitutional one which in substance amounted to a representative government under the rule of law and provided for a far-reaching protection of human rights, among which those of property and free enterprise ranked prominently.

These ideas found expression in the work of the outstanding defender of the Glorious Revolution, John Locke. The administrator of a commercial empire, Locke experienced exile and confiscation of his property for political reasons. Yet he did not just defend economic rights, high as these rights ranked in his view. He advocated the rights of man in general, emphasizing the natural rights of "life, liberty and property"[201] and considering their protection the

198. See ibid., 40 ff. The quotation is on 41.

199. *Commons' Journals* 1 (May 21, 1604):218.

200. Laski, *The Rise of European Liberalism,* 44. See Henri Pirenne, *Les périodes de l'histoire sociale du capitalisme* (Brussels, 1922).

201. According to Locke (*Two Treatises of Government,* ed. Peter Laslett, [Cambridge, 1960], 368–69) man, leaving the state of nature, "seeks out, and is willing to joyn in Society with others who are already united, or have a mind to unite for the mutual *Preservation* of the Lives,

very rationale for government. He favored a representative government by the majority in which the legislature as the dominant branch would ensure that laws were made with the consent of the governed. "Rationalism, toleration, constitutional government, without excess in any, these were his watchwords."[202] While Locke resented big government, he opposed anarchy. Maintaining that even the state of nature was not one of lawlessness, he left no doubt that constitutional government, no matter how much it was limited for the sake of the rights of the individual, was still a government that had to protect these rights effectively—a trust for freedom, law, and order.[203]

Locke supplied a theory on free government. A generation later, Blackstone, in his commentaries on the laws of England, described how that government actually worked in his country. There no longer was much doubt that liberalism was viable. Monarchical despotism came under attack in France. Obviously, liberal Frenchmen were impressed by what they observed across the Channel.[204] The best known among them was Montesquieu.

Liberties and Estates, which I call by the general Name, *Property.* The great and *chief end* therefore, of Mens uniting into Commonwealths, and putting themselves under Government, is *the Preservation of their Property.*" See also ibid., 294, 307, 325, 339, 341 ff., 347 ff., 352, 355, 368, 370–71, 373, 375 ff., 425, 430, 433.

202. Laski, *European Liberalism,* 77.

203. See Laslett's introduction to Locke's *Two Treatises of Government,* 112–116. In the Second Treatise, the following sections deal with the idea of trust: 22, 111, 142, 149, 155, 156, 164, 171, 210, 221, 226, 227, 231, 239, 240, 242.

204. See Joseph Dedieu, *Montesquieu et la tradition politique anglaise en France* (Paris, 1909). Chapter 1 is entitled "La connaissance des idées anglaises à la fin du XVIIe siècle."

CHAPTER II

ASPECTS OF MONTESQUIEU'S LIBERALISM

Introduction

Montesquieu has been considered the most important, after Rousseau, of all French political philosophers in the eighteenth century.[1] He was born in 1689, the year Locke published the first of his *Letters Concerning Toleration,* two years after the publication of Newton's *Principia,* at the time of the Glorious Revolution. Events during his life were conducive to a liberal creed. He lived under Louis XIV and his successor and had a first-hand knowledge of the *ancien régime.* A member of the aristocracy, Montesquieu resented the curtailing of the rights of the nobility by the king. Enjoying provincial eminence, he opposed the centralization of France.[2] A student of law and a member of the robe who was *président à mortier* in the parlement of Guyenne, one of the ancient judicial organizations that had assumed political significance, Montesquieu could see how absolute monarchy violated the ancient constitution of France. His participation in the Academy at Bordeaux, his being accepted in Paris by the Society of Regency, and in salons such as that of Mme. Lambert, and discussion clubs such as the Club l'Entresol, as well as his election to the

1. Sabine, *History of Political Theory,* 551. See also Walter Jellinek, *Verwaltungsrecht,* 2nd ed. (Berlin, 1929), 6–7.

2. Cf. E. Levi-Malvano, *Montesquieu e Machiavelli* (Paris, 1912), esp. the chapter entitled "L'antimachiavellismo de Montesquieu"; Pierre Barrière, *Un grand provincial: Charles-Louis de Secondat, baron de la Brède et de Montesquieu* (Bordeaux, 1946).

French Academy in 1728 were to liberally widen his horizon. So were his comprehensive studies in comparative government, travels to Austria, Hungary, Italy, Germany, Holland, and a long sojourn in England, whose freedom he admired.

For many commentators "Montesquieu is the very prototype of a liberal, different from Locke only in details."[3] This is due to his love of freedom.

Liberty

Liberty is a predominant value in Montesquieu's thought.

Few names are as much connected with freedom, and hardly any as immediately with political freedom, as that of Montesquieu. Given his praise of liberty which reached a climax in book 11 of *On the Spirit of the Laws,*[4] a book concerned with the English constitution, and that he was deeply impressed and strongly influenced by the liberal heritage and institutions of England, it can be said that previous discussions by English authors on the importance of freedom culminate in Montesquieu's work. His work also became a major source for the

3. Melvin Richter, *The Political Theory of Montesquieu* (Cambridge, 1977), 9. This evaluation has come under attack. Ibid., 9–10, and Louis Althusser, *Montesquieu, La politique et l'histoire,* 4th ed. (Paris, 1974), esp. chap. 6, "Le parti pris des Montesquieu," 109 ff. It has been argued that "Montesquieu was a reactionary landowning magistrate and aristocrat who detested Louis XIV because of his curbing of the nobility and his success in creating a centralized national administration. Seen from such a perspective, there was nothing progressive, nothing moral about Montesquieu's condemnation of Louis XIV. . . . Thus when he portrayed Louis XIV as a despot who had violated the ancient constitution of France, when he condemned the Sun King for having impoverished his country by constant and indefensible resort to war as an instrument of national policy, it was only class propaganda." (Richter, *Political Theory of Montesquieu,* 9–10.) However, this is just tantamount to saying that there was nothing progressive, nothing moral in the barons' forcing King John to sign the Magna Carta. Clearly, a first step was taken here in liberalizing monarchical abuses, even if the beneficiary was the aristocracy rather than the people at large. The ancient constitution, much as it may have favored the aristocracy, still constituted a restraint on governmental power. Cf. J. G. A. Pocock, *The Ancient Constitution and the Feudal Law* (Cambridge, 1957). Montesquieu's favoring the nobility against the absolute king would still have amounted to an attack upon absolutism and a promotion of freedom from despotism.

4. In the following, references to *Les lettres persanes, Les considérations sur les causes de la grandeur des romains et de leur décadence,* and *De l'esprit des lois,* (abbreviated, respectively, *LP, C, EL*), will be to the Nagel edition of *Oeuvres Complètes de Montesquieu,* published under the direction of André Masson with the collaboration of Robert Shackleton, Alain Cotta, André Nouat, Odile Combes and Françoise Weil, volume I (Paris, 1950). That volume reproduces the three volumes of the *Oeuvres Complètes* of 1758, published posthumously with the corrections made by Montesquieu before his death in 1755. The first volume contains books 1–21, the second, books 22–31 of the *Spirit of the Laws,* and volume three, the *Persian Letters* and the *Considerations.* A reference, "*LP,* 14:35" is to *Persian Letters,* letter 14, page 35 of the Nagel edition; "*C,* 15:450," to *Considerations,* chapter 15; page 450; "*EL,* 21, 5:470," to *Spirit of the Laws,* book 21, chapter 5, page 470; "*EL,* 22, 6:46," to *Spirit of the Laws,* book 22, chapter 6, page 46. My references to writings of Montesquieu usually are in the indirect speech. Quotations are in my own translation.

spreading of ideas on liberty throughout the world. In Europe, Montesquieu's influence was greater than that of any other liberal, including John Locke and William Blackstone. The latter worked in an environment in which liberal ideas had become recognized by the government as the result of an evolution that for centuries had emphasized the protection of the rights of the individual and made England a relatively free nation. Within the English framework, the writings of Locke and Blackstone were not considered particularly new or courageous. Living under the absolutist *ancien régime,* Montesquieu, in voicing his advocacy of freedom, was considered a challenger of oppressive establishments, inciting the enthusiasm of all those who had to live under despotic governments, which on the continent were the order of the day. His influence was not confined to Europe; it is inseparable from the creation of free government in the United States.[5] Neither was it confined to the eighteenth century: it had a strong impact upon constitutionalist movements in the nineteenth century and has not lost its appeal to this day.[6]

Compte and Durkheim called Montesquieu the founder of the science of politics. Since that science in a large measure was understood to promote the protection of the individual from arbitrary government, Althusser's statement that nobody has seriously doubted that Montesquieu was its founder[7] suggests that liberty is the gist of Montesquieu's thought. Indeed, much as authors may have emphasized other aspects of that thought, especially after its liberalism had become taken for granted, there can be little doubt about the general significance attributed to Montesquieu's love of freedom. A recent edition of the *Spirit of the Laws* states that it has been said so often that political liberty is the central theme or the dominant idea of that work that one need not insist upon that fact.[8]

Helvetius and Voltaire, although critical of Montesquieu, paid "homage to

5. See Paul M. Spurlin, *Montesquieu in America* (Baton Rouge, 1940).

6. F. A. Hayek, *Law, Legislation and Liberty* (Chicago, 1973), 1:v, brings as a motto Montesquieu's statement, made in the beginning of his major work: "Intelligent beings may have laws of their own making; but they also have some which they never made." *EL,* 1, 1:2. Montesquieu is the first man mentioned in the text of Hayek's study. See pages 1, 4.

7. Louis Althusser, *Montesquieu: la politique et l'histoire,* 4th ed. (Paris, 1974), 11. In the eighteenth century and thereafter, political science often appeared as "police science," as the science of restricting the police of the "police state," of transforming that oppressive, bad police of the police state into a police restricted under laws, into a "good police" that was aiding individuals rather than oppressing them. In essay 9 of *The Federalist,* Alexander Hamilton lauds the "science of politics." In essay 37, James Madison speaks of "political science" and in essay 43, praises Montesquieu as the advocate of the separation of powers, "this invaluable precept in the science of politics." On the attitude of the political scientist Robert von Mohl toward bad and good police, see his *Die Polizei-Wissenschaft nach den Grundsätzen des Rechtsstaates.* Cf. Wilhelm Joseph Behr, *Allgemeine Polizei-Wissenschaftslehre oder pragmatische Theorie der Polizei-Gesetzgebung und Verwaltung. Zur Ehrenrettung rechtsgemässer Polizei, mittels scharfer Zeichnung ihrer wahren Sphäre und Grenzen* (Bamberg, 1848).

8. Robert Derathé, introduction to his edition of *De l'esprit des lois* (Paris, 1973), xlii.

his love of freedom and his detestation for arbitrariness and intolerance."[9] In his praising farewell to Montesquieu, Lord Chesterfield wrote: "A friend to mankind, he asserted their undoubted and inalienable rights with freedom."[10] At the beginning of this century, Faguet considered Montesquieu a liberal, the one who, his eyes fixed upon England, has invented human rights.[11] In his *avertissement* to a new edition of Montesquieu's works, Laboulaye writes that while in the bad days the works of Montesquieu are not read, they rebounce as soon as France cherishes liberty, that the name of Montesquieu disappears with liberty.[12] For Dedieu, political liberty is the truly dominant idea in the work of Montesquieu, and the analysis of guarantees of liberty remains attached to his name.[13] The importance of freedom in Montesquieu's work was stressed in contributions published for the bicentennial of the publication of the *Spirit of the Laws*.[14] For Sabine, Montesquieu's love of political liberty was the sole enthusiasm of an otherwise chilly temperament.[15] The appreciation of Montesquieu as a lover of freedom can be seen in the writings of contemporary authors. In the 1970s it was written that political liberty is the cornerstone of the whole theory of Montesquieu, that his whole "policy" is directed toward

9. Franz Neumann, introduction to *The Spirit of the Laws* (New York, 1949), xiii.

10. *London Evening Post*, Feb. 1755, as quoted by F. T. H. Fletcher, *Montesquieu and English Politics, 1750–1800* (London, 1939), 23, and by Neumann, *Spirit of the Laws*, ix. The quotation Neumann gives reads: "On the tenth of this month, died at Paris, universally and sincerely regretted, Charles Secondat, Baron de Montesquieu, and President à Mortier of the Parliament at Bordeaux. His virtues did honor to human nature, his writings to justice! A friend of mankind, he asserted their undoubted and inalienable rights with freedom, even in his own country, whose prejudices in matters of religion and government he had long lamented and endeavored, not without some success, to remove. He well knew and justly admired the happy constitution of this country where fixed and known laws equally restrain monarchy from tyranny and liberty from licentiousness. His works will illustrate his fame and survive him as long as right reason, moral obligations, and the true spirit of laws shall be understood, respected, and maintained."

11. Emile Faguet, *La politique comparée de Montesquieu, Rousseau et Voltaire* (Paris, 1902; New York, 1971), 14.

12. *Oeuvres complètes de Montesquieu* (Paris, 1875), 1:i.

13. Joseph Dedieu, *Montesquieu et la tradition politique anglaise en France: Les sources anglaises de l' "Esprit des Lois"* (Paris, 1909; New York, 1970), 3–4.

14. Institut de droit comparé de la faculté de droit de Paris, ed., *La pensée politique et constitutionelle de Montesquieu. Bicentenaire de l'esprit des lois 1748–1948* (Paris, 1948). See the contributions of Boris Mirkine-Guetzévitch, "De 'l'Esprit des lois' à la démocratie moderne," 13, 15; André Gardot, "De Bodin à Montesquieu," 49, where Montesquieu is referred to as "Montesquieu, ce grand seigneur libéral"; Jean Brèthe de la Gressaye, "L'histoire de 'l'Esprit des lois'," writes at 73: "son idéal: idéal de liberté, qui le fait vitupérer sans cesse les diverses formes de despotisme." See also Charles Eisenmann, "La pensée constitutionelle de Montesquieu," 113; René Cassin, "Montesquieu et les droits de l'homme," esp. 185; Jean Graven, "Montesquieu et le droit pénal," esp. 212: "Montesquieu établit tous ses principes, en matière criminelle, par rapport à la liberté des citoyens; il y ramènera tous ses raisonnements: 'La Liberté, ce bien qui fait jouir des autres biens'." At 213, Graven refers to liberty as "Ce mot magique, ce mot-clé."

15. George Sabine, *History of Political Theory*, 551. See also 553, 558.

untiring attempts to find practical means of guaranteeing liberty against any kind of despotism, wherever it may come from, and that he vigorously favored moderate governments because only in them is liberty possible.[16] It was stated that "Montesquieu had . . . blown an invigorating breath of freedom over his century."[17]

Our list of authors emphasizing the importance of liberty for Montesquieu is by no means complete. If, in addition, we take into account that many writers considered the separation of powers the Frenchman's most important idea and that they generally have seen in this doctrine a means for the protection of the freedom of the individual from governmental power, that list could be further augmented.[18] Perhaps our best reference that liberty was Montesquieu's major value is the Latin formula of Gravina inscribed in the catalogue of La Brède, Montesquieu's family seat, at the head of the enumeration of political writers: *Res est sacrosancta libertas et divini juris, ut eam tentare scelus sit, impium circumvenire, occupare nefarium;* "Liberty is something sacred; it is divine law to the point that attacking it is a crime, suppressing it, an impiety, and to make oneself its master, sacrilege."[19]

Montesquieu himself left no doubt about his appreciation of freedom. It can be noted throughout his writing. His *Persian Letters,* not known primarily as a treatise on government but hailed as "the masterpiece which serves as a prelude to the whole French literature of the 18th century,"[20] show the author's emphasis on the value of liberty. The idea of freedom stands at the very beginning and the very end of that work. In the first letter, the quest for freedom is evident when Usbek writes that he and Rica left Persia urged by the thirst for knowledge, that they abandoned the amenities of a tranquil life for a laborious search after wisdom, that, although they were born in a prosperous

16. Jacques Robert, *Montesquieu, de l'esprit des lois* (Paris, 1972), 25–26. He also writes: "L'*Esprit des Lois* est le couronnement éclatant d'un demi-siècle de réaction des esprits français contre l'absolutisme monarchique," referring to J.-J. Chevallier, "Montesquieu ou le libéralisme aristocratique," *Revue international de philosophie* (1955), 331.

17. Henri Peyre, foreword to the American edition of Emile Durkheim, *Montesquieu and Rousseau* (Ann Arbor, 1965), xiv.

18. Very clear Albert Ciria, *Montesquieu* (Buenos Aires, 1967), 15: "la obra toda alcanza su punto culminante en el libro XI ("De las leyes que forman la libertad politica en relación con la constitución"), y mas concretamente en el celebérrimo capítulo sexto ("De la constitución de Inglaterra"), donde el autor examina apologéticamente el sistema político británico e introduce su teoría de la "separación de las poderes", acaso el mayor lugar común por el que se recuerda casi exclusivamente a Montesquieu en colegios y universidades de todo el mundo." On page 26, Ciria adds: "Es bueno, as veces, hacer un alto en el sendero para reflexionar sobre los primeros principios y la [*sic*] formulaciones básicas, referidas en el caso de Montesquieu al liberalismo político." Neumann, *Spirit of the Laws,* x, writes that Montesquieu's "formula of the 'separation of powers' as a device for securing liberty enjoys more reverence today than perhaps ever before in history."

19. Paul Vernière, *Montesquieu et l'esprit des lois ou la raison impure* (Paris, 1977), 68.

20. Quoted by M. Komroff in his preface to *The Persian Letters* (New York, 1929), xi.

realm, they did not believe that its boundaries should limit their knowledge, and that the lore of the East alone should enlighten them.[21] This is a clear confession to the principle that knowledge liberates. Upon hearing from a friend back home that his departure caused some stir, Usbek writes of his free mind which prompted him to refuse to be corrupted by the power he enjoyed as a courtier and to leave the court.[22] In the end of the *Persian Letters,* Roxana, Usbek's favorite wife, writes that while she lived in servitude, she has always been free, that she remodelled his laws upon those of nature, and that her mind always maintained its independence.[23] As Usbek sought greater external freedom by leaving Persia, she kept her inner freedom even as a slave and takes her life because she always longed for freedom.[24]

As the *Persian Letters* are framed by the tribute to freedom at their beginning and at their end, the value of liberty is also stressed in-between. Staff and wives in the seraglio hope to enjoy greater freedom.[25] Usbek writes his wives that he wants to be their husband rather than their master, confident that he can abstain from restrictive measures so that they may enjoy greater freedom.[26] Those in servitude want to be free. Liberation is offered to them as a reward for fidelity.[27] Usbek advances arguments for the right to commit suicide and criticizes European laws prohibiting it.[28] He relates how the Troglodites killed an oppressive king and intolerable magistrates in order to be free,[29] how an old, venerated, and virtuous man who was asked to be their ruler cries that he shall die of sorrow, having known the Troglodites as freemen, to behold them subjected to a ruler.[30] In each state, glory increases and diminishes with the liberty of the subjects.[31]Usbek denounces tyranny[32] and makes it plain that if a prince oppresses his subjects, they are freed of all allegiance to him and can return to their natural liberty.[33] Rhedi regrets that the invention of bombs has deprived Europeans of freedom, and the invention of gunpowder, of refuges from injustice and violence.[34] He praises Greece for having thrown off the yoke of tyrants and made possible the emergence of prosperous republics. He is glad that the love of liberty and the hatred of kings extended from Greece to Asia Minor, Italy, Spain, Portugal, and Gaul and lauds the Germanic tribes for being free. Liberty is a priceless treasure which the Romans offered to the Cappadocians and which that "mean" nation refused.[35] Usbek states that

21. *LP,* 1:10.
22. *LP,* 8:19–20.
23. *LP,* 161:323.
24. Neumann, *Spirit of the Laws,* xviii. This letter was added by Montesquieu in 1754, shortly before his death, as if he wanted to make sure that the idea of liberty, standing at the beginning of the *Persian Letters,* would also stand at their end, perhaps in the most dramatic way conceivable: The denial of liberty prompts suicide, the kind of death that is unlikely to interfere with the liberty of others, in contrast to a fight for liberty against others at the risk of death.
25. *LP,* 47:91.
26. *LP,* 67:131.
27. Ibid., 143.
28. *LP,* 76:156 ff.
29. *LP,* 11:27.
30. *LP,* 14:35–36.
31. *LP,* 89:179.
32. *LP,* 103:205.
33. *LP,* 104:207.
34. *LP,* 106:211.
35. *LP,* 131:263 ff.

nothing attracts strangers more than liberty and its accompaniment, wealth. The latter is sought for itself, and our needs lead us to those countries in which we find the former.[36]

Montesquieu continued his emphasis upon liberty in his *Considerations on the Causes of the Greatness of the Romans and their Decline.* In that work, greatness means national power, the ability to coerce other nations. Decline is attributed to the waning of that power. However, national power does not imply for Montesquieu an absence of freedom within a strong nation. In the very first chapter he writes that the extension of Rome's power depended upon its liberty, and he considers liberty the soul that animates a powerful nation. Since the liberty of the citizen is a prerequisite for the state's power, it must be protected. Juxtaposing liberty to tyranny,[37] Montesquieu leaves no doubt that he prefers the former and that he favors restrictions of governmental power for the sake of the rights of the individual. To him, the most vicious source of the misfortune of the Greeks was that they never knew the nature or limits of ecclesiastical and secular power.[38] The government of Rome was admirable because abuses of power could always be corrected by its constitution, whether by means of the spirit of the people, the strength of the senate, or the authority of the magistrates. The laws of Rome wisely divided public power among a large number of magistracies which supported, checked, and tempered each other.[39] Montesquieu criticizes the republics of Italy for having abusive governments and no liberty. The government of England, on the other hand, is wise because it is a free government, continually examined by Parliament, which also examines itself with a view of protecting the freedom of Englishmen.[40] Sulla is criticized for having made it impossible for Rome to preserve its liberty.[41] Horrible exactions imposed upon the population are decried for being incompatible with freedom.[42] After writing that tyrannicide was accepted in Greece and Italy, Montesquieu asks whether the crime of Caesar could be punished in any other way than by assassination.[43] He scoffs at Augustus, writing that those who usurp sovereignty in a free state call whatever can establish the unlimited rule of one man, good order, and denounce whatever can maintain the honest liberty of the subject as commotion, dissension, or bad government.[44] Montesquieu thus indicates a distrust of order, even of authority, if they exist at the cost of liberty. As a general rule, there is no liberty in a republic in which everyone is tranquil: a free government is constantly subject to agitation.[45] Movement, activity, progression, and progress have liberty for their prerequisite.

If the importance Montesquieu attributes to liberty can be seen in the *Persian Letters* and the *Considerations,* it is even more obvious in the *Spirit of*

36. *LP,* 122:244.
37. *C,* 9:413; 11:430; 12:431.
38. *C,* 22:519.
39. *C,* 8:410; 11:421.
40. *C,* 8:410.
41. *C,* 11:419–20.
42. *C,* 18:485.
43. *C,* 11:431.
44. *C,* 13:121.
45. *C,* 8:410.

the Laws. In the first two works, the idea of freedom is important but usually has not been considered dominant. In the last, it is prevalent. The *Persian Letters* and the *Considerations* indicate the ever-existing presence of freedom in the minds of men and show ways in which liberty has been negated. The *Spirit of the Laws,* while continuing that approach, does more. It elevates the protection of freedom to a central position around which other considerations evolve and concentrates on showing what can be done for securing the rights of the individual. Montesquieu, who has been called a revolutionary in many respects[46] and a liberal fighting the absolutist régime,[47] aside from describing things, suggests what can be done for the sake of freedom. From a description of the causes of the rise and decline of the Romans—appreciation and abuse of liberty—Montesquieu turns to a prescription of measures that can cause liberty to prevail in modern society.

The importance attributed to human liberty in the *Spirit of the Laws* is indicated when the first chapter of the first book states that nature requires men to be free agents.[48] It follows from the central position freedom occupies in that work. To judge by the number of books, the chapters on political liberty are located in the center of the first volume, which Montesquieu considered the more important of the two volumes making up the work.[49]

46. John Millar saw in Montesquieu the founder of a philosophical history that looked for the basic laws governing human development and compared him with Bacon. *A Historical View of the English Government,* 4th ed. (London, 1818), 2:429–30. Similar Adam Ferguson, according to Melvin Richter, *The Political Theory of Montesquieu,* 5. Friedrich Meinecke considered Montesquieu a founder of historicism, which according to Richter is "a distinctly modern perspective characterized by its relativism, holism, emphasis upon the positive value of the irrational and customary, as well as the uniqueness of every case and period." See Meinecke, *Historism,* trans. J. A. Anderson (New York, 1922), 90 ff. Richter, *Political Theory of Montesquieu,* 5. Hegel thought that Montesquieu was among the first to explain institutions, laws and political attitudes from their social environment and thus a source for his own method. Georg Wilhelm Friedrich Hegel, *The Philosophy of Right,* trans. T. M. Knox (Oxford, 1942), 16. Comte and Durkheim saw in Montesquieu a precursor of sociology, and Aron and Runciman, the first practitioner of political sociology. Auguste Comte, *Cours de philosophie positive* (Paris, 1839), 5:243; Emile Durkheim, *Montesquieu et Rousseau précurseurs de la sociologie* (Paris, 1953), 26; Raymond Aron, *Main Currents in Sociological Thought* (New York, 1965), 1:55–56; G. W. Runciman, *Social Science and Political Theory* (Cambridge, 1963), 24. Ernst Cassirer and Franz Neumann indicate that Montesquieu used ideal-type analysis, brought to fruition by Max Weber. Ernst Cassirer, *The Philosophy of the Enlightenment,* trans. Fritz Koelln and James Pettegrove (Princeton, 1951), 212; Neumann, *Spirit of the Laws,* xl–xli. See also Sheila Mary Mason, *Montesquieu's Idea of Justice* (The Hague, 1975), 199. For Montesquieu's attitude toward the *ancien régime,* see Mark Hulling, *Montesquieu and the Old Regime* (Berkeley, 1976).

47. The *Persian Letters* were first published 1721 anonymously at Cologne, the *Considerations,* anonymously in Amsterdam in 1734. The *Spirit of the Laws* was first published in Geneva in 1748. In a word, none of Montesquieu's works relating to government was first published in absolutist France, his home country.

48. *EL,* 1, 1:3.

49. Cf., on the importance of the center Charles S. Singleton, "The Poet's Number at the Center," *Modern Language Notes* 80 (1965):1; Hans Sedlmayr, *Art in Crisis: The Lost Center* (London, 1957); Gottfried Dietze, *Magna Carta and Property* (Charlottesville, Va., 1965), 30.

Montesquieu moves toward a definition of freedom as if he wanted to slowly lead the reader to a climax. In none of the titles of the first ten books is the word "liberty" mentioned. Neither is it in any of the 132 titles of their respective chapters. Under all these headings he discusses laws and traditional governments, here and there touching on their consequences for liberty and showing their inadequacies for a satisfactory protection of freedom. He thus whets the reader's appetite for knowing what liberty is and what can be done for its protection.

In view of the announcement made at the beginning of the *Spirit of the Laws* that it is planned to examine how laws will relate to the degree of liberty a constitution will bear, the reader can expect Montesquieu to show the consequences of traditional governments for freedom more clearly in book 11, the first book with a title mentioning liberty. Or, since in the preceding books Montesquieu shows the inadequacy of traditional governments for the existence of liberty, it can be expected that Montesquieu will come up with a new type of constitution or government which is more devoted to the protection of liberty. Pointing to the title of book 11, which, with its express reference to political liberty, appears to harbor the promise of something new, Pangle asserts that Montesquieu did the latter.[50] However, even if Montesquieu considered the liberal constitution of England dealt with in book 11 the mere climax of a development toward constitutional government that began much earlier, the importance of liberty as a highlight of the *Spirit of the Laws* would be evident.[51]

Just as Montesquieu whetted the appetite for knowing the government most conducive to the protection of liberty, he seems to have done so with respect to a definition of liberty. Much as he emphasized freedom in the *Persian Letters* and the *Considerations,* he did not define it. We only get an inkling of what it means when it is compared with despotism and tyranny. We also get an idea of certain of its aspects: Women in a seraglio are not free; neither are slaves and family members under the jurisdiction of the father. In China, a law requiring people to cut their hair or their nails was felt to be incompatible with freedom.[52] Prohibition of divorce and free love is considered oppressive.[53] According to Rica's learned instructor, barbarians are not

50. Thomas L. Pangle, *Montesquieu's Philosophy of Liberalism* (Chicago, 1973), 107.

51. Ibid., 107, writes: "In his presentation of the traditional forms of government, Montesquieu has revealed the inadequacies of their particular principles and the aims which derive from those principles. He has thereby pointed to the desirability of a government having no other purpose than the security and comfort of its citizens. He finds the principles of this desired government in the modern constitution of England, properly understood and interpreted. Book XI is the presentation of this constitution, and the books which follow all deal in one way or another with its consequence for political life in all times and places." The thought occurs that Montesquieu's spirit of the laws is similar to Hegel's weltgeist, that he is interested in an increase of the freedom of the individual and that such an increase for him constitutes the rationale of history.

52. *LP,* 61:123.

53. *LP,* 116: 231 ff.; 117:233 ff.

free; those submitting to an absolute power have lost their "sweet liberty," which is in conformity with reason, humanity, and nature.[54] The crime of *lèse-majesté* is said to have abolished liberty at banquets, confidence among kindred, and fidelity in slaves.[55] Montesquieu advocates liberty of trade.[56]

Similarly, the reader gets just an inkling of what liberty is all about in the first ten books of the *Spirit of the Laws.* In the beginning of book 1, Montesquieu writes that nature requires men to be free agents. At its end, he speaks of the degree of liberty the constitution will bear. Subsequently, he states that a person habituated to veracity has an air of boldness and freedom and mentions the liberty to seek or reject employment.[57] He speaks of the relation set forms of justice bear to the liberty and security of the individual, and writes that the trouble, expense, delays, and dangers of existing judicial proceedings are the price each subject pays for his liberty. Absolute rulers are said to care little about the liberty of men. In republics and monarchies, formalities increase in proportion to the value that is set on the honor, fortune, liberty, and life of the subject. Montesquieu mentions the loss of liberty in Florence and says that under Justinian the judges no longer were free to administer justice. In almost all states of Europe, penalties have increased or diminished in proportion to their governments' favoring or discouraging liberty. Persons aiming at the subversion of liberty were afraid of writings that might revive the spirit of freedom. Scylla confounded tyranny, anarchy, and liberty.[58] In monarchies, liberty results in luxury. Women are subject to little restraint: in court life, they assume a spirit of liberty, which is almost the only spirit tolerated there. In despotic governments, they are afraid lest their liberty should expose them to danger. In republics, women are free under the laws and restrained by manners.[59] Montesquieu writes that the greater the advantages people seem to derive from their liberty, the more they approach losing it; that petty tyrants arise who possess all the vices of a single tyrant; that what remains of liberty soon becomes insupportable. Syracuse labored under the alternate succession of liberty and servitude. Phillip II tempted the French with the allurement of liberty. When the Romans were free, they had contempt for power. The greater their power, the less considerate they were. In the end, they became their own tyrants and slaves and lost the strength of liberty to fall into the weakness of licentiousness. The sole aim of Lacedaemonia was liberty, the sole advantage of her liberty, glory. Athens had the ambition of commanding a free people rather than of governing slaves.[60] The conqueror who reduces people to servitude ought always reserve to himself the means of letting them get out of it. While the Spaniards in Mexico might have freed slaves, they made freemen slaves. If a democratic republic subdues a nation, it exposes its own liberty because it

54. *LP,* 136:274.
55. *C,* 14:445.
56. *C,* 20:501–2; 23:526.
57. *EL,* 4, 2:40–41, 43.
58. *EL,* 6, 2:99 ff.; 5:103, 106–7; 9:110; 15:119–20.
59. *EL,* 7, 4:134; 9:139–40.
60. *EL,* 8, 3:152–53; 9:158; 12:162; 16:165.

entrusts too great a power to those who are appointed to magistrate in the conquered state.[61]

In book 11, entitled "Of the Laws which Establish Political Liberty with regard to the Constitution," Montesquieu first mentions different meanings of the word *liberty* and thus adds to the confusion and mystery surrounding that concept. Perhaps he does so in order to increase the demand for a precise definition. He writes: "There is no word that has received more meanings and made more different impressions on the minds, than that of 'liberty'. Some have taken it as a means for deposing a person on whom they had conferred a tyrannical power; others, for the faculty of choosing a superior whom they are obliged to obey; others, for the right of bearing arms and the power of using violence; these, for the privilege of being governed only by a man from their own nation, or by their own laws. Certain people for a long time took liberty to mean the custom of wearing a long beard. (The Moscovites could not bear it that Peter made them cut theirs.) Some have attached this name to one form of government and excluded it from others; those who liked republican government have given it to monarchy. Finally, everybody has called 'liberty' the government that conformed to his customs or inclinations: And since in a republic, one does not always have before the eyes the bad things of which one complains and since even the laws seem to speak of it more, and the executors of the law, less, one ordinarily places liberty in republics and excludes it from monarchies. Finally, since in democracies, people seem to do pretty much what they like, one has deemed these governments free and confounded the power of the people with the liberty of the people."[62] After reading these lines, the reader is about as clever as he was before with respect to the meaning of liberty. When he then sees the title of the next chapter, "What Liberty Is," he gets new hope of finding out; but he is disappointed again when first he reads what liberty is not and that political liberty does not consist in doing what one wants to do. Finally, Montesquieu moves toward lifting the secret: "In a state, that is, in a society where there are laws, liberty can only consist in being able to do what one ought to want, and in not being forced to do what one ought not to want." Again, this is not too precise a definition of liberty. That definition presumably comes later, after we are urged to remember always that liberty is not identical to independence: "Liberty is the right of doing whatever the laws permit."[63]

Montesquieu's giving us just an inkling of what liberty is in the *Persian Letters,* the *Considerations* and the first ten books of the *Spirit of the Laws* perhaps symbolizes his own long search for the meaning of freedom. According to his preface for the *Spirit of the Laws,* he followed his object without any fixed plan and often found the truth only to lose it again. However, once he had discovered his principles, everything he searched for came to him.[64] And a

61. *EL,* 10, 3:186; 4:187; 6:189.
62. *EL,* 11, 2, 204–5.
63. *EL,* 11, 3, 205–6.
64. *EL,* preface, lxii.

major thing he searched for and found was that liberty is defined by law and exists according to law.

However, is that definition as precise as Faguet indicates?[65] All Montesquieu stated with some precision is what liberty is not: it is not independence. In an affirmative sense, his definition of freedom is precise only insofar as the laws are precise. It could be argued that laws are precise by definition because a case can be decided according to the laws in only one way. But that would apply merely to laws with a sanction. However, it has been asked whether Montesquieu, when he wrote that liberty exists according to the laws, had in mind just positive laws, which Jellinek thought of when he stated that law is an ethical minimum.[66] To this question we now turn.

Liberty under Law

High as liberty ranks for Montesquieu, it is not unlimited: it is defined by the laws. Is it limited not just by the laws that are enforced by the state, but also by nonpositive laws?

Since Montesquieu, when he writes that liberty is the right of doing what the laws permit, does not specify what he understands under the "laws," the question arises as to what laws he has in mind. His use of the plural indicates that he may mean all the laws there are. Some observers will argue that, given the fact that he uses the plural "laws" also in the title of his major work, the laws in question are all the laws mentioned in that work. They will maintain that in view of Montesquieu's general reference to "laws," he thinks of "Laws in General," as discussed under that heading in book 1 of the *Spirit of the Laws.* In what has been considered the most discussed paragraph of the whole study,[67] paragraph one of chapter one of book 1, Montesquieu states that all beings have their laws, the Deity His laws, the material world its laws, the intelligences superior to man their laws, the beasts their laws, man his laws.

The laws of man are, according to book 1, quite comprehensive. They include laws "particular intelligent beings" had before they made laws, as well as the laws they made. At the end of the first chapter, Montesquieu adds that man is, like other bodies, governed by invariable laws, that as an intelligent being, he incessantly transgresses the laws established by God and changes those of his own making. He is reminded of his duty by God through the laws of religion, by philosophy through the laws of morality, by legislators through political and civil laws.

Montesquieu then devotes chapters to the laws of nature and to positive

65. Faguet, *La politique comparée,* 14.

66. Georg Jellinek, *Die sozialethische Bedeutung von Recht, Unrecht und Strafe,* 45.

67. See J. Robert Loy, *Montesquieu* (New York, 1968), 89 ff.; Mark H. Waddicor, *Montesquieu and the Philosophy of Natural Law* (The Hague, 1970), 181 ff.; Althusser, *Montesquieu,* 28 ff.; Sheila Mary Mason, *Montesquieu's Idea of Justice,* 183 ff.

laws. Before the founding of society, man is under the laws of nature, which include the laws inclining men toward their Creator, the laws of self-preservation, of securing peace, nourishment, and procreation, and the laws due to the desire to live in society. In society, man loses the sense of his weakness and becomes aware of his strength. When a state of war begins between different societies and among the individuals composing societies, it gives rise to positive laws, to the law of nations relating to the intercourse among nations, to political laws concerning the relations between the rulers and the ruled, and to civil laws, regulating the behavior of individuals within societies.

Since Montesquieu favors free governments[68] that correspond to nature, it can be argued that he considers best those positive laws that conform to the laws of nature, and that, according to him, liberty exists in conformity with natural and positive laws. This argument could be supported by the fact that even in the chapter on positive laws, Montesquieu writes that law in general is human reason in as much as it governs all the inhabitants of the earth and that the political and civil laws of each nation ought to be only particular applications of human reason: Diverse as positive laws may be, they are part of a uniform law that is prior to positive law.

On the other hand, it will be asserted that the liberty defined by Montesquieu is merely one according to positive laws. This argument will be based upon his mentioning the expression "l'ESPRIT DES LOIX" for the first time in the chapter under the heading "Of Positive Laws."[69] It will also be based upon the organization of book 1, which proceeds from a chapter "Of the Relation of Laws to Different Beings" to one "Of the Laws of Nature" to one "Of Positive Laws." It will be said that this sequence, leading to and climaxing in a chapter on positive laws, indicates that Montesquieu wants to move away from the laws described in chapters 1 and 2, that he wants to move toward positive law, that the following discussion continues to be concerned with positive law only. It will be added that according to Montesquieu, the laws of each nation should be

68. After this definition of liberty and after having pointed out the importance of freedom in books 11 and 12, Montesquieu stresses that importance later on. He mentions the great advantages of liberty (13, 15:298), the inconveniences of lost liberty (13, 16:299). He argues that a freeman cannot sell himself because his freedom constitutes part of the public liberty, in a democratic state even a part of sovereignty. To sell one's freedom is so repugnant to all reason as can scarcely be supposed in any man. If liberty may be rated with respect to the buyer, it is beyond all price to the seller (15, 2:326 ff.). Given Montesquieu's defense of the right to suicide, he here perhaps puts liberty over life, although he argues in mere positivist fashion that if it is not lawful for a person to kill himself because he robs his country of his person, for the same reason he is not allowed to barter his freedom. For Montesquieu, there must be a certain minimum of liberty. The minute freedom of the Muscovites is not worth keeping (15, 6:331). In moderate governments, political liberty adds to the value of civil liberty. As slaves living among freemen come close to beasts, they are the natural enemies of society and their number must be dangerous (15, 13:338). In mountainous countries, liberty is the only thing worth defending (18, 2:379). Countries are cultivated in proportion to liberty, not fertility (18, 3:380).

69. *EL,* 1, 3:9.

adapted so much to the people for which they are made that it would be rare if the laws of one nation would suit another. Laws should reflect the nature and principle of each particular society and government and relate to the physical conditions of the land inhabited, its climate, its soil, its location and extension as well as to the nature of the people. Laws should be relative to the degree of liberty the country's constitution will bear, to the religions of its inhabitants, to their inclinations, their riches, their number, their commerce, their mores, their manners.[70] All this, it will be said, suggests adjustments of laws to existing conditions, something usually characteristic of positive laws.

Those inclined to think that liberty according to the laws for Montesquieu means primarily liberty according to natural law, will use the same passage in support of their opinion. They will argue that his statement clearly distinguishes between the intent of the lawmaker and the "natural" conditions he ought to take into consideration, such as geography, mores, morals, and manners.

The friends of natural law will point to Montesquieu's intent not to examine the laws, but their spirit, and consider that intent an indication of his being not just a positivist, but also a believer in prepositive law. Those seeing in Montesquieu a positivist will answer that positive laws have as much of a spirit as natural laws.[71] They will support their argument by the fact that many legal codes provide that their norms ought to be interpreted not according to the letter, but the spirit, of the law. Again, Montesquieu's statement in chapter 3 that he is going to examine all the relations of laws and that these relations constitute the spirit of the laws, can be used to support arguments that Montesquieu favored positive, respectively natural, law.

The uncertainty as to whether for Montesquieu freedom exists according to metapositive or positive laws can also be seen in book 11. According to chapter 6, judges ought to come from the people in the manner prescribed by, and the criminal ought to choose his judges in concurrence with, the law. A few lines later one reads that judicial decisions must conform to the precise text of the law.[72] All this seems to show Montesquieu as a positivist. On the other hand, he indicates a distinction between precisely formulated written law and other law. Chapter 6 deals with the constitution of England, which is not just a written document, but a conglomeration of older and newer, natural, customary, and common law, of written documents such as the Magna Carta, the Petition of Right, the Bill of Rights, acts of Parliament, and court decisions. Because all these in a large measure correspond to the common law and that

70. Ibid.

71. See *LP,* 97:193–94: "Que les législateurs ordinaires nous proposent des loix, pour régler les sociétés des hommes; des loix aussi sujettes au changement, que l'esprit de ceux qui les proposent, & des peuples qui les observent: ceux-ci ne nous parlent que des loix générales, immunables, éternelles, qui l'observent sans aucune exception, avec un ordre, une régularité, & une promptitude infinie, dans l'immensité des espaces."

72. *EL,* 11, 6:210.

law, according to Bracton's statement, *non sub homine sed sub Deo et lege,*[73] to the law of God, the ancient constitution of England[74] has strong meta-positivist undertones. Later on, Montesquieu writes that the law is at the same time *clairvoyante* and blind. In certain cases, it could be too rigorous. He adds that the House of Lords is to moderate the law in favor of the law itself and make it less rigorous. Clearly, if the law can be made less rigorous for the sake of the law, there must exist principles according to which this can be done, principles more lenient and liberal. And the principles usually considered conducive to a mitigation of the harshness of positive laws are those of higher law. For Montesquieu, liberty is established under English laws, whether Englishmen actually enjoy it or not.[75] This suggests occasions on which the laws are discarded by the executive, the judiciary, and the legislature. It implies that legislative fiat might not be in conformity with English laws securing the rights of individuals or with higher law principles as was argued by the American colonists when they asserted that acts of Parliament interfered with their rights as Englishmen and their rights as men.

In book 12, Montesquieu again recognizes metapositive as well as positive laws. He calls liberty triumphant when punishments correspond to the nature of the crime, stating that all penalties must be derived from the nature of the crime, a principle he repeats several times.[76] He writes that nature defends its rights. Sweet, lovable, and charming, it has strewn pleasures with a liberal hand, filled us with delights, and prepared us for even greater satisfactions.[77] It would be absurd to disregard the rules of decency in the punishment of crimes. Some Japanese laws subvert all ideas of human reason—something by which positive laws actually ought to be oriented.[78]

Montesquieu's appreciation of metapositive as well as positive laws is evident in other parts of the *Spirit of the Laws.* There is hardly a book in which it is not indicated. Even in the parts that are the most obviously concerned with positive laws, Montesquieu shows his appreciation of natural law. In book 13, concerned with taxation, he asks whether tax laws are just and reasonable[79] and mentions a rule derived from nature that taxes increase in proportion to liberty.[80] Tax exemptions must not ruin the state, but must be reasonable and just.[81] In book 26, "Of Laws in the Relation They Must Have with the Order of Things which They Determine," Montesquieu, remindful of book 1, refers to the several kinds of law. Using "droit" interchangeably with "loi," he writes that men are governed by "the law of nature; by divine law, which is that of religion; by ecclesiastical law, otherwise called canon law, which is that of religious polity [*police*]; by the law of nations, which one can consider as the civil law of the universe . . . ; by the general political law, which is concerned

73. Bracton, *De legibus et consuetudinibus angliae,* folio 5.
74. Cf. Pocock, *The Ancient Constitution and the Feudal Law.*
75. *EL,* 11, 6:217, 221.
76. *EL,* 12, 4:253, 255.
77. *EL,* 12, 6:259.
78. *EL,* 12, 14:267; 17:270.
79. *EL,* 13, 7:291.
80. *EL,* 13, 12:295.
81. *EL,* 13, 18:301.

with that political wisdom which has founded all societies; by the particular political law which concerns each society; by the law of conquest, founded on the fact that a people has wanted to, has been able to, or had to, do violence to another; by the civil law of each society, under which a citizen can defend his goods and his life against every other citizen; finally, by domestic law, which is derived from a society's being divided into several families which stand in need of a particular government."[82] In the following chapters delineating what laws apply under various circumstances, Montesquieu stresses that men, while they are under positive laws, are also under metapositive ones. He criticizes positive laws for being in conflict with other types of laws. He writes of civil laws which are contrary to the law of nature in chapters 3 and 4. When he desires the application of positive law, he clearly favors its principles not to the point of destroying nonpositive law, for principles imply exceptions.[83] He states that the matters that ought to be regulated by the principles of civil law can seldom be regulated by the laws of religion. This means that sometimes they may be regulated by the latter.[84] Chapter 10 discusses in what case it is necessary to follow the civil law which permits, and not the religious law which prohibits, leaving no doubt that in other cases the religious laws ought to be followed. Similarly, according to chapter 14, marriages between relatives can be regulated by the laws of nature and by civil laws.[85]

In book 29, on the manner of composing laws, Montesquieu deals with the spirit of the legislator. He states in the very first sentence of chapter 1 that he undertook the writing of his major work with no other purpose but that of proving that the legislator ought to be guided by the spirit of moderation—a clear exhortation to those who make positive laws. He continues saying that the political good, just as the moral good, always finds itself between two limits. He warns of too much legislation: "The formalities of justice are necessary for liberty. But their number could be so great as to hurt the end of the laws . . . . There would be no end to proceedings; property would be uncertain; the goods of one party would be given to another without examination, or they would both be ruined due to examination [*à force d'examiner*]. The citizens would lose their liberty and security; the accusers would no longer have the means to convict, nor the accused those of justifying themselves."[86]

Montesquieu's fear of too many positive laws is thus matched by his warning against bad legislation at the beginning of the book on the manner of

82. *EL,* 26, 1:126.

83. *EL,* 26, 2:127–28, the title of the chapter being, "Of Divine Laws and of Human Laws"; 2:128–29, the title of the chapter being, "Of Civil Laws which are contrary to Natural Law"; 5:131, the title of the chapter being, "Case in which one Can Judge according to the Principles of Civil Law, by Modifying the Principles of Natural Law"; 6:132 ff., the title of the chapter being, "That the Order of Succession Depends upon Principles of Political or Civil Law, and not upon Principles of Natural Law."

84. *EL,* 26, 9:137.

85. *EL,* 26, 10:139; 14:142 ff.

86. *EL,* 29, 1:269.

composing laws. It also is evident throughout the whole book. Montesquieu does not spare with criticism of lawmakers. They make laws so little understood by them that they are contrary to the very end the legislators had in mind.[87] He urges that laws be composed the right way and mentions examples of improper composition and enactment. A law on ostracism, he writes, produced a thousand mischiefs because it was imprudently made.[88] Chapter 16 deals with things to be observed in composing the laws. It urges that only those with sufficient genius should give laws to their nation or to another nation, although even they must be careful when making laws. Laws ought to be concise and simple, not subtle. They ought to convey to everybody the same ideas, to be as free of exceptions and limitations as possible, not to be contrary to the nature of things, and characterized by candor. Montesquieu shows how legislative enactments have not corresponded to these principles.[89] The next chapter of book 29 criticizes human legislators. Plato is said to have been incensed against the people of Athens; Aristotle, to have indulged in his jealousy against Plato and in his passion for Alexander. Machiavelli, Montesquieu writes, was full of his idol, the Duke of Valentinois. Thomas More rather spoke of what he read than of what he thought and wanted to govern all states with the simplicity existing in a Greek city. Harrington saw nothing but the republic of England, and a crowd [*foule*] of writers found disorder everywhere except in monarchies. The chapter ends: "The laws always meet [*recontrent*] the passions and prejudices of the legislator. Sometimes they pass them by and are merely tinctured by the latter, sometimes these passions and prejudices remain with, and become incorporated in, the laws."[90]

One would expect that with this strong warning of legislation concluding a book on the manner of composing the laws, a book introduced with the remark that the *Spirit of the Laws* was undertaken to prove that the spirit of the legislator ought to be one of moderation, Montesquieu would conclude his doubts about irresponsible positive laws. For, given his introductory remark, that book can be considered the last important book of his major work. However, he seems to be so occupied with the possibility of bad positive laws that in later books on feudal laws he does not abstain from criticizing positive laws. He writes that these man-made laws have done infinite good but also infinite mischief, that they produced a rule with a bias toward anarchy, anarchy with a tendency toward order and harmony.[91] This observation is complemented by subsequent remarks indicating fears of positive laws, remarks which show how fears of bad man-made laws constantly weighed on Montesquieu's mind.

These fears also can be seen in the emphasis upon justice and equity, concepts he ranks highly.[92] Usbek states that the law, made in order to make us

87. *EL,* 29, 16:283; 4:271.
88. *EL,* 29, 7:273.
89. *EL,* 29, 16:283 ff.
90. *EL,* 29, 19:290–91.
91. *EL,* 30, 1:292.
92. Cf. Mason, *Montesquieu's Idea of Justice;* J. Wróblewski, "La théorie du droit de Montesquieu," in Polska Akademia Nauk/Komitet Nauk Prawnych ed., *Monteskiusz i jego dzielo* (War-

more just, often makes us more guilty.[93] Criminal laws may, or may not, serve justice.[94] In self-interest—an interest which can be, and often is, expressed by positive laws—men will commit injustices. Justice is eternal and independent of human conventions—including man-made laws. If such laws, or other human behavior, interfere with justice, there is, fortunately, a principle within men which takes the side of justice by fighting for the protection of the weaker from the stronger.[95] Doubts are voiced on the justice of justice meted out under the laws.[96] Public law is a science that teaches princes to what degree they can violate justice.[97] Rica writes that the abundance of adopted laws oppresses justice.[98] Usbek complains that legislatures often followed the ideas of logic rather than those of natural equity.[99] Legal behavior can be unjust on account of odious laws.[100] Montesquieu denounces Romans for being unjust legislators.[101] Justinian's tax laws are said to have done general injustice to his subjects.[102] Excessive imposts in France are considered unjust.[103] Germanic laws are just because they protect the criminal against the injured party.[104]

Montesquieu's doubts about positive laws also follow from his remarks on virtue, another high value of his.[105] Usbek writes that the most just Troglodite told others that positive laws are less demanding than virtue.[106] This means that they may well conflict with virtue. He expresses disgust about unvirtuous acts, even though they are permitted by the laws.[107] He denounces the "detestable conspiracy" to acquire wealth, not by honest labor and generous industry but by the ruin of the prince, the state, and of fellow-citizens, by a behavior which is in accordance with the laws, but not with morals and virtue.[108] In the *Considerations,* Montesquieu states that assassination of a usurper is virtuous,[109] even though it is usually not in conformity with the laws. According to the *Spirit of the Laws,* the Greeks, living under a popular government, recognized no other support for that government than virtue.[110] People (including lawmakers) ought never to swerve from adhering to old institutions, for ancient maxims make people virtuous.[111] Rome experienced a decline of virtue when the magistrates and principal citizens abused their power,[112] a power they may well have exercised under positive laws.

---

saw, 1956); Jean Brethe de la Gressaye, "La philosophie du droit de Montesquieu," *Archives de philosophie du droit* 7 (1962) 199 ff.

93. *LP,* 33:68–69.
94. *LP,* 90:182–83.
95. *LP,* 83:169–70.
96. Rica in *LP,* 86:174–75; Usbek in 90:182–83.
97. *LP,* 94:187–88.
98. *LP,* 100:200.
99. *LP,* 129:258.
100. *LP,* 146:307.
101. *C,* 6:398–99.
102. *C,* 20:500.
103. *EL,* 20, 13:456.
104. *EL,* 30, 20:333.

105. According to Pangle, *Montesquieu's Philosophy,* 107 ff., Montesquieu subordinates virtue to freedom. Montesquieu's opinions on virtue are dealt with in Henry J. Merry, *Montesquieu's System of Natural Government* (West Lafayette, Ind., 1970), 10 ff., 69, 171–72, 174–75, 187–88, 197 ff., 245, 280, 376.

106. *LP,* 14:36.
107. *LP,* 48:98.
108. *LP,* 146:308–9.
109. *C,* 11:430 ff.
110. *EL,* 3, 3:27.
111. *EL,* 5, 7:64.
112. *EL,* 8, 14:164.

Montesquieu's emphasis upon virtue, often complemented by emphases upon morals,[113] is further complemented by his attributing to religion the quality of a check upon positive laws. He sees in the Christian religion a source of the best political and civil laws which according to him "are, next to that religion, the greatest good men can give and receive."[114]

Liberty as defined by positive laws is not all the liberty conceivable, but only a fraction. That fraction is not necessarily just a liberal minimum, for a free constitution can go quite far in guaranteeing aspects of freedom.[115] However, the sum total of these aspects will not amount to a liberal maximum either, since positive laws imply restrictions—including those of liberty. Already in the *Persian Letters,* Montesquieu made plain that there is a comprehensive liberty irrespective of governments and their particular laws.[116] He did not change his opinion later on. Depending upon governments, positive laws provide only for certain aspects of freedom. Even under the government of England, which in Montesquieu's opinion provided for more freedom than any other government, there could be more freedom still.

Montesquieu's concept of freedom under law is shrouded in mystery. However, this does not imply the unreality of liberty. Concrete realizations of aspects of freedom indicate that a comprehensive freedom exists. Credited with having given a definition of freedom by stating that liberty exists according to the laws, Montesquieu has not unravelled the mystery, and mysticism, of the general concept of freedom. This should not be held against him. He was merely unable to achieve something nobody succeeded in achieving before or after him. Perhaps he did not even want to try to find out what freedom in its totality is in order to retain, with its mystery, its fascination as a goal to be longed for.[117] This would be another proof of the high value he assigns to liberty.

Since Montesquieu conceived freedom to be under the imperatives ranging from those of religion and virtue to those prescribed by human rulers, there is a large span of laws according to which liberty can exist. Broadly speaking, this span has been said to range from natural to positive law. Shortly after the publication of the *Spirit of the Laws,* the spirits were divided as to Montesquieu's concept of laws. Critics like the Abbé Fontaine de la Roche and the Sorbonne, were indignant that Montesquieu had abandoned natural law.[118]

113. *LP,* 129:258; *C,* 5:382; 8:408.

114. *EL,* 24, 1:81.

115. While he writes that the minute freedom the Muscovites enjoy is not worth keeping (*EL,* 15, 6:331), he also makes plain that a certain degree of freedom exists even under despotic forms of government in *C,* 22:519.

116. *LP,* 12, 13, 14, on the lives of the Troglodites.

117. At the end of book 11 of the *Spirit of the Laws,* Montesquieu writes that he would like to inquire into the degree of liberty that is enjoyed by various moderate governments. "But it is not always necessary to exhaust a subject, and to leave no work for the reader. My business is not to make people read, but to make them think." *EL,* 11, 20:248–49.

118. See Waddicor, *Montesquieu,* 17.

The historian Crevier complained that this work reduces natural law to almost nothing.[119] Others seem to have seen in Montesquieu a believer in natural law and its moral values. De la Beaumelle, Voltaire, and Lord Chesterfield praised his contribution to the cause of humanity.[120] From about the middle of the nineteenth century on, Franck considered natural law the very basis of the *Spirit of the Laws;* Béchard stated that Montesquieu believed in the same immutable principles as Bossuet and Domat; and Janet and Sorel praised Montesquieu for his service to humanity.[121] On the other hand, Maine saw in Montesquieu a destroyer of the school of natural law.[122] Positivists such as Auguste Comte and Alengry considered Montesquieu a precursor of their ideas, as did, in the twentieth century, Dedieu and Oudin.[123] Animated also by the positivist spirit are contemporary authors such as Fletcher, Starobinski, Vernière, Althusser, Shackleton, and Loy.[124] In 1909, Charaux complained about Montesquieu's not paying sufficient tribute to natural law.[125] A few years later, Lanson claimed a natural law content for Montesquieu's writings, as did Marcel Raymond, Groethuysen, and Barrière.[126] More recently, the importance of natural law in the writings of Montesquieu has been stressed by Aron, Crocker, Ehrard, Meyer, Waddicor, and Mason.[127]

119. Jean-Baptiste-Louis Crevier, *Observations sur le livre, de l'Esprit des lois* (Paris, 1764), 4.

120. Laurent Angliviel de La Beaumelle, *Suite de la Défense de l'Esprit des lois, ou examen de la réplique du gazetier ecclésiastique à la Défense de l'Esprit des lois,* (1751) in *Oeuvres complètes de Montesquieu,* ed. Edouard Laboulaye (Paris, 1875–79), 6:250. François-Marie Arout de Voltaire, *Siècle de Louis XIV, Catalogue de la plupart des écrivains français qui ont paru dans le siècle de Louis XIV,* in *Oeuves complètes de Voltaire,* ed. Louis Emile Moland (Paris, 1877–85), 14:107.

121. Paul Janet, *Histoire de la science politique dans ses rapports avec la morale* (1858, 3rd ed., Paris, 1887), 2:379; Albert Sorel, *Montesquieu* (Paris, 1924), 108.

122. Henry J. S. Maine, *Ancient Law* (1861; London, 1930), 97.

123. Auguste Comte, *Cours de philosophie positive* (Paris, 1908), 4:127–28; Franck Alengry, "Montesquieu," in *Essai historique et critique sur la sociologie chez Auguste Comte* (Paris, 1900), 389 ff.; Joseph Dedieu, *Montesquieu et la tradition politique anglaise en France* (Paris, 1909), 169; *Montesquieu* (Paris, 1913), 184; *Montesquieu l'homme et l'oeuvre* (Paris, 1943), 27–28, 132 ff.; Charles Oudin, *Le Spinozisme de Montesquieu* (Paris, 1911), 63.

124. Frank T. H. Fletcher, *Montesquieu and English Politics (1750–1800)* (London, 1939), 271; Jean Starobinski, *Montesquieu par lui-même* (1953; Paris, 1961), 86–87; Paul Vernière, *Spinoza et la pensée française avant la Révolution* (Paris, 1954), 2:456–57; Althusser, *Montesquieu,* 8 ff.; Robert Shackleton, *Montesquieu: A Critical Biography* (Oxford, 1961), 247 ff.; Loy, *Montesquieu,* 112.

125. Auguste Charaux, "Montesquieu," *Etudes franҫiscaines* (1909), 615.

126. Gustave Lanson, "Le déterminisme historique et l'idéalisme social dans l'*Esprit des lois*" (1916), in *Etudes d'histoire littéraire* (Paris, 1929), 135 ff.; Marcel Raymond, "L'Humanisme de Montesquieu," in *Génies de France* (Neuchâtel, 1942), 124 ff.; Bernard Groethuysen, *Montesquieu* (Geneva and Paris, 1947), 45 ff.; Pierre Barrière, "L'Humanisme de l'*Esprit des lois,*" *IIe centenaire de l'Esprit des lois de Montesquieu, conférences organisées par la ville de Bordeaux* (Bordeaux, 1949), 31 ff.

127. Raymond Aron, *Les grandes doctrines de sociologie historique: Montesquieu, Auguste Comte, Karl Marx, Alexis de Tocqueville, les sociologues et la révolution de 1848* (Paris, 1960), 14 ff.; Lester Crocker, *Nature and Culture: Ethical Thought in the French Enlightenment* (Baltimore,

Schools emphasizing the influence of natural law upon Montesquieu thus have been matched by those maintaining that he broke with that law and inclined toward positivism. Perhaps George Sabine strikes a happy compromise when he wrote that Montesquieu's "love of liberty was in its early phase mainly ethical, bred of his study of the classics and reflecting an admiration for the ancient republic similar to that of Machiavelli, Milton, and Harrington," calling Montesquieu "a moralist for whom the eternal verities had begun to wear thin but who lacked the constructive power to get on without them."[128] Much as Montesquieu may have emphasized positive laws, he seems to have remained the captive of natural law.

Montesquieu was a pioneer and one of the greatest representatives of comparative government. He compared the laws of different societies in the course of history and in his own time. These laws were primarily positive laws. His favorite political system, that of England, was a concrete, specific government. Yet the relationship of the English constitution to higher, older, natural law and the law of God has always been emphasized and Montesquieu was aware of it. While he believed in positive laws to the point that even bad laws had to be obeyed as long as they were on the books, he preferred positive laws that conformed to natural law, to justice, virtue, morals, and religion. The latter values were always on his mind. He could not well be expected to escape them. After all, his century was that of natural law, much as toward its end, when Montesquieu had been dead for some decades, the age of legislation began. If Montesquieu could do something for the freedom of the individual, he would do so. A Frenchman living under an absolutist regime, he would do so especially in France, by pointing out how the positive laws of other nations, especially those of England, provided for greater freedom than those of his home country. However, he also felt that he would aid the cause of freedom by appealing to the old truths of natural law and its many ethical and moral contents. His approach was thus similar to that of the American colonists who first asserted their rights of Englishmen under the English constitution and then, from the Declaration of Independence on, their rights of man under older, higher, natural law and the law of God.

For Montesquieu, the rule of law, due in a large measure to his belief in concepts of natural law, implies restrictions upon governmental power for the sake of the freedom of the individual. However, it also implies, given the need for laws that can be enforced, for positive political and civil laws and the strict enforcement of these laws, even when they do not conform to natural law principles as much as Montesquieu would have liked them to.

1963), 25 ff.; Jean Ehrard, *L'idée de nature* (Paris, 1963), 2:718 ff.; *Politique de Montesquieu* (Paris, 1965), 10–11.

128. Sabine, *History of Political Theory,* 553. Similar Isaiah Berlin, "Montesquieu," *Proceedings of the British Academy* (Oxford, 1955), 290 ff.

Law as a Limitation upon Government

An advocate of constitutional government, Montesquieu desired a government limited by law.

It has been said that "despotism is his particular *bête noire*."[129] Indeed, it appears that Montesquieu's denunciations of arbitrary and unchecked governmental power is the alter ego of his praise of liberty under law. In the *Persian Letters,* Usbek denounces the arbitary rule existing under pashas.[130] He regrets that the French parliament yielded to the absolute authority of the king.[131] According to him, the unlimited power of the sultans produces monstrocities.[132] He denounces the custom that Persian princes can have those who incur their displeasure put to death.[133] A European whom Usbek considers quite sensible complains of the tyrannies of the East.[134] Rhedi regrets that Asia and Africa generally have been oppressed by despots, that in the Roman empire, the governors of the provinces had all too much authority, that laws preventing tyranny were not observed.[135] Rica writes that upon the death of Louis XIV, Frenchmen, tired of his tyranny, set up a new administration that divided governmental power and probably was the most sensible France ever had.[136]

In the *Considerations,* Montesquieu continues to show his wariness of despotism. He complains of Philip's tyranny, of the cruelty of Egyptian kings,[137] and of the Romans' creating a new kind of tyranny by levying excessive taxes on a conquered prince forcing him to oppress his subjects.[138] There were abuses of power in Rome itself, which fortunately were corrected by the Roman constitution. There are now such abuses in the various Italian states.[139] Montesquieu denounces man as a being whose greed for power grows with the power he possesses.[140] He rebukes Caesar for having usurped everything,[141] and Augustus, for establishing durable servitude in Rome.[142] Commenting on Tiberius, he writes that the most cruel tyranny is practiced in the shadow of the laws and under the colors of justice.[143] The people, the "*plebs,*" of Rome at times enjoyed the fruits of the tyranny of emperors under whom the great families were despoiled.[144] Powerful Roman rulers are called "monsters,"[145]

129. Lawrence Meyer Levin, *The Political Doctrine of Montesquieu's Esprit des Lois: Its Classical Background* (New York, 1936), 112, with references to P. Janet, *Histoire de la science politique, dans ses rapports avec la morale,* 3rd ed. (Paris, 1887), 2:328; E. Fournol, *Bodin, prédécesseur de Montesquieu* (Diss., Paris, 1896), 148; Henri Barckhausen, *Montesquieu, ses idées et ses oeuvres, d'après les papiers de la Brède* (Paris, 1907), 65; E. Levi-Malvano, *Montesquieu et Machiavelli* (Paris, 1912), 99; V. Klemperer, *Montesquieu* (Heidelberg, 1914), 1:4.

130. *LP,* 19:43.
131. *LP,* 92:184.
132. *LP,* 94:187.
133. *LP,* 102:203.
134. *LP,* 103:205.
135. *LP,* 131:264–65.
136. *LP,* 138:278.
137. *C,* 5:383–84, 388.
138. *C,* 6:392.
139. *C,* 8:410.
140. *C,* 11:427.
141. *C,* 11:427.
142. *C,* 13:439.
143. *C,* 14:446.
144. *C,* 15:452.
145. *C,* 15:453; 16:460.

and Caligula, Nero, Domitian, and Caracalla, tyrants.[146] Despots would give themselves up to the military and leave the citizens exposed to violence and rapine. Montesquieu mentions tyrannical acts of Charlemagne and regrets tyrannies in the succession of the Roman empire.[147] He denounces the power of Justinian's wife. Under the emperors, dissensions did not lead to the reestablishment of the laws and the end of abuses. Justinian protected a party infringing upon the laws and committed all sorts of despotic acts, selling judgments and laws alike.[148] According to Montesquieu, power is dangerous not only in the hands of temporal rulers, but also in those of monks. Bad as it is, it is never unlimited. Even the most immense power always is curtailed by some kind of limitations.[149]

Montesquieu's fear of despotism and arbitrary governmental power is also evident in the *Spirit of the Laws.* If in a republic a private citizen rises to exorbitant power, there comes into existence not just a regular monarchy, but some kind of supermonarchy in which the abuse of power is greater than in a regular monarchy because the laws make no provision against such an abuse. In all magistracies, power must be compensated and neutralized by brevity of the duration of office.[150] Ecclesiastical power is dangerous in a republic because it is, after all, power, and Montesquieu is a skeptic of power. However, as a counterpoise to monarchical power, it is appropriate in monarchies, especially in those approaching despotism.[151] The principle of despotism is fear. In despotic regimes, the immense power of the prince devolves entirely upon those he is pleased to entrust with it. In distinction to moderate governments supported by their own liberal laws, these regimes are maintained by the sheer power of the prince and his caprice. Montesquieu writes that one cannot mention these monstrous governments without horror and gives examples of them in Persia and in Rome.[152] They require an extreme obedience by the subjects, who cannot suggest modifications to the government's decrees. "Man is a creature who obeys to a creature who wants something." Under despotism, men can no longer represent their fears of a future event, nor impute their failures to the capriciousness of fortune. Men's portion here is, like that of the animals, instinct, compliance, and punishment. It is of no use to have appeal to natural sentiments, filial respect, parental or conjugal tenderness, to the laws of honor or one's state of health: once one has received an order, it is to be complied with. In Persia, when the king has condemned a person, it is no longer possible to mention him or to intercede in his favor. Even if the prince were intoxicated or out of his mind, his decree must be executed. Otherwise the prince would contradict himself, and his law cannot contradict itself. This way of thinking has always existed: the order that Ahasuerus gave to extermi-

146. *C,* 16:464.
147. *C,* 16:467, 470.
148. *C,* 20:499, 500, 501.
149. *C,* 22:513, 519.
150. *EL,* 2, 3:18, 19.
151. *EL,* 2, 4:21. See also, on a pope, 2, 5:23–24.
152. *EL,* 3, 9:35–36.

nate the Jews could not be revoked.[153] In despotic countries, a superior is not supposed to be addressed without making him a present, and Montesquieu says the emperor of Mogol never received requests from his subjects unless they gave him something.[154] Petty tyrants have all the vices of a single tyrant. In a tyranny, the people lose everything, even the advantages reaped from their corruption.[155] Monarchy is destroyed when a prince believes his power is better demonstrated by changing the order of things rather than by adhering to it, when he deprives people of their natural functions in order to assign these functions to others.[156] Monarchy is corrupted by arbitrary power. The corruption of the power of the monarch is as big a crime as that of *lèse-majesté*.[157] Most European nations are still governed by morals [*mœurs*]. However, if from a long abuse of power despotism should come about, neither morals nor climate would be able to withstand its baleful influence.[158]

Montesquieu shows that despotism has existed at all times, that it can exist anywhere. Oriental states were its chief models; however, the occident also had its share, from Rome to a Germanic country like Sweden.[159] Furthermore, while he makes it clear that despotism, next to the republican and monarchical forms of government, is a specific form of rule, he leaves no doubt that republics and monarchies also may become despotic. He describes all kinds of despotic features under the various tyrannies. Yet they all have one thing in common: concentrated governmental power is used to the detriment of the freedom of the individual.

It is, therefore, not surprising that Montesquieu, being a friend of constitutionalism, ranks the concentration of power about as low as he ranks freedom high, that for the sake of freedom he would suggest a deconcentration of governmental power in order to deprive power of its despotic possibilities and probabilities. He thus arrives at the mechanism of the separation of powers, a doctrine that made him famous and to him implies the separation of the executive, legislative, and judicial branches of the government. And whereas in his opinion despotism has existed throughout the ages all over the world, the separation of powers and its protection of the rights of the individual can be found only under "the constitution of England," a title he gives to chapter 6 of the famous book 11 of the *Spirit of the Laws*. In providing for the separation of powers, that constitution secures the freedom of the individual. From Montesquieu's interpretation of the English constitution, the French derived a general rule which can be found in Article 16 of the Declaration of the Rights of Man and Citizen of August 26, 1789: "A society, in which the guarantee of rights is not secured and the separation of powers not definitely accepted [*déterminée*], has no constitution." While the English constitution provides for the separation of powers as a means for the protection of freedom, the protection of

153. *EL*, 3, 10:36–37. See also 5, 14:78 ff.
154. *EL*, 5, 17:89.
155. *EL*, 8, 2:151.
156. *EL*, 8, 6:155.
157. *EL*, 8, 7:156–57.
158. *EL*, 8, 8:157.
159. *EL*, 5, 14:79.

rights and the separation of powers appear to be prerequisites for the existence of a constitution in the sense of constitutionalism, under which the individual's freedom is considered the end of government.

The restriction of that power through its division can be considered the core of book 11 of the *Spirit of the Laws,* the book in which Montesquieu defines freedom as freedom under the laws. In that book, he clearly connects the protection of liberty with the separation of powers. Right after the definition of freedom in chapter 3, chapter 4 turns to governmental power and its abuse. It does so amidst remarks on liberty. Neither democracy nor aristocracy are by their nature free. Political liberty can be found in moderate governments only if there is no abuse of power. However, it is an eternal experience that every man who possesses power is apt to abuse it as much as he can. Even virtue stands in need of limitations. To prevent an abuse of power, it follows from the nature of things that power should check power. The next sentence again mentions liberty under law. We read that a constitution can be such that no person shall be compelled to do things which the law does not oblige him to do and not to do things which the law permits.[160]

The idea of the protection of liberty through checks upon governmental power by means of the separation of powers is evident in book 11. When the legislative and executive powers are united in the same person or the same body of magistrates, there is no liberty because apprehensions arise lest the same monarch or the same senate make tyrannical laws or execute them in a tyrannical manner. Again, there is no liberty if the judicial power is not separated from the legislative and executive powers. If it were joined to the former, the power over the life and the liberty of the citizen would be arbitrary, for the judge would be the legislator. If it were joined to the executive, the judge could have the force of an oppressor. Everything would be lost if the same man or the same body of leaders, be they noble or common, would exercise these three powers. Turkey, where these powers are vested in the sultan, experiences a terrible despotism. In the republics of Italy, where they are also united, there is less liberty than in the majority of European monarchies in which the king possesses legislative and executive powers but leaves the judicial power to the citizens. The governments in the Italian republics are obliged to have recourse to violent methods for their support. The lot of the citizen is pitiful. The government can ruin the state and destroy every citizen. The people feel the effects of despotism every moment. Princes who wanted to make themselves despots always started out by uniting in their person all the magistracies and great offices of the state.[161]

After these remarks on the danger of combining all three powers, Montesquieu makes many statements on the threat to freedom by a combination of any two powers, always considering power combinations steps toward despotism.

160. Art. 16 of the Declaration of the Rights of Man and Citizen of August 26, 1789.
161. *EL,* 11, 6:208–9.

If the legislature leaves to the executive the right to imprison those who can give security for their good behavior, liberty would no longer exist. If people are arrested in order to answer without delay an accusation for an act considered a capital crime by the law, they are really free because they are subject to the law. If the executive power is committed to a certain number of persons elected from the legislative body, there would be no liberty. The two powers actually would be united because the same persons would sometimes possess, and always be able to have, a share in both. If the legislature would not meet for a considerable period of time, its legislative function could be assumed by the executive power which thereby would become absolute. The legislature ought not to have the power to judge the person and conduct of the executive, because the moment he is accused or judged, the legislature would become tyrannical and there would be an end to liberty. If the monarch took part in the legislative process of determining the content of the laws, liberty would be lost. It also would be lost were the executive power to determine the raising of public money, because the executive would then become a legislature with respect to the most important aspect of legislation.[162]

Montesquieu's fear of governmental power does not end there. He is also afraid that any one of the three powers might be too powerful, even in the case of a separation of powers. In order to prevent this, he wants the powers to check each other and thus combines his doctrine of the separation of powers with that of checks and balances. As a matter of fact, before he mentions the idea of separation, he states that to prevent an abuse of governmental power, "power should check power."[163] Thereupon, remarks on the danger of combining the branches of government are matched by those urging that these powers check each other not just by being divided, but also by participating in each other's functions. He wants the legislature to be divided into two houses, one representative of the nobles and the other of the people, each constituting a check upon the other. To prevent it from becoming despotic, the executive should have the right to halt legislative endeavors. If the legislature could confer upon itself all the power it can imagine, it would destroy the other powers. In a free state, the legislature should have the right and the means of examining in what way the laws are executed. The executive ought to have a share in legislation by its right of rejecting bills. "This is, then, the basic constitution of the government we are speaking of. The legislative body being composed of two parts, one will enchain the other by its faculty of checking and preventing. Both are restrained by the executive power, as the latter is by the legislative power."[164]

In the passage just quoted Montesquieu does not mention the judicial power. Perhaps he omits it because he feels that that power which, generally speaking, he considers "so terrible," under the constitution he describes is, not

162. *EL,* 11, 6:210–11, 214, 216, 218, 219.
163. *EL,* 11, 4:206.
164. *EL,* 11, 6:213, 215–16, 216, 218–19.

being attached to any particular estate or profession, "so-to-speak invisible and null." This is because it is not exercised by a permanent body but by persons coming from the people at large at certain times, in the manner prescribed by the law and being in session only when necessary. However, while the individual need not fear an ever-present judicial establishment, he fears the judicial magistracy which can always be called into courts that judge according to the precise text of the law. Ad hoc tribunals disperse after judgement is rendered.[165]

In the book entitled "Of the Constitution of England," Montesquieu shows how a constitution provides, for the sake of the freedom of the individual, for the separation of, and checks and balances among, the various branches of the government, be they permanently in existence, like the executive and the legislature, or temporarily, like the courts. Whatever the difference among those powers, they all are under a constitution. It is interesting to note that while chapter 6 according to its title supposedly deals with a specific constitution, namely, that of England, Montesquieu generally abstains from referring to that constitution. Rather, he seems to talk about a desirable constitution in general. He does not describe what is, but exhorts what ought to be.[166] The reader gains the impression that, perhaps on account of observa-

165. *EL,* 11, 6:210. See also 213: "Des trois puissances dont nous avons parlé celle de juger est, en quelque façon, nulle."

166. In the first 25 paragraphs, England is not mentioned at all. Montesquieu starts out by speaking of "chaque état" (207), then refers to "la plupart des royaumes de l'Europe," to the Turks, to Italy, and Asia (208–9). After mentioning the despotic "magistrature des *éphores*" and the "*inquisiteurs d'état* de Venise," he speaks of "un état libre," of "les grands états," "les petits," of representation in Germany (211–12). Only in paragraph 26, after mentioning Holland, does he mention England (212). Then, after just another sentence which could, but probably does not, refer to England, he discusses the situation in ancient republics, only to state afterwards that "dans un état" there are always people distinguished by birth, riches, or honors (213). On the same page, he speaks of "un état libre," without reference to England. He refers to Rome, to "l'état" (214), to Rome, Crete, Lacedemonia (216). On the same page, he speaks of "l'état" in which the legislature has the right to try the executive, of the advantage of a government [ce gouvernement] in which the legislature can try executive officials over the government "de *Gnide*" (216). Quite generally, he states that "les juges de la nation ne sont, comme nous avons dit, que la bouche qui prononce les paroles de la loi" (217). Then he speaks of the advantage of "ce gouvernement" (quite generally, a government in which the people cannot be, at the same time, accuser and judge), over the majority of ancient republics, and mentions Rome (218). Only then does he state "Voici donc la constitution fondamentale du gouvernement dont nous parlons." Does he mean that of England, or some ideal form of government? At any rate, after a few lines, he speaks of "some ancient republics," of Rome, of Holland, of Venice, of the Germanic tribes described by Tacitus, of which the English have derived the idea of their political government (218–21). And then, he states: "Comme toutes les choses humaines ont une fin, l'état dont nous parlons perdra sa liberté, il périra. *Rome, Lacédémone & Carthage* ont bien péri. Il périra, lorsque la puissance législative sera plus corrompue que l'exécutrice. Ce n'est point à moi à examiner si les Anglois jouissent actuellement de cette liberté, ou non. Il me suffit de dire qu'elle est établie par leurs loix, & je n'en cherche pas davantage. Je ne prétends point par-là ravaler les autres gouvernemens, ni dire que cette liberté politique extrême doive mortifier ceux qui n'en ont qu'une modérée." (221). The latter statement was made in the last

tions of the English constitution, Montesquieu depicts a concrete form of government that appears to him ideal, just as John Locke in his *Second Treatise,* while defending the Glorious Revolution and the government it brought about, avoided direct references to that government and thus gave his ideas a more general validity. Perhaps chapter 6 of book 11 can also be seen as a combination of the approaches of Locke and Blackstone, the latter making plain that he commented on the specific constitution of England. Be this as it may, there can be little doubt that for Montesquieu, governmental power, or the separation of the various branches of the government as well as their checks and balances, are due to a constitution, that is, bound by constitutional provisions limiting the government for the sake of the freedom of the individual. This is said in so many words at the end of chapter 6 when Montesquieu writes that it is not his task to examine whether the English actually enjoy liberty; that it is sufficient to state that liberty is established by their laws.[167]

The laws providing for liberty are many. This stands in stark contrast to the situation under despotism. A person rendering himself an absolute ruler immediately longs for a simplification of the laws and reduces them by streamlining because he does not care about the liberty of his subjects. There are more laws in freer governments, in monarchies and republics, and these laws increase with the appreciation of the honor, fortune, life, and liberty of the citizens. The restriction of the government under the laws and the ensuing liberty probably is the greatest in republics because here the individuals are everything, whereas under despotism, they are nothing.[168] In the following chapter, Montesquieu goes even further. He states flatly that in despotic states, there are no laws and the judge is his own rule. In monarchies, there is one law. If it is precise, the judge conforms to it; otherwise, he looks for its spirit. In republics, judges follow the letter of the law. The citizen's goods, honor, or life cannot be jeopardized through an interpretation of a law.[169] Following his emphasis in book 11 upon the separation of powers under the constitution, Montesquieu in

---

but one paragraph of chapter 6. In the last paragraph, he writes: "*Arrington,* dans son *Oceana,* a aussi examiné quel étoit le plus haut point de liberté où la constitution d'un état peut être portée. Mais on peut dire de lui, qu'il n'a cherché cette liberté qu'après l'avoir méconnue; & qu'ila [*sic*] bâti Chalcédoine, ayant le rivage de Bysance devant les yeux."—Imperative, as distinguished from descriptive, formulations can be seen on 210, 212, 215, 216.

167. *EL,* 11, 6:221.

168. *EL,* 6, 2:100–101: "Aussi, lorsqu'un homme se rend plus absolu (*a*), songe-t-il d'abord à simplifier les loix. On commence, dans cet état, à être plus frappé des inconvéniens particuliers, que de la liberté des sujets, dont on ne se soucie point de tout. On voit que, dans les républiques, il faut pour le moins autant de formalités que dans les monarchies. Dans l'un & dans l'autre gouvernement, elles augmentent en raison du cas que l'on y fait de l'honneur, de la fortune, de la vie, de la liberté des citoyens." "Les hommes sont tous égaux dans le gouvernement républicain; ils sont égaux dans le gouvernement despotique: dans le premier, c'est parce qu'ils sont tout; dans le second, c'est parce qu'ils ne sont rien." The reference under (a) is to "César, Cromwell, & tant d'autres."

169. *EL,* 6, 2:101.

book 12, "On the Laws which Form Political Liberty in its Relation with the Citizen," deals with various laws restricting the government for the sake of the individual's liberty, concentrating on laws that generally are believed to threaten the individuals the most, namely, criminal laws.[170]

In book 19, Montesquieu returns to a discussion of the "free people" of whom he has "spoken in the eleventh book" and mentions the various aspects of freedom under the English constitution and its separation of powers. In England, every citizen has a will of his own and can assert his independence at his pleasure. All the passions being free, hatred, envy, jealousy, the ardor to enrich and distinguish oneself appear to their full extent. Acting freely according to one's passion is considered a sign of strength and health. As a result of liberty, a party composed of freemen can dominate another party composed of freemen. The situation will reverse after the strength of the subordinate party has been increased by citizens rallying to its aid in order to prevent the perpetual omnipotence of one party and to keep the body politic strong by virtue of competition. Montesquieu compares this behavior with the act of eliminating infirmities of the human body. This way, there can always be hatred between the two parties, for it always will be harmless due to the citizens' watchfulness and their freedom to support the party out of power. The independent individual will follow his caprices and fantasies and often change his party affiliation. By abandoning his party, he leaves all his friends in order to align himself with another party, in which he will find all his former enemies. Thus the laws of friendship and hatred can often be disregarded. The English monarch acts like the individuals in his realm. Often he will be obliged in this general atmosphere of liberality to confide in those who have offended him the most and to disgrace those who have served him the best, acting that way by necessity rather than choice.[171]

If a power violates the fundamental laws, everyone would unite against it to the point of a revolution, which would neither alter the present form of government nor the constitution for revolutions prompted by liberty are nothing but confirmations of liberty. In order to enjoy liberty, everyone must be able to say what he thinks. A citizen will say and write everything the laws do not expressly prohibit. Always in ferment on account of their freedom, the English could be more easily prompted by passions than by reason. They are fabulously fond of liberty: Because no citizen is dependent upon another, each sets a greater value on his own liberty than on the glory of one or a number of citizens. Freed from destructive prejudices, England became a commercial nation in which opulence was extremely great. In search of plenty, some inhabitants even went to countries of servitude. A commercial nation has a number of great and little particular interests. In pursuit of these, it may injure and be injured in indefinite ways. England's colonies were designed to extend commerce rather than

170. *EL,* 12, 1–30:250 ff. Cf. Pangle, *Montesquieu's Philosophy,* 139. See also *EL,* 6, 2:99 ff.
171. *EL,* 19, 27:433 (I sometimes translated "passion" by "desire"). See also *LP,* 104:206–7.

the empire. Prompted to establish its system abroad, England gave to the people in the colonies her own form of government and, with it, her prosperity. England's commercial system, netting prosperity and the fulfillment of individual desires, is aided by the absence of fortresses and an army. Aside from freedom of speech, of the press, and of commerce, she enjoys freedom of religion. The latter may and did result in indifference toward, and fanaticism over, religion, in an adherence to the established state religion or in a great variety of religious sects as well as in believing in no religion at all. In this land of liberty, men are esteemed for real qualities, of which two are most recognized, riches and personal merit. There is solid luxury, founded on real needs. People enjoy great abundance. Some of them, having more wealth than expenses, will employ their wealth in a bizarre manner. Since one will always be occupied with one's own interests, one would not have those polished manners which are founded on leisure and not much time to spare. There prevails a restless spirit with many persons; they have extended views of things. In a nation where every man in his own way takes part in the administration of the state, the women scarcely live with the men who, without gallantry, throw themselves into debauchery, which leaves them all their liberty and leisure.[172] Because laws are not made for one individual more than for others, each citizen regards himself as a monarch. Men are confederates rather than fellow-citizens. The nobles share this general spirit; so do intellectuals. Historians betray the truth because they are at liberty to do so, and enjoy a liberty that produces divisions. Each historian can thus be the slave of his faction.[173]

Following his discussion of the freedom of the individual in commercial England, Montesquieu considers the individualistic aspects of commerce irrespective of national affiliation. According to him, the spirit of commerce, while it may unite nations, does not unite individuals. In countries where the people are only motivated by commerce alone, all human action as well as moral virtue constitute part of traffic. Due to the demand from men, the most trifling things are made and given for money. The spirit of commerce produces a certain sense of "exact justice."[174] In monarchies, commerce ordinarily is carried on not just for the necessities of life but for the sake of luxury. Its main objective is to procure for the nation everything that can contribute to its pride and its inhabitants' pleasures and fantasies. In republics, commerce usually is founded on economy rather than luxury. It implies incessant profit-making. One kind of commerce leads to another, the small commerce to a moderate one and the latter, to large-scale commerce. He who makes a small profit raises himself to a station where he can make much more. In republics, there is greater intrepidity than in monarchies. Based on free entrepreneurship, republics are the homes of great and powerful enterprises. In commercial republics, there is a great certainty of prosperity. It prompts people to make money with respect to about

172. *EL,* 19, 27:436, 437, 438, 440, 441, 442. See Pangle, *Montesquieu's Philosophy,* 153–54.
173. *EL,* 19, 27:441–42, 444.
174. *EL,* 20, 2:446.

everything. If one believes to safely possess what one has acquired, one dares to expose one's goods in order to acquire more. Risk becomes a means for further acquisition. Men expect much of their fortune.[175] Commerce is tied up with liberty, and this tie is the most evident in England. It is a desirable tie to Montesquieu. For him, the English know better than any other people in the world to highly value at the same time three great things—religion, commerce, and liberty. While other nations have subordinated commercial to political interests, England always has subordinated political interests to those of trade. As a result, Parliament has felt free to frequently change tariffs or customs, and her government has been reluctant to bind itself by treaties. Commerce is tied up with liberty; it is an aspect of liberty. Montesquieu likes the combination of commerce and liberty that is obvious in England.[176] The purpose of commerce is the export and import of merchandise in favor of the state. So that the inhabitants may enjoy freedom of commerce, commerce should not be interfered with by the customs. Through injustice, vexations, and excessive import duties, the ministry of finance destroys commerce. Even more so does it destroy commerce by the difficulties it causes and by red tape. In England, the latter problem has been reduced because there the customs are handled with speed. A word in writing accomplishes the greatest business affairs. The merchant does not lose much time and does not need special aides to help him obviate the difficulties made by the bureaucrats, or to submit to them.[177] The effects of commerce are riches, the effects of riches, luxury, and those of luxury, the perfection of the arts.[178] Under despotic governments, the liberalizing and enriching effects of commerce will be felt throughout the country.[179]

The Necessity of State Law

Montesquieu's advocacy of the separation of governmental powers for the sake of the rights of the individual does not imply a desire for an absence of government. A division of power does not abolish power. Neither does his advocacy of freedom imply a maximum of freedom. Believing in a government of law, Montesquieu is, of course, opposed to anarchy.[180] He also indicates the need for a great variety of legal restraints upon freedom.

In the *Persian Letters,* Usbek voices severe doubts about too much egoism. It creates a situation where the people are swayed by their own savage instincts and comes close to anarchy. He resents those saying, "Why should I kill myself with work for those about whom I don't care? I shall think only of myself. I shall live happily. What do I care whether others do? I will provide for my own necessities. As long as these are satisfied, I don't care whether all others live in

175. *EL,* 20, 4:448–49. 176. *EL,* 20, 7:452. 177. *EL,* 20, 13:456–57.
178. *EL,* 21, 6:471. See also 16:509. 179. *EL,* 22, 14:28–29.
180. Cf. *C,* 9:414; 11:423; 13:439. *EL,* 23, 23:73. It goes without saying that Montesquieu's opposition to anarchy follows from his advocacy of the rule of law.

misery."[181] He denounces extreme forms of free enterprise and notes with satisfaction that the Troglodites perished on account of meanness and injustice, which he considers corollaries of their egoism. Two families were less egoistic and more community-conscious, and this worked for their mutual benefit: they led a happy life. The sad end of their egoistic countrymen led them to see that the interest of the individual was bound up with that of the community, that to desire isolation from the community meant to court ruin. Usbek paints an idyllic picture of their lives: they were happy because they lived for the well-being of the community and their fellowmen.[182]

Men commit injustices because they have an interest in doing so and because they prefer their own satisfaction to that of others, for "interest is the greatest monarch on earth."[183] Usbek writes that most legislators are men of limited abilities whom mere chance has exalted over others. They consult nearly nothing but their prejudices and fantasies and do not seem to have a sense of the greatness and dignity of the laws they make. They amuse themselves by making childish institutions, suited to small minds but discrediting people with good sense. They fling themselves into useless details and give their attention to particular interests, all of which shows a narrow genius that grasps things piecemeal and does not take a general view.[184] Still, there are some wise laws restricting freedom. For instance, it must be admitted that lawmakers have shown much wisdom by giving fathers authority over their children. Nothing relieves magistrates more, nothing tends more to keep the tribunals of justice empty, in short, nothing is more conducive to the tranquility of the state.[185] Usbek approves of Roman penalties for those who rebelled against marriage and "wanted to enjoy a liberty so much opposed to the public good."[186] Rica favors laws against slander of one's nation, a crime which according to him deserves a thousand deaths.[187]

In the *Considerations,* Montesquieu expresses himself in favor of legislation that makes better citizens.[188] In the *Spirit of the Laws,* he writes that to fight depopulation, Europe needs laws favoring population growth.[189] Praising ordinances of Louis XIV providing for pensions for those who had ten children, Montesquieu writes that in addition, general rewards and penalties should be provided for with a view of increasing the population.[190] While he

181. *LP,* 11:27. 182. *LP,* 11–13:27 ff.

183. *LP,* 83:169. The quotation is from 106:212. In *EL,* 3, 6:34, Montesquieu writes that in monarchies, in which honor is the principle of government, "everybody advances the public good in the belief to advance his own particular interests."

184. *LP,* 129:257. On the other hand, Montesquieu calls it a misfortune of the human condition that legislators should be obliged to make laws which are repugnant to natural sentiments and which favor society rather than the citizen, and the citizen rather than the man, and sacrifice the citizen and the man by thinking of the republic only. *EL,* 27, 1:170. See also 29, 19:290–91.

185. *LP,* 129:258. 186. *LP,* 117:234. 187. *LP,* 127:252.

188. *C,* 13:439–40. 189. *EL,* 23, 26:75. See also 16–25:54 ff.

190. *EL,* 23, 27:76.

favors rates of interest for the lending of money, he advocates laws making these rates modest and preventing usury.[191] In commercial nations, where many people have no other subsistence but their arts and crafts, the state often is obliged to provide for the needs of the old, the sick, and the orphans. A well-policed [*bien policé*] state draws that support from the arts themselves. It gives to some people employment they are capable of performing and teaches others how to work. Montesquieu obviously considered these state activities desirable, adding: "Some alms one gives to the naked man in the street do not replace the obligation of the state, which owes to all citizens a secure subsistence, nourishment, convenient clothing, and a kind of life not incompatible with health." A rich state ought to build hospitals. The state is obliged to give to those suffering prompt aid in order to prevent suffering or a revolt. Hospitals or some equivalent regulations are necessary for the prevention of that misery. While Montesquieu thus comes out in favor of hospitals and state health care in rich nations, he stresses that this ought not to be overdone and prefers transient assistance to perpetual establishments. Given the fact that accidents are temporary, aid for them should be of the same nature and applied to particular accidents. He remarks that in poor countries hospitals may well inspire laziness and thus augment the general, and thus particular, poverty. Monks, by offering hospitality, encourage laziness with an infinite number of idle persons who spent their lives running from convent to convent. Henry VIII is credited with having abolished this kind of abuse by destroying monastery orders and by doing away with hospitals where the poor found subsistence, thereby establishing the spirit of commerce and industry.[192]

Mention of the situation in England and its spirit of commerce makes one wonder whether, in view of the role Montesquieu assigns to the state for aiding the individual and to laws restricting individual action for the sake of the public, he favors as rugged an individualism as is often believed. The answer is that while he desires a society composed of free individuals, he wants them to be responsible. Book 5 makes plain that commerce does not imply unlimited laissez faire. We read that if a democracy is based upon commerce, it can very well be that the individuals living in it will become very rich without a corruption of morals and customs. "The spirit of commerce brings in its train the spirit of frugality, economy, moderation, work, prudence, tranquility, order, rule." Thus while it subsists, the riches it produces have no ill effect.[193] Commercial nations have more laws than agricultural and nomadic ones. Therefore, merchants are more restricted than farmers and hunters.[194] "The liberty of commerce does not imply that merchants can act as they please; if they would, one could rather speak of the bondage of commerce. What constrains merchants does not restrain commerce. It is in free countries that the merchant finds innumerable obstacles in his way, and he never is less crossed by the laws

191. *EL,* 22, 19:33–34. 192. *EL,* 23, 29:78–79. 193. *EL,* 5, 6:62.
194. *EL,* 18, 8:384.

there than in countries of bondage. England . . . constrains the merchant, but for the sake of commerce."[195] The spirit of commerce is not automatically self-perpetuating.[196] Montesquieu advocates a role of the government: "To maintain the spirit of commerce, it is necessary that the principal citizens themselves engage in it; that this spirit alone rules and is not frustrated by another spirit; that all the laws favor it; that these very laws by their disposition divide the fortunes in the measure commerce increases them and make each citizen poor in sufficient ease so that he can work like the others, and each citizen rich in such a modest manner that it is necessary for him to work in order to conserve or acquire." It is "a very good law in a commercial republic, that all children are given an equal portion of the inheritance of their fathers. Thereby, whatever fortune the father has made, his children, always less rich than himself, are led to flee luxury and work like him."[197] For Montesquieu, work ethics accompany profit-making. While because of their freedom, the English enjoy physical comfort and satisfaction, their commercial wealth will not lead to corruption. Men are esteemed for real qualities. Frivolous talents or attributes are not appreciated. Solid luxury will be based not upon the refinement of vanity, but upon real needs. People will enjoy great opulence, but frivolous things will be proscribed.[198]

Montesquieu considers the protection of the English way of life from foreign enemies and a corresponding role of the government necessary. Possessing a great commerce, England should have all kinds of facilities in order to be powerful on the seas. The preservation of liberty will require that there are no military forts and land forces. However, she will stand in need of a navy [*armée de mer*] to guarantee protection from invasions. Her naval forces will be superior to those of all other powers, which will have to spend their money on land forces and therefore not have enough funds for a navy.[199] It has been pointed out that, although Montesquieu wanted the range of affairs supervised by a liberal republican government, he still saw a need for a vigorous government that is able to defend a large nation against foreign enemies and domestic dangers and thought that management of population growth and of the economy, administration of relief for the poor, and other such projects are included in the task of providing security.[200]

For the sake of security, Montesquieu assigns an important role to taxation. In many respects, he considers public revenues a sine qua non for the security of liberty and property. He begins his discussion on the relation of taxes to liberty with the statement that "the revenues of the state are a portion of what every citizen gives of his property, in order to secure the rest or to enjoy

195. *EL,* 20, 12:455–56.

196. Cf. Pangle, *Montesquieu's Philosophy,* 149.

197. *EL,* 5, 6:631. 198. *EL,* 19, 27:441–42. 199. *EL,* 19, 27:438.

200. Cf. Pangle, *Montesquieu's Philosophy,* 133–34; *EL,* 20, 18:460; 22, 3:5–6, 10:11 ff.; 23, 18–19:57–58.

it in an agreeable manner."[201] He writes that in fixing revenues, due regard must be given to the necessities of the state and of the citizens. The real needs of the people ought not to give way to the imaginary ones of the government, flowing from the passions and weaknesses of those in power, the charm of some extraordinary project, the vain desire for glory and a certain impotence of the mind to withstand fantastic temptations. Montesquieu warns that often those of a restless disposition imagined that the desires of their own little souls were those of the state. Public revenue should not be measured by the people's ability to give, but by considerations of what they ought to give.[202] On the face of it, this looks like an acknowledgement of a strong position of the individual within society. On the other hand, Montesquieu's opinion that the real needs of the people should not be inferior to the imaginary ones of the state can imply that the former are inferior to the nonimaginary needs of the state. Furthermore, if it is taken into account that he writes that in the fixing of revenues, consideration should be given to the necessities of the state and to those of the citizens, the fact that he mentions the necessities of the state first indicates that he considers taxation for the real, as distinguished from the imaginary, requirements of the state important. This could be because Montesquieu does not see a discrepancy between the interest of the state and that of the citizen as far as taxation is concerned. To him, a large state possessing industry, manufacture, and art makes regulations securing the advantages deriving from these possessions. England can encourage industry, manufacture, and art through rules and regulations which do not necessarily conflict with the interests of the inhabitants. The wealth of the state, partly brought about through increased taxes, is in the interest of the individuals.[203] It is an inspiration for the ambitious individual and productive of labor and income,[204] which augment the national wealth. "If the state proportions its fortune to that of the individuals, the ease of the individuals will soon make its fortune rise."[205] Taxation is compatible with the liberty of the citizens. As a general rule, taxes can be levied in proportion to the liberty of the subjects and must be decreased in proportion to their becoming less free. This always has been and always will be. It is a rule derived from nature and never varies. In moderate states, there is an indemnity for the weight of taxes, namely, liberty. Under despotic rule, there is an equivalent for liberty, namely, the lightness of taxes.[206]

In the first chapter of book 13 on the revenue of the state, there is a sentence that perhaps can be considered not just making reference to taxation but to all kinds of state intervention: "Nothing requires more wisdom and prudence than the regulation of that portion of which the subjects are de-

201. *EL,* 13, 1:285. 202. *EL,* 13, 1:285.

203. See *EL,* 5, 3:56: "Good democracies, by establishing domestic frugality, have opened the door for public expenses, as in Athens and Rome, where magnificence and profusion arose from the very fund of frugality."

204. *EL,* 13, 2:286. 205. *EL,* 13, 7:290. 206. *EL,* 13, 12:295.

prived, and of that they are suffered to retain."[207] Since "*règler*" obviously means regulation by the state, it could imply that the state can regulate not only the amount of taxes the subjects pay, but whatever the subjects ("*sujets,*" not "*citoyens*"!) are permitted to keep. Here is a general clause which could be interpreted as a sanction for far-reaching regulations of the property of the individual in society, the strength of which, according to Montesquieu, will be conducive to the well-being of those composing it. Be this as it may, for Montesquieu, even divided governmental power remains an effective power which not only protects the intercourse among individuals according to civil laws, but is also regulating their freedom and property for the sake of society and the state.

The necessity of state law and its execution is expressed on other occasions. Montesquieu maintains that even bad laws, as long as they are valid, must be obeyed and executed. Usbek writes that whatever religion one may believe in, the observation of the laws, the love of mankind and reverence toward parents are the first commandments.[208] Men must observe the duties of charity and humanity toward their fellow-men and not in the least violate the laws under which they live.[209] "I am obliged to obey the laws while I live under the laws."[210] Usbek regrets tumults leading to an overthrow of authority, writing that once authority providing for too severe penalties is set aside, nobody can restore it.[211] After complaining about the poor quality of legislators, Usbek writes: "Whatever the laws may be, they always must be obeyed and regarded as the public conscience to which that of the individuals [*particuliers*] always must conform."[212]

In the *Considerations,* Montesquieu points out that the situation in Rome worsened once the laws were no longer strictly observed.[213] He draws attention to the fact that the tyranny of a prince does no more to ruin a state than does indifference to the common good in a republic. There is a greater danger in the laws being avoided in a free state than in their being violated by a prince who, always being the foremost citizen, has a greater interest in preserving the state. In Rome, governed by laws, the people allowed the senate to direct affairs. In Carthage, governed by abuse, the people wanted to do everything themselves.[214] A reason for the fall of Rome was the decline of the people's authority and the laws.[215] "Those who no longer fear power can still respect authority."[216]

In the *Spirit of the Laws,* we read that it is bad to be free to act against the laws.[217] Nothing gives greater force to the laws than the extreme subordination of the citizens to the magistrate.[218] Montesquieu refers to Cicero's statement that the force of the people without a ruler is terrible because the people in

207. *EL,* 13, 1:285.
208. *LP,* 46:88.
209. *LP,* 48:88–89.
210. *LP,* 76:157.
211. *LP,* 80:165.
212. *LP,* 129:258.
213. *C,* 3:366.
214. *C,* 4:370–71.
215. *C,* 9:414.
216. *C,* 15:455.
217. *EL,* 3, 3:28.
218. *EL,* 5, 7:66.

their impetuosity are ignorant. People who live under a good police [*bonne police*] are happier than those who, without rule and leaders, err around the forests.[219] Censors must prevent the elusion and weakening of the laws.[220] If one examines the cause of all permissiveness [*relâchemens, (sic)*], one will find that it is the impunity of crimes. When people no longer observe the laws, corruption begins.[221] If the principles of government are sound, even bad laws have the effect of good ones and must be obeyed.[222] Montesquieu quotes Theodoric ordering his generals to follow the Roman law and to return fugitive slaves to their masters for the sake of the protection of that property secured by that law. For that reason, "the defender of liberty must not favor an abandonment of servitude."[223] In the very last book, Montesquieu again emphasizes how important the execution of the laws is, as if he wanted the reader not to lose sight of that fact. Charlemagne is praised for making good laws and, "what is more, having them executed."[224] Obedience to the law is also required of legislators, who must obey fundamental laws and will be forced by a united nation to do so.[225]

Conclusion

Montesquieu's writings reveal him as a man of measure.

He favors freedom, but not an unqualified freedom, only one according to the laws. He conceives of the rule of law as a limitation upon the government. Yet that rule is also a means in the hands of the rulers for the enforcement of law and order. He proposes a separation of powers for the sake of the liberty of the individual. Yet he does not want an absolute separation, but one qualified by checks and balances. In spite of the division of powers, governmental power remains a force to be reckoned with in the promotion of national defense and strength, be it through the enforcement of civil law affecting the commerce among individuals or through public law.[226] While Montesquieu expresses himself in favor of free trade, he is not in favor of unlimited laissez faire. Aside from restrictions of commerce, he proposes government activity for the sake of the public good.

219. *EL,* 5, 11:75–76, 77.

220. *EL,* 5, 19:95.

221. *EL,* 6, 12:114–15.

222. *EL,* 8, 11:159.

223. *EL,* 30, 11:305. In the very last book of his most important work, Montesquieu again emphasizes how important the execution of the laws is, as if he wanted the reader not to lose sight of that importance.

224. *EL,* 31, 18:397.

225. *EL,* 19, 27:435.

226. In book 26, chap. 15, entitled "That we Should not Regulate by the Principles of Political Law the Things which Depend on the Principles of Civil Law," Montesquieu lays down as a "maxim that whenever the public good is the matter in question, the public good never consists in depriving an individual of his property, or even in retrenching the least part of it by a law or a political regulation. In this case, it is necessary to follow the civil law which is the palladium of property" (148).

The idea of measure appears in a great variety of aspects. Usbek praises the happy means between joy and frugality during celebrations and favors a mild and temperate diet.[227] He considers intemperance the most poisonous source of a monarch's injustices and cruelties and opposes alcoholic excesses and licentious debauchery.[228] He complains about the low morality at Paris.[229] According to Rica, modesty is a virtue, needed by those whom heaven has endowed with great talents.[230] He denounces foreign eccentricities unknown in Persia, where one has not bent toward what is odd and extravagant and where one always endeavors to shape simple customs and naive manners in the mould of nature.[231] Usbek expresses himself in favor of punishments which are in proportion to the crime, and against those that are too severe penalties.[232] Rhedi writes that almost all monarchies have been founded on the ignorance of the arts and destroyed by their overcultivation.[233] Usbek expresses concern that for the luxury of one individual many others have to toil.[234] He is glad that nature works in a temperate way and never without rule and measure.[235] Rica ridicules the "Quidnuncs," busybodies without common sense who are utterly useless to society.[236]

Montesquieu quotes Livy saying that the augmentation of luxury and riches of the Romans have not made them greater.[237] Getting rich too soon means getting corrupted soon.[238] In the beginning of his reign, Philip won the love and confidence of the Greeks by virtue of his moderation. The Aetolians are rebuked for always going to extremes and for seeking to correct their follies by still other follies. Nature has given certain limits to states in order to mortify the ambitions of men.[239] Montesquieu denounces an "immoderate desire for liberty" and praises Roman censors for preventing excesses. The government of Rome was admirable because abuses of power could always be corrected.[240] The constancy of the Roman senate is favorably distinguished from the behavior of the people who always swing from extreme ardor to extreme weakness. A republic should hazard nothing that exposes it to good or bad fortune. It should steer a middle course for the perpetuation of its condition.[241] Complaining about the limitless luxury and profusion of the Romans, Montesquieu states that possessions beyond the needs of private life make it difficult to be a good citizen.[242] "The laws of Rome had wisely divided public power among a large number of magistracies, which supported, checked, and tempered each other, and, since they all had only a limited power, every citizen was qualified for these magistracies. The people, seeing many persons pass before them one after the other, did not grow accustomed to any in particular."[243] He com-

227. *LP,* 12:32; 19:43.
228. *LP,* 33:68–69.
229. *LP,* 48:98.
230. *LP,* 50:100
231. *LP,* 73:152–53.
232. *LP,* 80:164 ff.; 95:188 ff.; 102:203. Rica in 141:289.
233. *LP,* 105:209.
234. *LP,* 106:212.
235. *LP,* 114:227.
236. *LP,* 130:259–60.
237. *C,* 3:268.
238. *C,* 4:370.
239. *C,* 5:383–84, 385–86.
240. *C,* 8:405, 408, 410.
241. *C,* 9:412.
242. *C,* 10:418.
243. *C,* 11:421.

plains of man whose greed for power keeps increasing with the growth of his power and who desires all because he already possesses much. Moderation shown by someone after he usurped power does not deserve great praise.[244] Trajan, who possessed all virtues without being extreme in any, was the most accomplished prince in the annals of history, the man most suitable for honoring human nature and representing the divine.[245] It was the most vicious source of all the misfortunes of the Greeks that they never knew the limits of ecclesiastical and secular power.[246]

In the *Spirit of the Laws,* Montesquieu talks about the absence of genius in the legislators of Sparta, Lycurgus blending the hardest slavery with extreme liberty, the most atrocious sentiments with the greatest moderation.[247] Even moderation must not go to extremes. The moderation he likes is founded on virtue and does not derive from the cowardice and laziness of the soul. It is the soul of aristocracy, the form of government between that of monarchy and democracy and a happy mean.[248] Montesquieu clearly distinguishes between moderate and despotic governments, favoring the former.[249] The idea of measure and moderation does not only apply to aristocracies. In democracy also moderation ought to prevail. Here the love of equality limits ambition to the sole desire, to the sole happiness, of serving one's country, while the love of frugality limits desires to keeping only what is necessary for one's family and to donating the rest to society. Riches provide for power which a citizen cannot use for himself if he wants to remain equal. Thus good democracies, by establishing domestic frugality, make way for public spending. The good sense and the happiness of individuals consist greatly in the mediocrity of their talents and fortunes.[250] In an aristocracy, two things are pernicious: the extreme poverty and the exorbitant riches of the nobles.[251] Monarchical government has a great advantage over despotism because it is more lasting [*fixé*], its constitution is more firm and those who govern are more secure. Montesquieu quotes Cicero as saying that the violence of a headless people is more terrible than that of a despot.[252] "To form a moderate government, one must combine the powers, regulate them, temper them, set them in motion; give, so to speak, a ballast to one in order to put it in a postition to resist another."[253] Montesquieu likes the idea that in moderate countries, the law is wise in all its parts, is known everywhere and can be followed by the pettiest magistrates. This stands in contrast to despotism, under which the law is nothing but the will of the prince which cannot be known.[254] He favors moderate punishments.[255] He denounces the incontinence of women and the frightful dissolution of morals (*moeurs*) in Rome.[256] He discusses extremes in the various forms of govern-

244. *C,* 11:427.
245. *C,* 15:457.
246. *C,* 22:519.
247. *EL,* 4, 6:47.
248. *EL,* 3, 4:30; 5, 8:67–68.
249. *EL,* 3, 10:36 ff.
250. *EL,* 5, 3:55–56.
251. *EL,* 5, 8:71.
252. *EL,* 5, 11:75–76.
253. *EL,* 5, 14:84.
254. *EL,* 5, 16:88.
255. *EL,* 6, 6:118 ff.
256. *EL,* 7, 13:143 ff.

ment and their results in the form of corruption, writing as to extreme equality and liberty: "The true spirit of equality is as distant from that of extreme equality as is heaven from earth. . . . The natural place of virtue is close to liberty, but is not closer to excessive liberty than to servitude."[257] Great successes, especially those to which the people contributed, intoxicate them to such a degree that it is no longer possible to lead them.[258] When the nobility becomes hereditary, they can hardly show moderation any longer.[259] "When the Romans had lost their principles, the more power they had, the less prudent was their conduct until in the end, upon becoming their own tyrants and slaves, they lost the strength of liberty to fall into the weakness of license."[260] Montesquieu praises Alexander's frugality and private economy.[261] Book 11, especially chapter 6 on the constitution of England, is a treatise on the desirability of moderate government *par excellence,* as is book 12, dealing in a large measure with moderation and proportion of punishments, a theme Montesquieu takes up again in subsequent books.[262] He also favors moderation and proportion with respect to taxes. This is made plain by the title of chapter 12 in book 13, "Of the Relation of the Extent of Taxes to Liberty," a chapter in which he brings forth his general rule that taxes can go up with the degree of liberty the individual enjoys.[263] Similarly, the title of chapter 14 is "That the Nature of Taxes Is Relative to the Government." Montesquieu warns that due to governmental immoderacy and abuse of the individual's liberty, liberty has produced excessive taxes, resulting in servitude and a diminished tax income for the state.[264] Later on, Montesquieu points out that too much liberty produces disorder.[265] He is also glad to note, with respect to another extreme: "One has begun to cure oneself of Machiavellism, and recovers from it every day. More moderation has become necessary in the councils. What formerly was called coups d'état now would be, independent of the horror it would occasion, highly imprudent. Happy it is for men to be in a situation in which, though their passions prompt them to be wicked, they are interested in not being that way."[266] He favors a balance between the state as a creditor and the state as a debtor.[267] He praises the Stoics for not indulging in excesses, for carrying to excess only those things in which there is grandeur—the contempt of pleasure and pain.[268] As a man of measure, Montesquieu distinguishes between work and laziness, the good and the extraordinary, frugality and avarice, rejecting the latter extremes.[269] He desires harmony and proportion between law and religion.[270] He regrets that on account of a misfortune attached to the human

257. *EL,* 8, 3:152–53.
258. *EL,* 8, 4:153.
259. *EL,* 8, 5:154.
260. *EL,* 8, 12:162.
261. *EL,* 10, 14:200.
262. *EL,* 13, 8:292; 20, 14:457; 21, 11:495–96.
263. *EL,* 13, 12:295. See also 13:296, where Montesquieu writes that one can augment taxes in a monarchy because the moderation of the government can produce riches there.
264. *EL,* 13, 15:298.
265. *EL,* 16, 10:359.
266. *EL,* 21, 20:516.
267. *EL,* 22, 18:31.
268. *EL,* 24, 10:89.
269. *EL,* 24, 12:91.
270. *EL,* 24, 14:93.

condition, great men that are moderate are rare.[271] Toward the end of his major work, the author of the *Spirit of the Laws* devotes a book on the manner of composing laws. At its beginning, he writes: "I say it, and methinks I have undertaken this work with no other view than to prove it: the spirit of the legislator ought to be that of moderation; political, like moral good, always lies between two extremes [*limites*]."[272]

The fact that Montesquieu, the French liberal who had an enormous impact upon the creation of limited government throughout the world, was a man of measure, has been recognized by his students. Komroff, dealing with the *Persian Letters,* remarks that Montesquieu "showed that combination of satire tempered by the tolerance of wisdom that was later to place him in the front rank of French philosophical writers."[273] An author evaluating the *Considerations* states that in spite of his objective detachment, Montesquieu "sees that the immoderate liberty and power of the people is a great evil. In short, Montesquieu seems to favor a republic where the people have enough power to protect themselves against grave injustices but insufficient power to direct the state."[274] Neumann writes in his introduction to the *Spirit of the Laws:* "Both friend and enemy liked him, his dignity, urbanity, his love for friendship, his taste, his sincerity and, above all, his moderation."[275]

Moderation can be considered natural in those who belong to the aristocracy, often a link between the ruler and the people, as well as in those who study life in previous and contemporary societies. Montesquieu is an outstanding representative of the discipline of comparative government, which he dealt with in breadth and depth. As the title of his best known work indicates, the Frenchman, trained as he was as a jurist, was mainly concerned with the laws. For him, they constituted a moral minimum over which the moral maximum hovers as a constant reminder for human lawmakers to be fair and just. Most people have seen in Montesquieu a liberator from the rules and regulations of absolute monarchy. While he favored a great variety of rights, he was aware that in his time oppression in a large measure was due to interference in the individual's economic rights, that mercantilism was a major aspect of des-

271. *EL,* 28, 41:259.

272. *EL,* 29, 1:269.

273. Introduction to *The Persian Letters* (New York, 1929), xi.

274. David Lowenthal, introduction to *Considerations on the Causes of the Greatness of the Romans and their Decline* (New York, 1965), 12.

275. Neumann, *Spirit of the Laws,* xiii. Neumann refers to H. Carré in Lavisse, *Histoire de France* (Paris, 1911), 8:175. In his eulogy on Montesquieu before the Akademie der Wissenschaften in Berlin, Maupertius said on June 5, 1755: "Cet esprit de modération avec lequel il voyait les choses dans le repos de son cabinet, il l'appliquoit à tout, et le conservoit dans le bruit du monde et dans le feu des conversations. . . . Son maintien modeste et libre ressemblait à son conversation. . . . Il fut fort négligé dans ses habits et méprisa tout ce qui étoit au dela de la propriété; il n'étoit vêtu que des étoffes les plus simples et n'y faisoit jamais ajouter ni or ni argent. La même simplicité fut dans sa table et dans tout le reste de son économie." In Edouard Laboulaye, ed., *Oeuvres complètes de Montesquieu* (Paris, 1875), 1:24.

potism. It remained for Adam Smith to emphasize the latter fact and to show the importance of free enterprise for the wealth of nations.[276] In doing so, the professor of moral philosophy in the University of Glasgow did not lose sight of morals, as is evident from his first work, *The Theory of Moral Settlements,* on. Although primarily known as a political economist, Smith was interested also in that moral minimum which can effectively prescribe and proscribe mercantilism and oppress and secure the rights of man—the law.

276. Cf. Nicos E. Devletoglou, *Montesquieu and the Wealth of Nations* (Athens, 1963).

CHAPTER III

ASPECTS OF SMITH'S LIBERALISM

Introduction

Although Smith was influenced by Montesquieu's writings,[1] he is not generally known as a legal philosopher. The numerous titles of secondary literature on him do not as a rule suggest that he had a particular interest in the law.[2] In conferences commemorating the bicentennial of the publication of his best known work,[3] no paper was specifically concerned with his legal philosophy.[4] Yet it would be strange indeed if the author whose main—and last—work was

1. See Robert Maynard Hutchins, ed., *Adam Smith* (Chicago, 1952), v.

2. Exceptions are Walther Eckstein, "Adam Smith als Rechtsphilosoph," *Archiv für Rechts- und Wirtschaftsphilosophie* 20 (1926–27):378 ff.; C. A. Cooke, "Adam Smith and Jurisprudence," *The Law Quarterly Review* 51 (1935):326 ff.; Henry J. Bittermann, "Adam Smith's Empiricism and the Law of Nature," *The Journal of Political Economy* 48 (1940):487 ff., 703 ff.; Luigi Bagolini, *La simpatia nella morale e nel diritto: Aspetti del pensiero di Adam Smith* (Bologna, 1952); the last chapter, entitled "Hegel e Smith," in Pasquale Salvucci, *La filosofia politica di Adam Smith* (Urbino, 1966).

3. Adam Smith, *An Inquiry into the Nature and Causes of the Wealth of Nations,* was published in London on Mar. 9, 1776. In the following, quotations from that work will be from the Modern Library edition of the edition by Edwin Cannan, with an introduction by Max Lerner (New York, 1937, 1965).

4. For instance, in the conference at Eastern Kentucky University, out of 27 titles only 2 indicate a concern with the rule of law: David Levy, "Is Smith's 'Law of Nature' Exogenous or Endogenous to a Contractual Society?" and Leonard Billet, "The Justice of Inequality: Adam Smith on Property and the Purpose of Government."

considered "the most valuable contribution ever made by a single man towards establishing the principles on which government should be based,"[5] and said to have "exercised a power and beneficent influence on the public opinion and legislation of the civilised world, which has never been attained by any other work,"[6] if the man John Ruskin referred to as "the half-bred and half-witted Scotchman who taught the deliberate blasphemy: 'Thou shalt hate the Lord, thy God, damn his laws and covet his neighbour's goods,'"[7] would not have dealt with the law. After all, Smith was awarded an honorary LL.D. from the University of Glasgow for "the ability with which he had for many years expounded the principles of jurisprudence."[8] Quite correctly, it was pointed out in 1935 that "his works contain views of direct interest to jurists on the relation of legal and economic ideas, and on the relation of law to the social order."[9] Five years later, an article was published on Adam Smith and the law of nature.[10] In his last work, Hayek writes that Smith was a legal philosopher.[11]

Smith's concern with the law seems natural. He was an admiring student of Francis Hutcheson, who had "lectured first on Ethics, next upon what might very well be called Natural Jurisprudence, and thirdly upon Civil Polity."[12] Smith read Pufendorf and Grotius. Upon the illness of Craigie, he succeeded his teacher in the chair of moral philosophy at Glasgow. In 1758 his friend David Hume wanted him to stand for the Chair of Law of Nature and Nations at Edinburgh.[13] Later on he "handed on to Millar the torch taken over from Hutcheson,"[14] being instrumental in the appointment in 1761 of his lawyer friend to a professorship of civil law in Glasgow. The study of jurisprudence and the law was constant in the Scotland of his day and common among all those interested in governmental and social affairs.[15]

It has been said that "Smith's own approach to political economy was from moral philosophy through jurisprudence."[16] It may be added that concern with the law is evident throughout his writing, from the beginning to the end. This was already evident at the start of his career in Edinburgh. He was asked to give lectures there by a group that included many lawyers; they commissioned him to give a course in the philosophy of law. "In this course he probably surveyed

5. Henry Thomas Buckle, *History of Civilization in England,* 2d ed. (New York, 1888), 1:154.

6. Quoted in Edwin R. A. Seligman's "Introduction" to *The Wealth of Nations* (London, 1970), v.

7. Ibid.

8. J. R. McCulloch, "Sketch of the Life of Dr. Smith," in his edition of *The Wealth of Nations* (Edinburgh, 1828), 1:xxiv, quoting from the minutes of the Academic Senate.

9. Cooke, "Adam Smith and Jurisprudence," 326.

10. Bittermann, "Adam Smith's Empiricism and the Law of Nature."

11. F. A. Hayek, *Law, Legislation and Liberty,* vol. 1, *Rules and Order* (Chicago, 1973), 67.

12. Cannan, "Editor's Introduction," *The Wealth of Nations,* xliv.

13. Cooke, "Adam Smith and Jurisprudence," 327.

14. C. R. Fay, *Adam Smith and the Scotland of his Day* (Cambridge, 1956), 92.

15. A. L. Macfie, *The Individual in Society* (London, 1967), 25.

16. Cooke, "Adam Smith and Jurisprudence," 326.

the whole evolution of law in Western Europe, beginning with the Roman Empire and going through the development of feudalism, the effects of the crusades upon the distribution of property and trade, the rise of towns and the increase of liberty."[17] Another biographer wrote that Smith's course at Edinburgh was on jurisprudence and was continued in the Glasgow lectures.[18]

Of these lectures, John Millar, who listened to them, wrote that their course was divided into four parts: "The first contained Natural Theology; in which he considered the proofs of the being and attributes of God, and those principles of the human mind upon which religion is founded. The second comprehended Ethics, strictly so called, and consisted chiefly of the doctrines which he afterwards published in his Theory of Moral Sentiments. In the third part, he treated at more length of that branch of morality which relates to *justice,* and which, being susceptible of precise and accurate rules, is for that reason capable of a full and particular explanation. Upon this subject he followed the plan that seems to be suggested by Montesquieu; endeavoring to trace the gradual progress of jurisprudence, both public and private, from the rudest to the most refined ages, and to point out the effects of those arts which contribute to subsistence, and to the accumulation of property, in producing correspondent improvements or alterations in law and government."[19] Millar added that in the last part of his lectures, Smith examined those political regulations that are founded upon the principle of expediency and calculated to increase the riches, the power, and the prosperity of a state. He dealt with the political institutions relating to commerce, to finances, to ecclesiastical and military establishment, subjects later discussed in *The Wealth of Nations.* Smith's interest in the law is evident also in a student's notes of 1763, with a title page of 1766 stating the topic, *Juris Prudence, or Notes from the Lectures on Justice, Police, Revenue, and Arms.*[20]

Smith also dealt with the law in the books he published. *The Theory of Moral Sentiments* contains chapters on "the sense of Justice," on the "Authority of the general Rules of Morality" which "are justly regarded as the Laws of the Deity." Further chapters examine when "the Sense of Duty ought to be the sole principle of our conduct." They deal with "the order in which individuals are recommended by nature to our care and attention," with "the order in which societies are by nature recommended to our beneficence," and "licentious systems." One cannot well advance a theory on moral sentiments and ignore justice and the law. Discussion of the law dominates the last pages. He

17. E. G. West, *Adam Smith* (New Rochelle, N.Y., 1969), 48–49.

18. William Robert Scott, *Adam Smith as Student and Professor* (Glasgow, 1937), 112.

19. Quoted in Dugald Stewart, "Account of the Life and Writings of Adam Smith, LL.D.," in Adam Smith, *The Theory of Moral Sentiments* (London, 1759; new edition, London, 1853; reprinted New York, 1966), xvii. Unless noted otherwise, quotations will be from this edition.

20. Adam Smith, *Lectures on Justice, Police, Revenue and Arms,* edited with an introduction and notes by Edwin Cannan (Oxford, 1896).

concludes: "I shall, in another discourse, endeavor to give an account of the general principles of law and government, and of the different revolutions they have undergone in the different ages and periods of society, not only in what concerns justice, but in what concerns police, revenue, and arms, and whatever else is the object of law. I shall not, therefore, at present enter into any farther detail concerning the history of jurisprudence."[21]

During the year before his death Smith wrote that in *The Wealth of Nations,* on the title page of which his name is followed by the letters "LL.D.," he "partially executed this promise, at least so far as concerns policy, revenue and arms."[22] He admitted, then, that he had not yet discussed justice the way he had planned to. We hear that in his later years, Smith "was also reported to be engaged upon another work, which, judging from some hints in the *Moral Sentiments,* was probably a treatise on jurisprudence after the manner of Montesquieu; but the materials which he had collected for this work were destroyed at his own order shortly before his death."[23] Still, given the fact that Smith included police,[24] revenue, and arms among the subjects that are "the object of the law," it is obvious that *The Wealth of Nations* deals with various aspects of the law by his own account. The reader becomes easily aware that it also is concerned with justice. A discussion of legal matter—it has been said that *The Wealth of Nations* started out as an "essay in conjectural history," that is, a "systematic study of the effects of legal, institutional and general environmental conditions upon human progress"[25]—cannot well ignore the problems of justice. Besides, a part of a chapter is devoted to that subject.[26]

Millar's account of the Glasgow lectures shows that Smith discussed justice between ethics and expediency. It has been pointed out that the omission of a published work on justice constitutes a gap between *The Theory of Moral Sentiments* and *The Wealth of Nations.*[27] "The Adam Smith problem," concerned with the consistency of these two books,[28] might not have come into existence had Smith filled that gap through a publication. On the other hand, his omission cannot be interpreted as a lack of interest in the law. Perhaps the central position of justice in his lectures indicates that he attributed a great deal

21. *Theory of Moral Sentiments,* 503.

22. Adam Smith, *The Theory of Moral Sentiments,* 6th ed. (London, 1790), preface.

23. Glenn R. Morrow, "Adam Smith: Moralist and Philosopher," in *Adam Smith, 1776–1926—Lectures to Commemorate the Sesquicentennial of the Publication of "The Wealth of Nations"* (Chicago, 1928), 159.

24. For the relation of "police" to "policy," see Smith, *Lectures,* 154.

25. West, *Adam Smith,* 19.

26. "Of the Expence of Justice," *Wealth of Nations,* 669–81.

27. Cooke, "Adam Smith and Jurisprudence," 326–27.

28. Cf. August Oncken, "Das Adam Smith-Problem," *Zeitschrift für Socialwissenschaft* 1 (1898):25 ff., 101 ff., 276 ff. A survey on how authors have tried to solve the problem is provided by Hans Gustav Müller, *Die Nationalökonomie Adam Smiths als Ende der weltanschaulichen Emanzipation des naturalistischen Selbstinteresses in der europäischen Geistesgeschichte* (Diss. Tübingen, 1969), 506–12.

of relevance to it.[29] It may well be that he considered it so important that he felt he could not handle the subject through discussion, for which he conceded a definite need, be it by mentioning, at the end of *The Theory of Moral Sentiments,* his plan of dealing with the law in the future, or by partly realizing that plan in *The Wealth of Nations.* The rather abrupt ending of the discussion of the law at the end of his first book and the admission (probably with regrets) that in *The Wealth of Nations* only some aspects of the law were dealt with, point in that direction.[30] Perhaps he felt badly about not having said more on the law which to him may well have been the element pervading natural theology, ethics, and political economy and not just the link between moral philosophy and political economy.

In spite of this omission, there is enough in Smith's lectures and writings to show his concepts of the rule of law. Throughout his career, he was in one way or another concerned with the law as the proper measure of freedom and order. Some forty years ago, it was said that "his works contain views of direct interest to jurists on the relation of legal and economic ideas, and on the relation of law to the social order. Nor are these views without relevance today, when economists are urging the use of their own standards as legal criteria."[31] Smith's views on law, private liberty, and public order probably are even more relevant today when liberty, order, and the rule of law guaranteeing them are in jeopardy.

Liberty

Freedom is a predominant value in Smith's thought.

Few names are as much connected with freedom and none as immediately with economic freedom as that of Adam Smith. It has been said that with Smith, the development of the earlier English ethics culminates.[32] It also has been stated that he is the founder of the science of political economy.[33] It may

29. See Cooke, "Adam Smith and Jurisprudence."

30. Smith's discussion of the law concludes in *The Theory of Moral Sentiments,* the last part, "Of Systems of Moral Philosophy." It is dealt with in just a few pages and one gets the impression that its discussion is not completed. The fact that jurisprudence may well have been the pervasive element in Smith's thought is indicated by Cooke, "Adam Smith and Jurisprudence," esp. 328. It has been suggested that Smith regarded *The Theory of Moral Sentiments* and *The Wealth of Nations* "as complementary or as parts of a larger whole to be completed by a study of jurisprudence and political theory." It is added: "It seems likely that Smith had written part of this third treatise by 1790. The manuscript may have been among the papers he ordered destroyed just before his death." Henry J. Bittermann, "Adam Smith's Empiricism and the Law of Nature," 508.

31. Cooke, "Adam Smith and Jurisprudence," 326.

32. Wilhelm Wundt, *Ethics,* Washburn trans. (London, 1897), 2:82.

33. Seligman, "Introduction," v, quotes Lord Mahon for having stated that "*The Wealth of Nations* not only founded, but also almost completed political economy"; and Jean Baptiste Say: "Read Adam Smith as he deserves to be read and you will perceive that before him no political economy existed."

be added that Smith brought to a conclusion the English striving for freedom and initiated an age in which liberty resulted in unmatched prosperity. His work, falling into a time when Americans were striving for independence, can be said to have been a milestone in the evolution of constitutional government, like the Magna Carta, the Petition of Right, the Bill of Rights, the Act of Settlement, and the Declaration of Independence. It was in line with the ideas of the Barons, of Coke and Harrington, Locke and Blackstone, the latter being Smith's fellow-student at Oxford. Smith's economic liberalism has been considered a complement to the religious liberalism of Voltaire and the political liberalism of Rousseau.[34] The Scotsman stands between two other great liberals—Montesquieu and Kant.[35] Smith's thought was the fountain-head for modern liberalism in its different variations. It was admired by "the semi-liberal aristocrat Stein and the semi-conservative bourgeois Gentz," by the Prussian reformer who brought about the "liberation-legislation" (*Befreiungsgesetzgebung*) and by the adviser of Metternich, the leader of the Restoration.[36] It influenced political economists throughout the liberal era and thereafter.

Comments on Smith generally consider freedom his most prominent value. This is evident in encyclopedias.[37] It can be seen in scholarship. Years after Smith's death Dugald Stewart could write that the "fundamental doctrines of Mr. Smith's system are now so generally known, that it would be tedious to offer any recapitulation of them." Nevertheless, he observed that the great and leading object of Smith's speculations is the idea that freedom leads to wealth.[38] Smith's emphasis upon freedom is evident in J. R. McCulloch's remarks in his edition of *The Wealth of Nations,* a work he considered "a full and masterly exposition of the benefits arising from the freedom of industry," to be placed "in the foremost rank of those works that have helped to liberalize, enlighten, and enrich mankind."[39] After the era of modern liberalism had drawn to a close in most continental countries, Viner, in a volume commemorating the 150th anniversary of the publication of *The Wealth of Nations,* wrote that the "system of individual liberty is much in evidence among the interpreters of Smith."[40] Palyi's comprehensive account of Adam Smith's influ-

34. Morrow, "Adam Smith," 161.

35. See Walther Eckstein, "Einleitung" to his German translation, *Theorie der ethischen Gefühle* (Leipzig, 1926), 1:xxxiii; Macfie, *The Individual in Society,* 68, 91.

36. Melchior Palyi, "The Introduction of Adam Smith on the Continent," in *Adam Smith, 1776–1926,* 181.

37. For instance, the *Encyclopedia Americana,* 25 (1968): 111, speaks of the "basic contention . . . that national progress is the best secured by freedom of private initiative within the bounds of justice." *Der Grosse Brockhaus,* 10 (Wiesbaden, 1956): 761, states that in *The Wealth of Nations,* Smith has "als erster die individualistischen und liberalen Wirtschaftslehren des 18. Jahrhunderts geschlossen dargestellt."

38. Stewart, "Account," liv.

39. McCulloch, ed., *The Wealth of Nations,* 1:viii, xxviii.

40. Jacob Viner, "Adam Smith and Laissez Faire," in *Adam Smith, 1776–1926,* 120. Heinrich Waentig, in his "Einleitung" to the German translation of *The Wealth of Nations,* refers to Smith

ence in Europe deals about exclusively with the spreading of economic liberalism. "Everybody knows today that all over the world the name of Adam Smith, for three generations at least, became synonymous with economic liberalism in its fundamental aspects."[41] The general acceptance of the opinion that Adam Smith was an advocate of economic freedom has not changed to this day. An oration given at Glasgow in 1938 mentioned "his characteristic doctrine of freedom of enterprise and Free Trade," just as in a lecture given in America twenty years later, Smith was called "a great individualist . . . the great interpreter of those forces of individualism and free enterprise."[42] The year after, West's biography of Smith was published in an "Architects of Freedom Series." A speech commemorating the 250th anniversary of the birth of Adam Smith stated that "of course, Smith is now chiefly remembered for his contribution to economics where he is firmly associated with certain distinctive points of view." The enumeration of these points of view clearly shows their connection with freedom: the importance of competition as the only effective form of economic discipline; capitalism; the invisible hand; government as an unfortunate necessity, an impediment to the free action of individuals and therefore to a growth process otherwise limitless in its potential. The lecturer stated that "these are popular views," adding that "precisely because they are such it may be useful to confirm their validity and at the same time to introduce some necessary qualifications."[43] Although he wants to qualify these popular views, he treads cautiously, because these views are basically correct. This is characteristic of research on Smith. However authors may have interpreted Smith's emphasis upon freedom and free trade—they have not shaken the widespread belief that economic freedom ranks high with Smith, a belief that is the central theme of a film made to commemorate the bicentennial of *The Wealth of Nations.*[44]

Smith himself left no doubt about his appreciation of liberty. As early as 1749, he advocated "leave alone" in a lecture: "Projectors disturb nature in the course of her operations on human affairs, and it requires no more than to leave her alone and give her fair play in the pursuit of her ends that she may establish her own design. . . . Little else is required to carry a state to the highest degree of affluence from the lowest barbarism but peace, easy taxes, and a tolerable administration of justice; all the rest being brought about by the natural course of things. All governments which thwart this natural course, which force things

as "vornehmster Herold der wirtschaftlichen Freiheit"—"the most noble herald of economic freedom." *Eine Untersuchung über Natur und Wesen des Volkswohlstandes,* 3rd ed. (Jena, 1923), iv.

41. Palyi, "The Introduction of Adam Smith on the Continent," 225.

42. W. R. Scott, *Adam Smith—An Oration* (Glasgow, 1938); J. M. Clark, "Adam Smith and the Spirit of '76," in Carl L. Becker, ed., *The Spirit of '76 and Other Essays* (New York, 1966), 69.

43. Andrew S. Skinner, *Adam Smith and The Role of the State* (Glasgow, 1974), 5–6.

44. *Adam Smith and The Wealth of Nations,* produced by Liberty Fund, Inc., and Charles Barker Films. Narrator is Benjamin A. Rogge.

into another channel, or which endeavor to arrest the progress of society at a particular point, are unnatural, and, to support themselves, are obliged to be oppressive and tyrannical."[45]

In *The Theory of Moral Sentiments,* Smith writes in the first chapter of "fear and anxiety, the great tormentors of the human breast." While the child is protected from them, neither reason nor philosophy can protect it when it is growing up.[46] Nostalgically, he writes of "a life like what the poets describe in the Fortunate islands, a life of friendship, liberty, and repose; free from labor, and from care, and from all the turbulent passions which attend them."[47] However, freedom can exist not only in the Garden of Eden, man may also enjoy it in the state—by abstaining from being ambitious and interested in rank.[48] He can do so also by being ambitious and achieving rank. Ranking men can be free men, even though they obtain rank through a loss of liberty. They enjoy the respect and sympathy of mankind,[49] unless, like "a Borgia or a Nero," they become "scourges of mankind," "insolent and inhuman oppressors."[50] Smith believes not only in the freedom of the individual, but also in that of groups, "orders and societies into which the state is divided."

He resents too many regulations by lawmakers, fearing they would be "destructive of all liberty, security, and justice."[51] He favors a government that basically leaves alone institutions and rights as they have freely and gradually developed: "The man whose public spirit is prompted altogether by humanity and benevolence, will respect the established powers and privileges even of individuals, and still more those of the great orders and societies into which the state is divided. Though he should consider some of them as in some measure abusive, he will content himself with moderating, what he often cannot annihilate without great violence. When he cannot conquer the rooted prejudices of the people by reason and persuasion, he will not attempt to subdue them by force, but will religiously observe what by Cicero is justly called the divine maxim of Plato, never to use violence to his country, no more than to his parents. He will accommodate, as well as he can, his public arrangements to the confirmed habits and prejudices of the people, and will remedy, as well as he can, the inconveniencies which may flow from the want of those regulations which the people are averse to submit to. When he cannot establish the right, he will not disdain to ameliorate the wrong; but, like Solon, when he cannot establish the best system of laws, he will endeavor to establish the best that the people can bear."

Smith continues, denouncing planning and regulation: "The man of system, on the contrary, is apt to be very wise in his own conceit, and is often so

45. Quoted in John Rae, *Life of Adam Smith* (New York, 1895), reprinted, with an introduction by Jacob Viner (New York, 1965), 62–63.

46. Smith, *Theory of Moral Sentiments,* 8.

47. Ibid., 40.

48. Ibid., 72, 80.

49. Ibid., 72, 80, 81, 424–25.

50. Ibid., 107.

51. Ibid., 116.

enamoured with the supposed beauty of his own ideal plan of government, that he cannot suffer the smallest deviation from any part of it. He goes on to establish it completely in all its parts, without any regard either to the great interests or to the strong prejudices which may oppose it: he seems to imagine that he can arrange the different members of a great society with as much ease as the hand arranges the different pieces upon a chess-board; he does not consider that the pieces upon the chess-board have no other principle of motion besides that which the hand impresses upon them; but that, in the great chess-board of human society, every single piece has a principle of motion of his own, altogether different from that which the legislature might choose to impress upon it. If those two principles coincide and act in the same direction, the game of human society will go on easily and harmoniously, and is very likely to be happy and successful. If they are opposite or different, the game will go on miserably, and the society must be at all times in the highest degree of disorder."

Smith adds: "Some general, and even systematical, idea of the perfection of policy and law, may no doubt be necessary for directing the views of the statesman. But to insist upon establishing, and upon establishing all at once, and in spite of all opposition, every thing which that idea may seem to require, must often be the highest degree of arrogance. It is to erect his own judgment into the supreme standard of right and wrong. It is to fancy himself the only wise and worthy man in the commonwealth, and that his fellow-citizens should accommodate themselves to him, and not he to them. It is upon this account that of all political speculators sovereign princes are by far the most dangerous. This arrogance is perfectly familiar to them. They entertain no doubt of the immense superiority of their own judgment. When such imperial and royal reformers, therefore, condescend to contemplate the constitution of the country which is committed to their government, they seldom see any thing so wrong in it as the obstructions which it may sometimes oppose to the execution of their own will. They hold in contempt the divine maxim of Plato, and consider the state as made for themselves, not themselves for the state. The great object of their reformation, therefore, is to remove these obstructions—to reduce the authority of the nobility—to take away the privileges of cities and provinces, and to render both the greatest individuals and the greatest orders of the state as incapable of opposing their commands as the weakest and most insignificant."[52]

It has been stated that in *The Theory of Moral Sentiments,* "Smith develops his system of ethics on the basis of a doctrine of a harmonious order in nature guided by God, and in an incidental manner applies his general doctrine with strict consistency to the economic order."[53] Freedom is valued highly in both orders. As in his lecture of 1749, Smith in his first book strongly asserts

52. Ibid., 342–44.

53. Viner, "Adam Smith and Laissez Faire," 119.

laissez-faire,[54] showing the consistency of the two documents. Harmony is suggested also by the equilibrium of liberty indicated in the latter work. *Rien pour rien:* The more the ambitious individual gives up what could be called "inner liberty," the more he gains what could be called "outer liberty." He has a choice and may do whatever he considers his self-interest. The rather passive type of liberty existing in the "Fortunate islands," surrounded by friendship and repose, can be replaced in the fortunate state of the "great society" by a liberty complemented by competition and activity. The former type of liberty is as natural as the latter.[55] The liberty in friendship and repose diminishes as that gained by virtue of active competition grows. Both types of liberty may be enjoyed by the same person at the same time. The ambitious and active as well as the reposed and passive, he maintains in disputing the Stoics, can "breathe the free air of liberty and independency."[56] Moral sentiment and self-interest may prompt one person to prefer freedom in repose, and another, to prefer it in competition, or a little of each. Both act virtuously.[57] The Smithian equation on liberty, allowing the different types of freedom, makes Smith's first book perhaps less rigid than has been asserted.[58] At any rate, there can be no doubt about Smith's high evaluation of liberty in *The Theory of Moral Sentiments.*

Smith's advocacy of liberty also is obvious in his *Lectures.* According to the student who took notes, Smith maintains that "a person has a right to have his body free from injury and his liberty free from infringement unless there be proper cause, nobody doubts."[59] With regrets, he describes how liberty was lost and with satisfaction how it was restored.[60] He likes the idea that "the king's revenue . . . depends so much on the concurrence of the parliament that it never can endanger the liberty of the nation," speaks of "a happy mixture of all the different forms of government properly restrained, and a perfect security to liberty and property," and points out "other securities to liberty."[61] He

54. Smith does not use the French expression. Given the fact that in "1755 Smith had publicly asserted his claim to priority, as against some unnamed rival, in applying to the economic order the system of natural liberty" by citing the lecture of 1749, in which he suggests a "leave alone" policy (Viner, "Adam Smith and Laissez Faire," 118–119), it is possible that he refrained from using "laissez faire" in order to avoid the impression that he borrowed that term from the French economists, or physiocrats. According to Ernest Belfort Bax, the term *laissez faire, laissez passer* was introduced by Jean de Gournay; Introduction to his edition of *The Wealth of Nations* (London, 1887), 1:xxx. See August Oncken, *Die Maxime Laissez faire et laissez passer, ihr Ursprung, ihr Werden* (Bern, 1886).

55. Smith's use of the words "natural" and "nature" is discussed by Bittermann, "Smith's Empiricism and the Law of Nature," esp. 703–34.

56. Smith, *Theory of Moral Sentiments,* 424–28.

57. Cf. Joseph Cropsey, *Polity and Economy: An Interpretation of the Principles of Adam Smith* (The Hague, 1957).

58. Viner, "Adam Smith and Laissez Faire," 120. On the problem of the consistency of Smith's two books, see Cropsey, *Polity and Economy,* and the review of that book by A. L. Macfie, in *The Individual in Society,* 126–29.

59. Smith, *Lectures,* 8.

60. Ibid., 26–43, 43–72.

61. Ibid., 44–46.

praises the law of England for being "always the friend of liberty," and shows the importance of impartial juries for the security of "life, liberty and property."[62] A tyrant "is one who deprives the people of their liberty, levies armies and taxes, and puts the citizens to death as he pleases."[63] To Smith, "nothing can be more absurd than perpetual entails."[64] He praises the advantages of free commerce, advocating that "Britain should by all means be made a free port, that there should be no interruptions of any kind made to foreign trade, that if it were possible to defray the expenses of government by any other method, all duties, customs, and excise should be abolished, and that free commerce and liberty of exchange should be allowed with all nations, and for all things." Holland is well off with corn, "entirely owing to the free export and import they enjoy."[65] These quotations are examples in which he expressly uses words such as "free" and "liberty." They do not imply that he would not advocate freedom in other passages.

All of his lectures are interspersed with his advocacy of liberty, as is *The Wealth of Nations.* It has been pointed out that *The Theory of Moral Sentiments* led to *The Wealth of Nations.* Also, the editor of the *Lectures* has shown how much of the material discussed in them reappears in his best known work.[66] Regardless of how one may feel about the consistency of, and continuity in, the various works of Smith, one cannot entertain much doubt that his high evaluation of freedom in *The Theory of Moral Sentiments* leads to the system of natural liberty which generally has been considered the core of *The Wealth of Nations.*[67] The latter fact, aside from considerations of space, makes it unnecessary to give detailed quotations on Smith's advocacy of liberty in his best known work. "Flaws in the natural order" of liberty, much as they may disturb the harmony of that order, only confirm the importance of freedom.[68] Where they seem to harm liberty, they are exceptional. Even then, however, they often exist in the public interest and thus are, in the last analysis, conducive to the "great society" in which freedom thrives. They only confirm the rule of the preeminence of liberty. Viner stated: "From his examination of the operation of self-interest in specific phases of the economic order and of the consequences of government interference with the free operation of self-

62. Ibid., 51–52. 63. Ibid., 55. 64. Ibid., 124.

65. Ibid., 206, 209, 230–231.

66. Cannan prepared a comprehensive table of parallel passages. Ibid., xxxv–xxxix.

67. See Viner, "Adam Smith and Laissez Faire," 120.

68. These "flaws" are pointed out by Viner, ibid., 134–38. Smith is reluctant to restrict freedom in order to do away with these flaws for the sake of a more perfect harmony: "People of the same trade seldom meet together, even for merriment and diversion, but the conversation ends in a conspiracy against the public, or in some contrivance to raise prices. It is impossible indeed to prevent such meetings, by any law which either could be executed, or would be consistent with liberty and justice. But though the law cannot hinder people of the same trade from sometimes assembling together, it ought to do nothing to facilitate such assemblies; much less to render them necessary." *Wealth of Nations,* 128.

interest, Smith arrives at an extensive program for the extension of the system of natural liberty through the abolition of existing systems of governmental regulation, though he nowhere brings the several items in that program together." He added that Smith advocates four main reforms: the establishment of free choice of occupations through the repeal of existing apprenticeship regulations and settlement laws; free trade in land through the abolition of entails, primogenitures, and other restrictions hindering the free transfer of land by gift, devise, or sale; internal trade through the abolition of local customs taxes; free international trade through the abolition of duties and bounties, of mercantilist prohibitions and trading monopolies of chartered companies.[69] Viner was correct in stating that the four programs mentioned are the *main* measures Smith favors for the sake of liberty. For there are, throughout *The Wealth of Nations,* many other detailed propagations of freedom. "We trust with perfect security that the freedom of trade, without any attention of government, will always supply us with the wine which we have occasion for: and we may trust with equal security that it will always supply us with all the gold and silver which we can afford to purchase or to employ, either in circulating our commodities, or in other uses."[70] This statement by Smith shows that for him, not only precious metals, but goods in general, including luxuries such as wine, become available through freedom. The latter is for Smith more than a means for securing wealth; it is a formidable driving force of human action. This is evident in a passage said to be "really the text of the polemical portion of the *Wealth of Nations.*"[71] That passage reads: "The natural effort of every individual to better his own condition, when suffered to exert itself with freedom and security, is so powerful a principle, that it is alone, and without any assistance, not only capable of carrying on the society to wealth and prosperity, but of surmounting a hundred impertinent obstructions with which the folly of human laws too often incumbers its operations; though the effect of these obstructions is always more or less either to encroach upon its freedom, or to diminish its security."[72] In the last page of the polemic portion, before Smith turns to book five, concerned with the duties of the sovereign which for the common weal may legitimately necessitate restrictions of the citizens' freedom, Smith, as a concluding emphatic note, again confesses his advocacy of liberty: "All systems either of preference or of restraint, therefore, being thus completely taken away, the obvious and simple system of natural liberty establishes itself of its own accord. Every man, as long as he does not violate the laws of justice, is left perfectly free to pursue his own interest his own way, and to bring both his industry and capital into competition with those of any other man, or order of men. The sovereign is completely discharged from a duty, in the

69. Viner, "Adam Smith and Laissez Faire," 133.
70. *Wealth of Nations,* 404.
71. Cannan, "Editor's Introduction," *Wealth of Nations,* liv.
72. *Wealth of Nations,* 508.

attempting to perform which he must always be exposed to innumerable delusions, and for the proper performance of which no human wisdom or knowledge could ever be sufficient; the duty of superintending the industry of private people, and of directing it towards the employments most suitable to the interest of the society." In this state of affairs, there exists what Smith calls "a great society."[73] It is a happy society,[74] one in which freedom is not unduly encroached upon by "the folly of human laws"—the laws made by those whom Smith denounced in *The Theory of Moral Sentiments,* by men who arrogate to themselves to move human beings the way they move the figures on a chessboard—by the planners of human design.

Liberty under Law

The importance of freedom in Smith's scale of values must not blind us to the fact that to him, liberty is under law and exists according to the laws. In saying so, we have in mind not only the restraints imposed upon freedom by the law of nature, but also by human laws.[75]

Liberty is, first, restricted by natural laws. It has been a widely accepted opinion that Smith was strongly influenced by writers on natural law and

73. Ibid., 651.

74. Stewart, "Account of the Life and Writings of Adam Smith," xiii, speaks of Smith's "ruling passion of contributing to the happiness and the improvement of society." In *The Theory of Moral Sentiments,* 235, Smith writes: "The happiness of mankind, as well as of all other rational creatures, seems to have been the original purpose intended by the Author of Nature when he brought them into existence. No other end seems worthy of that supreme wisdom and divine benignity which we necessarily ascribe to him; and this opinion, which we are led to by the abstract consideration of his infinite perfections, is still more confirmed by the examination of the works of Nature, which seem all intended to promote happiness, and to guard against misery. But, by acting according to the dictates of our moral faculties, we necessarily pursue the most effectual means for promoting the happiness of mankind, and may therefore be said, in some sense, to co-operate with the Deity, and to advance, as far as in our power, the plan of providence. By acting otherwise, on the contrary, we seem to obstruct, in some measure, the scheme which the Author of Nature has established for the happiness and perfection of the world, and to declare ourselves, if I may say so, in some measure the enemies of God." Morrow, "Adam Smith: Moralist and Philosopher," 179, concludes his essay with this quotation from Smith, which clearly shows that Smith always asked the paramount question "wherein consists the happiness and perfection of a man, not only as an individual, but as a member of a family, of a state, and of the great society of mankind." From these quotations one may well conclude that freedom, economic freedom, and free trade were seen by Smith as prerequisites for the happiness and perfection of man and a guard against misery.

75. Smith speaks of "all laws, both human and divine," and distinguishes "positive law" from "natural jurisprudence." *Theory of Moral Sentiments,* 33, 501. He distinguishes "jurisprudence," "natural jurisprudence," from "the constitution of states and the principles of civil laws"; *Lectures,* 1. In the latter work, he divides part one, concerned with "Justice," into the following divisions: "Of Public Jurisprudence," "Domestic Law," "Private Law." The original index of the *Lectures* under "Law" shows the following entries: "its general principles," "of Nations," "Cannon Law," "Domestic," "Private."

jurisprudence such as Cicero, Grotius, Pufendorf, Locke, Shaftesbury, and Hutcheson.[76] Given the fact that his time was characterized by far-reaching governmental controls and restrictions, it could perhaps be expected that Smith would go out of his way to emphasize that freedom is natural and that its curtailments are incompatible with nature and the will of God. However, like his teachers, he refrained from favoring an abolition of all restrictions upon freedom. While he asserts the basic naturalness of freedom, he leaves no doubt that liberty, much as natural law may suggest its extension, is still under the law of nature, or God.

In *The Theory of Moral Sentiments,* Smith makes clear that nature, manifesting itself through the operation of its forces, be they external, physical phenomena, or human propensities, is not in chaos but constitutes a harmonious whole. It is an order with "unalterable laws."[77] It is designed and guided by "God,"[78] "the Deity,"[79] the "all-wise Being"[80] who is "the Author of Nature,"[81] "the all-wise Author of Nature,"[82] "the great Director of nature,"[83] "the great Director of the universe,"[84] "the great Superintendent of the universe,"[85] "the great Conductor of the universe,"[86] "the all-seeing Judge of the world."[87] The absence of absolute freedom is obvious. Where there is a director, a superintendent, a conductor, and, especially, a judge, there must be law and order. Freedom exists within the harmony of the universal order and its laws.

Moral sentiments "were plainly intended to be the governing principles of human nature, the rules which they prescribe are to be regarded as the commands and laws of the Deity, promulgated by those viceregents which he has thus set up within us. All general rules are commonly denominated laws: thus the general rules which bodies observe in the communication of motion, are called the laws of motion. But those general rules which our moral faculties observe in approving or condemning whatever sentiment or action is subjected to their examination, may much more justly be denominated such. They have much greater resemblance to what are properly called laws, those general rules which the sovereign lays down to direct the conduct of his subjects. Like them they are rules to direct free actions of men: they are prescribed most surely by a lawful superior, and are attended too with the sanction of rewards and punishments. Those viceregents of God within us never fail to punish the violation of them by the torments of inward shame and self-condemnation; and, on the

76. For authors who believed that Smith was influenced by natural law philosophers, see Bittermann, "Smith's Empiricism and the Law of Nature," 488–90. Even Bittermann, who emphasizes that Smith was an empiricist influenced by Hume, admits the impact of natural law upon Smith.

77. *Theory of Moral Sentiments,* 208.

78. Ibid., 153, 346.

79. Ibid., 232, 251.

80. Ibid., 345, 346; "that divine Being," 219, 347.

81. Ibid., 109, 235, 436. (On 109 and 436, "nature" is not capitalized.) On 240, Smith speaks of "the great Author of our nature."

82. Ibid., 185.

83. Ibid., 110.

84. Ibid., 346.

85. Ibid., 427.

86. Ibid., 347.

87. Ibid., 176, 187.

contrary, always reward obedience with tranquility of mind, with contentment, and self-satisfaction."[88]

Obedience to divine and natural laws, to moral sentiments, is aided by "the great demigod within the breast, the great judge and arbiter of conduct."[89] Human behavior and conduct are supposed to exist not in total liberty, but "according to those restrained and corrected emotions which the great inmate, the great demigod within the breast prescribes and approves of," according to "the authority of the judge within the breast" who provides for, or is even identical to, "the sense of propriety."[90] To Smith, "this demigod within the breast appears, like the demigods of the poets, though partly of immortal, yet partly too of mortal extraction. When his judgments are steadily and firmly directed by the sense of praiseworthiness and blameworthiness, he seems to act suitably to his divine extraction: but when he suffers himself to be astonished and confounded by the judgments of ignorant and weak man, he discovers his connection with mortality, and appears to act suitably rather to the human than to the divine part of his origin."[91] Another guide for human behavior is what Smith refers to as "the ideal man within the breast,"[92] "the man within,"[93] "the man within the breast."[94] The latter two may well be more human and more fallible than the former, or they may not. Whatever the concrete meaning of the various expressions may be—and Smith does not appear to be too specific about it—there can be no doubt that they stood for a law within us which would induce the individual to refrain from licentious uses and abuses of freedom. The same can be said of the role of "the spectator," a figure which, like that of the "demigod" and the "man within the breast," appears in a great variety of shades,[95] and seems to be connected with these figures.[96]

88. Ibid., 234–35.

89. Ibid., 363. See also 185, 194, 385.

90. Ibid., 359, 360.

91. Ibid., 187.

92. Ibid., 222.

93. Ibid., 186, 194, 195.

94. Ibid., 185, 206, 216, 333, 428. Smith also speaks of "the judge within the breast," 360; "the great judge within the breast," 363; "the great inmate of the breast," 385. He indicates a relationship between these figures and his "demigod" when he speaks of "this demigod within the breast" (187) and "the great demigod within the breast" (359, 363).

95. Smith speaks of "the spectator" (73, 112), of "a spectator" (165), "the spectators" (120), "the indifferent spectator" (52, 222), "the most indifferent spectator" (350), "every generous spectator" (115), "the impartial spectator" (27, 120, 141, 172, 206, 208, 314, 331, 335, 356, 426, 427), "every impartial spectator" (209, 486), "every impartial bystander" (275), "the impartial spectators" (167), "any other fair and impartial spectator" (162), "every intelligent and impartial spectator" (366, 415), "the cool and impartial spectator" (50), "every human spectator" (239), "the real spectator" (216), "the real spectators" (207), "the real and impartial spectator" (221), "the real, revered, and impartial spectator" (219), "the real or supposed spectator" (203), "the supposed impartial spectator" (191, 333, 385, 386), "the abstract and ideal spectator" (216). Cf. the chapter "The Impartial Spectator" in Macfie, *The Individual and Society,* 82–100.

96. "The man within the breast, the abstract and ideal spectator of our sentiments and conduct, requires often to be awakened and put in mind of his duty, by the presence of the real spectator: and it is always from that spectator, from whom we can expect the least sympathy and indulgence, that we are likely to learn the most complete lesson of self-command." *Theory of Moral*

Smith's natural order is not a metaphysical order, but the order of this world. He did not like "this cobweb science of Ontology, which was likewise sometimes called Metaphysics," composed as it was of "subtleties and sophisms."[97] Already in *The Theory of Moral Sentiments,* the "great end" is "the order of the world, and the perfection and happiness of human nature."[98] This order is composed of smaller orders, such as the state, and smaller "orders and societies into which the state is divided." The individual's liberty is restricted by whatever concrete order he is in. This means that it is restricted not only by ethical and moral considerations, by divine and natural law, but also by norms set by men. The great eclectic who speaks of God, of the "demigod" partaking of both divine and human features, of "the ideal man within the breast," of just "the man in the breast," of the "ideal" and the "real" spectator, makes another transition in upholding positive law as distinguished from natural jurisprudence. He maintains: "Every system of positive law may be regarded as a more or less imperfect attempt towards a system of natural jurisprudence, or towards an enumeration of the particular rules of justice." Yet he feels that, in spite of positivist abuses, systems of positive law "deserve the greatest authority" and "the public magistrate is under a necessity of employing the power of the commonwealth to enforce the practice" of the virtue of justice. "Without this precaution, civil society would become a scene of bloodshed and disorder, every man revenging himself at his own hand whenever he fancied he was injured."[99] Smith's advocacy of the positive enforcement of practical justice, of the known and enforceable specific "laws of society"[100] which possibly differ from "the commands and laws of the Deity"[101] which conform to ideal justice, thus is mentioned in one breath with a desirable restriction of the freedom of the individual. Liberty was to be under law[102] so that justice could prevail.

Justice is a *sine qua non* for the survival of society and the actual freedom the societal order secures. Much as Smith goes out of his way to emphasize the moral value of beneficence, he makes it clear that it is less important than justice, which is more of a result of (enforceable) law: "Beneficence . . . is less essential to the existence of society than justice. Society may subsist, though not in the most comfortable state, without beneficence; but the prevalence of injustice must utterly destroy it." Beneficence "is the ornament which embellishes, not the foundation which supports the building, and which it was, therefore, sufficient to recommend, but by no means necessary to impose.

Sentiments, 216. See also ibid., 333. The connection of the "man within the breast" to the "demigod" can be seen on 359, 363.

97. *Wealth of Nations,* 726. Bittermann, "Smith's Empiricism and the Law of Nature," 498, likens Smith to the later positivists.

98. *Theory of Moral Sentiments,* 239.

99. Ibid., 501–2.

100. Ibid., 3, 41, 107.

101. Ibid., 232, 234.

102. Cf. Macfie, *Individual in Society,* 91, writing about Smith, that in his basic argument "for the (suitably controlled) freedom of the individual he was the eternal radical."

Justice, on the contrary, is the main pillar that upholds the whole edifice. If it is removed, the great, the immense fabric of human society, that fabric which, to raise and support, seems, in this world, if I may say so, to have been the peculiar and darling of nature, must in a moment crumble into atoms. In order to enforce the observation of justice, therefore, nature has implanted in the human breast that consciousness of ill desert, those terrors of merited punishment, which attend upon its violation, as the great safeguards of the association of mankind, to protect the weak, to curb the violent, and to chastise the guilty."[103]

Speaking of "the sense of Justice," Smith gives an idea on what the individuals are not free to do. They must not commit a breach of contract. Still worse is a breach of property, such as theft and robbery. Worst of all is murder. "The most sacred laws of justice, therefore, those whose violation seems to call loudest for vengeance and punishment, are the laws which guard the life and person of our neighbour; the next are those which guard his property and possessions; and last of all come those which guard what are called his personal rights, or what is due to him from the promises of others."[104] It also does not correspond to "the sense of justice" of the classic advocate of free enterprise to be free to do harm to one's neighbor: "To disturb his happiness merely because it stands in the way of our own, to take from him what is of real use to him merely because it may be of equal or more use to us, or to indulge, in this manner, at the expense of other people, the natural preference which every man has for his own happiness above that of other people, is what no impartial spectator can go along with." Neither is man free to unfairly compete: "In the race for wealth, and honours, and preferments, he may run as hard as he can, and strain every nerve and every muscle, in order to outstrip all his competitors. But if he should justle, or throw down any of them, the indulgence of the spectators is entirely at an end."[105]

We dealt at some length with Smith's first book because it contains the bulk of his writing on the idea that freedom is under the law.[106] Also, in view of the fact that he brought out a new edition of that work shortly before his death, it can be assumed that he wanted its contents to complement his other writing, including *The Wealth of Nations.* In what he produced since *The Theory of Moral Sentiments* was first published, Smith only seems to confirm that freedom is under the rule of law.

103. *Theory of Moral Sentiments,* 125. See also 250: "The rules of justice may be compared to the rules of grammar; the rules of the other virtues to the rules which critics lay down for the attainment of what is sublime and elegant in composition. The one are precise, accurate, and indispensable. The other are loose, vague, and indeterminate, and present us rather with a general idea of the perfection we ought to aim at, than afford us any certain and infallible directions for acquiring it."

104. Ibid., 121.

105. Ibid., 119.

106. Eckstein's article, "Adam Smith als Rechtsphilosoph," is drawing nearly exclusively upon *The Theory of Moral Sentiments.*

When, in his *Lectures,* he starts out the first part, dealing with justice, by saying that the end of justice is to secure from injury and then enumerates the various ways how an individual can be injured "as a man . . . as a member of a family . . . as a member of a state," he sounds a keynote for the general theme that freedom exists under law. A few pages later he says that freedom is under the law for the sake of its protection and for that of utility.[107] He approves the fact that the legislative power "makes laws for the public good: the judicial . . . obliges private persons to obey these laws, and punishes those who disobey."[108] His considering judicial tenure and courts of justice as "securities to liberty" amounts to saying that liberty exists according to, or under, the laws.[109] When he says that the law of England always has been the friend of liberty, he implies that liberty has been secured by, and under, that law.[110] Smith gladly notes that "the laws of every country are particularly careful of securing" liberty, even though he writes: "Nothing is more difficult than perfectly to secure liberty."[111]

In *The Wealth of Nations* Smith again shows plainly that liberty—even "natural liberty"—can exist only under a legal order. "According to the system of natural liberty," the sovereign—as the head of a system of positive law—has "the duty of protecting the society from the violence and invasion of other independent societies." In other words, the sovereign has the duty of protecting liberty as it exists in and under the peace provided for the legal order of society from violent invasions by external forces. He also must protect liberty from invasion by internal enemies, having "the duty of protecting, as far as possible, every member of the society from the injustice or oppression of every other member of it, or the duty of establishing an exact administration of justice." The "great society" is one in which the law restricts unlimited liberty, or license, for the sake of the legally protected, concrete liberty of the individual.[112] Smith devotes considerable space defending the expenses the sovereign must make for purposes of defense and justice, always having in mind the need for the peaceful existence of a liberal[113] order under law. Law protects property rights. Without law and its enforcement, property rights are unsafe. "It is only under the shelter of the civil magistrate that the owner of that valuable property, which is acquired by the labour of many years, or perhaps of many successive generations, can sleep a single night in security. He is at all times surrounded by unknown enemies, whom, though he never provoked, he can never appease, and from whose injustice he can be protected only by the powerful arm of the civil magistrate continually held up to chastise it."[114]

107. *Lectures,* 9–10.

108. Ibid., 17.

109. Ibid., 45–46.

110. Ibid., 51.

111. Ibid., 144.

112. *Wealth of Nations,* 651.

113. Smith uses the word "liberal" when he speaks of the "liberal reward of labour," "the liberal system of free exportation and free importation," "the most liberal wages," "the liberal or loose system." *Wealth of Nations,* 73, 506, 532, 746.

114. Ibid., 670.

Without law and its enforcement, liberty is unsafe, for "upon the impartial administration of justice depends the liberty of every individual, the sense which he has of his own security."[115] Even "perfect liberty" is not an absolute, unrestricted liberty, but one under law.[116]

When he says that freedom is under law, he in a large measure is thinking of law with sanction, that is, of positive law. However, his stating with regrets that positive law is only a more or less imperfect attempt toward natural jurisprudence and his mentioning positivistic abuses shows that he appreciates a positive law that approaches natural jurisprudence, a law that conforms to the principles of justice and natural law and the law of God. Influenced as he was by the natural law school, his idea on the rule of law is close to that of natural law philosophers. It corresponds to Bracton's statement, *non sub homine sed sub Deo et lege,*[117] or to Harrington's wish for an empire of laws and not of men.[118] Smith wants a law, customary or legislative, which would limit the power of the government for the sake of liberty. He favored a law that corresponds to the principles of natural justice and gives justice priority to the state, as symbolically expressed by the German term *Rechtsstaat.*

But Smith also states that positive law, even though it may not correspond to natural jurisprudence, was entitled to authority. For him, the rule of law does not merely imply restrictions upon the rulers. It also means the strict enforcement of existing laws, even though they may not absolutely conform to natural jurisprudence. To him, there can be no constitutionalist, or liberal, aspects of the rule of law unless these aspects are made and recognized by state law, or *Staatsrecht.*[119]

Smith, then, believes in two concepts of the rule of law. He believes in the rule of law in the sense of constitutional government, implying a limitation of governmental power for the sake of the freedom of the individual. He also believes in the rule of law implying the enforcement of the law by the state for the sake of public order. It is obvious that both concepts can conflict. State law could damage and negate the law state. However, they also can be quite

115. Ibid., 681.

116. For Smith, "perfect liberty" exists where the individual "may change his trade as often as he pleases." He speaks of "a society where things were left to follow their natural course, where there was perfect liberty, and where every man was perfectly free both to chuse what occupation he thought proper, and to change it as he thought proper." *Wealth of Nations,* 56, 99. He mentions "perfect liberty" (ibid., 62, 118), "the most perfect freedom" and "the most perfect liberty" (ibid., 114, 118). These terms are always used in the context of life in existing legal orders.

117. Bracton, *De legibus et consuetudinibus angliae,* folio 5.

118. "Government (to define it [*de jure*] or according to *ancient Prudence*) is an Art whereby a Civil Society of men is instituted and preserved upon the foundation of common right or interest, or (to follow *Aristotle* and *Livy*) it is the *Empire of Lawes* and not of Men." James Harrington, *The Common-wealth of Oceana* (London, 1656), 2.

119. The term *Staatsrecht* is used here not in the narrow sense in which it recently has been used by German jurists, meaning a part of public law, but in a broader sense, meaning all the positive laws of a state, or nation.

compatible if state law transmutes the ideas of the law state, or natural jurisprudence, into positive norms. In the following, it will be examined in greater detail how Smith felt about the two concepts of law.

Law as a Limitation upon Government

Smith believed in a government limited by law.

This follows from his belief in constitutional government.[120] In the last paragraph of the first part of *The Theory of Moral Sentiments,* a part concerned with propriety, Smith makes a statement that shows his wariness of governmental power and expresses strong fears lest government is above the law. After discussing the corruption of moral sentiments, which is due to a disposition to admire the rich and the great, Smith writes that, in order to become powerful and admired, "the candidates for fortune too frequently abandon the paths of virtue." The ambitious man flatters himself that "in the splendid situation to which he advances, he will have so many means of commanding the respect and admiration of mankind, and will be enabled to act with such superior propriety and grace, that the lustre of his future will entirely cover, or efface, the foulness of the steps by which he arrived at that elevation." With a view to the dangers of big government unrestrained by law, Smith adds: "In many governments the candidates for the highest stations are above the law; and, if they can attain the object of their ambition, they have no fear of being called to account for the means by which they acquired it. They often endeavor, therefore, not only by fraud and falsehood, the ordinary and vulgar arts of intrigue and cabal, but sometimes by the perpetration of the most enormous crimes, by murder and assassination, by rebellion and civil war, to supplant and destroy those who oppose or stand in the way of their greatness." While these men "commonly gain nothing but the disgraceful punishment which is due to their crimes," Smith admits that they may be fortunate enough to attain that wished-for greatness. He proceeds to denounce their kind of government, a government which is "polluted and defiled by the baseness of the means" through which they rose to it. In such a government, there is likely to exist a "profusion of every liberal expense," an "excessive indulgence in every profligate pleasure, the wretched, but usual, resource of ruined characters." In order to make his subjects forget the illegitimacy of his power, the ruler is likely to hurry public business or to go to war. Smith decries "all the gaudy pomp of the most ostentatious greatness; . . . the venal and vile adulation of the great and of the learned; . . . the more innocent though more foolish, acclamations of the common people," which exists under this type of a government.[121]

Elsewhere in his first book Smith warns of governmental power which

120. See the unpublished paper by E. G. West, "Adam Smith's Economics of Politics" (1975).
121. *Theory of Moral Sentiments,* 88–90.

seems to captivate all those who possess it and which few will be able to escape. He refers to "the perfidy and cruelty of a Borgia or a Nero," rulers who obviously did not consider themselves restrained by the law. He sympathizes with "the persons whom those scourges of mankind insulted, murdered, or betrayed" and calls them, with indignation, "insolent and inhuman oppressors of the earth." He is sympathetic to those whom these oppressors hurt, saying that "we enter with more eagerness into all their schemes of vengeance, and feel ourselves every moment wreaking, in imagination, upon such violators of the laws of society, that punishment which our sympathetic indignation tells us is due to their crimes." Smith thus indicates a right of resistance to rulers whose cruelty shows that they do not consider themselves bound by the rule of law.[122] He regrets that rulers of foreign powers, when they occupy enemy territory, do not consider themselves bound by the rule of law: "Whenever it suits the conveniency of the public enemy, . . . the goods of the peacable citizens are seized . . . their lands are laid waste, their houses are burnt, and they themselves, if they presume to make any resistance, are murdered or led into captivity."[123] He resents that people are disturbed whenever it suits the conveniency of the public enemy and complains that the law of nations makes this possible. Clearly, an admission of the principle, *tel est Notre plaisir,* a principle characteristic of despotism which implies the very negation of the idea that governments are under the rule of law, must be unacceptable to him *a fortiori:* "That kings are the servants of the people, to be obeyed, resisted, deposed, or punished, as the public conveniency may require, is the doctrine of reason and philosophy."[124]

According to his *Lectures* Smith was as outspoken about the need for the ruler's respect for the law and proposed a right of resistance to despots. He notices with approval that military monarchs, such as the Roman emperors, did not alter the institutions of the civil law upon their assumption to power, that Cromwell did the same in England. Asiatic governments are quite different. Arabians and Tartars "and other barbarous nations who had no regular system

122. Ibid., 107–8. The quotation is on 107.

123. Ibid., 218.

124. Ibid., 74. Smith continues, "but it is not the doctrine of nature. Nature would teach us to submit to them for their own sake, to tremble and bow down before their exalted station, to regard their smile as a reward sufficient to compensate any services, and to dread their displeasure, though no other evil were to follow from it, as the severest of all mortifications. To treat them in any respect as men, to reason and dispute with them upon ordinary occasions, requires such resolution, that there are few men whose magnanimity can support them in it, unless they are likewise assisted by familiarity and acquaintance. The strongest motives, the most furious passions, fear, hatred, and resentment, are scarce sufficient to balance this natural disposition to respect them: and their conduct must, either justly or unjustly, have excited the highest degree of all those passions, before the bulk of the people can be brought to oppose them with violence, or to desire to see them either punished or deposed. Even when the people have been brought this length, they are apt to relent any moment, and easily relapse into their habitual state of deference to those whom they have been accustomed to look up as their natural superiors. They cannot stand the mortification of their monarch."

of laws," did not respect the laws of the countries they conquered. "A Turkish bashaw or other inferior officer is decisive judge of everything, and is as absolute in his own jurisdiction as the Signior. Life and fortune are altogether precarious, when they thus depend on the caprice of the lowest magistrate. A more miserable and oppressive government cannot be imagined."[125]

In a section, "How Liberty was Restored," Smith describes how England moved from absolute government, in which the monarch determined the law, to one that protected liberty, because the law limited the government. He is glad to note that the king's power is curtailed by that of Parliament, and that, furthermore, the legislature is divided into a House of Lords and a House of Commons. "Here is a happy mixture of all the different forms of government properly restrained, and a perfect security to liberty and property." The proper restraint of governmental power by the rule of laws aids the security of liberty and property under that rule. After mentioning other features of English government which show the existence of legal limitations of the government, such as judicial tenure, the liability of the king's ministers to impeachment, the Habeas Corpus Act, the method of election, Smith notes that "these established customs render it impossible for the king to attempt anything absolute."[126] Customary law secures the kind of a balance of power and protection of liberty for the individual which Smith, here obviously influenced by Montesquieu, considers an important feature of constitutionalism. Smith also praises the law of England for providing for impartial juries, and thereby serving the cause of liberty. After voicing doubts about courts established by the king, such as the court of high commission, the star chamber and the court of wardship, he is pleased that the king can no longer establish a new court without the consent of parliament. For the establishment of new courts runs the risk of jeopardizing the rule of law. "In no other country of Europe is the law so accurate as in England, because it has not been of so long standing. The parliament of Paris was only erected about the time of Henry VIII of England. . . . All new courts disdain to follow the rules that were formerly established. All new courts are a great evil, because their power is first not precisely determined, and therefore their decisions must be loose and inaccurate."[127]

In another paragraph, devoted to the rights of subjects, Smith deals with "the crimes of the sovereign against the subject, or the limitations of his power." It is here that Smith favors a right of resistance in case of abuses of governmental power. After pointing out how difficult it is to precisely say how far the power of the sovereign may go—even in England, where "it can be exactly ascertained when the king encroaches on the privileges of the people, or they on that of the king"—Smith writes that there are "certain abuses which no doubt make resistance in some cases lawful, on whatever principle government be founded." He mentions specific cases: "Suppose that government is found-

125. *Lectures,* 30–32.

126. Ibid., 45–46.

127. Ibid., 51–53. The quotation is on 53.

ed on contract, and that these powers are entrusted to persons who grossly abuse them, it is evident that resistance is lawful, because the original contract is now broken." Smith thus follows Locke. But Smith, who does not accept the idea that governments are based upon contract, also maintains that a right of resistance exists when, as he believes, government is founded on the principles of utility and authority: "Whatever be the principle of allegiance, a right of resistance must undoubtedly be lawful, because no authority is altogether unlimited. Absurdity of conduct may deprive an assembly of its influence as well as a private person, an[d] imprudent conduct will take away all sense of authority. The folly and cruelty of the Roman emperors make the impartial reader go along with the conspiracies formed against them." Smith states that the right of resistance is more frequently asserted in absolute monarchies because one man is more apt to fall into imprudent measures than a number. He again follows Locke, to whom he refers, when he considers popular resistance lawful if the king of England raises taxes against the will of the people. Then he states more generally: "Exorbitant taxes no doubt justify resistance, for no people will allow the half of their property to be taken from them." Yet, again in a Lockean vein, he is reluctant to admit resistance for slight causes, saying that "though the highest propriety be not observed, if they have any degree of moderation, people will not complain. No government is quite perfect, but it is better to submit to some inconvenience than make attempts against it." While he states that it is "hard to determine what a monarch may or may not do," he, again considering the particular situation in England, states that "when the *summa potestas* is divided as it is in Britain, if the king do anything which ought to be consented to by the parliament, without their permission, they have a right to oppose him. The nature of parliamentary right supposes that it may be defended by force, else it is no right at all. If the king impose taxes or continue them after the time is expired, he is guilty of breach of privilege." Smith then proceeds to denounce various activities of James II for being incompatible with the rule of law, ending up with the statement that "King James, on account of his encroachments on the body politic, was with all justice and equity in the world opposed and rejected."[128]

Smith's belief in the law state is even shown by a passage we find under part 2 of the *Lectures,* a part dealing with the police: "Law and government . . . secure the individual who has enlarged his property, that he may peaceably enjoy the fruits of it. By law and government all the different arts flourish, and that inequality of fortune to which they give occasion is sufficiently preserved. By law and government domestic peace is enjoyed and security from the foreign invader. Wisdom and virtue too derive their lustre from supplying these necessities . . . the establishment of law and government is the highest effort of human prudence and wisdom."[129] All these statements use the sequence, "law and government," not "government and law." This indicates that Smith gave

128. Ibid., 66–72, passim.

129. Ibid., 160.

priority to law, not government, a priority that is also evident in the German *Rechtsstaat.* Law was not to primarily express the wishes of the government, and certainly not those of an arbitrary government. Rather, government was to be conducted according to the law. It was under the rule of law.

Smith confirms his belief in restrictions of the government by the rule of law in *The Wealth of Nations.* Perhaps it cannot be expected that he would elaborate this theme in his last book. It was, after all, to be dealt with in his planned work on jurisprudence. On the other hand, *The Wealth of Nations* is generally regarded as the gospel of free trade. Therefore, it probably can be considered a treatise on legal restraints of governmental power for the sake of freedom anyway.

Smith makes specific statements in support of this. As he reportedly did in his *Lectures,* he speaks of "law and government," as prerequisites for the protection of the arts, again using a sequel that shows the priority of the law before the government.[130] He regrets that in ancient Greece law did not develop as a science and that in the various republics, particularly in Athens, "the ordinary courts of justice consisted of numerous, and therefore disorderly, bodies of people, who frequently decided almost at random, or as clamour, faction and party spirit happened to determine. The ignominy of an unjust decision, when it was to be divided among five hundred, a thousand, or fifteen hundred people (for some of their courts were so very numerous), could not fall very heavy upon any individual." He is pleased that in Rome a legal science developed very early and that the courts, consisting "either of a single judge, or of a small number of judges, whose characters, especially as they deliberated always in public, could not fail to be very much affected by any rash or unjust decision." Smith shows the beginning of the law of precedent in Rome and notices with satisfaction that this kind of law influenced other legal systems: "In doubtful cases, such courts, from their anxiety to avoid blame, would naturally endeavour to shelter themselves under the example, or precedent, of the judges who had sat before them. . . . This attention to practice and precedent, necessarily formed the Roman law into that regular and orderly system in which it has been delivered down to us; and the like attention has had the like effects upon the laws of every other country where such attention has taken place." And then he continues, saying that the superiority of character in the Romans over that of the Greeks was probably mainly due to the better constitution of their courts of justice.[131] For Smith, the rule of law is a supreme principle, to be protected and gradually developed by independent courts who are its guardians.

Basically, that rule consists of customary law, which is likely to be more liberal than legislative or executive enactments. Smith denounces many of the latter, which often are characteristic of mercantilism. He complains about the law of settlements, about legislative enactments in favor of masters or about

130. *Wealth of Nations,* 532.

131. Ibid., 731–32.

workers; of laws prohibiting the manufacturer from exercising the trade of a shopkeeper, and obliging farmers to be corn merchants, of legislation favoring woolen manufacturers and hurting sheep farmers and growers of wool; of restrictions of the inland trade and the coastal trade. These enactments, and many others, are incompatible with natural liberty.[132] They reflect the "folly of human laws": "The natural effort of every individual to better his own condition, when suffered to exert itself with freedom and security, is so powerful a principle, that it is alone, and without any assistance, not only capable of carrying on the society to wealth and prosperity, but of surmounting a hundred impertinent obstructions with which the folly of human laws too often encumbers its operations; though the effect of these obstructions is always more or less either to encroach upon its freedom, or to diminish its security."[133]

In a common law country like Great Britain, the limitation of the government through law and the resultant protection of freedom is greater than in civil law countries. Smith continues the passage just quoted: "In Great Britain industry is perfectly secure; and though it is far from being perfectly free, it is as free or freer than in any other part of Europe." Freedom is aided by "the balance of the constitution,"[134] by the division of governmental power, from which even the colonies profit.[135] The situation is different under the "absolute governments of Spain, Portugal, and France." Here, the sovereign in the capital "overawes" his inferior officers and, of course, his subjects. The situation is worse in the colonies, for "the discretionary powers which such governments commonly delegate to all their inferior officers are . . . exercised there with more than ordinary violence."[136] Smith resents "that insidious and crafty animal, vulgarly called a statesman or politician, whose councils are directed by the momentary fluctuations of affairs"[137] rather than by the stable rules of

132. Ibid., 132, 141, 142, 497, 612, 615. See also 61 (monopolies), 134 (statute of apprenticeship, privileges of corporations), 421 (regulation of commerce), 651 ("All systems either of preference or of restraint").

133. Ibid., 508.

134. Ibid., 589.

135. Ibid., 538–42. Smith speaks of "the genius of the British constitution which protects and governs North America" (73). "In every thing, except their foreign trade, the liberty of the English colonists to manage their own affairs their own way is complete. It is in every respect equal to that of their fellow-citizens at home, and is secured in the same manner, by an assembly of the representatives of the people, who claim the sole right of imposing taxes for the support of the colony government. The authority of this assembly over-awes the executive power, and neither the meanest nor the most obnoxious colonist, as long as he obeys the law, has any thing to fear from the resentment, either of the governor, or of any other civil or military officer in the province" (551).

136. Ibid., 552. See also 541. On 555 we read: "The policy of Europe . . . has very little to boast of, either in the original establishment, or, so far as concerns their internal government, in the subsequent prosperity of the colonies of America. Folly and injustice seem to have been the principles which presided over and directed the first project of establishing those colonies."

137. Ibid., 435. On 423 Smith writes: "What is the species of domestic industry which his capital can employ, and of which the produce is likely to be of the greatest value, every individual, it is evident, can, in his local situation, judge much better than any statesman or lawgiver can do for

customary law that over generations have proved to be conducive to freedom. He speaks of "natural liberty which it is the proper business of law, not to infringe, but to support,"[138] and considers the proper administration of justice by an independent judiciary a prerequisite for freedom and an important feature of the rule of law.[139]

The Necessity of State Law

In spite of his skepticism toward legislation and regulation, Smith concedes important functions to them.

Following the passage just quoted Smith writes that "exertions of the natural liberty of a few individuals, which might endanger the security of the whole society, are, and ought to be, restrained by the laws of all governments; of the most free, as well as the most despotical. The obligation of building party walls, in order to prevent the communication of fire, is a violation of natural liberty, exactly of the same kind with the regulations of the banking trade which are here proposed." This passage is symbolic of Smith's thinking. The great advocate of the restriction of governmental power through the rule of law leaves no doubt that his advocacy is not unqualified. It permits governmental regulations. This was pointed out by Viner when the sesquicentennial of *The Wealth of Nations* was celebrated;[140] it was emphasized in 1960 and a few years before the bicentennial of that publication in 1973.[141]

---

him. The statesman, who should attempt to direct private people in what manner they ought to employ their capitals, would not only load himself with a most unnecessary attention, but assume an authority which could safely be trusted, not only to no single person, but to no council or senate whatever, and which would nowhere be so dangerous as in the hands of a man who had folly and presumption enough to fancy himself fit to exercise it."

138. Ibid., 308.

139. Ibid., 680–81. The last paragraph of his discussion "Of the Expence of Justice" reads: "When the judicial is united to the executive power, it is scarce possible that justice should not frequently be sacrificed to, what is vulgarly called, politics. The persons entrusted with the great interests of the state may, even without any corrupt views, sometimes imagine it necessary to sacrifice to those interests the rights of a private man. But upon the impartial administration of justice depends the liberty of every individual, the sense which he has of his own security. In order to make every individual feel himself perfectly secure in the possession of every right which belongs to him, it is not only necessary that the judicial should be separated from the executive power, but that it should be rendered as much as possible independent of that power. The judge should not be liable to be removed from his office according to the caprice of that power. The regular payment of his salary should not depend upon the good-will, or even upon the good economy of that power." See also 862, where Smith writes that a regular administration of justice is a prerequisite for commerce and manufactures.

140. Viner, "Adam Smith and Laissez Faire," 138 ff.

141. Nathan Rosenberg, "Some Institutional Aspects of the *Wealth of Nations*," *The Journal of Political Economy* 48 (1960):557 ff.; M. Blaug, introduction to *The Wealth of Nations* (Homewood, Ill., 1963), esp. v; Andrew S. Skinner, *Adam Smith and The Role of the State* (Glasgow, 1974).

In *The Theory of Moral Sentiments* Smith sets the keynote for regulation: "Foreign war and civil faction are the two situations which afford the most splendid opportunities for the display of public spirit," he writes. After stating that the glory of the hero who wins a foreign war is likely to be greater than that of a successful leader of a civil faction, Smith continues: "The leader of the successful party, however, if he has authority enough to prevail upon his own friends to act with proper temper and moderation (which he frequently has not), may sometimes render to his country a service much more essential and important than the greatest victories and the most extensive conquests. He may re-establish and improve the constitution, and from the very doubtful and ambiguous character of the leader of a party, he may assume the greatest and noblest of all characters, that of the reformer and legislator of a great state; and, by the wisdom of his institutions, secure the internal tranquillity and happiness of his fellow-citizens for many succeeding generations."[142]

Smith devotes the whole second part of his *Lectures* to a discussion of police, which to him means "the regulation of the inferior parts of government, viz:—cleanliness, security and cheapness or plenty." He thinks that the former two are "too mean" to be considered in detail: the need for them is too obvious to warrant much discussion.[143] When he elaborates "cheapness or plenty," he admits regulations. Taxes are proper. To him, "the English are the best financiers in Europe, and their taxes are levied with more propriety than those of any country whatever."[144] Some regulations are "not very inconvenient."[145]

Likewise, *The Wealth of Nations* mentions quite a few regulations that Smith does not consider very inconvenient. A general clause states the principle of governmental activity: "According to the system of natural liberty, the sov-

142. *Theory of Moral Sentiments,* 340–41. Smith continues: "Amidst the turbulence and disorder of faction, a certain spirit of system is apt to mix itself with that public spirit which is founded upon the love of humanity, upon a real fellow-feeling with the inconveniencies and distresses to which some of our fellow-citizens may be exposed. This spirit of system commonly takes the direction of that more gentle public spirit, always animates it, and often inflames it, even to the madness of fanaticism. The leaders of the discontented party seldom fail to hold out some plausible plan of reformation, which, they pretend, will not only remove the inconveniencies and relieve the distresses immediately complained of, but will prevent in all time coming any return of the like inconveniencies and distresses. They often propose, upon this account, to new-model the constitution, and to alter in some of its most essential parts that system of government under which the subjects of a great empire have enjoyed, perhaps, peace, security, and even glory, during the course of several centuries together. The great body of the party are commonly intoxicated with the imaginary beauty of this ideal system, of which they have no experience, but which has been represented to them in all the most dazzling colours in which the eloquence of their leaders could paint it. Those leaders themselves, though they originally may have meant nothing but their own aggrandizement, become, many of them, in time the dupes of their own sophistry, and are as eager for this great reformation as the weakest and foolishest of their followers. Even though the leaders should have preserved their own heads, as, indeed, they commonly do, free from this fanaticism, yet they dare not always disappoint the expectation of their followers, but are often obliged, though contrary to their principle and their conscience, to act as if they were under the common delusion."

143. *Lectures,* 154.
144. Ibid., 245.
145. Ibid., 246.

ereign has only three duties to attend to; three duties of great importance, indeed, but plain and intelligible to common understandings: first, the duty of protecting the society from the violence and invasion of other independent societies; secondly, the duty of protecting, as far as possible, every member of the society from the injustice or oppression of every other member of it, or the duty of establishing an exact administration of justice; and, thirdly, the duty of erecting and maintaining certain public works and certain public institutions, which it can never be for the interest of any individual, or small number of individuals, to erect and maintain; because the profit could never repay the expence to any individual or small number of individuals, though it may frequently do much more than repay it to a great society."[146]

The latter "are chiefly those for facilitating the commerce of the society, and those for promoting the instruction of the people."[147] From among the former, he first discusses government activities necessary for promoting commerce in general, such as highways, bridges, navigable canals, harbors, the coinage, and postal services. He then deals with public works and institutions that facilitate particular branches of commerce. Trade with barbarous nations requires forts, and trade with other nations, ambassadors. Extraordinary expenses which the protection of any particular branch of commerce may occasion should be defrayed by taxes, fines, and duties. Smith approves of regulations of trading companies.[148] While he basically opposes legal monopolies, he permits temporary monopolies when a company risks a new trade with a remote and barbarous nation. He indicates approval of patent and copyright, and supports the participation by the government in the education of the young and the old.[149]

Defense falls within the sphere of government action. "THE first duty of the sovereign . . . can be performed only by means of a military force." And although "the expence both of preparing this military force in time of peace, and of employing it in time of war, is very different in the different states of society, in the different periods of improvement,"[150] in modern society it is definitely with the government. The state has the right to enforce military exercises and service or to make the trade of the soldier a separate one, that is, to establish a militia or a standing army. Smith prefers the latter. "A militia, . . . in whatever manner it may be either disciplined or exercised, must always be much inferior to a well-disciplined and well-exercised standing army."[151]

146. *Wealth of Nations,* 651.

147. Ibid., 681.

148. Ibid., 682–89, 690–716.

149. Ibid., 716–766.

150. Ibid., 653.

151. Ibid., 661. Smith continues: "The soldiers, who are exercised only once a week, or once a month, can never be so expert in the use of their arms, as those who are exercised every day, or every other day; and though this circumstance may not be of so much consequence in modern, as it was in ancient times, yet the acknowledged superiority of the Prussian troops, owing, it is said, very much to their superior expertness in their exercise, may satisfy us that it is, even at this day, of very considerable consequence. The soldiers, who are bound to obey their officer only once a week or

Smith elaborates this thesis at some length. Like Rousseau, he does not want liberty for the individual at the cost of national defense.

Smith approves of many other government regulations. Some of them do not fall within his general categories, but are mentioned in passing when he discusses policies that do fall within these categories. When he stresses the duty of the government to fight the growth of cowardice, he writes that "it would deserve its most serious attention to prevent a leprosy or any other loathsome and offensive disease, though neither mortal nor dangerous, from spreading."[152] From this can be concluded that he would have favored governmental control of dangerous diseases *a fortiori.*

"In many instances Smith supported government restrictions on private initiative where neither justice nor defense was involved, and where the sole aim was to improve upon the direction which private initiative gave to the investment of capital, the course of commerce, and the employment of labor."[153] He feels that the public registration of mortgages and all rights to immovable property is advantageous to the people and thus permissible. Stamp duties upon cards and dice, newspapers and periodical pamphlets are proper taxes upon consumption.[154] He approves of the prevailing restriction of the maximum rate of interest to 5 percent. If a rate "was fixed so high as eight or ten per cent., the greater part of the money which was to be lent, would be lent to prodigals and projectors, who alone would be willing to give this high interest. Sober people, who will give for the use of money no more than a part of what they are likely to make by the use of it, would not venture into the competition. A great part of the capital of the country would thus be kept out of the hands which were most likely to make a profitable and advantageous use of it, and thrown into those which were most likely to waste and destroy it. Where the legal rate of interest, on the contrary, is fixed but a very little above the lowest market rate, sober people are universally preferred, as borrowers, to prodigals and projectors."[155] It has been said that Smith here admitted "that the majority of investors could not be relied upon to invest their funds prudently and safely, and that government regulation was a good corrective for individual stupidity."[156]

once a month, and who are at all other times at liberty to manage their own affairs their own way, without being in any respect accountable to him, can never be under the same awe in his presence, can never have the same disposition to ready obedience, with those whose whole life and conduct are every day directed by him, and who every day even rise and go to bed, or at least retire to their quarters, according to his orders. In what is called discipline, or in the habit of ready obedience, a militia must always be still more inferior to a standing army, than it may sometimes be in what is called the manuel exercise, or in the management and use of its arms. But in modern war the habit of ready and instant obedience is of much greater consequence than a considerable superiority in the management of arms."

152. Ibid., 739.
153. Viner, "Adam Smith and Laissez Faire," 150.
154. *Wealth of Nations,* 814–15.
155. Ibid., 339–40.
156. Viner, "Adam Smith and Laissez Faire," 151.

Smith also makes concessions to mercantilist regulations of foreign trade. Under certain circumstances, export restrictions on corn may be warranted.[157] Such restrictions are not necessarily good but may be required out of expediency: "The laws concerning corn may every where be compared to the laws concerning religion. The people feel themselves so much interested in what relates either to their subsistence in this life, or to their happiness in a life to come, that government must yield to their prejudices, and, in order to preserve the public tranquility, establish that system which they approve of. It is upon this account, perhaps, that we so seldom find a reasonable system established with regard to either of those two capital objects."[158] While a prohibition of the exportation of wool cannot be justified, a small export duty on wool is permissible because it would produce revenue for the government and afford advantages to British manufacturers of woolens over their foreign competitors.[159] Smith favors moderate taxes on foreign manufactured goods so that "our own workmen might . . . have a considerable advantage in the home market, and many articles, some of which at present afford no revenue to government, and others a very inconsiderable one, might afford a very great one."[160]

Smith's willingness to make concessions to governmental regulation of natural liberty can also be found in some of his comments on taxes. Landlords who, "instead of raising the rent, take a fine for the renewal of the lease," a practice which "is in most cases the expedient of a spendthrift," is frequently harmful to landlord and tenant alike and "always hurtful to the community," ought to be penalized by heavier taxation. In order to discourage leases that prescribe to the tenant a certain mode of cultivation, a practice "which is generally a foolish one," rents from such leases ought to be taxed. Rents in kind should be taxed more heavily than money rents: "Such rents are always more hurtful to the tenant than beneficial to the landlord." The landlord who cultivates a part of his own land should get tax advantages because it is important that the landlord, in view of his greater command of capital and his greater willingness and capacity to risk experiments, should be encouraged to actively participate in agriculture.[161]

Smith does not oppose a tax on the retail sale of liquors so adjusted as to "give some discouragement to the multiplication of little ale-houses."[162] He favors a heavy tax on distilleries as a sumptuary measure against spiritual

157. *Wealth of Nations,* 507. "In a Swiss canton, or in some of the little states of Italy, it may, perhaps, sometimes be necessary to restrain the exportation of corn. In such great countries as France or England it scarce ever can. To hinder, besides, the farmer from sending his goods at all times to the best market, is evidently to sacrifice the ordinary laws of justice to an idea of public utility, to a sort of reasons of state; an act of legislative authority which ought to be exercised only, which can be pardoned only in cases of the most urgent necessity. The price at which the exportation of corn is prohibited, if it is ever to be prohibited, ought always to be a very high price." Ibid.

158. Ibid.

159. Ibid., 618–19.

160. Ibid., 834.

161. Ibid., 783–84.

162. Ibid., 804.

liquors and wants a reduction of the tax on healthy beverages like beer and ale.[163] He seems to favor legislation for what today is often called "social justice," from luxury goods to ordinary income. Luxury carriages ought to pay heavier highway tolls than carriages of necessary use, so that "the indolence and vanity of the rich is made to contribute in a very easy manner to the relief of the poor, by rendering cheaper the transportation of heavy goods to all the different parts of the country."[164] The gains of monopolists are the most proper for taxation.[165] Ground rents are "a more proper subject of peculiar taxation than even the ordinary rent of land."[166] He indicates sympathy to progressive taxation: "A tax upon house-rents . . . would in general fall heaviest upon the rich; and in this sort of inequality there would not, perhaps, be any thing very unreasonable. It is not very unreasonable that the rich should contribute to the public expence, not only in proportion to their revenue, but something more than in that proportion."[167]

Smith, much as he resented governmental interference with natural liberty, was willing to occasionally concede such interference. There are times when one has the feeling that he was ill at ease in doing so. For instance, shortly after he admitted the regulations concerned with the relationship between landlord and tenant, he makes an assertion of laissez-faire: "The principal attention of the sovereign ought to be to encourage, by every means in his power, the attention both of the landlord and of the farmer; by allowing both to pursue their own interest in their own way, and according to their own judgment; by giving to both the most perfect security that they shall enjoy the full recompence of their own industry; and by procuring to both the most extensive market for every part of their produce, in consequence of establishing the easiest and safest communications both by land and by water, through every part of his own dominions, as well as the most unbounded freedom of exportation to the dominions of all other princes."[168] To Smith, natural liberty was the rule.[169] As an empiricist, however, he realized that there is no rule without exceptions. The Scotsman could not follow his French contemporary Quesnay, who seemed to have imagined that the body politic "would thrive and prosper only under a certain precise regimen, the exact regimen of perfect liberty and perfect justice." He counters: "If a nation could not prosper without the enjoyment of perfect liberty and perfect justice, there is not in the world a nation which could ever have prospered. In the political body, however, the wisdom of nature has fortunately made ample provision for remedying many of the bad effects of the folly and injustice of man."[170]

This leads us to a discussion of the remaining general field which Smith

163. Ibid., 842. 164. Ibid., 683. 165. Ibid., 844.
166. Ibid., 796. 167. Ibid., 794. 168. Ibid., 785.
169. See Viner, "Adam Smith and Laissez Faire," esp. 139–40, and Skinner, *Adam Smith and The Role of the State.*
170. *Wealth of Nations,* 638.

wanted to be directed by the sovereign—the administration of justice. Smith goes further than admitting state law in the form of legislation and regulation. To him, that law is a prerequisite for the rule of law. Without state law, there can be no law state and, therefore, no protected liberty.

The rule of law implies not only a restriction upon rulers but also the protection of individuals from others through the strict enforcement of the laws. The latter is what Smith basically understands as "justice." It will be remembered that he assigned to the government "the duty of protecting, as far as possible, every member of the society from the injustice of oppression of every other member of it, or the duty of establishing an exact administration of justice." The administration of justice must be exact. As was just shown, it need not—and cannot—be perfect. The laws must be clear and precise. They need not—and cannot—protect perfect liberty. This is perhaps the meaning of the statement that the government must protect every member of the society *as far as possible:* The contents of the laws must reflect natural liberty in a more or less, but not a completely, perfect manner. They may be more or less perfectly just by such criteria as "higher justice," "social justice," or "fairness," whatever they may mean. Justice, as generally understood by Smith, simply seems to imply what is right under the concrete legal order, an order that is enforceable and enforced for the protection of individuals from attacks by their fellow men. To Smith, the rule of law implies law and order. He, the liberal, was not inclined toward anarchy. He did not believe that the individual should take the law into his own hands. This is evident in his attitude toward criminal as well as private law.

Smith's defense of law and order is obvious in his first book. The basis for this defense is his realization that man, much as he may be an individualist, has obligations toward his fellow-men. "Mankind . . . have a very strong sense of the injuries that are done to another. The villain . . . is as much the object of our indignation as the hero is that of our sympathy and affection. We . . . delight as much in the punishment of the one, as we are grieved at the distress of the other." If an individual is attacked, people "rejoice to see him attack in turn, and are . . . gratified by his revenge, provided it is not immoderate, as if the injury had been done to themselves." Speaking of man's passions that are likely to produce desires of revenge and render it dangerous to insult or injure him, Smith acknowledges their utility "to the public, as the guardians of justice."[171]

Public order is a prerequisite for society. "Society . . . cannot subsist among those who are at all times ready to hurt and injure one another. The moment that injury begins, the moment that mutual resentment and animosity take place, all the bands of it are broken asunder, and the different members of which it consisted, are . . . dissipated and scattered abroad by the violence and opposition of their discordant affections. If there is any society among robbers

171. *Theory of Moral Sentiments,* 44–45.

and murderers, they must at least . . . abstain from robbing and murdering one another. Beneficence, therefore, is less essential to the existence of society than justice. Society may subsist . . . without beneficence; but the prevalence of injustice must utterly destroy it." Two pages later, Smith writes that "society cannot subsist unless the laws of justice are tolerably observed, as no social intercourse can take place among men who do not generally abstain from injuring one another."[172] The guardianship of justice is in the hands of the public magistrate: "As the violation of justice is what men will never submit from one another, the public magistrate is under a necessity of employing the power of the commonwealth to enforce the practice of this virtue."[173]

Man must be considerate and not demonstrate too much hatred and resentment toward others, lest he lose his place in society: "Too violent a propensity to those detestable passions, renders a person the object of universal dread and abhorrence, who, like a wild beast, ought, we think, to be hunted out of all civil society."[174] In another passage, Smith writes: "The very existence of society requires that unmerited and unprovoked malice should be restrained by proper punishments; and, consequently, that to inflict those punishments should be regarded as a proper and laudable action."[175] For Smith, to whom the "peace and order of society is of more importance than even the relief of the miserable,"[176] "[a] prison is certainly more useful to the public than a palace; and the person who founds the one is generally directed by a much more just spirit of patriotism, than the one who builds the other" which "may serve to promote luxury, and set the example of the dissolution of manners."[177] Smith favors penalty as a deterrent, and capital punishment. He indicates a justification of the principle "an eye for an eye, and a tooth for a tooth."[178] His community-consciousness is evident in the fact that he feels that the traitor, who "fancies he can promote his own little interest by betraying to the public enemy that of his native country . . . appears to be of all villains the

172. Ibid., 124–25, 127.

173. Ibid., 501. Smith continues: "Without this precaution, civil society would become a scene of bloodshed and disorder, every man revenging himself at his own hand whenever he fancied he was injured. To prevent the confusion which would attend upon every man's doing justice to himself, the magistrate, in all governments that have acquired any considerable authority, undertakes to do justice to all, and promises to hear and to redress any complaint of injury."

174. Ibid., 54.

175. Ibid., 109. 176. Ibid., 331. 177. Ibid., 46.

178. Ibid., 96: ". . . if the person who had . . . murdered our father or our brother . . . should soon afterwards die of a fever, or even be brought to the scaffold upon account of some other crime, though it might soothe our hatred, it would not fully gratify our resentment. Resentment would prompt us to desire, not only that he should be punished, but that he should be punished by our means, and upon account of that particular injury which he had done to us. Resentment cannot be fully gratified, unless the offender is not only made to grieve in his turn, but to grieve for that particular wrong which we have suffered from him. He must be made to repent and be sorry for this very action, that others, through fear of the like punishment, may be terrified from being guilty of the like offence. The natural gratification of this passion tends, of its own accord, to produce all the political ends of punishment; the correction of the criminal, and the example to the public."

most detestable."[179] Smith, the liberal, warns of altering the established forms of government.[180]

The picture does not change in the notes of his *Lectures*. From among the "four great objects of law," namely, "justice, police, revenue, and arms," Smith is reported to have mentioned "justice" first, the object of which "is the security from injury." It is "the foundation of civil government."[181] In nations that were "almost lawless, and under no authority, depredations were continually committed up and down the country, and all kinds of commerce stopped."[182] A principle that induces men to obey the civil magistrate is utility. "Every one is sensible of the necessity of this principle to preserve justice and peace in the society. By civil institutions the poorest may get redress of injuries from the wealthiest and most powerful; and though there may be some irregularities in particular cases, . . . yet we submit to them to avoid greater evils." Not only individuals profit from obedience, but also the society. Smith's community-consciousness is evident when he says: "It is the sense of public utility, more than of private, which influences men to obedience. It may sometimes be for my interest to disobey, and to wish government overturned, but I am sensible that other men are of a different opinion from me, and would not assist me in the enterprise. I therefore submit to its decision for the good of the whole."[183] The protection of individuals from their fellow-men through an enforcement of the laws is conducive to incentive and the accumulation of stock, and will benefit individuals and society.[184]

The Wealth of Nations continues the discussion on the need of law enforcement with respect to private law. Smith praises the "present admirable

179. Ibid., 335. On 238 Smith writes that "human laws, the consequences of human sentiments, forfeit the life and the estate of the industrious and cautious traitor, and reward, by extraordinary recompenses, the fidelity and public spirit of the improvident and careless good citizen."

180. "The support of the established government seems evidently the best expedient for maintaining the safe, respectable, and happy situation of our fellow-citizens—when we see that this government actually maintains them in that situation. But in times of public discontent, faction, and disorder, . . . even a wise man may be disposed to think some alteration necessary in that constitution or form of government which, in its actual condition, appears plainly unable to maintain the public tranquility. In such cases, however, it often requires, perhaps, the highest effort of political wisdom to determine when a real patriot ought to support and endeavour to re-establish the authority of the old system, and when he ought to give way to the more daring, but often dangerous, spirit of innovation." Ibid., 340.

181. *Lectures*, 3.

182. Ibid., 35.

183. Ibid., 10–11.

184. "In the infancy of society . . . government must be weak and feeble, and it is long before its authority can protect the industry of individuals from the rapacity of their neighbours. When people find themselves every moment in danger of being robbed of all they possess, they have no motive to be industrious. There could be little accumulation of stock, because the indolent, which would be the greatest number, would live upon the industrious, and spend whatever they produced." Ibid., 223.

constitution of the courts of justice in England," with "each judge endeavouring to give . . . the speediest and most effectual remedy, which the law would admit, for every sort of injustice." He is pleased to note that whereas originally the courts gave damages only for breach of contract, the court of chancery took upon it to enforce the specific performance of agreements.[185] In the last chapter, which also is the last chapter of his total written work, Smith emphasizes the utility of obedience to the law and of law enforcement to trade and industry: "Commerce and manufactures can seldom flourish long in any state which does not enjoy a regular administration of justice, in which the people do not feel themselves secure in the possession of their property, in which the faith of contracts is not supported by law, and in which the authority of the state is not supposed to be regularly employed in enforcing the payment of debts from all those who are able to pay. Commerce and manufactures, in short, can seldom flourish in any state in which there is not a certain degree of confidence in the justice of government."[186]

Smith, who, in *The Wealth of Nations,* warns of state interference into the economy, wants the law of the state to protect the free economy. State power is dangerous, state authority is not. On the contrary, authority is a prerequisite for the rule of law and the liberty that rule protects. This is in tune with what he wrote in *The Theory of Moral Sentiments:* "He is not a citizen who is not disposed to respect the laws and to obey the civil magistrate; and he is certainly not a good citizen who does not wish to promote, by every means in his power, the welfare of the whole society of his fellow-citizens."[187] Without the promotion of the welfare of society, there is no good citizenship. Without obedience to the laws, there is no citizenship at all. Obedience to that ethical minimum, the law, is the *conditio sine qua non* for man's social minimum, namely, citizenship. The right of the citizen to be protected in his natural freedom from undue inroads by the government is matched by his obligation to obey the law. One concept of the rule of law is complemented by the other.

Conclusion

Smith's ideas on the rule of law reveal him as a man of measure.

The Theory of Moral Sentiments was published in 1759; its sixth edition, the last work Smith saw through the press, in 1790. In the 1760s Smith gave his *Lectures; The Wealth of Nations* came out in 1776. Smith thus was active when the American and French revolutions were in the making. He wrote during a revolutionary period, but was he a revolutionary?

Clark suggests that Smith's system can be best understood in terms of what Smith reacted against: "He was the interpreter of the forces of economic liberty

185. *Wealth of Nations,* 679.
186. Ibid., 862.
187. *Theory of Moral Sentiments,* 339.

against certain types of restraints prevalent in the mid-eighteenth century."[188] This indicates that Smith was a revolutionary. Lerner writes that "Smith's system of thought took its shape from his intense reaction against the elaborate apparatus of controls which the surviving feudal and mercantilist institutions were still imposing on the individual. . . . Adam Smith was, in his own day and his own way, something of a revolutionary. His doctrine revolutionized European society as surely as Marx's in a later epoch. He was, on the economic side, the philosopher of the capitalist revolution, as John Locke was its philosopher on the political side."[189] West devotes the first chapter of his book to "Adam Smith's Revolution."[190] However, all these authors, representing a broad spectrum of thought, agree that Smith was a revolutionary with measure. "Fortunately," Clark writes, "Smith has set the example, not of dogmatic and universal absolutes, but of a sane and balanced treatment of conflicting interests, consciously adjusted to the conditions and needs of his own time."[191] Lerner points out that while Smith was "an unconscious mercenary in the service of a rising capitalist class . . . [h]is own personal sympathies were not entirely with the capitalist . . . there runs through *The Wealth of Nations* a strain of partisanship for apprentices and laborers, for farmers, for the lowly and oppressed everywhere, and a hostility to the business corporations, the big-businessmen of the day, the ecclesiasts and the aristocrats."[192] According to West, "Smith was not as doctrinaire as is sometimes believed. Prepared to consider exceptions to general rules, he was a careful *advocate,* and not, like the subsequent writers in the Manchester School, an *apostle* of free trade."[193]

The measure that characterizes Smith the economist is also evident in Smith the jurist. This is not surprising. The study of law and economics was closely connected in the Scotland of his time and elsewhere. Economic possibilities existed in the legal mechanism of society.[194] Smithian legal measure can be seen in various ways.

It has been said that Smith tempered Hume's doctrine of self-interest by a Hutchesonian humanity, that his theory of the individual interest is always qualified in its practical application by Hutcheson's sense of justice.[195] Five years later, when Smith's empiricism was emphasized over his belief in the law of nature, Hutcheson's thought was depicted as being tempered by the influence of Hume.[196] Whatever may be closer to the truth, there cannot be much

188. John Maurice Clark, "Adam Smith and the Currents of History," in *Adam Smith, 1776–1926,* 58.

189. Max Lerner, Introduction to *The Wealth of Nations,* ix–x.

190. West, *Adam Smith,* 11–24.

191. Clark, "Adam Smith and the Currents of History," 58.

192. Lerner, Introduction, ix–x. Cf. Eli Ginzberg, *The House of Adam Smith* (New York, 1934).

193. West, *Adam Smith,* 24.

194. Cook, "Adam Smith and Jurisprudence," 332.

195. Ibid., 330.

196. Bittermann, "Adam Smith's Empiricism and the Law of Nature."

doubt that Smith was influenced by both his teacher and his friend and congested the intake in a measured way.

Smith considered feudal and mercantilist laws incompatible with the free order prescribed by natural law. He also believed that customary law was more likely to reflect natural law and its protection of freedom than legislative acts and administrative decrees. Yet, man of measure that he was, he was not absolutely opposed to legislation. Realizing that existing laws were bad, he asked for their abolition by legislation. Furthermore, he was careful not to be an all-out advocate of legislation even in an age in which legislation was becoming fashionable as a means of promoting freedom, demonstrating a measureful reluctance of being swept away by vogues.

Smith attacked privileges. He favored equal rights for all the members of society; however, he would not go so far as to propose an equal share in the goods of the earth. He was interested in eliminating norms that were advantageous to some groups and disadvantageous to others. On the other hand, the existing legal order, insofar as it established general rules for all men and did not impose unnecessary restrictions upon economic liberty, was to remain untouched, even though it had led to an unequal distribution of wealth and would do so in the future.[197] Smith was as much, and as little, a revolutionary as John Locke. The right of revolution should be exercised with measure and as a last resort, only after a long abuse of governmental power. Private law and its protection of property should not be injured in a revolution.

Smith favored the predominance of private law. In the age of mercantilism and absolutism, he could not fail to recognize the oppressive nature of public law. Yet he was reluctant to deny the merits of public law altogether. He thought it could play a significant role for the well-being and survival of a free society. While he feared big government, he wanted the public power to be active in minor cases and in such broad fields as defense, public works, and the administration of justice. The opponent of absolutism resented the police state. Yet he did not want to abolish the police, which he felt was necessary for the maintenance of public order.

Smith considered that government best that governs least. This, without any doubt, is the underlying theme of his work. However, it is dubious whether he wanted "anarchy plus a constable," an expression coined by Carlyle and said to describe the unregulated and individualistic capitalist economy.[198] Smith's individualism was community-conscious. Sympathy and benevolence toward other men, described in *The Theory of Moral Sentiments,* did not disappear in *The Wealth of Nations.* Neither was Smith's liberal society to be "unregulated." It was under the rule of law. And while this rule implied the maximum of freedom that was possible in society, it also implied the enforce-

197. Alexander Leist, "Savigny und Adam Smith," *Schmollers Jahrbuch für Gesetzgebung, Verwaltung und Volkswirtschaft im Deutschen Reiche* 41 (1917):146–147.

198. Lerner, Introduction to *Wealth of Nations,* ix.

ment of the moral minimum of the law[199] that was necessary for the existence of a free society.

Much as Smith left no doubt about his rejection of an uninhibited individualism, his emphasis in his last, and best known, book on the merits of free enterprise has been conducive to conveying the idea of laissez-faire, especially in times of economic expansion. People like to take from great works what furthers their interests. They would overlook Smith's warnings of sheer egoism, the more so since these warnings, appearing here and there in *The Wealth of Nations,* ran the risk of being considered mere reminders of his *Theory of Moral Sentiments,* an earlier treatise felt by many to have been superseded by the later one. This attitude is understandable in view of the fact that Smith's moral writings, as those of the Scotch Enlightenment, were hedonistic calculations. It remained for Immanuel Kant, whose kind of liberalism is similar to that of Smith in many respects,[200] to elucidate that man must acknowledge value judgments as valid a priori and accept the existence of a norm as absolute and unrelated to any further end.[201]

199. Jellinek, *Die sozialethische Bedeutung von Recht, Unrecht und Strafe,* 45.

200. See August Oncken, *Adam Smith und Immanuel Kant—Der Einklang und das Wechselverhältnis ihrer Lehren über Sitte, Staat und Wirtschaft* (Leipzig, 1877).

201. See Carl J. Friedrich, Introduction to *The Philosophy of Kant* (New York, 1977), xxxiv.

CHAPTER IV

ASPECTS OF KANT'S LIBERALISM

Introduction

After Montesquieu and Smith, Kant was probably the outstanding liberal of the eighteenth century. The works of these authors show sustained attacks upon absolutism. The *Persian Letters* was published in 1721, the *Considerations* in 1734, the *Spirit of the Laws* in 1748, the *Theory of Moral Sentiments* in 1759, the *Wealth of Nations* in 1776. Kant's *Critique of Pure Reason* appeared in 1791, his *Anthropology,* in 1798. Between 1791 and 1798, Kant published other writings demonstrating his liberalism.[1]

1. Kant's political philosophy can be found in the following works: *Idee zu einer allgemeinen Geschichte in weltbürgerlicher Absicht* (1784); *Beantwortung der Frage: Was ist Aufklärung?* (1784); *Recensionen von J. G. Herders Ideen zur Philosophie der Geschichte der Menschheit* (1785); *Muthmaßlicher Anfang der Menschengeschichte* (1786); *Recension von Gottlieb Hufeland's Versuch über den Grundsatz des Naturrechts* (1786); *Was heißt: Sich im Denken orientieren?* (1786); *Kritik der praktischen Vernunft* (1788); *Kritik der Urteilskraft* (1790); *Die Religion innerhalb der Grenzen der bloßen Vernunft* (1793); *Über den Gemeinspruch: Das mag in der Theorie richtig sein, taugt aber nicht für die Praxis* (1793); *Das Ende aller Dinge (1794); Zum ewigen Frieden* (1795); *Verkündigung des nahen Abschlusses eines Tractats zum ewigen Frieden in der Philosophie* (1796); *Metaphysische Anfangsgründe der Rechtslehre* (1797); *Metaphysische Anfangsgründe der Tugendlehre* (1797); *Der Streit der Facultäten* (1798); *Anthropologie in pragmatischer Hinsicht abgefaßt* (1798). References are to volumes 5–8, Königlich Preußische Akademie der Wissenschaften (ed.), *Kant's Werke* (Berlin, 1907–12). Kant is considered difficult to understand. Often referring to his statements in the indirect speech, I was tempted to quote him a length in German in the notes. However, I refrained from doing that because such quotations are amply available in Dietze, *Kant und der Rechtsstaat* (Tübingen, 1982).

On account of Montesquieu's institutional restrictions of governmental power and Smith's fight against mercantilism, the Frenchman and the Scot have always been considered political thinkers, the more so since their opinions on freedom, law, and order can be found in well-known works. The evaluation of Kant was different. For a long time, he was known mainly for his three critiques. So important were his philosophical writings, notably the revolution brought about by the *Critique of Pure Reason*[2] that Kant's political ideas were thought to be relatively insignificant. They were said to constitute not more than 5 percent of his total output[3] and were only occasionally obvious in his better known writings. Furthermore Kant, usually disposed toward a systematic approach, seems to have given his political philosophy only a peripheral treatment.[4] It was pointed out that he commented on political questions only after he turned seventy. In addition, he gladly permitted Richter, an obscure professor, to systematize and spread his political thoughts in order to get rid of a task he himself could no longer fulfill.[5]

All this does not necessarily mean that Kant considered political philosophy of little importance. The publication of his political opinions late in his life might be due to the fact that he felt them to be so important that he should wait to make them known until he had reached the wisdom of old age. It must not be forgotten that his *Critique of Pure Reason* came out only when he was fifty-six. Besides, censorship made the printing of political critiques risky.[6]

Toward the end of the 1920s, Borries wrote on Kant the politician.[7] During the past decades, Kant's political philosophy has been emphasized. According to Jaspers, the continuity of numerous little treatises and remarks in major works show that Kant's interest in politics was not of a minor nature. He states that a philosophy like Kant's, which asks primarily what man is, must be a political one. He calls Kant a first-class political thinker[8] and devotes about one fourth of his study of Kant to the latter's political thoughts. In the following years, works on these thoughts were published in France.[9] Later on, a student of Jasper's set out to elaborate them in a two-volume work. In the foreword of

2. Karl Jaspers, *Die grossen Philosophen* (Munich, 1957), 1:615; Carl J. Friedrich, *The Philosophy of Kant* (New York, 1949), xi ff.

3. Hans Saner, *Kant's Political Thought* (Chicago, 1973), 1.

4. Ibid.

5. Ibid., 1–2.

6. See Kant's preface to *Streit der Fakultäten,* 7:5 ff.; Lewis White Beck, *Essays on Kant and Hume* (New Haven, 1978), 172.

7. Kurt Borries, *Kant als Politiker* (Leipzig, 1928).

8. Jaspers, *Die grossen Philosophen,* 534.

9. Pierre Hassner, "La philosophie politique de Kant," *Archives de philosophie du droit* 4 (1959), 216 ff.; George Vlachos, *La pensée politique de Kant* (Paris, 1962); Institut international de philosophie politique, ed., *La philosophie politique de Kant* (Paris, 1962), with contributions by E. Weil, Théodore Ruyssen, Michel Villey, Pierre Hassner, Norberto Bobbio, Lewis White Beck, Carl J. Friedrich, Raymond Polin.

that work he argues that Kant's is a political philosophy through and through.[10]

Liberty

Freedom occupies an important position in Kant's writing.

Schiller, a great fighter for freedom, expressed his thanks to Kant.[11] In his lectures at the University of Berlin on the occasion of the centennial of Kant's death, Simmel stated that the basic motive of Kant's philosophy is the concept of individuality and that the evolution of the freedom of the individual reached a high point in Kant's work.[12] Kroner, whose interpretation follows that of the Heidelberg School, interprets Kant's Weltanshauung as an understanding in which the use of freedom crowns man's ability and duty.[13] Chamberlain, an admirer and friend of Wagner, wrote that Kant had the liberation of man in mind as well as the development of the sublime hidden in human nature.[14] According to Friedrich, "the problem of freedom, the freedom of the human personality to unfold and fulfill its higher destiny, is the central issue of all of Kant's philosophizing."[15] Hayek emphasized Kant's significance for liberalism, stating that "German writers usually place Kant's theories at the beginning of their accounts of the movement toward the *Rechsstaat* . . . he undoubtedly gave those ideas the form in which they exerted the greatest influence in Germany."[16] Carnois's book on the coherence of Kant's doctrine of liberty starts out with the remark that for Kant the idea of liberty occupies a preferred position.[17]

Kant himself left no doubt about his high evaluation of freedom. A reference of his to the *Critique of Pure Reason* refers to the concept of freedom as "the keystone of the whole building of a system of pure, even speculative, reason," joined by the concepts of God and immortality, which owe their being and objective reality to freedom. Among all the ideas of speculative reason, freedom is the only one we can possibly know a priori.[18] The *Critique of*

10. Hans Saner, *Kants Weg vom Krieg zum Frieden,* vol. 1: *Widerstreit und Einheit: Wege zu Kants politischem Denken* (München, 1967). K. H. Volkmann-Schluck, *Politische Philosophie* (Frankfurt, 1974), deals with Kant and de Tocqueville.

11. Houston Stewart Chamberlain, *Immanuel Kant* (3. Aufl., München, 1916), 3, remarks, " 'Kant und seinen Auslegern' gelten bekanntlich Schillers Verse:

> Wie doch ein einziger Reicher so viele Bettler in Nahrung
> Setzt! Wenn die Könige bau'n, haben die Kärrner zu tun."

12. Georg Simmel, *Kant* (Leipzig, 1904), 178–179.

13. Richard Kroner, *Kants Weltanschauung* (Tübingen, 1914).

14. Chamberlain, *Immanuel Kant,* 6.

15. Friedrich, *The Philosophy of Kant,* xiii.

16. Hayek, *Constitution of Liberty,* 196–97.

17. Bernard Carnois, *La cohérence de la doctrine kantienne de la liberté* (Paris, 1973), 11.

18. *Krit.d.prakt.V.,* 5:4. We read further "Damit man hier nicht Inconsequenzen anzutreffen wähne, wenn ich jetzt die Freiheit die Bedingung des moralischen Gesetzes nenne, und

Practical Reason states that one cannot do without the concept of freedom, that "key to the most sublime practical principles for *critical* moralists who thereby come to realize that they must necessarily proceed *rationally.*" To Kant, the autonomy of the will is the only principle of all moral laws and the duties corresponding to them. On account of his freedom, man is the subject of the holy moral law. Kant mentions the "wonderful opening up . . . of an intelligible world through the realization of the . . . concept of freedom." Among all the ideas of pure speculative reason, it is the concept of freedom which greatly enlarges the field of the metasensual [*Übersinnlichen*]. It exclusively possesses great fertility. "It is *a priori* (morally) necessary, to *produce* the *highest good with the freedom of the will.*"[19] At the end of the *Critique of Judgment,* Kant emphasizes that the moral law is contingent upon freedom. Among the three ideas of reason, namely, God, freedom, and immortality, freedom has an important, unique function. The concept of freedom is the "basic concept of all unqualified practical laws."[20]

Kant's appreciation of liberty can also be seen in his noncritical writings. In 1784 Kant states that nature gave man reason and based his freedom of will upon it so that he could be free to become happy and perfect.[21] Two years later Kant describes the evolution of man as a transition from the tutelage of nature to the status of freedom.[22] Morality [*Sittlichkeit*] is the highest good possible in the world. It is possible only through freedom.[23] In 1793 he remarks that neither nature nor inclination can rule freedom.[24] His treatise on eternal peace shows that men are members of a society only insofar as they live according to the principles of a constitution providing for freedom. Freedom and the moral law based upon it furnish the context of the concept of right [*Rechtsbegriff*].[25]

The freedom discussed in the preceding paragraphs is an inner freedom.[26] Man is free because his reason permits him to determine his moral values. His freedom grows with autolimitation made in the awareness of duty.[27]

Kant also favors liberty from restrictions by others. Liberty decreases with

---

in der Abhandlung nachher behaupte, daß das moralische Gesetz die Bedingung sei, unter der wir uns allererst der Freiheit bewußt werden können, so will ich nur erinnern, daß die Freiheit allerdings die *ratio essendi* des moralischen Gesetzes, das moralische Gesetz aber die *ratio cognoscendi* der Freiheit sei. Denn wäre nicht das moralische Gesetz in unserer Vernunft eher deutlich gedacht, so würden wir uns niemals berechtigt halten, so etwas, als Freiheit ist, (ob diese gleich sich nicht widerspricht), anzunehmen. Wäre aber keine Freiheit, so würde das moralische Gesetz in uns gar nicht anzutreffen sein."

19. Ibid. 5:7–8, 33, 87, 94, 103, 113.
20. *Krit.d.U.,* 5:473, 474.
21. *Gesch.in weltb.A.,* 8:19.
22. *Anf.d.Menschengesch.,* 8:115.
23. *Denken orient.,* 8:139.
24. *Gemeinspruch,* 8:288.
25. *Frieden,* 8:349–50, 372.
26. For Kant's use of this term, cf. *Streit,* 7:67, 72; *Anthropologie,* 8:267.
27. *Denken orient.,* 8:145; *Religion,* 6:57–58; *Tugendlehre,* 6:382.

the growth of those restrictions.[28] Favoring the individual's protection from the state, he denounces "provisions and formulas" as "footshackles of a perpetual minority." The people can enlighten themselves "if left free to do so." Kant mentions curtailments of freedom by the government, the military officer, the revenue official, the clergyman and makes plain that men are not permitted to deprive posterity of freedom.[29] Two years later he speaks of the advantages of the "inestimable good of freedom." Without freedom "there is no diligence which can produce wealth." He regrets that in "Sina" all traces of freedom were extinguished.[30] In 1793 Kant praises the coexistence of free individuals in society. Every individual has unalienable rights that he cannot give up even if he wants to and that only he himself is permitted to judge. In every community there must be a "spirit of freedom."[31] Kant condemns the opinion that some men are not ready for freedom.[32] In 1797 he writes that the individuals who give up their external freedom in an original social contract, immediately get it back as members of the community. The citizens of conquered states do not lose their liberty as a result of conquests.[33]

Kant goes on to emphasize the various aspects of freedom. He remarks that nature cares the most tenderly for the desire of free thinking. Gradually, free thought influences the mentality of the people, increasingly enabling them to act freely. Finally, it even has an impact upon the government, which will find it to its own advantage to treat man, who is now more than just a machine, according to his dignity.[34] Freedom of thought cannot really exist as long as the government restricts its expression.[35] Later on, Kant emphasizes "public freedom of thought." One reason for its defense is that scholars can only expect the community to have confidence in their findings if they make their interpretations available to everybody and are always open and receptive to better insights.[36]

In tune with his opinion that a true freedom of thought cannot exist if it cannot be made public, Kant stresses freedom of speech and pen. Curtailing the latter means robbing people of an important part of freedom and depriving the ruler of the opportunity to be informed about their complaints.[37] The *Anthropology* explains why learned people cry for the freedom of the pen: If that freedom is denied, we cannot examine the correctness of our own judgments and are prone to error.[38] In the same year Kant comes out in favor of a popular enlightenment [*Volksaufklärung*] which, however, must not be arranged by the state.[39]

28. *Tugendlehre,* 6:382.
29. *Aufklärung,* 8:35–37. See also 39.
30. *Anf.d.Menschengesch.,* 8:120–21.
31. *Gemeinspruch,* 8:290, 304, 305, 306.
32. *Religion,* 6:188.
33. *Rechtslehre,* 6:348.
34. *Aufklärung,* 8:41–42.
35. *Denken orient.,* 8:146.
36. *Religion,* 6:114.
37. *Gemeinspruch,* 8:304.
38. *Anthropologie,* 7:128–29.
39. *Streit,* 7:89: "Volksaufklärung ist die öffentliche Belehrung des Volks von seinen Pflichten und Rechten in Ansehung des Staats, dem es angehört. Weil es hier nur natürliche und

Kant also advocates academic freedom. An officer on duty must execute an order and not criticize it in front of his subordinates. On the other hand, he ought to be permitted to publish learned critiques. Revenue inspectors must collect taxes but must be allowed to criticize finance policy in a learned way. A clergyman must obey the statutes of his church, but as a scholar he has the right and duty to freely publish his thoughts on church and religion.[40] For the sake of scholarship and the publication of learned ideas, there ought to be faculties of philosophy which can criticize prevailing ideas and make their thoughts available to the public.[41]

Kant, who had a pietist education at home and at school, fought for religious freedom. His treatise on enlightenment concludes mentioning the place where it was written—Königsberg, Prussia. He was obviously proud to reside in a city whose name contained the syllable "king" and to live in a state ruled by Frederick the Great, a king known for his religious tolerance. According to Kant, a contract binding clergymen to an unchangeable symbol in order to permanently exercise tutelage over the members of their parishes and thus over the people is "absolutely impossible. Such a contract, concluded in order to prevent for good all further enlightenment of the human race, simply is null and void even if it is confirmed by the supreme power, by Reich Diets and the most solemn peace treaties." The government should stay out of religious disputes. Under no circumstances may it support the despotism of some clergymen over the people.[42] In 1793 Kant writes that the state may have the church run by scholars and men of a good moral reputation, but must not interfere with their disputes and try to teach them. He opposes state interference in religious matters in the orient and the occident. Since the government is in no position to prevent thinking to begin with, it looks funny when it asserts that it does not interfere with freedom of conscience by prohibiting its public expression while not preventing anybody to secretly think whatever he likes. Statutes forcing individuals to believe in certain things are a "yoke." The opinion that some people are not ready for religious freedom is wrong.[43]

---

aus dem gemeinen Menschenverstande hervorgehende Rechte betrifft, so sind die natürlichen Verkündiger und Ausleger derselben im Volk nicht die vom Staat bestellte amtsmäßige, sondern freie Rechtslehrer, d.i. die Philosophen, welche eben um dieser Freiheit willen, die sie sich erlauben, dem Staate, der immer nur herrschen will, anstößig sind, und werden unter dem Namen Aufklärer als für den Staat gefährliche Leute verschrieen; obzwar ihre Stimme nicht vertraulich ans Volk (als welches davon und von ihren Schriften wenig oder gar keine Notiz nimmt), sondern ehrerbietig an den Staat gerichtet und dieser jenes sein rechtliches Bedürfniß zu beherzigen angefleht wird; welches durch keinen andern Weg als den der Publicität geschehen kann, wenn ein ganzes Volk seine Beschwerde (*gravamen*) vortragen will. So verhindert das Verbot der Publicität den Fortschritt eines Volks zum Besseren, selbst in dem, was das Mindeste seiner Forderung, nämlich bloß sein natürliches Recht, angeht."

40. *Aufklärung,* 8:37–38.

41. *Streit,* 7:28–29. See also 67.

42. *Aufklärung,* 8:38–41.

43. *Religion,* 6:113, 130–31, 133–34, 179, 188.

Kant pleads for the freedom of the arts and sciences.[44] He opposes discriminatory taxes.[45] He favors free trade. "Bourgeois freedom [*bürgerliche Freiheit*] cannot now well be touched without disadvantages in all kinds of business, notably trade and the ensuing weakening of the state in foreign relations." "If the citizen cannot look after his welfare the way he sees fit, something that must be in conformity with the freedom of others, the liveliness of human action and, thereby, the strength of the whole, is hampered."[46] Approvingly, Kant describes the beginning of laissez-faire.[47] Without freedom there can be no activity that can produce wealth.[48]

Whereas Kant mentions various aspects of freedom, he does not clearly define freedom. Next to inner freedom,[49] mainly two types of "external" freedom recur in his writings, the unlimited or wild freedom of the state of nature and the legal freedom in a community.

"Internal" freedom, discussed at length in the *Critique of Practical Reason,* is not really defined there.[50] Neither is it in other publications. The *Critique of Judgment* merely states that the moral law with all its might over motivations exists for the sake of inner freedom.[51] In 1797 Kant writes that virtue is "a compulsion according to a principle of inner freedom, that is, to the mere conception of duty in tune with the formal law of that freedom": Inner freedom corresponds to inner lawmaking and can mean different things. Kant speaks of the extension of the concept of duty beyond that of external freedom, of the latter's restriction in order that inner freedom may exist on account of the ability of autolimitation on the basis of pure practical reason. Virtue, "the moral strength of the will of a *human being* doing his *duty* . . . orders and accompanies its imperatives by a moral compulsion (which is possible on account of inner freedom)." We again miss a definition of inner freedom, as we do when we read: "Inner freedom requires two things: in a given case to *master* oneself (*animus sui compos*) and to *rule* oneself (*imperium in semetipsum*), that is, to *tame* one's affects and to *govern* one's passions." The man of dignity must not deprive himself of his inner freedom.[52] What this freedom consists of, however, Kant does not tell us. In the *Anthropology,* inner freedom is dis-

44. *Aufklärung,* 8:41.

45. *Gemeinspruch,* 8:298.

46. *Gesch.in weltb.A.,* 8:27–28.

47. *Streit,* 7:19–20; see also *Aufklärung,* 8:41.

48. *Anf.d.Menschengesch.,* 8:120.

49. See *Streit,* 7:67, 72; *Anthropologie,* 8:267.

50. We read: "Das Herz wird doch von einer Last, die es jederzeit ingeheim drückt, befreit und erleichtert, wenn an reinen moralischen Entschließungen, davon Beispiele vorgelegt werden, dem Menschen ein inneres, ihm selbst sonst nicht einmal recht bekanntes Vermögen, die innere Freiheit , aufgedeckt wird, sich von der ungestümen Zudringlichkeit der Neigungen dermaß en loszumachen, dass gar keine, selbst die beliebteste nicht, auf eine Entschließung, zu der wir uns jetzt unserer Vernunft bedienen sollen, Einfluß habe." *Krit.d.prakt.V.,* 5:161.

51. *Krit.d.U.,* 5:271.

52. *Tugendlehre,* 6:394, 396, 405, 407–8, 420.

tinguished from affect and passions,[53] but no satisfactory definition of it can be found.

According to the *Idea for a Universal History* man is very much inclined toward unlimited freedom. That freedom, characteristic of the state of nature, brings about great suffering and soon convinces men that they no longer can live in "wild freedom." The "wild man" is forced "to give up his brutal freedom and to look for peace and security under a legal constitution." Kant fears "barbaric devastations" and "lawless freedom." The danger is similar with respect to nations. Kant denounces the "barbaric freedom of existing states," to arm and wage war. He complains about the "confused gamble of human events" under an "unruly freedom."[54] In 1786 Kant expresses doubts about a lawless use of reason.[55] In 1793 he denounces the "state of a lawless external (brutal) freedom and independence from compulsory laws" as one of "injustice and of war of all against all."[56] He criticizes "the state of complete lawlessness (*status naturalis*) in which all law ceases to be effective," denounces "anarchy with all its atrocities," and regrets that it is perhaps impossible to tame human liberty.[57] Two years later he mentions "with deep contempt" the "predisposition of wild people toward lawless freedom, toward fighting incessantly with one another rather than subordinating themselves to a lawful compulsion constituted by themselves, and preferring rational freedom to a rabid one," considering this predisposition the "lawless freedom" of men and attacking anarchy.[58] Similarly, in 1793 he complains of the wild lawlessness of men, of "lawless (brutal) freedom."[59] In 1797 he mentions "an externally lawless freedom" in which men fight each other. Man left "the wild, lawless freedom totally to again find his undiminished freedom under laws." Kant criticizes wild people who consider themselves noble on account of the "lawless freedom they have chosen."[60] A year later he is of the opinion that the passionate inclination toward freedom is the greatest with natural man because he cannot avoid having arguments with others.[61] But whatever Kant may have said about freedom in the state of nature, he did not define it.

Men leave the state of nature by entering an original contract[62] under which all give up their external freedom in order to immediately regain it as members of a community. Thus by entering a state men do not sacrifice part of the external freedom they are born with. They give up wild, lawless freedom in order to regain undiminished freedom under law. The freedom under law is undiminished because men's dependence upon laws derives from their own

53. *Anthropologie,* 7:267.

54. *Gesch.in weltb.A.,* 8:22, 24, 25, 26, 30.

55. *Denken orient.,* 8:145.

56. *Religion,* 6:97.

57. *Gemeinspruch,* 8:301, 302, 306.

58. *Frieden,* 8:354, 367.

59. *Religion,* 6:27, 97.

60. *Rechtslehre,* 6:307, 316.

61. *Anthropologie,* 7:268.

62. Cf. Polin, "Les relations du peuple avec ceux qui le gouvernent dans la politique de Kant," in *La philosophie politique de Kant,* 163 ff.

legislative will.[63] For Kant, therefore, external freedom does not only exist in a state of nature. It also exists in the state.[64]

Kant writes in 1784 that the highest task of nature for the good of the human race must be to build a society in which there is freedom under external laws combined, to the greatest possible degree, with irresistible power. This makes a completely just bourgeois constitution [*bürgerliche Verfassung*].[65] In 1793 he states that external law absolutely derives from the concept of freedom with respect to the external relations among men. It has nothing to do with men's natural desire for happiness and with rules concerning the means of achieving it. The bourgeois constitution is a relationship among free individuals under external laws that constitute public law.[66] Two years later people could read that external freedom is legal freedom, "the right not to obey any external law except those to which I have been able to consent."[67] In 1797 Kant speaks of "external freedom in conformity with general laws."[68] However, much as he may have mentioned external freedom, he did not define it.[69]

Neither do Kant's connections of freedom with moral law, a law important to him,[70] lead to a definition of freedom. He writes that man recognizes his freedom, which without moral law would have remained unknown to him. He considers the autonomy of the will the "only principle of all moral laws and the duties corresponding to them." He identifies the awareness of freedom with that of moral law, a "law of causality through freedom," "erected as a principle of the deduction of freedom," something positive in itself, namely, the form of an intellectual causality, of freedom. Kant praises "the wonderful discovery which pure practical reason lets us make through the moral law: the discovery of an intelligible world through the realization of the otherwise transcendent concept of freedom, and thereby of the moral law itself." The moral law is "the only determining basis of the pure will." Freedom is "postulated through, and for the sake of, moral law." Moral thinking gives an awareness of freedom.[71] In the *Critique of Judgment* we read that "the high esteem for the moral law

63. *Rechtslehre,* 6:315 f.

64. For Kant's connecting external freedom in the state of nature and in the state, cf. *Anf.d.Menschengesch.,* 8:118; *Rechtslehre,* 6:257–58, 267, also 246, 251, 256, 347; *Anthropologie,* 7:269.

65. *Gesch.in weltb.A.,* 8:22.

66. *Gemeinspruch,* 8:289–90.

67. *Frieden,* 8:350.

68. *Tugendlehre,* 6:396.

69. Kant often juxtaposes inner and external freedom in the same sentence or paragraph without a clear definition. Cf. *Herder,* 8:57; *Tugendlehre,* 6:380, 394, 396, 406.

70. The "reine Sittengesetz" is "heilig." The moral law is "etwas an sich Positives . . . , nämlich die Form einer intellectuellen Causalität d.i. der Freiheit," an object of "Achtung," der "größten Achtung." It exists "in seiner feierlichen Majestät" and is embellished by "Herrlichkeit." "Achtung fürs moralische Gesetz ist . . . die einzige und zugleich unbezweifelte moralische Triebfeder." The moral law is the supreme practical law of rational beings. *Krit.d.prakt.V.,* 5:32, 73, 77, 78, 93.

71. Ibid., 5:30, 33, 46, 47, 48, 73, 94, 109, 124, 133, 160. See also 132.

presents to us absolutely freely, according to the rule of our own reason, the final purpose of our destiny."[72] In 1793 Kant writes that freedom becomes known to man when his will is determined by the absolutely moral law. It is no secret, for everybody can become aware of it. However, the *Grund* of freedom is a secret because we cannot find out what it is. But freedom, applied to the final object of practical reason, namely, the realization of the idea of the moral end, unavoidably leads us to holy secrets.[73] In 1796 Kant mentions the concept of freedom and the law of the categorical imperative derived from it. He speaks of the spontaneity of freedom and its moral-practical laws, of the "moral categorical imperative" that "first makes us know" freedom.[74] Kant probably comes closest to a definition of freedom when he writes that the moral law is so inseparably connected with freedom "that practical freedom also could be defined as the independence of the will from every other will except the moral law." But he immediately adds that freedom of an active cause, especially in the world of the senses, cannot be known at all. He considers himself happy to find it sufficiently certain that there is no proof of its impossibility. Therefore, because of the moral law which postulates freedom, we are forced and entitled to assume that freedom exists. Kant speaks of the unexplorable potential of freedom.[75] Again, there is no satisfactory definition of freedom.

Liberty under Law

The preceding statements show that for Kant, freedom is a product of the moral law or that it creates the moral law by which in turn it is restricted. At any rate, the individual must use his freedom in accordance with the moral law.

In 1786 Kant writes that the pure practical use of reason consists in the prescription of moral laws. He indicates the connection of freedom to these laws and denounces a use of reason opposed to moral laws. If reason—and freedom—do not want to be under these laws, they of necessity must be under laws that are not necessarily moral and perhaps very harsh, "for without any law whatsoever nothing, not even the greatest nonsense, can be active for a long time. Therefore, the unavoidable result of *declared* lawlessness in thinking (a liberation from the restrictions posited by reason) is that the liberty to think in the end is lost and literally forfeited because not misfortune, but a veritable hybris can be blamed for that lawlessness." Kant condemns the licentious freedom of thinking, rapture, and irrationalism. The last is a troublesome state of the human mind. It first prevents moral laws from moving the heart, then deprives them of all authority and finally brings about *Freigeisterei,* the principle of no longer recognizing any duty. People ought not to deny to reason what makes it the highest good on earth, namely the privilege of being the last test of

72. *Krit.d.U.,* 5:481. 73. *Religion,* 6:138.
74. *Verkündigung,* 8:416, 417. Cf. H. J. Paton, *The Categorical Imperative* (Chicago, 1948).
75. *Krit.d.prakt.V.,* 5:93–94, 47.

the truth. One should use freedom according to the law and for the best of the world.[76]

Restrictions of freedom by the moral law can be considered the core of the idea of practical reason. This law humiliates "unavoidably every man who compares his natural sensuous inclination with it." Moral thinking must be free from all sensual desires. Kant speaks of "a highest being, or one free of all sensuality." The moral interest is a pure interest, one free of sensuous desires. It demands respect through the free subordination of the will to it. The individual must act only for the sake of moral law. "For . . . a most perfect being that law is one of *holiness,* for . . . finite rational beings, one of *duty,* of moral compulsion and the determination of their actions out of *respect* for this law and esteem for one's duty." Duty and obligation alone should count in our relationship to the moral law. Although we are lawmaking members of a moral empire made possible through freedom and esteemed for practical reason, we are, at the same time, the subjects, not the sovereign, of that empire. Therefore, not recognizing our low status as created beings and vainly refusing to recognize the prestige of the holy law amounts to denying that law in spirit, even if its letter is fulfilled. We should try "in an uninterrupted, but indefinite progress" to follow the "law of all laws," the command, "*love God above everything and your neighbor as yourself.*" It stands in contrast to the principle of one's own happiness, "*love yourself above everything, but God and your neighbor for your own sake.*" By virtue of the autonomy of his freedom man is the subject of the moral law, which is holy. It is the supreme practical law of rational beings. Freedom is the ability "to usually follow the moral law. It is *independence from inclinations.*" "The moral law is holy (unforgiving) and demands the holiness of customs." It demands from me to act with a view of achieving the highest possible good in a world. My will must be determined by the moral law, not by my own happiness. That law always obliges everybody because it is a command, not just a clever rule. Inclinations toward happiness ought to be subordinated to it. A person's value depends solely upon the moral value of his actions. Without promising anything for sure or threatening us, the moral law within us demands our unegoistic respect. Thinking of our freedom, we follow the moral law and thus have "esteem *for ourselves,* being conscious of our freedom." In the conclusion of *Critique of Practical Reason* we read the famous words: "Two things fill the mind with ever new and increasing awe and admiration the more frequently and continuously reflection is occupied with them; *the starred heaven above me and the moral law within me.*"[77]

The *Critique of Judgment* leaves no doubt either that the moral law limits the inner freedom of man. There, Kant speaks of that law's power over our passions. That power exists for the sake of our inner freedom; it is so strong that it does not even permit us to look for other motives for our actions. He

76. *Denken orient.,* 8:139, 145, 146–47.
77. *Krit.d.prakt.V.,* 5:74, 76, 79, 80, 82, 83, 87, 93, 117, 128, 161.

speaks of the original being as the legislative sovereign in a moral realm of purposes. In that realm, the existence of rational beings under moral laws is the highest, only possible good. Man must judge himself as being in this world under moral laws. It can be considered certain that only man under moral laws can be the final aim of the supreme cause. We find in ourselves and still more so in the concept of a rational free being a moral teleology that can be considered necessary and is connected with the nomoethics of freedom. Even the most common human reason must agree with the principle that if there is a final purpose that reason must designate a priori, it can only be "*man* (every rational world-being) *under moral laws.*" Kant emphasizes: "I say on purpose: *under* moral laws, not man *according to* moral laws." We read further: "The moral law alone, as a formal rational condition for the use of our freedom, binds us without being dependent upon any material purpose; but it also determines—*a priori*—our final purpose and obliges us to strive for it. That purpose is the *highest good in the world* made possible through freedom. Happiness is the subjective condition under which, according to the law just mentioned, man can set himself a final aim. Consequently, the highest physical good possible in the world and, as far as we are concerned, to be promoted, is *happiness.*" The highest physical good is "the worthiness of being happy under the objective condition of the conformity of man with the law of *morality.*" Thus the freedom to strive for happiness is restricted by moral law. The idea of a final purpose of the use of freedom under moral laws possesses "subjective *practical* reality." In contrast to happiness, morality [*Sittlichkeit*], as far as its possibility is concerned, is set a priori. It is dogmatically certain. We must promote and bring about the final purpose under moral laws. Kant speaks of the "concept of man's freedom under moral laws together with the final purpose which the former prescribes through the latter." The concept of freedom demonstrates its reality through the causality of reason and the moral law it unrefutedly postulates.[78]

In 1793 Kant begins his foreword to the first edition of his study on religion within mere reason with the words "Die Moral." Throughout that work it is evident that freedom is circumscribed by morals. We read that through reason man is bound by unconditioned laws to respect morality, that moral law alone orders without qualifications. It demands that we must achieve the highest good we possibly can even if it implies a loss of happiness. Kant praises the Rigorists who are not inclined to make concessions at the cost of morals. He calls the moral law the law of freedom which must be used according to that law. The moral law is the "commanding law per se" [*das schlechthin gebietende Gesetz*]. Man's inclination toward evil is morally evil. The moral law deserves to be considered divine law. Kant mentions the morality of law found by reason and adds that man ought not to deprive the "unambiguous moral feeling" of its dignity by relating it to any other fantastic one. He

78. *Krit.d.U.,* 5:271, 275, 444–45, 447–48, 448–49, 450, 453, 460, 470–71, 474.

speaks of the moral laws that have to be executed in the world. The law of morality is so close to everyman, even the most naive individual, that it is as if it were literally written into his heart. Freedom must be determined by the moral law.[79]

In the same year Kant writes that we must see to it that the world conforms to moral purposes, that in view of our relationship to this world we must always obey the moral law.[80] In 1795 he praises that step toward morality to do one's duty for its own sake irrespective of rewards.[81]

His study on the metaphysical bases of legal theory again emphasizes the importance of the moral law in us. In the foreword to the treatise on the metaphysical bases of the theory of virtue we read that if the principle of happiness rather than that of freedom would determine inner lawmaking, the gentle death of all morality would follow. Kant rebukes all those who fight and suspect the moral concept of freedom and states with satisfaction that their attempts will fail in the end. Insofar as virtue is based upon inner freedom, it contains the command to subordinate all one's abilities and inclinations to the power of reason and thereby to exercise power over oneself. This command is complemented by the prohibition to permit oneself to be controlled by one's feelings and inclinations. Man must act under the principles of moral inner freedom. He ought not to permit himself to be deprived of the privileges of a moral being. He ought not to make himself "into a play of mere inclinations, that is, into a mere thing." Kant speaks of the "moral imperative restricting our freedom."[82]

In the *Dispute of the Faculties,* it is stated that human action must result from the use of moral forces. We are subordinated to moral laws. This moral disposition is in us, inseparable from humanity. The public use of the Bible is good because it promotes the invigoration of moral motives, to which all other intentions must be secondary. The moral law propels the actions of the free will. God is the originator of the moral law within us.[83]

According to the *Anthropology,* affect may cause an immediate end of freedom and self-discipline, passion may give it up and delight in a slave mentality; however, "reason with its demand for inner freedom," that is, with its command to act according to the moral law, does not subside.[84]

As did Montesquieu and Smith, Kant thinks of a judge within man who, like an inner voice, complements the moral law. He mentions "judicial voices of that wonderful ability in us which we call conscience," the "inner magistrate's bench."[85] Transgressions of duty bring about earnest self-reproaches that speak in us "as if they were the voice of a judge." There is a voice men hear

79. *Religion,* 6:3, 4, 5–6, 22, 23–24, 26, 37, 113–14, 114, 171, 181, 191.

80. *Gemeinspruch,* 8:280.

81. *Frieden,* 8:376.

82. *Rechtslehre,* 6:355; *Tugendlehre,* 6:378, 408, 420, 437.

83. *Streit,* 7:42, 68, 72, 73–74.

84. *Anthropologie,* 7:267.

85. *Krit.d.prakt.V.,* 5:98, 152.

within themselves when they have not behaved correctly.[86] In 1793 Kant mentions the "accuser in us" asking for a verdict of condemnation. He speaks of the judgment of a future judge, of the awakening conscience in one breath with the empirical way of knowing oneself. "If one asks the judge within man, he will give a severe verdict for he cannot bribe his reason." "Reason, heart and conscience teach and demand that man is called on by the moral law to lead a good life, that he find fulfillment in his innate unextinguishable respect for the moral law, his confidence in that good spirit and in the hope to do it justice regardless of what happens. Always connecting the latter expectation with the former strict command, he always must examine whether he can justify his behavior before a judge."[87] Dishonesty is lack of the honesty to confess before one's inner judge. "Everyman has a conscience and finds himself observed, threatened and generally kept in awe . . . by an inner judge. This power, watching the laws in himself, is not (arbitrarily) *created* by him, but is an ingredient part of his being."[88] A year later Kant writes that whenever he wrote his studies, he would imagine a judge within himself, standing by him.[89]

Kant's categorical imperatives and concepts of duty are tied up with the moral law. That law is a categorical imperative in that it exists unconditionally. Everybody can fulfill it: "To live up to the categorical command of morality is at all times in everybody's power."[90] In 1793 Kant writes "that, *if* we have certain moral relationships to the things in this world, we must obey the moral law everywhere. Furthermore, we have a duty to see to it as much as possible that there exists such a relationship (a world appropriate to moral highest purposes)." He presents man's duty as a moral necessity and connects it with the moral-good state of affairs. The purity of an unegoistic exercise of duty is the true value. The absence of the will to strive for such a purity is the death of morality.[91]

The connection of duty and morality follows from the tribute to duty in the *Critique of Practical Reason,* which derives duty from the moral law.[92] It is

86. *Krit.d.U.,* 5:458.

87. *Religion,* 6:76–77, 144–45.

88. *Tugendlehre,* 6:430, 438. Kant continues: "Es folgt ihm wie sein Schatten, wenn er zu entfliehen gedenkt. Er kann sich zwar durch Lüste und Zerstreuungen betäuben oder in Schlaf bringen, aber nicht vermeiden dann und wann zu sich selbst zu kommen oder zu erwachen, wo er alsbald die furchtbare Stimme desselben vernimmt. Er kann es in seiner äußersten Verworfenheit allenfalls dahin bringen, sich daran gar nicht mehr zu kehren, aber sie zu hören, kann er doch nicht vermeiden." See also the following paragraphs.

89. *Streit,* 7:9.

90. *Krit.d.prakt.V.,* 5:32, 36–37, 134. *In Tugendlehre,* 6:396, Kant speaks of the "moralischen Imperativ." Cf. also *Frieden,* 8:375–377; *Tugendlehre,* 6:388–89, 392–93, 394–95.

91. *Gemeinspruch,* 8:280, 283, 284, 285.

92. *Krit.d. prakt.V.,* 5:86: "Pflicht! du erhabener, großer Name, der du nichts Beliebtes, was Einschmeichelung bei sich führt, in dir fassest, sondern Unterwerfung verlangst, doch auch nichts drohest, was natürliche Abneigung im Gemüthe erregte und schreckte, um den Willen zu bewegen, sondern blos ein Gesetz aufstellst, welches von selbst im Gemüthe Eingang findet, und doch sich selbst wider Willen Verehrung, (wenn gleich nicht immer Befolgung) erwirbt, vor dem

emphasized in the rest of that work. The moral law requires that the promotion of happiness can never be a direct duty and even less the principle of all duty. Kant connects the duty to advance the highest good with the moral way of thinking, with the moral law. "The *value* of an opinion *totally* in tune with the moral law is infinite. For in the judgment of a wise and omnipotent distributor of such opinions all possible happiness has no other limitation than the failure of rational beings to fulfill their duty." Only acts done out of duty have a moral value. The moral law requires to be followed from a feeling of duty, not from one of desire. It requires to put "the holiness of duty alone above everything else and to become conscious that this *can* be done because our own reason recognizes this as a command and says that one *ought* to do it, to totally rise above the world of the senses." The consciousness of the moral law is inseparable from one's ability to master sensuousness. Shortly before the end of the second critique, Kant again connects duty with the moral way of thinking.[93]

In the *Critique of Judgment* we read that the fulfillment of duty consists of the earnest desire to act according to the moral law. Kant demands that we do what the moral law posits as the final purpose for us to fulfill. He sees in the moral law a formal practical principle that leads categorically, the basis of duty.[94] In the first sentence of his study on religion within the limits of mere reason, Kant again connects duty and morality. According to that work, it is a general duty of the human race to "*rise* . . . to the ideal of moral perfection, i.e., to the original example of moral ways of thinking." Acting out of duty is something purely moral. In connection with the moral law Kant writes that duty prompts us to see that the unification of rational world-beings in an ethical state is something good. To recognize what is moral is a general duty of men. We do not live up to our duty if we do not obey the holy law that has been recognized by us. "*Religion* (subjectively seen) means recognizing all our duties as divine commands." Kant regrets that men pass by their true moral duty and compensate for it by fulfilling their obligations toward a church.[95] In the same year he mentions as an aspect of the moral law the "concept of freedom in all its purity" in contrast to the striving for happiness and material gain. He speaks of "a pure moral way of thinking which honors duty above everything, fights and conquers innumerable evils of life and the most seductive allurements (for one assumes with justification that man is able to demonstrate this way of thinking.)"[96] In 1794 he again mentions duty in connection with the moral

---

alle Neigungen verstummen, wenn sie gleich ingeheim ihm entgegen wirken: welches ist der deiner würdige Ursprung, und wo findet man die Wurzel deiner edlen Abkunft, welche alle Verwandtschaft mit Neigungen stolz ausschlägt, und von welcher Wurzel abzustammen, die unnachlaßliche Bedingung desjenigen Werths ist, den sich Menschen allein geben selbst können?"

93. Ibid., 5:92–93, 125–26, 142–43, 144, 128, 147–48, 158, 159, 160–61.

94. *Krit.d.U.,* 5:465, 485.

95. *Religion,* 6:61, 118, 138–39, 140, 153, 160.

96. *Gemeinspruch,* 8:286–87.

law,[97] as he does in the following year when he speaks of the duty to bring about peace.[98] In 1797 he connects the moral law with the duty to promote peace. The pursuit of happiness, often distinguished by Kant from obedience to the moral law, is no duty to him. "Virtue is . . . the moral strength of a *man's* will to do his *duty,* which is a moral *compulsion* through his own legislative reason, in so far as the latter constitutes itself into a power which *executes* the law." Man, aware of the sublimity of his moral potential, has the duty of self-esteem. Kant mentions the command of reason man must obey against all conflicting inclinations. Duty means to act under the law of reason, reason directly compelling men to act that way. The moral "Ascetik" obligates man to remain morally healthy.[99]

Later on, Kant connects duty with moral law. The *Dispute of the Faculties* emphasizes the duty to create a legally and morally good constitution that prevents aggressive wars.[100] At the very beginning of the *Anthropology,* Kant rebukes the moral egoist "who finds useful only those things that are useful to him and whose . . . will is mainly determined by his own happiness, and not by considerations of duty." Later on he continues: "Virtue is the *moral strength* of doing one's duty. It never ought to become a custom, but always ought to be newly and originally produced from one's way of thinking. Dutiful choice serves the promotion of morality. Man has the moral duty of creating good out of evil.[101]

Kant makes plain that categorical imperatives also require obedience to positive laws. The state possesses autonomy. It creates and sustains itself with legislative, executive, and judicial powers according to laws of freedom. It profits from "the greatest conformity of the constitution with principles of law . . . the striving for which reason demands through a *categorical imperative.*" While the state forms itself according to the moral law, it may for its preservation require obedience to positive laws. Thus positive criminal law must be obeyed unconditionally.[102]

As early as 1784 Kant speaks of the citizen's duty to obey state laws.[103] He repeats this advice in 1790.[104] In 1793 he writes that church-going, thought of as a solemn external service to God, is a citizen's duty for the sake of the community which here on earth lives in a state that can be thought of as a divine institution.[105] In his remarks against Hobbes, Kant argues that the bourgeois society is an "unqualified and first duty." It serves a purpose which is the *conditio sine qua non* of all external duties, namely, "the *law* [*Recht*] of

97. *Ende aller Dinge,* 8:338.

98. *Frieden,* 8:368.

99. *Rechtslehre,* 6:354–55; *Tugendlehre,* 6:386–87, 405, 420, 435, 481–82, 484–85.

100. *Streit,* 7:85.

101. *Anthropologie,* 7:130, 147, 244, 329.

102. *Rechtslehre,* 6:318, 331–32. In some passages, Kant's imperatives can refer to moral as well as positive laws: *Frieden,* 8:375–77; *Tugendlehre,* 6:388–89, 392–93, 394–95.

103. *Aufklärung,* 8:37–38.

104. *Krit.d.U.,* 5:367.

105. *Religion,* 6:198.

men *under public compulsory laws* which define to each his own and through which it can be secured from anybody else."[106] Man has the duty to obey the positive laws of society.[107]

Kant comments on the restriction of the freedom of the individual by positive law in other connections. In 1794 he speaks of "a society in which *freedom under external laws* is combined to the highest possible degree with irresistible power," that is, "a perfectly *just bourgeois constitution,* nature's highest task for the human race."[108] He thinks it is compatible with the enlightenment that soldiers, taxpayers, and church visitors do not rationalize [*räsonieren*], but exercise, pay, and pray as commanded by positive laws. In the official positions entrusted to them, state employees may act only within the framework of the laws which can restrict their freedom considerably.[109] Two years later Kant wrote that nature has provided men with reason in order to restrict their freedom by a "general external legality which is called *bourgeois law.*"[110] Obligations according to natural law are considered superfluous and often misleading. By contrast, bourgeois law is binding.[111] Although Kant favors a far-reaching protection of freedom of thought, he justifies its restriction through laws if people take unreasonable advantage of it, do not make a judicious use of it and thus introduce "the greatest disorder in the citizens' affairs."[112]

The opinion that freedom can be restricted by positive laws is also evident in the publications of the nineties. In 1790 Kant speaks of "public freedom and justice in a country," of "legal communal living by which people create a permanent community, having mastered the great difficulty of uniting freedom (and thus equality) and compulsion (respect and subordination out of duty rather than fear)."[113] From 1793 we read: "*Law* [*Recht*] is the restriction of everybody's freedom in a way that everybody else also may be free, in so far as this is possible under a general law. *Public law* consists of *external laws* which make such a harmony possible."[114] The bourgeois state as a legal state is based upon positive laws that restrict the freedom of the individual and play an important role. Positive laws make subjects citizens by restricting their freedom. All law [*Recht*] depends upon laws [*Gesetzen*] and consists in the limita-

106. *Gemeinspruch,* 8:289.

107. *Rechtslehre,* 6:260; *Tugendlehre,* 6:392. Sometimes, when Kant speaks of duty, it can mean obedience to moral as well as positive laws, see *Denken orient.,* 8:146; *Gemeinspruch,* 8:300, 305, 313; *Frieden,* 8:350, 376, 377, 385; *Tugendlehre,* 6:388, 394; *Streit,* 7:29, 31–32, 91; *Anthropologie,* 7:259.

108. *Gesch.in weltb.A.,* 8:22, 23, see also 24–25.

109. *Aufklärung,* 8:37.

110. *Anf.d.Menschengesch.,* 8:118.

111. *Hufeland,* 8:128.

112. *Denken orient.,* 8:145–46.

113. *Krit.d.U.,* 5:256, 367.

114. *Gemeinspruch,* 8:289–90.

tion of freedom.[115] Public laws determine what is legally permitted. "The sentence, *salus publica suprema civitatis lex est* continues to enjoy its undiminished value and prestige. However, the public weal which is to be considered *first,* requires a legal constitution that secures everybody's freedom through laws. He is free to pursue his happiness any way he sees fit as long as he does not violate the general legal freedom, that is, the rights of his fellow-subjects."[116] A year later Kant writes: "If internal problems would not compel people to subject themselves to the compulsion of public laws, war would do so." Nations are in a state of nature, exercising pressure upon each other. Therefore, people must combine so that they may have the power to defend themselves against neighbors.[117]

Legal freedom is a freedom restricted by positive external laws to which the individual consented. A state constitution is possible only under a legal compulsion according to principles of freedom.[118] Basically, freedom is to be respected. Exceptionally, it must be curtailed by positive laws. The citizen possesses the "legal *freedom* not to obey any law to which he did not consent." People are "under bourgeois law." Kant quotes: "The best constitution is one where not men, but laws rule."[119] The *Dispute of the Faculties* speaks of a bourgeois society's laws on freedom and means its positive laws.[120] According to the *Anthropology,* everybody can claim freedom under positive laws, i.e., not an absolute freedom. "*Freedom* and *law* (restricting the former) are the two linchpins around which bourgeois society turns."[121]

115. Ibid., 8:290, 291; on 292 he writes: "Denn da alles Recht bloß in der Einschränkung der Freiheit jedes Anderen auf die Bedingung besteht, daß sie mit der meinigen nach einem allgemeinen Gesetze zusammen bestehen könne, und das öffentliche Recht (in einem gemeinen Wesen) bloß der Zustand einer wirklichen, diesem Princip gemäßen und mit Macht verbundenen Gesetzgebung ist, vermöge welcher sich alle zu einem Volk Gehörige als Unterthanen in einem rechtlichen Zustand (*status iuridicus*) überhaupt, nämlich der Gleichheit der Wirkung und Gegenwirkung einer dem allgemeinen Freiheitsgesetze gemäß einander einschränkenden Willkür, (welches der bürgerliche Zustand heißt) befinden: so ist das angeborne Recht eines jeden in diesem Zustande (d.i. vor aller rechtlichen That desselben) in Ansehung der Befugniß jeden andern zu zwingen, damit er immer innerhalb den Gränzen der Einstimmung des Gebrauchs seiner Freiheit mit der meinigen bleibe, durchgängig gleich."

116. Ibid., 8:294, 298. 117. *Frieden,* 8:365–66. 118. Ibid., 8:350, 374.

119. *Rechtlehre,* 6:314, 318, 355. Kant speaks of the "äußeren Freiheit" under positive law, to have a thing "als das Meine" and to make any use whatsoever of it. (*Rechtslehre,* 6:246). He speaks of "Gesetzen der Freiheit" and "Freiheitsgesetzen," and means positive law, which is concerned with the "äußeren Mein und Dein" (ibid., 6:248–49). He mentions the physical possession of soil according to "dem Gesetz der äußeren Freiheit," i.e., according to freedom under positive law (ibid., 6:251). When in his remarks on possession he speaks of "Freiheit nach allgemeinen Gesetzen," he has in mind positive laws. The bourgeois state of affairs exists "unter einer allgemeinen äußeren (d.i. öffentlichen) mit Macht begleiteten Gesetzgebung" (ibid., 6:256). The "Gesetz der äußeren Freiheit" concerning possession is positive, as is the state "einer öffentlich gesetzlichen Freiheit" (ibid., 6:257–58, 263) and the "Axiom der äußeren Freiheit" (ibid., 6:268).

120. *Streit,* 7:91. 121. *Anthropologie,* 7:273, 330.

Kant leaves no doubt that some positive laws are bad. He complains about laws providing for armament,[122] about regulations restricting free thought,[123] about laws that need improvement, about bad constitutions.[124] He speaks of men as "victims of the law."[125] Nevertheless, in all these cases, he justifies the execution of the laws.

An ideal society, in which the freedom of the individual is determined by positive laws, is the legal-bourgeois [*rechtlich-bürgerliche*] society.[126] This is already made plain in the fifth sentence of Kant's *Idea for a Universal History: "The greatest problem for the human race which nature forces it to solve, is the achievement of a* bourgeois society *administering justice in a general way.* Only in a society that enjoys the greatest freedom—a continuous antagonism of its members combined with the most exact definition and security of the limits of freedom so that the freedom of one may exist with that of others—can achieve nature's highest intention for humanity, namely, the development of all its potential. Nature also demands that society itself achieve this purpose. . . . Therefore, nature's highest task for the human race must be a society in which there exists *freedom under external laws,* combined to the greatest possible degree with irresistible power, that is, a completely *just bourgeois constitution.* Only by achieving that goal can nature achieve its other intentions with mankind."[127] This sentence, preceded and followed by four sentences and thus being central, probably is the core of Kantian liberalism. The idea of the greatest possible freedom, which does not jeopardize society but finds its limitations in the laws, and is protected by their execution, is evident.[128]

In his later publications, Kant adheres to this concept of a bourgeois society.[129] We first consider Kant's statements concerning curtailment of the

122. *Gesch.in weltb.A.,* 8:26. In the closing remarks of *Anf.d.Menschengesch.,* 8:121, we read: "Es ist aber von der größten Wichtigkeit: mit der Vorsehung zufrieden zu sein (ob sie uns gleich auf unserer Erdenwelt eine so mühsame Bahn vorgezeichnet hat): theils um unter den Mühseligkeiten immer noch Muth zu fassen, theils um, indem wir die Schuld davon aufs Schicksal schieben, nicht unsere eigene, die vielleicht die einzige Ursache aller dieser Übel sein mag, darüber aus dem Auge zu setzen und in der Selbstbesserung die Hülfe dagegen zu versäumen."

123. *Denken orient.,* 8:146.

124. *Frieden,* 8:372.

125. *Anthropologie,* 7:259.

126. Kant speaks of the "rechtlich-bürgerlichen" society in contrast to the "ethisch-bürgerliche" (*Religion,* 6:94, 95). However, usually he calls "rechtlich-bürgerlich" just "bürgerlich." The bourgeois state of affairs is a "politischer" (*Religion,* 6:95). He also speaks of a "juridisch-bürgerlichen Staate" (ibid., 6:140), of a "bürgerlich-gesetzlichen Zustande" (*Frieden,* 8:349).

127. *Gesch.in weltb.A.,* 8:22.

128. As to the significance of central positions in Magna Carta and with Dante, see Gottfried Dietze, *Magna Carta and Property* (Charlottesville, 1965), 29–30.

129. Kant considers "eine vollkommene bürgerliche Verfassung" as "das äußerste Ziel der Cultur" (*Anf.d.Menschengesch.,* 8:117). He sees "das Vornehmste" in man's "Anstalt zur bürgerlichen Verfassung und öffentlichen Gerechtigkeit, zuerst freilich nur in Ansehung der größten Gewaltthätigkeiten, deren Rächung nun nicht mehr wie im wilden Zustande Einzelnen, sondern

freedom of the individual in that society. By 1785 he had made it plain that human rights are ordered by the constitution of the state.[130] Nature gives man freedom and reason "to restrict that freedom by . . . *bourgeois law.*" Under a bourgeois constitution the individual is no longer free to take revenge on others. He must leave his protection to the government.[131] The freedom to think is opposed by bourgeois compulsion. *Freigeisterei,* an excess of freedom, is for the sake of order restricted by the authorities.[132] In 1790 Kant states that the legal power of bourgeois society restrains the freedom of individuals fighting with each other.[133] In his treatise against Hobbes, Kant argues that a bourgeois constitution restricts "the *right* of men *under public compulsory laws* giving to each his own and securing it from the attacks by others."[134] *Bürgerliches Recht* or *Staatsrecht* subordinates individuals and thus curtails their freedom.[135] Authorities define what is permitted.[136]

In 1795 Kant mentions that while bourgeois society consists, "first, according to the principles of the *freedom* of the members of a society (as men)" he immediately qualifies this remark by saying that it consists, "secondly, according to the principle of the *dependence* of all from one unique common legislation (as subjects)." In a "bourgeois-legal state" the individual may show animosity toward someone else only if he has been physically attacked. The government granting men security also restricts their freedom.[137] In such a state the evil in human nature is veiled by governmental compulsion limiting freedom. In each bourgeois constitution it must be assumed that the head of

---

einer gesetzmäßigen Macht, die das Ganze zusammenhielt, d.i., einer Art von Regierung überlassen war, über welche selbst keine Ausübung der Gewalt statt fand. . . . Von dieser ersten und rohen Anlage konnte sich nun nach und nach alle menschliche Kunst, unter welcher die der Geselligkeit und bürgerlichen Sicherheit die ersprießlichste ist, allmählich entwickeln" (ibid., 8:119). A bourgeois constitution is a "durchgängig rechtliche Verfassung" (*Gemeinspruch,* 8:297), characterized by "souveräne Gewalt" (*Rechtslehre,* 6:344). Kant speaks of "einer bürgerlichen, das Volk unter Disciplin haltenden (politischen). . . . Regierung" (*Streit,* 7:67), of "Hinstreben zu einer bürgerlichen, auf dem Freiheits-, zugleich aber auch gesetzmäßigen Zwangs-Princip zu gründenden Verfassung" (*Anthropologie,* 7:328). Kantians lead an exemplary life and subordinate themselves to "jede bürgerliche Ordnung" (*Streit,* 7:75). Kant mentions the "mechanische Einhelligkeit . . . einer bürgerlichen Verfassung" (ibid., 7:80), speaks of "einer bürgerlichen Verfassung, welche der höchste Grad der künstlichen Steigerung der guten Anlage in der Menschengattung zum Endzweck ihrer Bestimmung ist" (*Anthropologie:* 7:327), of "Hinstreben zu einer bürgerlichen auf dem Freiheits-, zugleich aber auch gesetzmäßigen Zwangs-Princip zu gründenden Verfassung" (ibid., 7:328). "Das Verstandeswohl, die Erhaltung der einmal bestehenden Staatsverfassung, ist das höchste Gesetz einer bürgerlichen Gesellschaft überhaupt; denn diese besteht durch jene" (ibid., 7:331).

130. *Herder,* 8:64.
131. *Anf.d.Menschengesch.,* 8:118, 119.
132. *Denken orient.,* 8:146.
133. *Krit.d.U.,* 5:446.
134. *Gemeinspruch,* 8:289. See also p. 292.
135. Ibid., 8:312.
136. *Religion,* 6:154.
137. *Frieden,* 8:349. On the other hand, Kant on p. 350 explains "äußere (rechtliche) Freiheit" as "die Befugniß, keinen äußeren Gesetzen zu gehorchen, als zu denen ich meine Beistimmung habe geben können." Similar *Rechtslehre,* 6:314, "seine Beistimmung gegeben hat."

state possesses "*irresistible* sovereignty." The people have no right to riot.[138] In 1797 Kant writes that only under a power that gives law, i.e., in a bourgeois state, a legal state, can one have property. This state, in which freedom exists according to general laws, provides for restrictions of the freedom to deprive others of their property. The individual owns only what he brings under his control according to the laws. With respect to real estate, the distributive law of mine and thine (*lex iustitiae distributivae*) according to the axiom of external freedom can derive only from the bourgeois state which alone determines what is right and legal [was *recht,* was *rechtlich* und was *Rechtens ist*]. Kant juxtaposes the natural state (*status naturalis*) to the bourgeois state (*status civilis*), the latter being "a society under a distributive justice" in which freedom is limited by positive laws. Individuals living in a bourgeois state have a share in saying what is right under a constitution and thus may act as they see fit only within the limits of that law. The state possesses autonomy. It constitutes and sustains itself according to the laws of liberty, according to laws that restrict the freedom of the individual. He speaks of the "*best* of the state (*salus reipublicae suprema lex est*). It does not mean the *well-being* of its citizens and their *happiness* . . . but the greatest conformity of the constitution with the principles of law that reason makes us to strive for *through a categorical imperative.*" Kant criticizes Beccaria who opposed capital punishment "out of a sympathetic sentimentality deriving from an affected humanity." To Kant, the legislator is holy even if he orders penalties. "In an association of citizens," all are under criminal law. Freedom is even restricted under a constitution "which makes *freedom* alone a principle, even the condition of all *compulsion* necessary in a legal constitution in the true sense of the state," because freedom is only a principle and exists under positive compulsory laws. The freedom of the acting individual must exist with the freedom of every other individual according to a general law.[139]

A year later Kant writes that people are content with a constitution providing for an autocratic rule but they nevertheless want a government which rules "in a republican fashion, i.e., in the spirit of republicanism and in analogy to it." The "external norm for all bourgeois constitutions" is the "idea of a constitution that conforms to the natural rights of men," a constitution under which those who are supposed to make laws must also obey the law.[140] Members of a nation who exempt themselves from bourgeois laws are "the wild crowd in that people," the *rabble* (*vulgus*) whose lawless association is *rioting* (*agere per turbas*), a behavior disqualifying a citizen of the state." Kant is glad that men subject themselves to the discipline of bourgeois compulsion.[141]

138. *Frieden,* 8:355, 382.
139. *Rechtslehre,* 6:255–56, 264, 267, 306–7, 311, 318, 334–35, 340; *Tugendlehre,* 6:382.
140. *Streit,* 7:90–91.
141. *Anthropologie,* 7:311, 329.

Law as a Limitation upon Government

Kant favors the bourgeois *Rechtsstaat* with its restrictions of governmental power through laws.

His curtailment of the freedom of the individual by positive laws does not conceal the fact that in the state, he desires the government to be limited by laws. He writes that "as long as a state is in danger of being absorbed by other states, it cannot be expected to discard its constitution even if it is despotic (something that secures greater strength with respect to external enemies)."[142] Nevertheless, there can be no doubt that Kant condemns despotism.[143] Much as he denounces war in 1784,[144] he writes two years later that the threat of war at least mitigates despotism, that the end of that threat results in the despotism of mighty tyrants.[145] In the *Critique of Judgment* we read that a state ruled by a single absolute will is represented as a mere machine.[146] In 1793 he states, "*a paternal government* (*imperium paternale*) is the greatest conceivable *despotism* (constitution which does away with all the freedom of the subjects who thereafter have no rights). For it treats the subjects like minor children who cannot distinguish between what is truly useful or damaging to them, are forced to behave passively and are to know the way they should be happy only from the head of state and . . . his beneficence." The principle of happiness results in evil not only in morals, but also in the law of the state [*Staatsrecht*] whenever the sovereign, who wants to make the people happy according to his taste, becomes a despot. Kant fears that superpowers under one head of state could endanger freedom and bring about the "most terrible despotism."[147] In 1795 he opposes the consolidation of states under a universal monarchy, a "soulless despotism" that, "having exterminated the seeds of the good, ends up in anarchy." This "despotism (on the cemetary of freedom)" leads to a "weaken-

142. *Frieden,* 8:373.

143. As to the definition: "Der Republikanism ist das Staatsprincip der Absonderung der ausführenden Gewalt (der Regierung) von der gesetzgebenden; der Despotism ist das der eigenmächtigen Vollziehung des Staats von Gesetzen, die er selbst gegeben hat, mithin der öffentliche Wille, sofern er von dem Regenten als sein Privatwille gehandhabt wird" (*Frieden,* 8:352). "Eine Regierung, die zugleich gesetzgebend wäre, würde despotisch zu nennen sein im Gegensatz mit der patriotischen, unter welcher aber nicht eine väterliche (*regimen paternale*), als die am meisten despotische unter allen (Bürger als Kinder zu behandeln), sondern vaterländische (*regimen civitatis et patriae*) verstanden wird, wo der Staat selbst (*civitas*) seine Unterthanen zwar gleichsam als Glieder einer Familie, doch zugleich als Staatsbürger, d.i. nach Gesetzen ihrer eignen Selbstständigkeit, behandelt, jeder sich selbst besitzt und nicht vom absoluten Willen eines Anderen neben oder über ihm abhängt" (*Rechtslehre,* 6:316–17). Kant distinguishes the mechanism under despotic compulsory laws from a legal compulsion that exists only on account of principles of freedom. (*Frieden,* 8:374).

144. *Gesch.in weltb.A.,* 8:24–25.

145. *Anf.d.Menschengesch.,* 8:120.

146. *Krit.d.U.,* 5:364.

147. *Gemeinspruch,* 8:291, 302, 311.

ing of all forces." Kant regrets that despotising [*despotisierende*] . . . moralists often act against reason of state by too hastily made or praised measures.[148] Two years later he remarks that despotism cannot be hidden and can be discovered in the means a minister uses.[149] In 1798 Kant denounces the assertion that England enjoys constitutional restrictions of the monarch as hypocritical and claims that the English king is an absolute monarch.[150]

Kant goes on to condemn particular manifestations of despotism. He mentions the "spiritual despotism which can be found in all established churches, irrespective of how modest and popular they make themselves appear."[151] It also can be found in the state. A constitution that demands subordination under church statutes is always despotic, be it monarchical, aristocratic, or democratic in form. "Wherever statutes of the faith are considered part of constitutional law [*Constitutionalgesetz*], there is a rule by the *clergy*. They believe that they can do without reason and even a learned knowledge of the scriptures because, as the only authorized preservers and interpreters of the will of the invisible lawgiver they have to exclusively administer the articles of faith and, with that power, may *only order,* not convince."[152] In 1795 Kant considers democracy a form of state that is of necessity despotic: "Among the three forms of state that of *democracy* in the genuine understanding of the word is necessarily *a despotism.* For it establishes an executive power through which all rule over, and in all cases also against, one (who does not agree with them). Therefore all, who, however, are not all, decide: the general will contradicting itself and freedom." The despotism under the rule of one is the most bearable despotism. Kant opposes the opinion that one ought not to have high titles for a monarch, such as "Godly anointed," or "administrator of God's will on earth." "It is absolutely wrong to think that they make the ruler conceited. If he has brains (something one surely ought to take for granted), they must humiliate him to his soul. For he will think about having taken an office that is too great for a man and is the holiest thing God has on earth, namely, to administer *justice to men* [*das Recht der Menschen*]. He always will worry over having hurt that apple of the eye of God just a little too much."[153] On the other hand, Kant also says of the "*Autokrator*" or "*self-ruler,*" of him "who possesses *all* power," that he is, as the most simple form of government in the handling of the law, probably "the best, but, with respect to *justice* itself, probably the most

148. *Frieden,* 8:367, 373.

149. *Rechtslehre,* 6:319. Kant here sees in despotism a means of maintaining the laws and considers the belief that through their deputies the people curtail the power of the monarch, something blinding, "Blendwerk." Cf. also ibid., 322.

150. *Streit,* 7:90.

151. *Religion,* 6:175. Für Kant, "der schwärmerische Religionswahn" is "der moralische Tod der Vernunft, ohne die doch gar keine Religion, als welche wie alle Moralität überhaupt auf Grundsätze gegründet werden muß, statt finden kann."

152. Ibid., 6:180.

153. *Frieden,* 8:352–53.

dangerous for the people because this form of government very much invites despotism."[154] At the end of the *Anthropology* we read, following the remark that freedom and law are the linchpins around which bourgeois lawmaking turns, that for the law to be effective and not just an empty program praised to the audience, there also must be a power which, tied to freedom and law, assures the success of these principles. Kant considers four combinations of freedom, law, and power. In an anarchy, there are law and freedom without power; in a despotism, law and power without freedom; under barbarism, power without freedom and law; in a republic, power with freedom and law. Only the last combination deserves "to be called a true bourgeois constitution."[155]

Kant's emphasis upon a "true bourgeois constitution" at the end of his life's work indicates its importance to him.[156] Other references to this can be found earlier and they recur. Whenever Kant speaks of a bourgeois constitution, he generally has in mind a republican one, which he considers the true bourgeois constitution. But he did not explicitly state that only a republican constitution qualifies as a true bourgeois constitution.

Kant often speaks of the republican constitution. It is his favorite form of government, the right opposite to anarchy, despotism, and barbarism. It restricts the freedom of the individual as well as that of the government of the state, through laws. Kant's desire for a limitation of the state is evident when he speaks quite generally of a bourgeois constitution of society. In sentence eight of his *Idea for a Universal History,* he mentions, after having denounced undue interferences by absolute governments, "*enlightenment* as a great good which mankind must apply to its rulers' egoistic intentions of aggrandizement. Enlightenment and with it a certain disposition of the heart which cannot be avoided by the enlightened man who completely understands what is good, will gradually spread to the throne and even influence principles of government."[157] A year later Kant suggests that the real purpose of destiny is a constitution of a state, according to the principles of human rights, which leaves no doubt that it is binding upon the rulers. It would bring about an "always continuing and growing activity and culture."[158] In 1793 Kant emphasizes that the people possess "rights vis-à-vis the head of state they cannot lose."[159] Two years later he warns that it would be wrong to see in the "true sentence *fiat iustitia, pereat mundus* a permission to use one's own right with the greatest rigor, for this would be incompatible with one's ethical duty."

154. *Rechtslehre,* 6:339.

155. *Anthropologie,* 7:330–31. See also *Rechtslehre,* 6:354.

156. Cf. Carl J. Friedrich, *Inevitable Peace* (Cambridge, Mass., 1948), 41; Jaspers, *Die grossen Philosophen,* 546 ff.; Charles W. Hendel, "Freedom, Democracy, and Peace," in Charles W. Hendel, ed., *The Philosophy of Kant and Our Modern World* (New York, 1957), 110, referring to *Kritik der reinen Vernunft, B373–374.*

157. *Gesch.in weltb.A.,* 8:27–28.

158. *Herder,* 8:64.

159. *Gemeinspruch,* 8:303.

Rather, that sentence implies an "obligation of those in power not to refuse, out of dislike or compassion, to anybody his right against others or to reduce that right. . . . This is best secured by a constitution of the state made according to pure principles of law."[160] In 1797 Kant writes that the state must treat its subjects "as state citizens, i.e., according to laws securing their independence." Although the ruler has "no (compulsory) duties" toward the subjects to the fulfillment of which he can be forced, he has duties nevertheless. The sovereign does not have "the right to lead his subjects into war as if it was a hunt and into a battle as if it was an amusement party." Man, especially the citizen, always must be considered a fellow-legislator, "not just as a means, but as an end." Therefore, he "freely must assent through his representatives to the conduct of war as well as to every particular declaration of war. . . . Only under this condition can the state require him to perform dangerous service." "This right derives from the *duty* of the sovereign toward the people (not vice versa). The latter must be assumed to have consented. Although the people are passive and suffer to be ordered around, they also are active and sovereign."[161]

In 1798 Kant writes that the government considers it beneath its dignity to be concerned with scholarly disputes—a clear assertion of academic freedom. He hails a development that "at long last prepares for the elimination of all restrictions upon the freedom of public judgments by arbitrary government." He regrets that in Great Britain people no longer care about finding "the true constitution because it is assumed to already exist. Dishonest publicity deceives the people telling them that they enjoy a monarchy limited by laws of their own making, whereas the truth of the matter is that the people's deputies having been bribed, have subjected them to an *absolute monarch*."[162] The bourgeois constitution is based upon the principle of freedom which is binding upon the ruler.[163] Only a constitution based upon the principles of freedom can last.[164] Kant connects the bourgeois constitution with the *respublica*.[165]

In a similar fashion, he emphasizes the subordination of rulers to a republican constitution. In 1795 he warns readers not to confound the republican constitution with the democratic one. Like autocracy and aristocracy, democracy only tells us who rules. It does not say anything about the nature of ruling. The way "the state uses its omnipotence" either is "*republican* or *despotic*." "*Republicanism* is the principle of separating the executive power (of the government) from the legislative. Despotism exists if laws are executed by those who made them, if the public will is handled by the regent as his private will." The republican constitution is "the only one which completely corresponds to human rights [*dem Recht der Menschen*]," that is, one under which the ruler is bound to respect those rights. "A state also can already *rule* itself in a republican fashion although according to its present constitution it possesses

160. *Frieden,* 8:378–79.
161. *Rechtslehre,* 6:317, 345–46.
162. *Streit,* 7:34, 90.
163. *Anthropologie,* 7:328.
164. *Frieden,* 8:373.
165. *Streit,* 7:91.

despotic *power.* It can do so until people gradually become able to feel the impact of the authority of the law (as if it possessed physical power) and thereafter are considered capable of passing their own legislation (which has its original source in the law)." Here again, the subordination of the government under *Gesetz* and *Recht* is stressed. Similarly, Kant's comment on the problem of reason of state explains: "It is uncertain whether the people for a long time can be kept obedient and, at the same time, in abundance through severeness, or the temptation of vanity, or the supreme power of one individual, perhaps even just by means of a nobility in the king's service or by popular power within the state. . . . Throughout history, all forms of government have offered examples to the contrary." The only exception is the "genuine republican one, which, however can cross the mind of a moral politician only,"[166] obviously because he considers himself bound by the laws and refrains from Machiavellian methods.

In 1797 Kant proposes that "the *letter* [*littera*] of original lawmaking in a bourgeois state" serve the "*spirit*" of the original contract establishing a bourgeois society. "If a society cannot do so at once, it gradually and continually must change the *kind of government* so as to bring it, at least with respect to its effect, in line with the only legitimate constitution, namely, that of a pure republic. Furthermore, society must see to it that old empirical (statutory) forms which only brought about the *subjection* of the people, get transformed into the original (rational) form which has *freedom* alone for its principle, even as the condition of all *compulsion* necessary under a legitimate constitution, . . . and in the end will literally bring about such a constitution.—The only permanent constitution of a state is one where the *law* alone rules and is not dependent upon any one particular person; the final purpose of all public law is the state in which each can *peremptorily* be given his own."[167]

In 1798 Kant emphasizes: "To *rule* autocratically and yet to *govern* in a republican way, i.e., in the spirit of republicanism or in analogy to it, makes people content with their constitution." A little later, he speaks of the duty of monarchs to govern in a republican (not a democratic) fashion, much as they may rule *autocratically.*" That duty requires that people be treated according to principles which are in conformity with the spirit of laws on freedom [*Freiheitsgesetze*], which a mature people would give themselves.[168]

The government ought to be subject to laws to which the people consented. In 1795 Kant defines "external (legal) *freedom*" as "the right to obey only those laws to which I have been able to consent." Under a republican constitution—he praises the "honesty of its origin, its having sprung from the pure fountain of the concept of law"—it is imperative that the citizens are asked whether or not there should be war.[169] When Kant expresses the same

166. *Frieden,* 8:352–53, 366, 372, 377.
167. *Rechtslehre,* 6:340–41.
168. *Streit,* 7:87, 91.
169. *Frieden,* 8:350, 351.

idea speaking of bourgeois constitutions, he probably has republican ones in mind. Already in 1793 he writes that the citizen is a colegislator. "All who can vote," the majority of the individuals in the state, "must agree upon the law of public justice." For those who are not enfranchised he recommends "the principle to put up with that majority as if it were there by general consent, i.e., by a contract as the supreme basis of a bourgeois constitution." This contract is "an *original contract* on which alone a bourgeois, i.e., really legal, constitution can be founded among men and a community established." It is "a coalition of each particular and private will to form a common and public will." It is "a *mere idea* of reason, which however, has its undoubted (practical) reality. It binds every legislator to make laws as if they *could* have sprung from the united will of a whole people. It looks upon each subject, insofar as he wants to be a citizen, as if he agreed to that will, for this is the test of the justness of each public law. It is not just . . . if it is *impossible* that all the people *could* have agreed to it."[170]

In 1797 Kant distinguishes state-citizens from state-fellowmen [*Staatsbürger* from *Staatsgenossen*]. He emphasizes that positive laws made by the former must not deprive the latter of the opportunity to achieve citizenship. He speaks of a general ruler "who, according to the laws of freedom, can only be the united people itself."[171] Shortly thereafter we read that "whatever the whole people cannot decide concerning itself, the lawmaker cannot decide over the people."[172] Kant adds the principle: "Whatever the people (the whole mass of subjects) cannot decide concerning the rule over itself and its component parts, the sovereign cannot either." He speaks of the "citizen of the state . . . who within the state must be considered a member participating in lawmaking."[173]

In 1798 Kant again emphasizes that man, a being blessed with freedom, in the awareness of his freedom can demand for the people to which he belongs a government in which people can participate in lawmaking. One should strive "toward a constitution which cannot want war, namely, a republican one. It may be republican even in the form of the state [*Staatsform*] or only in the *kind of government* [*Regierungsart*]. In the latter case, characterized by monarchy, the state is administered in analogy to the laws." The idea of a constitution that reflects the natural rights of man is that all those who obey the law are cooperating in making the laws.[174]

For Kant, the fact that those who obey the laws also make laws does not necessarily imply direct democracy. In 1793 he writes that in a large nation those voting would not agree to laws directly but only through their representatives.[175] Four years later he mentions that the people possess legislative

170. *Gemeinspruch,* 8:294, 296–97, see also 299.
171. *Rechtslehre,* 6:315.
172. Ibid., 6:327.
173. Ibid., 6:329, 345–46.
174. *Streit,* 7:87–88, 90–91.
175. *Gemeinspruch,* 8:296.

power through their deputies. He speaks of the representatives of the people in parliament and jury.[176]

Aside from this kind of representation, Kant refers to representation in connection with the separation of powers as a characteristic feature of republicanism. "*Republicanism* is the state-principle [*Staatsprinzip*] of separating the executive power (of the government) from the legislative one. Despotism exists if the state itself executes the laws it made, if the regent handles the public will as if it were his private will. . . . Every form of government which is not *representative* actually is an *unform* [*Unform*] because the legislator can also be the executor." A republicanism characterized by this kind of representation is found in monarchies rather than aristocracies. It does not exist in a democracy, which is a despotism. While Kant admits that autocracy and aristocracy could be despotic, "it is at least possible that they adopt a government which is representative in spirit. For instance, Frederick II at least *said* that he was only the first servant of the state. . . . This attitude is impossible in a democracy because all desire to be master."[177] Kant maintains that the decrease of the number of rulers increases the possibility of republicanism.[178]

About the separation of powers we read: "Each state contains three *powers,* i.e., the general unified will exists in a triune person (*trias politica*): *the ruling power* (sovereignty) of the legislator, the *executive power* of the government (in accordance with the laws) and the *judiciary power* (giving to each his own according to the law) in the person of the judge (*potestas legislatoria, rectoria et iudiciaria*)." He adds: "All three powers in the state are dignified . . . *state-dignities* [*Staatswürden*]."[179] They are "moral persons" and as

176. *Rechtslehre,* 6:319, 322, 317. Siehe auch *Streit,* 7:90.

177. *Frieden,* 8:352–53.

178. Ibid., 8:353: "Man kann daher sagen: je kleiner das Personale der Staatsgewalt (die Zahl der Herrscher), je größer dagegen die Repräsentation derselben, desto mehr stimmt die Staatsverfassung zur Möglichkeit des Republikanism, und sie kann hoffen, durch allmähliche Reformen sich dazu endlich zu erheben. Aus diesem Grunde ist es in der Aristokratie schon schwerer als in der Monarchie, in der Demokratie aber unmöglich anders als durch gewaltsame Revolution zu dieser einzigen vollkommen rechtlichen Verfassung zu gelangen. Es ist aber an der Regierungsart . . . dem Volk ohne alle Vergleichung mehr gelegen, als an der Staatsform (wiewohl auch auf dieser ihre mehrere oder mindere Angemessenheit zu jenem Zwecke sehr viel ankommt). Zu jener aber, wenn sie dem Rechtsbegriffe gemäß sein soll, gehört das repräsentative System, in welchem allein eine republikanische Regierungsart möglich, ohne welches sie (die Verfassung mag sein, welche sie wolle) despotisch und gewaltthätig ist.—Keine der alten sogenannten Republiken hat dieses gekannt, und sie mußten sich darüber auch schlechterdings in dem Despotism auflösen, der unter der Obergewalt eines Einzigen noch der erträglichste unter allen ist."

179. *Rechtslehre,* 6:315. We read further: "Sie enthalten das Verhältniß eines allgemeinen Oberhaupts (der, nach Freiheitsgesetzen betrachtet, kein Anderer als das vereinigte Volk selbst sein kann) zu der vereinzelten Menge ebendesselben als Unterthans, d.i. des Gebietenden (*imperans*) gegen den Gehorsamenden (*subditus*)." On page 316 Kant continues: "Von diesen Gewalten, in ihrer Würde betrachtet, wird es heißen: der Wille des Gesetzgebers (*legislatoris*) in Ansehung dessen, was das äußere Mein und Dein betrifft, ist untadelig (irreprehensibel), das Ausführungs-Vermögen des Oberbefehlshabers (*summi rectoris*) unwiderstehlich (irre-

such are coordinated—"(*potestas coordinatae*), one complementing the other for the sake of the completion (*complementum ad sufficientiam*) of the state constitution." On the other hand they "also are *subordinated* (*subordinatae*) in order that one may not usurp the function of another one it aids, but have its own principle."[180] By means of the three powers the state forms and sustains itself according to the laws of freedom.[181]

Aside from the institutional division of powers, Kant mentions a natural pluralism, characteristic of republicanism and legally protecting the individual from the power of the state. The republican constitution is "the only one completely adequate to the rights of men. It also is the most difficult to achieve and, even more so, to sustain. Therefore, many people assert that it must be a state of *angels* because men with their egoistic inclinations are not able to live under a constitution with such a sublime form." The good organization of the state which can be achieved by men, opposes the egoistic inclinations and forces so "that the one halts or destroys the destructive effects of the other. Thus reason succeeds in that both appear to be non-existent and man is forced to be a good citizen although not necessarily a morally good individual."[182]

Egoistic inclinations are apparent in economic life. Kant favors a free economy under laws that restrain arbitrary state interferences. In 1786 he favors a "legal constitution which secures everybody's freedom by the laws. The individual is free to seek his happiness as he sees fit as long as he does not interfere with that general freedom which protects the rights of others." Laws seeking the citizens' wealth secure the state of law, especially against foreign enemies.[183] "A credit system infinitely increasing debts which, however, can always be paid back (because all creditors will not want to be satisfied at the same time), invented by a trading nation during this century, makes good sense." Kant praises the *spirit of trade* which cannot exist in times of war and which sooner or later will take hold of every people. He states that "among all means subordinated to the power of the state, the *power of money* is probably the most reliable."[184] In 1797 Kant writes that legal theory leaves it up to everybody's arbitrary will to set the aims for his own activities as long as his freedom can exist side by side with that of others according to general law.[185] In the *Dispute of the Faculties* Kant sides with the Frenchman who proposed laissez-faire and thus stresses the limits of state power and state regulations.[186] In the *Anthropology* we read that "since only public, not private, life can be reproached for luxury, the relationship of the citizen to the community with respect to free enterprise . . . should not really be burdened by prohibitions of spending." The invention of checks, banks, and lotteries as well as the freedom

sistibel) und der Rechtsspruch des obersten Richers (*supremi iudicis*) unabänderlich (inappellabel)." Ibid., 6:316.

180. Ibid., 6:316.
181. Ibid., 6:318.
182. *Frieden,* 8:366.
183. *Gemeinspruch,* 8:298.
184. *Frieden,* 8:345, 368.
185. *Tugendlehre,* 6:382.
186. *Streit,* 7:19–20.

the Gondolieri and Lazzaroni enjoy toward higher classes are considered good aspects of the Italians.[187]

The Necessity of State Law

In spite of his fear of state regulations Kant assigns to the state a number of functions.

Although he sees in the separation of powers an important means for the protection of the individual from the state, he emphasizes that it must not undermine governmental authority. Together, the three powers constitute the "*good* [*Heil*] of the state, not to be understood as the *welfare* of the citizens and their *happiness,* for that perhaps (as Rousseau would have it) can exist much more conveniently and in a more desirable fashion in the state of nature or under a despotic government. Rather, it is to be understood as the greatest harmony of the constitution with legal principles reason compels us to strive for *through a categorical imperative.*"[188] The three powers may check each other, but may not sabotage the constitution much as it may provide, for the sake of the freedom of the individual, for checks and balances. The three powers, which "derive from the concept of a *community* (*res publica latius dicta*) are only so many relationships of the united will of the people deriving *a priori* from reason and a pure idea of a head of state possessing objective reality."[189]

For the sake of the community, the authority of the republican government must not fall prey to pluralism. Already in 1786 Kant speaks of community [*Geselligkeit*] as the "greatest aim of human destiny."[190] "*Salus publica suprema civitatis lex est*" he writes in 1793 and emphasizes that the "*first* consideration" ought to be given to the public weal.[191] In spite of his fight for a strong position of the individual Kant has doubts about egoism. He remarks that "not every purpose (for example, not that favoring one's own happiness), is moral, but only the unegoistic one. . . . Therefore, what motivates man as a result of the idea of the highest good that can be achieved in the world through his collaboration, is not his own happiness. It is that idea itself, its pursuit as a duty. For that idea does not imply the prospect of happiness per se, but only a proportion between it and the dignity of the subject." Making up one's mind accordingly is "not *egoistic.*"[192] Two years later Kant criticizes the destructive effects of egoistic inclinations in a "people of devils." He denounces the "*political moralist* . . . who adjusts his morals so that they further the advantages of the statesman," who flatters rulers in order to seek his private advantage and who sacrifices the people and possibly the whole world. Kant in one breath

187. *Anthropologie,* 7:250, 317.

188. *Rechtslehre,* 6:318.

189. Ibid., 6:338. Carl Schmitt, *Verfassungslehre* (München und Leipzig, 1928), 182, speaks of a distinction of the powers.

190. *Anf.d.Menschengesch.,* 8:110.

191. *Gemeinspruch,* 8:298.

192. Ibid., 8:279–80.

speaks with contempt of the "egoistic inclination of men" which is not based upon maxims of reason and of the "untruthful and treacherous, but nevertheless intellectualizing [*vernünftelnden*] bad principle which in a deceptive manner justifies all transgressions from the weakness of human nature."[193] In the *Dispute of the Faculties* Kant mentions "black sheep . . . which because of their egoism can be found in every herd." He makes plain that a moral character is one from which egoism is absent, that "true enthusiasm always is directed toward *what is ideal* and toward the purely moral . . . and cannot be grafted upon egoism."[194] The *Anthropology,* under a heading "On Egoism," critically describes the various types of egoism. To Kant, a game is "a means of acquisition . . . establishing a certain convention of egoism to chat with the greatest politeness and elevating a total egoism . . . to a principle." At the end of that work he quotes Frederick the Great who spoke of "*cette maudite race à laquelle nous appartenons,*" and writes that the evil in man derives from egoism.[195] Men are not as pure as angels.[196] Earlier Kant had juxtaposed angels to "men with their egoistic inclinations,"[197] and stated that only unegoistic acts are moral.

Given these rejections of egoism it is not surprising that Kant, for the sake of individuals and society, permits certain governmental controls and activities. In 1784 he distinguishes between the acts of men in their capacity as scholars and as state officials. The former must be free, the latter can be regulated.[198] He warns of the individual's abuse of freedom, of a presumptuous confidence in the independence of their ability [*Vermögens*] from all restrictions. Authorities can curtail *Freigeisterei.*[199] Kant favors a public law [*Gesetz*] "which determines for all what they can, and cannot, do," the "act of a public will from which all law [*Recht*] derives and which therefore cannot be unjust to anybody." For the purpose of war, the government can tax the subjects. It can restrict their freedom to buy through import prohibitions.[200] State "restrictions, recruitments, etc.," are permitted as long as they equally distribute

193. *Frieden,* 8:372, 379.

194. *Streit,* 7:85–86. Thinking of the French Revolution, he continues on p. 86: "Durch Geldbelohnungen konnten die Gegner der Revolutionirenden zu dem Eifer und der Seelengröße nicht gespannt werden, den der bloße Rechtsbegriff in ihnen hervorbrachte, und selbst der Ehrbegriff des alten kriegerischen Adels (ein Analogon des Enthusiasm) verschwand vor den Waffen derer, welches das Recht des Volks, wozu sie gehörten, ins Auge gefaßt hatten . . . und sich als Beschützer desselben dachten."

195. *Anthropologie,* 7:332–33.

196. Ibid., 7:332.

197. *Frieden,* 8:366.

198. *Aufklärung,* 8:37–38. Also *Streit,* 7:18–19, 23 ff., 34. On page 33, Kant writes: "Denn statutarische Vorschriften der Regierung in Ansehung der öffentlich vorzutragenden Lehren werden immer sein müssen, weil die unbeschränkte Freiheit, alle seine Meinungen ins Publicum zu schreien, theils der Regierung, theils aber auch diesem Publicum selbst gefährlich werden müßte."

199. *Denken orient.,* 8:146.

200. *Gemeinspruch,* 8:294, 297–98.

the burdens. The state can abolish statutes permitting corporations, estates, and orders to leave real estate for the exclusive use of coming generations as long as it compensates the survivors.[201] "For the sake of the survival of the state there also is . . . its right of *inspection* (*ius inspectionis*) so that no association which can influence the *public* weal of society (*publicum*) can be kept secret (from the illumination by the state or by religion) and must make public its constitution if requested to do so by the police." In emergencies the police, authorized by a higher authority, may search private homes. "If the subject commits a crime and his presence spoils the communal life for fellow-subjects and the state," the sovereign has "the right to *banish* . . . i.e., to *deport,*" as well as to exile (*ius exilii*).[202] To protect the eyes of the people, the police should regulate the printing of books.[203] Kant considers the *Aufwandgesetze* passed by some countries, wise.[204]

Aside from desiring restrictions on individuals for the sake of the public good, Kant favors an active role for the state. In 1784 he regrets that "our rulers of the world until now have had no money to spare for public institutions of learning and, generally speaking, for anything that concerns the good of the world."[205] He writes that through armament, "the maternal care of the state for some people is transformed into a merciless hardship of demands" but considers armament justified because of threats from abroad.[206] In 1793 he justifies war taxes, even oppressive ones.[207] Two years later he opposes standing armies, but favors a periodical military drill of the citizens "in order to safeguard themselves and the fatherland from external attacks." The state can go into debt to aid "the land's economy (improving roads, new settlements, building magazines as safeguards against the threat of bad harvests, etc.)." The money may come from inside the country itself or from abroad.[208] In 1795 Kant writes that the state has the duty and the right to take care that "there is no want of scholars and men of good morals for the administration of the church system."[209] He mentions rights of governmental agencies concerned with the economy of the state, financial matters, and the police. The latter takes care of "public *security, leisureliness* and *decency.*" Kant continues: As a man who has taken over the duty of the people, "the supreme commander, possesses the *indirect* right to burden the people for the sake of their own maintenance by exacting tributes from them for the care of the *poor,* of *foundlings* and *churches,* otherwise known as mild or pious foundations."[210] The sovereign has the right to promote the immigration and settlement of foreigners.[211] In 1798 Kant writes that the government can provide for the eternal bourgeois and

201. *Rechtslehre,* 6:319, 324.
202. Ibid., 6:338.
203. *Streit,* 7:115.
204. *Anthropologie,* 7:209.
205. *Gesch.in weltb.A.,* 8:28.
206. *Anf.d.Menschengesch.,* 8:121.
207. *Gemeinspruch,* 8:297–98.
208. *Frieden,* 8:345.
209. *Religion,* 6:113.
210. *Rechtslehre,* 6:325–26.
211. Ibid., 6:338.

sanitary welfare of everybody by creating faculties of theology, law, and medicine. As to religion, the state may have an interest in regulating teaching so that it may have useful citizens, good soldiers, and, generally, faithful subjects. The government acts wisely by promoting the use of the Bible, "that great means of leading people," in order to further "their unity and tranquility in a state." In the end Kant regrets, as he did earlier, that the state has no money to spare for paying good teachers. Education has no coherence if it is not "designed, established and consistently maintained according to a considered plan of the supreme state power. This probably implies that from time to time the state reform itself and constantly seek progress, trying evolution instead of revolution."[212]

The state is important for the execution of the laws and the maintenance of law and order. Already in 1784 Kant writes that "a completely *just bourgeois constitution*" is "a society in which there can be found *freedom under external laws* to the greatest possible degree combined with irresistible force." He continues: "Generally much in favor of unlimited freedom, men are compelled to enter into this state of compulsion by need, to be more exact, by the greatest of all needs, one inflicted by men upon each other because due to their inclinations they cannot peacefully live in wild freedom for long."[213] In his review of Herders' ideas Kant emphasizes the state's importance for order. He considers "a state constitution ordered according to concepts of human rights" the proper aim of destiny in contrast to a "shadowy picture of happiness which everybody makes for himself."[214] In 1793 he writes of the authority of the state to enforce obedience to public laws. Kant calls "the power in the state which gives effect to the laws . . . *irresistible.* There is no legally existing commonwealth without such a power, putting down all internal resistance, occurring according to a maxim which, if made a general one, would destroy the whole bourgeois constitution and eliminate the state without which men cannot possess any rights."[215] In his treatise on eternal peace Kant denounces the lawless, rabid freedom of wild people and distinguishes it from the rational freedom under the legal compulsion of the state through public law. Kant speaks of the "idea of the authority of the law (as if it possessed physical force)." Concepts of reason demand "a legal compulsion according to principles of freedom . . . which alone make possible a rightfully existing constitution of a state." The evil in men is "veiled by the compulsion of bourgeois laws because the citizens' inclination to hurt each other is forcefully counteracted by the still greater power of the government and . . . the outbreak of illegal inclinations is

212. *Streit,* 7:60, 68, 93.

213. *Gesch.in weltb.A.,* 8:22.

214. *Herder,* 8:64.

215. *Gemeinspruch,* 8:299. On page 305: "Es muß in jedem gemeinen Wesen ein Gehorsam unter dem Mechanismus der Staatsverfassung nach Zwangsgesetzen (die aufs Ganze gehen), aber zugleich ein Geist der Freiheit sein, da jeder in dem, was allgemeine Menschenpflicht betrifft, durch Vernunft überzeugt zu sein verlangt, daß dieser Zwang rechtmäßig sei, damit er nicht mit sich selbst in Widerspruch gerathe."

checked." The "true sentence, *fiat iustitia, pereat mundus*" is understood "as a duty of those in power not to deny or decrease anybody's right vis-à-vis others out of disfavor or compassion."[216] In 1797 Kant says there is a state of lawlessness if in a legal dispute no competent judge can be found to render a valid verdict. The state exercises important functions through its branches of government, the ruling one by the legislator, the executive one by the government, the judicial one by the judge. "There are three powers (*potestas legislatoria, executoria, iudiciaria*) which give the state (*civitas*) its autonomy whereby it forms and maintains itself following the laws of freedom." The state must strictly execute criminal laws according to the principle of retribution (*ius talionis*), including capital punishment. "Even if the bourgeois society, with the consent of all its members, would dissolve (for instance, people inhabiting an island decide to part company to disperse all over the world), it would be necessary to first execute the last murderer in jail so that everybody would get what his deeds deserve. Otherwise the people, not having insisted on this punishment, would be guilty of participating in a public violation of justice and be burdened with having spilled blood [*Blutschuld*]. . . . Death must be suffered by all those who murdered and ordered or participated in murder. This is required by justice as ideal of judicial power according to general, *a priori* established laws." Among all rights of the sovereign, Kant considers that of granting pardons the most slippery one. The sovereign does not possess that right with respect to a crime committed by one subject against another. In that case, "impunity (*impunitas criminis*) is the greatest injustice." He can use it only if he himself is hurt (*crimen laesae maiestatis*). Even then he cannot do so if impunity would be detrimental to the security of the people. Whereas in a "pure republic" freedom is the principle and condition of compulsion, the latter nevertheless is "necessary for a legal constitution in the proper sense of the state."[217] At the end of his *Anthropology* Kant once again makes plain the necessity of state power when he depicts power as something that secures the success of freedom and the law.[218]

Conclusion

Kant's opinions on liberalism show him as a man of measure.[219]

His remarks on the execution of the laws indicate that he condemns revolts against the power of the state. The fighter against despotism is also opposed to revolution.[220] When, in 1784, Kant desires the emancipation of the people

216. *Frieden,* 8:354, 371, 372, 374, 375, 378–79.

217. *Rechtslehre,* 6:312, 313, 318, 333, 334, 337, 340.

218. *Anthropologie,* 7:330.

219. Vgl. Otto Friedrich Bollnow, *Mass und Vermessenheit des Menschen* (Göttingen, 1962).

220. Cf. Hendel, "Freedom, Democracy, and Peace," 95 ff.; Beck, "Kant and the Right of Revolution," in *La philosophie politique de Kant,* 171 ff.

from absolutism, he leaves no doubt that it has to evolve gradually. "A revolution may end personal despotism and an oppression out for personal gain and power. It will never truly reform thinking. New prejudices, as well as the old ones, will serve as guidelines for the senseless big crowd."[221] In 1793 Kant favors the suppression of all internal resistance by the state.[222] He remarks that if the revolutions by which Switzerland, the Netherlands, or Great Britain achieved their now happily praised constitutions, had failed, the readers of the history of these revolutions would see in the execution of their now so much praised instigators nothing but the deserved punishment of great criminals who committed crimes against the state."[223] Two years later he writes: "Should the vehemence of a *revolution,* generated by a bad constitution, illegally have led to a more legitimate constitution, it would no longer be permissible to lead the people back to the old regime, although during that regime everybody trying through violence or cunning to overthrow it would rightfully have been subject to the penalty of sedition."[224] In a word, even against a constitution resulting from a revolution, there is no right of revolution. Kant asks whether sedition is a lawful means people can use in order to shake off an oppressive tyrant. He admits that the rights of the people are hurt under such a ruler and that the latter would not suffer injustice if he was deposed. "Nevertheless, the subjects would act highly illegally if they sought their right that way and could not complain of being treated unjustly if they were punished severely after being defeated in that struggle.[225] In the treatise on the metaphysical beginnings of legal theory we read: "The origin of the supreme power is, for practical purposes, *inscrutable* for the people living under that power. That is, the subject *must not* go about to *strain his reason* [*werkthätig vernünfteln*] as to that origin with a view of finding out whether the right of that power to demand his obedience was a dubious one (*ius controversum*). The sentence, "all authority derives from God" implies "the obligation to obey the presently existing legislative power, be its origin what it may." Even if a regent acted against the laws, "the subject may answer this injustice with *complaints* (*gravamina*), but not with resistance." The constitution must not contain a provision enabling a power within the state to oppose the supreme commander if he transgresses the constitution.[226] "There is, therefore, no legal resistance of the people against the supreme legislator of the state; for a state of law is possible only by virtue of subordination to his general legislative will. There is thus no right of *sedition* (*seditio*), even less one of *rebellion* (*rebellio*). The least of all can it be permitted to act against him as a single person (monarch) under the pretense of an abuse of his power (*tyrannis*), by *seizing* his person, or even taking his life (*mon-*

221. Aufklärung, 8:36. Earlier, Kant writes of the possibility, even inevitability, that people enlighten themselves.

222. *Gemeinspruch,* 8:299.

223. Ibid., 8:301.

224. *Frieden,* 8:372–73.

225. Ibid., 8:382.

226. *Rechtslehre,* 6:318, 319.

archomachismus sub specie tyrannicidii). The slightest attempt to do so is *high treason* (*proditio eminens*). A traitor of this kind, being one who tries to *kill his fatherland,* must be punished by death."[227] A deficient state constitution can be changed only by reforms of the sovereign, not by the people through revolution. Kant again emphatically denies a right of revolution even if the existing situation results from a revolution: "If a revolution has been successful and a new constitution been founded, its illegality cannot free the subjects as good citizens from the obligation to put up with the new order. They cannot refuse to honestly obey the authority now in charge." Kant condemns the "pretense of revolutionaries . . . that the people have the right to change bad constitutions by the use of violence, that they once and for all can be unjust in order to found a more secure justice and let it prosper.[228]

A rejection of revolutions is also evident in Kant's last works. *The Dispute of the Faculties* expresses his fears that preachers and law officials will voice their objections to, and doubts about, spiritual and temporal legislation to the people and thus inveigle it against the government, "that the seed of seditions and factions will be sown and the government jeopardized." While Kant is skeptical of libelous sycophants who, thinking they are very important, consider innocent criticisms an "innovation-mania, Jacobinism and ganging" endangering the state, he warns of "revolution which always is unjust."[229] The *Anthropology* denounces the "public injustice of a revolutionary condition which has been declared legal (for example, the Committee for Public Welfare of the French Republic)." The illegal association of the rabble, the "*Rottiren* (*agere per turbas*)" is a behavior that excludes participants from state citizenship. Kant praises the Germans because among all civilized nations they are the least opposed to the established order.[230]

Kant demonstrates measure in other respects. *The Idea for a Universal History* speaks of necessary limitations of men and their freedom. Man will abuse his freedom if there is no authority above him ruling according to the laws.[231] Since the highest authority must be an embodiment of justice and yet a human being, a humble Kant considers the task of finding an ideal ruler "the most difficult of all: Yes, its complete solution is impossible: one cannot make something straight out of so crooked wood as man is made of." Nature also is moderate when it demands measure in man. Kant emphasizes that the role of

227. Ibid., 320. 228. Ibid., 6:322–23, 353.

229. *Streit,* 7:29, 34, 86–87.

230. *Anthropologie,* 7:259, 311, 317.

231. Kant considers man "ein Thier, das, wenn es unter andern seiner Gattung lebt, einen Herrn nöthig hat. Denn er mißbraucht gewiß seine Freiheit in Ansehung anderer Seinesgleichen; und ob er gleich als vernünfiges Geschöpf ein Gesetz wünscht, welches der Freiheit Aller Schranken setze: so verleitet ihn doch seine selbstsüchtige thierische Neigung, wo er darf, sich selbst auszunehmen. Er bedarf also einen Herrn, der ihm den eigenen Willen breche und ihn nöthige, einem allgemeingültigen Willen, dabei jeder frei sein kann, zu gehorchen." *Gesch.in weltb.A.,* 8:23.

man is very artificial and modest. We do not know the nature of the inhabitants of other planets. There "perhaps each individual completely achieves his destiny during his lifetime. It is different with us. Only the species can hope to do so." Kant denounces the "barbaric freedom" of states to arm for, and wage, war, as well as the resulting evils. They "force our species to find, in view of the basically good resistance of many states deriving from freedom, a law of balance and a united power which enforces that law, introducing a cosmopolitan public security for the states. That security must not be devoid of all *danger* so that men won't fall asleep but keep alert. On the other hand, it must not be without a principle of *equality* of their mutual *effect and countereffect,* so that the states won't destroy each other." Kant regrets: "We are *civilized* to a degree of being overburdened with respect to all kinds of social manners and fine behavior. But there remains much to be done to consider us *moralized.*"[232] The following year, Kant speaks of "philosophy which is achieved in the cutting rather than the growing of rampant sprouts." He warns of an "imagination lifted by metaphysics or sentiments" and favors a "reason extended in its planning, but cautious in its execution."[233] He praises the "maxims of care, impartiality and measure." He writes that there are limits to a rational use of experience, opposes intolerance[234] and speaks of "praiseworthy modesty."[235] In 1786 he criticizes the talkativeness of children and people without brains "who disturb the thinking part of the community by rattling, crying, whistling, singing and other noisy entertainments," as well as the lustfulness and dreams of "unnecessary, even unnatural inclinations under the name of luxuriance." He asks the thinking individual who, in contrast to those without thoughts is discontent with his fate, to be content. Man must not ask for too much. "It is of the greatest importance *to be content with fate* (although it has assigned us a toilsome road on this earth). We must be content in order to always have courage in spite of all adversity and blaming destiny for our misery, not lose sight of our own guilt, which perhaps is the only cause of all the evils we experience, against which we must seek help through self-improvement." Freedom can be curtailed in order to bring about a "motherly care of the state for all its members." That care, however, must not excessively result in a merciless harshness of exactions.[236] In 1786 Kant denounces "exuberant views in the name of faith upon which tradition and revelation can be grafted without the agreement of reason." Man ought not to judge if he does not know enough to render judgment. He must think, not dream. For Kant, *reiner Vernunftglaube* is "the guidepost or compass whereby the speculative thinker, roaming around in rational pursuits, can orient himself in the field of metaphysics whereas the man with a common, yet (morally) healthy reason can chart his road in theoretical as well as practical intention in a way that is completely adequate for the whole purpose of his destiny." Kant opposes the "admixture of all possible

232. Ibid., 8:23, 26.
233. *Herder,* 8:55.
234. Ibid., 8:56, 57.
235. Ibid., 8:59.
236. *Anf.d.Menschengesch.,* 8:110–11, 121.

delusions," an "arrogance transcending all boundaries," which leads Spinoza to "dreaming" [*Schwärmerei*]. If reason resents being under the law it gives to itself, it must bow to the yoke of laws given to it by someone else. Kant speaks of the measure of the law without which nothing can act for long, of the "cockiness" of the "*declared* lawlessness in thinking (a liberation from the limitations imposed by reason)," which forfeits freedom of thought. Urging measure, he adds: "Since human reason always strives for freedom, once it has broken its shackles, its first use of the long-absent freedom must degenerate in misuse and presumptuous overconfidence in the independence of its ability from all limitations."[237] In 1793 Kant favors the freedom of the pen, but "within the limits of a high esteem and love for the constitution wherein one lives and the subjects' liberal way of thinking. . . . Writers exercise self-control in order not to lose their freedom."[238] In 1794 he speaks of "incessantly growing injustice, oppression of the poor by the boisterous indulgence of the rich." He denounces "the moral decline and the fast growth of all sins together with the evils that accompany them." The "*liberal* way of thinking" is "as far from a slave's sense of submission as from the absence of all ties."[239] A year later he speaks of the duty of the moral politician "once faults are found in the constitution of a state or in the relationship among states, . . . to see to it that they are redressed as soon as possible according to natural law as it appears exemplary to us from the point of view of the idea of reason."[240] *The Dispute of the Faculties* warns that we should not expect too much of a human progress.[241] The *Anthropology* condemns an "egoism which is so excessive that it cannot conceive the genuine concept of duty." It condemns *hubris*.[242] We read: "Real understanding exists not so much on account of a great number of concepts, but rather because concepts are *adequate* to knowing the object." Kant denounces luxuriance and indulgence, distinguishing them from the good way of life, "the appropriateness of living well to communal life (–with taste)." He condemns passions.[243]

Kant is not opposed to innovation, but wants it to come about with measure. According to him, the name *Neologe* is hated for good reason, but misunderstood if believed to apply to every originator of something new. What

237. *Denken orient.*, 8:134, 136, 137, 142, 143, 145–46.

238. *Gemeinspruch*, 8:304.

239. *Ende aller Dinge*, 8:331–32, 338.

240. *Frieden*, 8:372.

241. *Streit*, 7:92–93.

242. *Anthropologie*, 7:130. On page 148 we read: "Was ist aber von dem ruhmredigen Ausspruche der Kraftmänner, der nicht auf bloßem Temperament gegründet ist, zu halten: 'Was der Mensch will, das kann er'? Er ist nichts weiter als eine hochtönende Tautologie: was er nämlich auf den Geheiß seiner moralisch-gebietenden Vernunft will, das soll er, folglich kann er es auch thun (denn das Unmögliche wird ihm die Vernunft nicht gebieten). Es gab aber vor einigen Jahren solche Gecken, die das auch im physischen Sinn von sich priesen und sich so als Weltbestürmer ankündigten, deren Rasse aber vorlängst ausgegangen ist."

243. Ibid., 7:197, 265 ff. For an exception, comp. *Rechtslehre*, 6:320.

is old is not necessarily, but usually, better.[244] Kant shows a certain skepticism toward fashion, accusing Herder of following it.[245] In 1794 he criticizes "the often self-contradictory designs for appropriate means, changed from time to time, *for making religion in a whole people at once pure and powerful,* so that one may well exclaim: Poor mortals, nothing is constant with you but inconstancy!" He humbly admits his inability to make new and happy attempts to change things and proposes to leave them the way they are and for nearly a generation have proved to be bearable.[246] In his treatise on eternal peace he opposes the destruction of a union of states before it can be replaced by a better constitution and condemns hasty amendments of a faulty confederation. However, those in power should at least believe in the maxim of the necessity of change and constantly try to make the best possible constitution under law.[247] A year later Kant favors reform, not revolution.[248] He seems to consider the French Revolution "a reform of a people's constitution."[249] He opposes the "present fashion" of bookprinters.[250] He is skeptical toward geniuses who "often go new ways and open up new prospects" and denounces "*geniusmen* (better geniusapes) [*Geniemänner* (*besser Genieaffen*)]."[251] He leaves no doubt about his condemnation of fashion.[252]

In ways that were not fashionable in his time, Kant went into new directions and opened up new prospects. His *Critique of Pure Reason* has been considered so important an innovation that ever since philosophy has been divided into pre- and post-Kantian periods. This first critique brought about a liberation of thinking. According to Kant, the faculty of philosophy, given its modesty to simply be free and let be free to find the truth for the sake of every

244. *Streit,* 7:34. In *Anthropologie,* however, Kant speaks out against customs; 7:147, 149.

245. *Herder,* 8:54.

246. *Ende aller Dinge,* 8:336–37.

247. *Frieden,* 8:372.

248. *Rechtslehre,* 6:322.

249. *Streit,* 7:88. Cf. Beck, "Kant and the Right of Revolution."

250. *Streit,* 7:115.

251. *Anthropologie,* 7:226: "Ob der Welt durch große Genies im Ganzen sonderlich gedient sei, weil sie doch oft neue Wege einschlagen und neue Aussichten eröffnen, oder ob mechanische Köpfe, wenn sie gleich nicht Epoche machten, mit ihrem alltägigen, langsam am Stecken und Stabe der Erfahrung fortschreitenden Verstande nicht das Meiste zum Wachsthum der Künste und Wissenschaften beigetragen haben (indem sie, wenn gleich keiner von ihnen Bewunderung erregte, doch auch keine Unordnung stifteten), mag hier unerörtert bleiben.—Aber ein Schlag von ihnen, Geniemänner (besser Genieaffen) genannt, hat sich unter jenem Aushängeschilde mit eingedrängt, welcher die Sprache außerordentlich von der Natur begünstigter Köpfe führt, das mühsame Lernen und Forschen für stümperhaft erklärt und den Geist aller Wissenschaft mit einem Griffe gehascht zu haben, ihn aber in kleinen Gaben concentrirt und kraftvoll zu reichen vorgiebt. Dieser Schlag ist, wie der der Quacksalber und Marktschreier den Fortschritten in wissenschaftlicher und sittlicher Bildung sehr nachtheilig, wenn er über Religion, Staatsverhältnisse und Moral gleich dem Eingeweihten oder Machthaber vom Weisheitssitze herab im entscheidenden Tone abspricht und so die Armseligkeit des Geistes zu verdecken weiß. Was ist hiewider anders zu thun, als zu lachen und seinen Gang mit Fleiß, Ordnung und Klarheit geduldig fortzusetzen, ohne auf jene Gaukler Rücksicht zu nehmen?"

252. Ibid., 7:245–46.

science [*Wissenschaft*], carries the torch leading other faculties.[253] If this statement is applied to human faculties in general, the philosophy of the bachelor of Königsberg, who toward the end of his life asserted that his never leaving that city and its neighborhood did not in the least detract from his knowledge of men and the world, can be considered one of the great liberators of humanity. In Luther people have seen, above all, a liberator from a powerful religion; in Montesquieu, one concerning politics; in Smith, one with respect to economics. Kant has been considered to be quite generally the liberator.[254] Schiller envisaged that the wealth of Kant's thinking would bear rich fruit. It has been said that Wagner's innovations led to modern music, those of Rodin, to modern sculpture, and those of Picasso, to modern painting. Perhaps it may be added that the works of all as well as other inventions were facilitated by Kant.

Kant obviously was aware of the enormous potential of his teachings. Probably never before did an author complement a work that was as liberating as the *Critique of Pure Reason* with one that was as limiting as the *Critique of Practical Reason*. The connection of the two demonstrates the togetherness of liberation and restriction and shows good measure midway in the work of the Prussian scholar.

Measure is the main feature of Kant's political thought, which deals with the freedom of the individual within the public order. When Kant spoke out, often disturbed by censorship,[255] liberalism, much as it may have been popular with some people, was officially rejected. There were many things which, as Schiller and Beethoven put it, were strictly divided by fashion. Only a few were able to enjoy freedom. Kant wrote that his contemporaries were living in an age of enlightenment, not in an enlightened age.[256] In that era, Kant, the liberator emphasizing categorical imperatives, perhaps was the political thinker of measure.

Kant lived to see the dawn of the century known as the liberal century, in which the French liberal de Tocqueville observed democracy in America about a hundred years after his compatriot Montesquieu had admired constitutional government in England. This prompts us to ask how the new world of liberalism fared in the New World of the United States. It suggests an examination of the opinions of the man often considered the father of American democracy, who lived through the first fifty years of the nation he helped to found, witnessing an enormous extension of the suffrage. Unlike the men discussed so far, Jefferson was not primarily an author of books and treatises. He was a politician, a revolutionary, a diplomat, a man in public service. Are his statements at the root of different meanings of liberalism in America and Europe?

253. *Streit,* 7:28.

254. Cf. Heinz Zimmermann, *Der Befreier* (München, 1930).

255. See *Streit,* 7:5 ff.

256. "Wenn den nun gefragt wird: Leben wir jetzt in einem aufgeklärten Zeitalter? so ist die Antwort: Nein, aber wohl in einem Zeitalter der Aufklärung." *Aufklärung,* 8:40.

CHAPTER V

ASPECTS OF JEFFERSON'S LIBERALISM

Introduction

The writings of great European liberals in the formative period of the historical movement known as liberalism show certain common beliefs. Opposing tyranny and absolutism, Montesquieu, Smith, and Kant advocated the freedom of the individual from excessive governmental restraints. Men with strong moral convictions, they favored the rule of law as an ethical minimum, binding the rulers as well as the ruled. While they emphasized the need for a restriction of governmental power, they recognized the importance of government for the preservation of peace and other services necessary for the welfare of the community. As men of measure, Montesquieu, Smith, and Kant favored a sound balance between the freedom of the individual and the power of the government.

In the following, whether the ideas expressed in the writings of Thomas Jefferson can be said to parallel those of the representative liberals in the Old World will be examined. It has been stated that the American tradition differs from that of Europe because America never experienced feudalism.[1] Does Jeffersonian liberalism differ from that of his European contemporaries who in a large measure reacted to feudalism and its aftermath, royal absolutism? Does "the Apostle of Americanism"[2] add another dimension to liberal thought because he was influenced by the American environment?

There is a certain consistency in the professional interests and lives of

1. Louis Hartz, *The Liberal Tradition in America* (New York, 1955), 3, 71–73.

2. Gilbert Chinard, *Thomas Jefferson: The Apostle of Americanism,* 2d rev. ed. (Ann Arbor, Mich., 1957).

Montesquieu, Smith, and Kant. Montesquieu held minor public offices only; he was an author on morality, freedom, and government. So were Smith and Kant, professors who lived up to their calling. But Jefferson tried his hand at many vocations. He started out as a lawyer; he was an architect who liked gadgets; the founder of a nation; a diplomat; a politician. "Probably the most widely read man of his time in America, Jefferson had a far broader range of interests—political, religious, economic, agricultural, aesthetic, and scientific—than did any other of the leaders."[3] While he was probably not better read than Montesquieu, Smith, and Kant, who are known for their literacy, he did not concentrate on any particular discipline and was engaged in more diverse activities than the Europeans who, attuned to the Old World way of life, essentially remained in a more restricted set of intellectual interests.

Jefferson's versatility may well have kept him from publishing major works. "Although a political philosopher, Jefferson never set forth his views in any formal treatise. . . . Jefferson did not write an ordered treatise on political economy. His ideas have mostly to be patched together from scattered remarks in public and private papers, each written for an occasion. For that reason many of them have assumed a form at once somewhat exaggerated and confused. His nature was markedly sanguine and affectionate. Particularly in his private letters he often expressed himself with heavy over-emphasis. It is quite unfair to treat many of these statements as though they had been deeply pondered and carefully worded for those who, unlike his friends, did not know the background of his mind and understand his mode of expression."[4]

It would be just as unfair to ignore these statements in an attempt to discover whether a liberalism similar to that of Montesquieu, Smith, and Kant

3. James Truslow Adams, *The Living Jefferson* (New York, 1936), 3. Karl Lehmann, *Thomas Jefferson, American Humanist* (New York, 1947), 9–10, writes: "Thomas Jefferson was a lawyer, politician, revolutionary, the author of the Declaration of Independence, wartime governor of his native state, writer of epoch-making bills, American minister to France, secretary of state, vice-president and, for two terms, president of the United States, founder and directing spirit of the University of Virginia. He was an assiduous farmer in the extensive manner of big eighteenth century landowners, supervising not only agriculture but also a sprawling home production of almost everything needed in a community of several hundred people. He was a great builder and creative architect, a manufacturer of nails, an enthusiastic gardener who gave much of his time to procuring plants and experimenting with them. He was a student of mathematics, an inventor of practical devices and gadgets, a naturalist, a meteorologist who made observations year after year, a collector of records about the Indians. He assembled the biggest private library in America and possibly of his age, and gave much time to its organization and cataloguing. He wrote so many letters that those hitherto published fill a score of volumes; he estimated that in one year their number amounted to twelve hundred. . . . All this is the record of only part, though a major part, of his interests and activities." See also Nathan Schachner, *Thomas Jefferson* (New York, 1951), 1:vii–ix. Cf. Eleanor Davidson Berman, *Thomas Jefferson among the Arts* (New York, 1947); William Howard Adams, *Jefferson and the Arts: an Extended View* (Washington, D.C., 1976); Frederick Doveton Nichols and Ralph E. Griswold, *Thomas Jefferson Landscape Architect* (Charlottesville, 1978); Edward T. Martin, *Thomas Jefferson: Scientist* (New York, 1952).

4. Adams, *The Living Jefferson,* 3–4.

emerges from Jefferson's writings. Sanguine and affectionate statements, while reflecting less rational thought, often reflect more ardent love. Enthusiastic comments expressed on the spur of the moment, may well contain the same ideas as those carefully reasoned and thought over. Human outbursts and outpourings are by no means of necessity less liberal than restrained, disciplined writings. And if the former occur again and again, they may demonstrate deep-seated, lifelong convictions.

Liberty

Freedom is a predominant value in Jefferson's thought.

Opposing mercantilism and favoring free trade, Adam Smith added a new dimension to English striving for freedom. Coming at a time when the American colonists were interested in independence from the mother country, his work can be considered another milestone in the evolution of free government, in line with the Magna Carta, the Petition of Right, the Bill of Rights, the Act of Settlement, with the works of Bracton, Coke, Locke, and Blackstone. Yet while an outstanding observer of English government like Montesquieu considered that government free because its substance was republican, it formally has remained monarchical to our day. It was in America that republican government was introduced in the English-speaking world both in practice and form. In this liberation Jefferson played a key role, setting an example for Bolívar, with whom he was ranked as a fighter for freedom.[5] He wanted his authorship of the Declaration of Independence to be noted on his tombstone, together with two other facts indicating his love of liberty, that the Virginia Statute for Religious Freedom went to his credit and that he was the founder of the University of Virginia, where academic freedom existed.

Jefferson's liberalism and his love of freedom have often been emphasized. A party song of 1801 runs:

> Rejoice! Columbia's sons, rejoice!
> To tyrants never bend the knee,
> But join with heart, and soul, and voice,
> For JEFFERSON and LIBERTY.[6]

Following his death on July 4th, the "dominant recognition of Jefferson in the encomium of 1826 was as the Apostle of Liberty."[7] It was stated that "the life of Jefferson was a perpetual devotion . . . to the pure and noble cause of public freedom. From the first dawning of his youth his undivided heart was given to the establishment of free principles—free institutions—freedom in all its varieties of untrammelled thought and independent action."[8]

5. Hendrik Willem van Loon, *Fighters for Freedom: Jefferson and Bolívar* (New York, 1962).
6. Quoted in Dumas Malone, *Thomas Jefferson as Political Leader* (Berkeley, 1963), 50.
7. Merrill D. Peterson, *The Jefferson Image in the American Mind* (1960, reprint New York, 1970), 9. See also 7.
8. Nicholas Biddle, *Eulogium on Thomas Jefferson* (Philadelphia, 1827), 51–52.

Connecting Jefferson with the love of freedom has continued down to our day. In 1834, Jefferson's works were credited with showing "the elements of the splendid structure of free government which he was instrumental in establishing," warranting "an extensive dissemination."[9] Under Jacksonian democracy, Jefferson's *Memoirs* were considered "text books of liberal political principles." Jefferson kindled in the people "that glow of feeling by which the true votary of liberty has ever been distinguished."[10] He was considered "the liberating scientist who had discovered the sum of political truth once and for all."[11] "Jefferson's object was *Liberty*. . . . The object of Mr. Jefferson through his life was . . . to increase and extend the influence of the great principle of *Liberty*, to which he had attached his faith, and which formed as it were his religion. . . . we do not well see how any judicious observer can feel himself authorized to attribute the course of Mr. Jefferson's political conduct to any other motive than an ardent zeal for liberty."[12] Four years later, the Democratic Young Men's Convention resolved that in Jefferson's life and writings "we learn the great lessons of human rights."[13] According to Alexander Hill Everett, Jefferson believed in freedom.[14] Hildreth criticized Jefferson for putting too much emphasis upon his vision of liberty, stating that Jefferson, who in 1769 "signalized his entrance into the [Virginia] Assembly by a motion giving to masters of slaves an unrestricted right of emancipation," was "a sincere and enthusiastic believer in the rights of humanity."[15] Shortly before the Civil War, the doctrine of individual freedom was considered the key to Jefferson's political thought.[16] Benjamin F. Hallett, a Democratic leader in New England, saw in Jefferson "the apostle of Freedom."[17] Lincoln wrote: "The principles of Jefferson are the definitions and axioms of a free society."[18]

In his eulogy of the martyred President, Bancroft saw Jefferson and Lin-

9. B. L. Rayner, *Life of Thomas Jefferson* (Boston, 1834), iv.

10. Quoted by Peterson, *The Jefferson Image,* 70.

11. Ibid., 79.

12. William Leggett, "Origin and Character of the old Parties," *North American Review* 39 (1834):246, 247, 252.

13. Quoted by Peterson, *The Jefferson Image,* 107.

14. Ibid., 133.

15. Richard Hildreth, *The History of the United States of America,* 6 vols. (New York, 1849–53; republished St. Clair Shores, Michigan, 1972), 2:549.

16. William Dorsheimer in his review of Henry S. Randall, *The Life of Thomas Jefferson* (New York, 1858) in *Atlantic Monthly* 2 (Nov., Dec., 1858):706 ff., 789 ff.

17. Quoted by Peterson, *The Jefferson Image,* 208.

18. To Henry L. Pierce and others, Apr. 6, 1859, in Roy P. Basler, ed., *The Collected Works of Abraham Lincoln* (New Brunswick, N.J., 1953), 3:375. On 376 we read: "All honor to Jefferson—to the man who, in the concrete pressure of a struggle for national independence by a single people, had the coolness, forecast, and capacity to introduce into a merely revolutionary document, an abstract truth, applicable to all men and all times, and so to embalm it there, that today, and in all coming days, it shall be a rebuke and a stumbling-block to the very harbingers of re-appearing tyranny and oppression."

coln as copartners in the progress of human liberty.[19] During the next decade, it was stated that Jefferson was so obsessed with liberty that he never realized that oppression could be derived from it and that he gave unqualified supremacy to private interests.[20] Toward the end of the nineteenth century, the Declaration of Independence was considered "a stately and a passionate chant of human freedom."[21]

Emphasis upon Jefferson's love of freedom did not subside during the twentieth century. In 1903 Senator George F. Hoar told the Thomas Jefferson Association that Jefferson was an expansionist of freedom.[22] At the end of World War I, it was said that Jefferson "will continue to serve his fellow-men so long as freedom is loved and fought for."[23] A sympathizer of the New Deal wrote that Jefferson's ideal was liberty, that he had a great love of freedom.[24] A year later, one could read that Jefferson "was, and still is, the greatest and most influential American exponent of both Liberalism and Americanism. . . . bound to insist upon freedom."[25] On April 13, 1943, President Roosevelt dedicated the Jefferson Memorial in Washington, D.C., celebrating the bicentennial of Jefferson's birth, with the words: "Today, in the midst of a great war for freedom, we dedicate a shrine to freedom. To Thomas Jefferson, Apostle of Freedom, we are paying a debt long overdue."[26] In a volume published that year, Jefferson was called "America's Apostle of Liberty," "The First Emancipator."[27]

19. George Bancroft, Memorial Address on the Life and Character of Abraham Lincoln, Feb. 12, 1866, in Charles R. Cushman, ed., *Memorial Addresses delivered before the two Houses of Congress on the Life and Character of Abraham Lincoln, James A. Garfield, William McKinley* (Washington, 1903), 14–15, 19.

20. David Wasson in *North American Review,* 118 (1874):405, esp. 408–10, 413. On 411, we read that "there was no special strength in Jefferson's character or mind. He had an eager curiosity to know something of all that was going on in the world; he dabbled in *omne scibile* of his day, but he studied nothing thoroughly. He soon tired of a subject and turned to another. He was a smatterer of the dangerous kind who feel that they have arrived at truth. Believing firmly in his intuitions, revelations of reason, he never knew when the oracle was *medizing.* When he changed his mind he rearranged his principles or invented new ones. Were he living now, he would be a 'sentimentalist,' with remedies for the cure of all our troubles deduced from 'principles of the purest morality and benevolence'; a visionary, impracticable, and mischievous; an uncompromising reformer and philanthro*pest.*"

21. Moses Coit Tyler, *The Literary History of the American Revolution* (New York, 1897), 1:521.

22. Andrew A. Lipscomb and Albert E. Bergh, eds., *Writings of Thomas Jefferson* (Washington, 1903–4), 1:vii–xiii. This edition will hereafter be cited as *Memorial ed.*

23. David Saville Muzzey, *Thomas Jefferson* (New York, 1918), viii.

24. Charles Maurice Wiltse, *The Jeffersonian Tradition in American Democracy* (Chapel Hill, N.C., 1935), 101, 210.

25. Adams, *The Living Jefferson,* 4.

26. Address at dedication of the Thomas Jefferson Memorial, Washington, D.C., Apr. 13, 1943, in Samuel I. Rosenman, *The Public Papers and Addresses of Franklin D. Roosevelt* (New York, 1950), 12 (1943):162.

27. By Herbert Bayard Swope and W. Warren Barbour, in James Waterman Wise, ed., *Thomas Jefferson Then and Now, 1743–1943* (New York, 1943), 7, 11.

In 1950 Jefferson was referred to as "the greatest liberal who took part in founding our government."[28] In his introduction to *The Jefferson Papers,* Boyd wrote that they should be regarded as the embodiment of the idea of freedom and self-government.[29] Three years later, the following comment was made: "Wherever man exists and has the aspiration to be free, he derives new hope and inspiration from the political philosophy of Thomas Jefferson."[30] In 1960 Jefferson was called "freedom's most inspiring American voice." It was added: "Into whatever remote niches the historians pursue Jefferson, they help to illuminate the American faith in freedom. Of freedom, Jefferson speaks to the present with the same urgency as to his own time, and with a voice as affirmative as it is authentic. . . . When so many of Jefferson's values have slipped away, he may yet go on vindicating his power in the national life as the heroic voice of imperishable freedoms."[31] According to Healey, Jefferson's "consistency lay in his continued striving for freedom."[32] Later in the sixties, it was written that "Freedom, 'the first-born daughter of science,' was fundamental to Jefferson's plan—freedom of religious faith, freedom of political expression, freedom from social cast and from inherent prejudice."[33] Studies were made of Jefferson and the foundation of American freedom,[34] and on Jefferson, the man of liberty.[35] In a work published in 1970 we read: "Whenever the reader dips into this book he will find that Jefferson, whether speaking of politics, religion, economics, science, or education, is concerned with one great objective: the freedom and happiness of man." Jefferson is said to be "an ever-living and ever-inspiring champion of man's inalienable rights."[36] A year later he again is referred to as "Apostle of Freedom."[37]

Jefferson himself left no doubt about the importance he attributed to freedom, which he considered natural to men. "Under the law of nature all

28. Anson Phelps Stokes, *Church and State in the United States* (New York, 1950), 1:338.

29. Julian P. Boyd, et al., eds., *The Papers of Thomas Jefferson* (Princeton, 1950–), 1:viii–xi. This edition is hereafter cited as *Papers.*

30. Caleb Perry Patterson, *The Constitutional Principles of Thomas Jefferson* (Austin, Tex., 1953), 62. He also writes: "World War II vindicated Jefferson's thesis that liberty is the supreme object of man and that it should never be sacrificed for standardization and regimentation, even in the interest of efficiency. . . . Thomas Jefferson was dedicated to fighting for the liberty of man. Liberty was his religion, and his services to liberty are immortal." 66, 188.

31. Peterson, *The Jefferson Image,* 442, 456, 457.

32. Robert M. Healey, *Jefferson on Religion in Public Education* (New Haven, 1963), 79. See also 88, 94.

33. Roy J. Honeywell, *The Educational Work of Thomas Jefferson* (New York, 1964), 147.

34. Saul K. Padover, *Thomas Jefferson and the Foundations of American Freedom* (Princeton, 1965).

35. Leonard Wibberley, *Man of Liberty: The Life of Thomas Jefferson* (New York, 1968).

36. Bernard Mayo, ed., *Jefferson Himself: The Personal Narrative of a Many-Sided American* (Charlottesville, Va., 1970), vi. Mayo points out that Jefferson's written material consists of "especially his thousands of letters written (as he said) 'in the warmth and freshness of fact and feeling' and forming 'the only full and genuine journal' of his life" (vi).

37. C. Randolph Benson, *Thomas Jefferson as Social Scientist* (Cranbury, N.J., 1971), 271.

men are born free," he wrote in 1770, reaffirming this idea in the same year as if to be sure the message was firmly implanted.[38] When the colonists' conflict with the mother country was approaching revolution, he puts liberty on a par with life. "The god who gave us life, gave us liberty at the same time: the hand of force may destroy, but it cannot disjoin them," we read in *A Summary View of the Rights of British America.*[39] During the following year he again emphasizes the importance of freedom, writing that "our attachment to no nation on earth should supplant our attachment to liberty. . . . We do then most solemnly, before god and the world declare, that, regardless of every consequence, at the risk of every distress, the arms we have been compelled to assume we will (*wage*) use with the perseverance, exerting to their utmost energies all those powers which our Creator hath given us, to (*guard*) preserve that liberty which he committed to us in sacred deposit, & to protect from every hostile hand our lives & our properties."[40] In his draft to the Declaration of Independence, liberty is listed among the "inherent and inalienable rights" all men are endowed with by their Creator.[41] The Declaration itself mentions liberty among men's unalienable rights and denounces the king for unduly curtailing many aspects of liberty. Three years later, liberty is considered good "for promoting the publick happiness . . . those persons, whom nature hath endowed with genius and virtue, should be rendered by liberal education worthy to receive, and able to guard the sacred deposit of the rights and liberties of their fellow citizens."[42] In 1780 he urges the President of Congress to postpone to the great object of liberty every smaller motive and passion.[43] The *Notes on Virginia* sound a reminder that freedom was God-given, asking, "can the liberties of a nation be thought secure when we have removed their only firm basis, a conviction in the minds of the people that these liberties are the gift of God?"[44] Five years later, disenchanted about the situation in America, he writes from Paris: "I own it astonishes me to find such a change wrought in the opinions of our countrymen since I left them, as that threefourths of them should be contented to live under a system which leaves to their governors the power of taking from them the trial by jury in civil cases, freedom of religion, freedom of

38. *Howell* vs. *Netherland,* Apr. 1770, in Thomas Jefferson, *Reports of Cases determined in the General Court of Virginia* (1829), 90–96, as quoted by Healey, *Jefferson on Religion,* 41. It was reaffirmed: "Under the law of nature, we are all born free."

39. "A Summary View of the Rights of British America," July 1774, in *Papers,* 1:135. See also Healey, *Jefferson on Religion,* 36, for a statement that to Jefferson, the day would come when God would liberate men on earth.

40. "Declaration of the Causes and Necessity for Taking Up Arms," Jefferson's Fair Copy for the Committee, July 1775, *Papers* 1:201, 202.

41. Ibid., 1:423.

42. "A Bill for the More General Diffusion of Knowledge," 1779, *Papers* 2:527.

43. Letter of Feb. 9, in Paul Leicester Ford, ed. *The Writings of Thomas Jefferson* (New York, 1892–99); 2:298, hereafter referred to as *Ford I.*

44. "Notes on Virginia," (1782), Query 18, Paul Leicester Ford, ed., *The Works of Thomas Jefferson,* Federal ed., 12 vols. (New York, 1904–5), 4:83. Hereafter cited as *Works.*

the press, freedom of commerce, the habeas corpus laws, and of yoking them with a standing army. This is a degeneracy in the principles of liberty to which I had given four centuries instead of four years."[45]

Jefferson advocates diffusing light and liberality among oppressors.[46] If this won't make the individuals free, they can have recourse to other means. He approves of uprisings in favor of freedom. Following Shays's Rebellion in Massachusetts he writes: "The commotions which have taken place in America . . . offer nothing threatening. They are a proof that the people have liberty enough, and I would not wish them less than they have. If the happiness of the mass of the people can be secured at the expence of a little tempest now and then, or even of a little blood, it will be a precious purchase. Malo libertatum periculosam quam quietam servitutem."[47] For the sake of freedom Jefferson does not shy away from stating even more strongly: "The tree of liberty must be refreshed from time to time with the blood of patriots and tyrants. It is it's natural manure."[48]

In view of these opinions it is not surprising that Jefferson has some positive things to say about the French Revolution. Under the *ancien régime,* when he travelled in France, he sadly states: "What a cruel reflection that a rich country cannot long be a free one."[49] After the revolution had started he writes enthusiastically to Madame d'Enville: "Heaven send that the glorious example of your country may be but the beginning of the history of European liberty, and that you may live many years in health and happiness to see at length that heaven did not make man in it's wrath."[50] The next year he expresses confidence that the success of the French Revolution would ensure the progress of liberty in Europe.[51] The year after he hopes that "God send that all the nations who join in attacking the liberties of France may end in the attainment of their own."[52] In 1793 Jefferson continues to be "eternally attached" to the principles of the French Revolution, hopeful that it would end in the establishment of some firm government, friendly to liberty and capable of maintaining it. If it did, he thinks, the world would become inevitably free.[53]

Observing the Paris scene did not mean that Jefferson would not continue to eagerly watch the developments in his home country. "The natural progress of things is for liberty to yeild, and government to gain ground," he wrote pessimistically when the constitution drafted in Philadelphia was up for ratification.[54] His reaction to seeing that document shows his enormous con-

45. To William Stephens Smith, Feb. 2, 1788, *Papers* 12:558.
46. To Jean Nicolas Démeunier, June 26, 1786, ibid., 10:63.
47. To Ezra Stiles, Dec. 24, 1786, ibid., 10:629.
48. To W. S. Smith, Nov. 13, 1787, ibid., 12:356.
49. Remarks on travels in France, Mar., 1787, ibid., 11:420.
50. To Madame d'Enville, Apr. 2, 1790, ibid., 16:291.
51. To Edmund Pendleton, July 24, 1791, *Works* 6:287.
52. To Joel Barlow, June 20, 1792, ibid., 7:123.
53. To J. P. Brissot de Warville, May 8, 1793, ibid., 7:322.
54. To Edward Carrington, May 27, 1788, *Papers* 13:208–9.

cern for freedom. He did not share Hamilton's idea that, given the checks and balances of the new supreme law, the constitution itself was a bill of rights and that there was no need for adding a formal bill,[55] but wanted to make doubly sure about guarantees for freedom, commenting that he "disapproved from the first moment . . . the want of a bill of rights to guard liberty against the legislative as well as executive branches of the government, that is to say to secure freedom in religion, freedom of the press, freedom from monopolies, freedom from unlawful imprisonment, freedom from a permanent military, and a trial by jury in all cases determinable by the laws of the land."[56] A few days later Jefferson, looking back, sees the need for the younger generation to recognize the importance of liberty and to keep the flame of liberty alive. Thinking of young scientists, he writes to Dr. Willard: "We have spent the prime of our lives in procuring them the precious blessing of liberty. Let them spend theirs in shewing that it is the great parent of science and virtue; and that a nation will be great in both always in proportion as it is free."[57] After the ratification of the Constitution Jefferson heralded hard work for extending freedom, writing that "the ground of liberty is to be gained by inches, and we must be contented to secure what we can get from time to time, and eternally press forward for what is yet to get. It takes time to persuade men to do even what is for their own good."[58] In tune with this idea, Jefferson remained an advocate of freedom for the rest of his life.

In the aftermath of the French Revolution he still considered himself "a warm zealot for the attainment & enjoiment by all mankind of as much liberty, as each may exercise without injury to the equal liberty of his fellow citizens," yet he "lamented that in France the endeavours to obtain this should have been attended with the effusion of so much blood."[59] Having experienced Jacobin terror, the man who had considered the blood of patriots and tyrants as the natural manure of the tree of liberty obviously had second thoughts on blood-letting for the sake of freedom, even though on balance he felt the French Revolution was a good thing and that its promotion had its price. Still, he is glad to note that in America the fight for liberty cost less blood, writing of the American Revolution: "The liberty of the whole earth was depending on the issue of the contest, and was ever such a prize won with so little innocent blood?"[60] Two years later he proudly states that it is the Americans' glory that they first put the ball of liberty in motion, and their happiness being foremost, they had no bad examples to follow.[61]

55. *The Federalist,* essay 84.

56. To Francis Hopkinson, Mar. 13, 1789, *Papers* 14:650.

57. To Dr. Willard, Mar. 24, 1789, ibid., 14:699.

58. To Rev. Charles Clay, Jan. 27, 1790, ibid., 16:129.

59. To M. de Meusnier, Apr. 29, 1795, *Works* 8:173.

60. To William Short, Jan. 3, 1793, ibid., 7:203.

61. To Tench Coxe, June 1, 1795, ibid., 8:183: "This ball of liberty, I believe most piously, is now so well in motion that it will roll around the globe. At least the enlightened part of it, for light

After he had become president, Jefferson, in spite of his newly acquired power, continued to be an advocate of the freedom of the individual. His First Inaugural is a document for liberty.[62] In the next year he gladly notes that "at every vibration between the points of liberty and despotism, something will be gained by the former."[63] He opposes joining "the confederacy of kings to war against the principles of liberty,"[64] trusting that Napoleon will give to the French liberty, "that first of blessings."[65] Upon reelection to the presidency, Jefferson proclaims to his countrymen: "I . . . will zealously cooperate with you in every measure which may tend to secure the liberty, property, and personal safety of our fellow citizens."[66] In 1807 he writes: "I sincerely pray . . . that all the members of the human family may, in the time prescribed by the Father of us all, find themselves securely established in the enjoyment of life, liberty, and happiness."[67] During the last year of his incumbency he assures political friends that his "affectionate concern for the liberty and prosperity of my fellow-citizens, will cease but with life to animate my breast."[68]

He lived up to that promise, affirming his belief in freedom again and again, often considering the spreading of liberty an American mission: "The preservation of the holy fire is confided to us by the world, and the sparks which will emanate from it will ever serve to rekindle it in other quarters of the globe, numinibus secundis,"[69] he writes in 1810. A year later he confirms: "The last hope of human liberty in this world rests on us. We ought, for so dear

---

& liberty go together. It is our glory that we first put it into motion & our happiness that being foremost we had no bad examples to follow."

62. First Inaugural, Mar. 4, 1801, ibid., 9:193 ff. In that speech, Jefferson expresses his pride that the presidential campaign demonstrated freedom of discussion and exertion. The speech states that the rights of the minority must be protected, mentions liberty as an important value and favors religious tolerance, and contains the famous phrase that error of opinion may be tolerated where reason is left free to combat it. It advocates a frugal government which "shall restrain men from injuring one another, shall leave them otherwise free to regulate their own pursuits in industry & improvement, and shall not take from the mouth of labor the bread it has earned." It defends freedom of religion, freedom of the press, freedom of person under the protection of habeas corpus, and trial by juries impartially selected (194–97).

63. To Thomas Cooper, Nov. 29, 1802, ibid., 9:403.

64. To Elbridge Gerry, Jan. 26, 1799, ibid., 9:18.

65. "If the hero [Napoleon] who has saved you from a combination of enemies, shall also be the means of giving you as great a portion of liberty as the opinions, habits and character of the nation are prepared for, progressive preparation may fit you for progressive portions of that first of blessings, and you may in time attain what we erred in supposing could be hastily seized and maintained, in the present state of political information among our citizens at large." To M. Cabanis on July 12, 1803, Henry A. Washington, ed., *The Writings of Thomas Jefferson,* 9 vols. (Washington, 1853–54), 4:496, hereafter cited as *Writings.*

66. Draft of Fifth Annual Message, Dec. 3, 1805. *Works* 9:197–198.

67. To Messrs. Thomas, Ellicot, and others, Nov. 13, 1807, *Writings* 8:119.

68. To the Democratic Citizens of the County of Adams, Pennsylvania, Mar. 20, 1808, ibid., 5:262.

69. To Rev. Mr. Knox, Feb. 12, 1810, ibid., 5:503.

a state, to sacrifice every attachment and every enemy."[70] In 1811 he remarked that "when we reflect that the eyes of the virtuous all over the earth are turned with anxiety on us, as the only depositories of the sacred fire of liberty, and that our falling into anarchy would decide forever the destinies of mankind, and seal the political heresy that man is incapable of self-government, the only contest between divided friends should be who will dare farthest into the ranks of the common enemy."[71] In 1817 Jefferson states: "That we should wish to see the people of other countries free, is as natural, and at least as justifiable, as that one King should wish to see the Kings of other countries maintained in their despotism."[72] Less than three years before his death he writes to John Adams, who survived Jefferson by five hours and whose last words were, "Thomas Jefferson still survives,"[73] a letter that again expresses his satisfaction with, and hope for, the spreading of liberty: "I will not believe our labors are lost. I shall not die without a hope that light and liberty are on steady advance."[74]

Jefferson did not define liberty. Being of the opinion that men would become freer and freer, he obviously was aware that this hope of an ever-increasing liberty for mankind precludes a definition of freedom. It has been said that in the encomium of 1826, liberty was the quintessence, and it was asked, in the same sentence, "but liberty in what sense?" The author gave this answer: "If the eulogies are read with an eye to their theoretical purport, they associated Jefferson with two contrasting, some may say contradictory, types of political liberty. One derived from the English legal heritage: the Whiggish liberty of individual rights. The other partook strongly of American and French revolutionary ideology: the democratic liberty of popular rule. Was Jefferson the conservative guardian of the law or the flaming prophet of democracy? The eulogists gave no clear-cut answer to the question. Nor was one requisite, since it was, after all, the fundamental question, the irresoluble ambiguity, in the American polity. Jefferson could be imagined either way. He embodied the ambiguity."[75]

The juxtaposition of Whiggish liberty and American revolutionary ideology and the seeming identification of the latter with French revolutionary thought may be open to debate. The American revolution has been considered a continuation of the English Whig revolution of the preceding century,[76] and to Jefferson, popular government was the best means—but still a means—for securing the freedom of the individual. Still, it is correct to say that Jefferson basically believed in two classes of individual liberty: the protection of the

70. To William Duane, Mar. 28, 1811, *Works* 11:193.

71. To John Hollins, May 5, 1811, *Writings* 5:597.

72. To Albert Gallatin, June 16, 1817, *Works* 12:71.

73. Quoted by Peterson, *The Jefferson Image,* 3.

74. To John Adams, Sept. 12, 1821, *Writings* 7:217–18.

75. Peterson, *The Jefferson Image,* 9–10.

76. Cf. Charles H. McIlwain, *The American Revolution, A Constitutional Interpretation* (New York, 1923).

individual from interferences by the government and his fellowmen and his rights to participate in government. Jefferson derived this broad concept of liberty from the law of nature early in his career. In 1770 he states: "Under the law of nature all men are born free, everyone comes into the world with a right to his own person, which includes the liberty of moving and using it at his will. This is what is called personal liberty, and is given him by the author of nature, because necessary for his own sustenance."[77] The freedom of the individual from interference is not just pleasant, it is necessary. Without that freedom, man could not sustain himself. And, to ensure that man had that freedom and the rights derived from it, there had to be self-government. This whole idea is expressed in what became the most often quoted words of the Declaration of Independence, "That all men are created equal, that they are endowed by their creator with certain unalienable rights; that among these are life, liberty and the pursuit of happiness; that to secure these rights governments are instituted among men, deriving their just powers from the consent of the governed." Jefferson's draft to these words does not merely state that all men are created equal, but they are created "equal & independent." He may well have meant "equally independent," considering the fact that he immediately adds "that from that equal creation they derive rights inherent & inalienable."[78] Be this as it may, if men derive their inherent rights from their equal creation, it is probable that for Jefferson, "the equality of men consisted in the 'rights' (or 'liberties' or 'freedoms') with which their benevolent Creator had endowed them."[79] Equality thus appears the alter ego of freedom, a kind of prerequisite for the existence of the individuals' rights or liberties or freedoms. The latter being but specific concrete aspects of the general concept of freedom, it seems as if equality is a mere aid for the promotion of general freedom. It is perhaps for this reason that Jefferson was praised as an apostle of freedom rather than equality.

As to the various rights to be left alone, some of the above quotations indicate what they include.[80] Authors have stressed that Jefferson preferred some of them to others.[81] There is little doubt, however, that he cherished all of

77. *Howell* v. *Netherland,* Apr. 1770, as quoted in Healey, *Jefferson on Religion,* 41–42, with reference to Marie Kimball, *Jefferson: The Road to Glory, 1743–1776* (New York, 1943), 94.

78. Jefferson's Rough Draft, *Papers* 1:423.

79. Healey, *Jefferson on Religion,* 41.

80. Cf. Julian P. Boyd, "Thomas Jefferson and the Police State," *North Carolina Historical Review* 15 (1948):233 ff.; "Thomas Jefferson's 'Empire of Liberty,'" *Virginia Quarterly Review* 24 (1948):538 ff.; Henry Steele Commager, "Jefferson and the Book-Burners," *American Heritage* 9 (1958):65 ff.; Adrienne Koch and Harry Ammon, "The Virginia and Kentucky Resolutions: An Episode in Jefferson's and Madison's Defense of Civil Liberties," *William and Mary Quarterly,* 3rd series, 5 (1948):145 ff.; Leonard W. Levy, *Jefferson & Civil Liberties: The Darker Side* (Cambridge, Mass., 1963); Dumas Malone, *Jefferson and the Rights of Man* (Boston, 1951); James Morton Smith, *Freedom's Fetters: The Alien and Sedition Laws and American Civil Liberties* (Ithaca, N.Y., 1956).

81. See Phillips Russell, *Jefferson: Champion of the Free Mind* (New York, 1956). Dumas

them. As other particular aspects of the general concept of freedom, he also favored the rights of individuals to govern themselves, in whatever variations they might appear.[82] All rights, including those to be free from interference and to participate in government, were for him merely among the rights of men, but by no means all of them, just as, in the Declaration of Independence, liberty is considered to be "among" certain unalienable rights with which men were endowed by their Creator. Even though only among the unalienable rights of man and not identical to them, freedom appears to be of paramount importance, conducive as it is for Jefferson to the pursuit of happiness. Fifty years after the Declaration of Independence, two weeks before his death, Jefferson reconfirmed his belief in the necessity of liberty, writing that "the mass of mankind has not been born with saddles on their backs, nor a favored few booted and spurred, ready to ride them legitimately by the Grace of God."[83] Jefferson never denied what he had written in 1791: "I would rather be exposed to the inconveniences attending too much liberty than those attending too small a degree of it."[84]

Liberty under Law

Much as Jefferson would rather be exposed to the dangers of too much liberty than too little a degree of it, he saw the risk of too much freedom. In 1813 he expresses to Madame Stael the hope that France may be "re-established in that temperate portion of liberty which does not infer either anarchy or licentiousness, in that high degree of prosperity which would be the consequence of such a government," a government France would have enjoyed under the constitution of 1789 "if wisdom could have stayed at that point the fervid but imprudent zeal of men, who did not know the character of their own countrymen."[85] Two years later, he continues in that vein in a letter to Lafayette.[86] After another five years, he speaks to him of the "disease of

Malone, *Thomas Jefferson as Political Leader* (Berkeley, 1963), 71, calls Jefferson "a champion of the freedom on which depend all other freedoms and the progress of mankind," namely, the freedom of the mind. The last sentence of that book reads: "What other political leader in our history or any other history ever did more to liberate and safeguard man's immortal mind?" See also Henry Wilder Foote, *Thomas Jefferson: Champion of Religious Freedom, Advocate of Christian Morals* (Boston, 1947); Frank L. Mott, *Jefferson and the Press,* (Baton Rouge, La., 1943).

82. See Charles M. Wiltse, "Jeffersonian Democracy: A Dual Tradition," *American Political Science Review* 28 (1934):833 ff.

83. To Roger C. Weightman, June 24, 1826, *Works* 12:477.

84. To Archibald Stuart, Dec. 23, 1791, ibid., 6:351.

85. Letter of May 24, 1813, *Writings* 6:120.

86. "A full measure or liberty is not now perhaps to be expected by your nation, nor am I confident they are prepared to preserve it. More than a generation will be requisite, under the administration of reasonable laws favoring the progress of knowledge in the general mass of the people, and their habituation to an independent security of person and property, before they will

liberty."[87] To Richard Rush he writes that "the boisterous sea of liberty is never without a wave."[88] Given these doubts about excessive liberty, it is not surprising that Jefferson would want certain restrictions. He favors "freedom in just pursuits"[89] a "rightful Liberty"—"unobstructed action according to our will, within the limits drawn around us by the equal rights of others."[90] He wants freedom limited through morality and natural and positive law.

Morality ranks high in Jefferson's values. As a young man Jefferson went through a religious crisis and thereafter was critical of religions, showing "reticence" about them.[91] By contrast, he never cast doubt upon morality and always was outspoken in urging it. He believed in God and rejected the accusation that he was an atheist,[92] while asserting that atheists could be highly moral.[93] He thought that Jesus "has told us only that God is good and perfect, but has not defined him" and that "we have neither words nor ideas adequate to that definition."[94] He refers to God in numerous ways, *inter alia* as the "Holy Author of religion" and the "Author of morality."[95]

To Jefferson, morality is more important than religious dogmas. True religion is moral.[96] Believing in religious freedom, Jefferson did not deny the right to deny the existence of God. In an advice on how to study religion, we read: "Religion . . . shake off all the fears and servile prejudices under which

be capable of estimating the value of freedom, and the necessity of a sacred adherence to the principles on which it rests for preservation. Instead of that liberty which takes root and growth in the progress of reason, if recovered by mere force or accident, it becomes, with an unprepared people, a tyranny still, of the many, the few, or the one." Letter of Feb. 14, 1815, *Works* 11:455.

87. To Lafayette on Dec. 26, 1820: "The volcanic rumblings in the bowels of Europe, from north to south, seem to threaten a general explosion, and the march of armies into Italy cannot end in a simple march. The disease of liberty is catching; those armies will take it in the south, carry it thence to their own country, spread there the infection of revolution and representative government, and raise its people from the prone condition of brutes to the erect altitude of man." Ibid., 12:190.

88. To Richard Rush, Oct. 20, 1820, *Writings* 7:182.

89. *Notes on Virginia,* Query 14, *Works* 4:62.

90. To Lewis Williams, Feb. 18, 1820, Jefferson Papers, Library of Congress, *217,* 38713, as quoted in Healey, *Jefferson on Religion,* 78.

91. See Peterson, *The Jefferson Image,* 25–26.

92. "As to the calumny of Atheism, I am so broken to calumnies of every kind . . . that I entirely disregard it." To James Monroe, May 26, 1800, *Works* 9:136.

93. "Diderot, D'Alembert, D'Holbach, Condorcet, are known to have been among the most virtuous of men. Their virtue, then, must have had some other foundation than the love of God." To Thomas Law, June 13, 1814, *Writings* 6:348–49.

94. To Ezra Styles, June 25, 1819, ibid., 7:127–28.

95. Healey, *Jefferson on Religion,* 27–28, also giving other names used by Jefferson, such as "God," "my God," "God of the universe," "God of justice," "Deity," "Almighty," "Supreme Being," "Creator," "our Creator," "benevolent Creator."

96. True religion "is more than an inner conviction of the existence of the Creator; true religion is morality." Jefferson thinks that "the moral precepts . . . the sublime doctrines of philanthropism and deism taught us by Jesus . . . constitute true religion." To John Adams, May 5, 1817, *Works* 12:89–90.

weak minds are servilely couched. Fix reason firmly in her seat, and call her tribunal every fact, every opinion. Question with boldness even the existence of a god; because, if there be one, he must more approve of the homage of reason, than that of blindfolded fear. . . . Do not be frightened from this enquiry by any fear of it's consequences. If it ends in the belief that there is no god, you will find incitements to virtue in the comfort and pleasantness you fell in it's exercise, and the love of others which it will procure you."[97] Whereas mankind for ages has disagreed on dogmas of religion, there has existed a certain consent on morality.[98]

Morality is superior to other disciplines. "I never submitted the whole system of my opinions to the creed of any party of men whatever in religion, in philosophy, in politics, or in any thing else where I was capable of thinking for myself. Such an addiction is the last degradation of a free and moral agent."[99] Much as Jefferson respected scientific thinking, he "was aware that science of itself is not always a power favoring the development of a moral society."[100] "As for France and England, with all their preëminence in science, the one is a den of robbers, and the other of pirates. And if science produces no better fruits than tyranny, murder, rapine and destitution of national morality, I would rather wish our country to be ignorant, honest, and estimable, as our neighboring savages are."[101]

If the religious superstructure Jefferson perceived as a child collapsed, his foundation of morality remained unshaken. "Jefferson took Bolingbroke's ad-

97. To Peter Carr, Aug. 10, 1787, *Papers* 12:15–16.

98. "On the dogmas of religion as distinguished from moral principles, all mankind, from the beginning of the world to this day, have been quarrelling, fighting, burning and torturing one another, for abstractions unintelligible to themselves and to all others, and absolutely beyond the comprehension of the human mind." To Matthew Carey, Nov. 11, 1816, *Works* 12:42. According to Healey, *Jefferson on Religion,* 244, Jefferson "believed he had arrived at an irreducible minimum of religious belief upon which all sects agree and those who held otherwise were dogmatizing venal jugglers." Jefferson distinguished between "moral man" and "dogmatising venal jugglers." To Francis A. Van der Kemp, Mar. 16, 1817, *Works* 12:54. Healey adds that Jefferson and Jesus "were alike in that vicious frauds had attacked them both for their uprightness and honesty, for their simple, universal, rational morality," *Jefferson on Religion,* 244. Jefferson writes, "my religious reading has long been confined to the moral branch of religion, which is the same in all religions; while in that branch which consists of dogmas, all differ, all have a different set. The former instructs us how to live well and worthily in society; the latter are made to interest our minds in the support of the teachers who inculcate them. Hence, for one sermon on a moral subject, you hear ten on the dogmas of the sect." To Thomas Leiper, Jan. 21, 1809, *Memorial ed.,* 12:236–37. "The result of your fifty or sixty years of religious reading, in the four words, 'Be just and good,' is that in which all our inquiries must end; as the riddles of all the priesthoods end in four more, '*ubi panis, ibi deus.*' What all agree in, is probably right. What no two agree in, most probably wrong." To John Adams, Jan. 11, 1817, *Works* 12:48. See also Healey, *Jefferson on Religion,* 100.

99. To Francis Hopkinson, Mar. 13, 1789, *Papers* 14:650.

100. Healey, *Jefferson on Religion,* 183.

101. To John Adams, Jan. 21, 1812, *Works* 11:220.

vice and built himself a philosophy of life involving personal discipline and scrupulously moral behavior. He also responded in Stoic tradition to the call of duty to the life of public service, and soon enlisted in the movement to bring about the amelioration of society and mankind. From ancient moralists such as Cicero, Seneca, and Marcus Aurelius, Jefferson derived a conception of patriotism and public duty which molded his life." And whereas Jefferson as a young man approved Bolingbroke's dictum that morality should be based on materials drawn from moralists of ancient Greece and Rome, this gave way to the conviction in his later years of the superior social value of the moral teachings of Jesus.[102]

Throughout his life Jefferson stressed that a moral faculty was innate in man. When his advice was requested on what to study in the field of moral philosophy, he replied: "I think it lost time to attend lectures in this branch. He who made us would have been a pitiful bungler if he had made the rules of our moral conduct a matter of science. . . . Man was destined for society. His morality therefore was to be formed to this object. He was endowed with a sense of right and wrong merely relative to this. This sense is as much a part of his nature as the sense of hearing, seeing, feeling; it is the true foundation of morality. . . . The moral sense, or conscience, is as much a part of man as his leg or arm. It is given to all human beings in a stronger and weaker degree, as force of members is given them in greater or less degree. It may be strengthened by exercise, as may any particular limb of the body. This sense is submitted indeed in some degree to the guidance of reason; but it is a small stock which is required for this."[103] In 1814 Jefferson states that morality is an innate element of the human constitution,[104] emphasizing that the Creator "has formed us moral agents . . . that we may promote the happiness of those with whom he has placed us in society, by acting honestly towards all, benevolently to those who fall within our way, respecting sacredly their rights, bodily and mental, and cherishing their freedom of conscience as we value our own."[105] He confirms the innateness of morality in men three years later.[106]

Proud that nature allotted to him the "field . . . of morals . . . the feelings of sympathy, of benevolence, of gratitude, of justice, of love, of friendship,"[107] he leaves no doubt about the importance of morality as compared to other faculties. He advises Peter Carr that "virtue can never be made up by all the other acquirements of body and mind. Make these then your first object. Give up money, give up fame, give up science, give up the earth itself and all it

102. Healey, *Jefferson on Religion,* 100, with reference to Jefferson's communication to Robert Skipwith. See Aug. 3, 1771, *Papers* 1:79 f.

103. To Peter Carr, Aug. 10, 1789, *Papers* 12:14–15.

104. To Thomas Law, June 13, 1814, *Writings* 6:348 ff.

105. To Miles King, Sept. 26, 1814, ibid., 6:388.

106. To John Adams, May 5, 1817, *Memorial ed.* 15:427.

107. To Maria Cosway, Oct. 12, 1786, *Papers* 10:450.

contains rather than do an immoral act."[108] Jefferson repeatedly "emphasized the need for unremitting moral behavior,"[109] and considered the lack of a moral sense more degrading than the most hideous of the bodily deformities.[110]

Jefferson believed that the moral sense is especially strong in agricultural America. Farmers to him are "the chosen people of God, if ever he had a chosen people, whose breasts he made his peculiar deposit for substantial and genuine virtue. . . . Corruption of morals in the mass of cultivators is a phenomenon of which no age nor nation has furnished an example."[111] He is happy to note that the morals of the American people could be made the basis of their government.[112]

Just as Jefferson does not define God, the "Author of morality," he refrains from defining morality. In 1787 he advises Peter Carr, "above all things lose no occasion of exercising your dispositions to be grateful, to be generous, to be charitable, to be humane, to be true, just, firm, orderly, courageous, &c. Consider every act of this kind as an exercise which will strengthen your moral faculties, and increase your worth."[113] The moral branch of religion instructs individuals "how to live well and worthily in society."[114] In 1816 Jefferson writes "fear god and love thy neighbor,"[115] and in 1817, "Be just and good."[116] Toward the end of his life he offers this advice: "Adore God. Reverence and cherish your parents. Love your neighbor as yourself, and your country more than yourself. Be just. Be true. Murmur not at the ways of Providence."[117] It can thus be said that to Jefferson, the moral man was a noble and good individual, considerate of the interests of others, remindful of Goethe's words, "Edel sei der Mensch, hilfreich und gut"—man be noble, helpful, and good.[118] Rank and standing did not matter. A farmer could answer moral questions as quickly and correctly as a professor, if not better.[119] Morality was not to be learned by studying many books and by reasoning too much

108. To Peter Carr, Aug. 19, 1785, ibid., 8:406. In 1787 he writes his daughter: "It is your future happiness which interests me, and nothing can contribute more to it (moral rectitude always excepted) than the contracting a habit of industry and activity." To Martha Jefferson, Mar. 28, 1787, *Papers* 11:250. Jefferson thus put morality over industry.

109. Healey, *Jefferson on Religion,* 160.

110. To Thomas Law, June 13, 1814, *Writings* 6:351.

111. Query 19, *Works* 4:85.

112. To John Adams, Feb. 28, 1796, ibid., 8:219.

113. To Peter Carr, Aug. 10, 1787, *Papers* 12:15. See also Jefferson's letter to Martha Jefferson, Mar. 28, 1787, ibid., 11:250 ff.

114. To Thomas Leiper, Jan. 21, 1809, *Works* 11:89.

115. To George Logan, Nov. 12, 1816, ibid., 12:43.

116. To John Adams, Jan. 11, 1817, ibid., 12:48.

117. To Thomas Jefferson Smith, Feb. 21, 1825, *Writings* 7:401.

118. First line of the poem "Das Göttliche."

119. To Peter Carr, Aug. 10, 1787, *Papers* 11:15.

over it. It was to be practiced ceaselessly,[120] to be guided by the example of exemplary figures.[121]

Thinking that man was destined for society, Jefferson considered utility for oneself and one's fellowmen the purpose of moral action. In 1787 he holds out the hope of life after death as an incentive to moral living. Such living would also benefit life on this earth: "Be good, be learned, and be industrious, and you will not want the aid of travelling to render you precious to your country, dear to your friends, happy with yourself."[122] The *Notes on Virginia* propose that the elements of morality should be taught by an open utilitarian appeal to reason, involving that happiness was among other things the result of good conscience.[123] In 1808 he advises Thomas Jefferson Randolph: "A determination never to do what is wrong, prudence and good humor, will go far towards securing you the estimation of the world."[124]

Jefferson believed that the utilitarian argument was very effective, that it would strengthen the normal moral sense. The rational demonstration that just and upright behavior was always in one's own interest would be useful in convincing students whose moral sense was deficient, to act morally.[125] Two years later the utilitarian argument again is evident. Jefferson looks upon "the moral precepts, innate in man, and made a part of his physical constitution, as necessary for a social being."[126] The idea of utility can be seen in the Rockfish Gap Report, which makes clear that the cultivation of morals is conducive to the happiness of the individual and, by example, to the happiness of others.[127] It is stated by Jefferson in so many words when he writes that "nature has constituted *utility* to man the standard and best of virtue. Men living in differ-

120. Healey, *Jefferson on Religion,* 168.

121. Jefferson hoped to shield his favorite grandson, living by himself in Philadelphia to complete his education, with this advice: "I had the good fortune to become acquainted very early with some characters of very high standing, and to feel the incessant wish that I could ever become what they were. Under temptations & difficulties, I would ask myself what would Dr. Small, Mr. Wythe, Peyton Randolph do in this situation? What course in it will insure me their approbation? I am certain that this mode of deciding on my conduct, tended more to its correctness than any reasoning, & with powers I possessed. Knowing the even & dignified line they pursued, I could never doubt for a moment which of two courses would be in character for them. Whereas, seeking the same object through a process of moral reasoning, and with the jaundiced eye of youth, I should often have erred. . . . these little returns into ourselves, this self-catechising habit, is not trifling nor useless, but leads to the prudent selection & steady pursuit of what is right." To Thomas Jefferson Randolph, Nov. 24, 1808, *Works* 11:79–80.

122. To Peter Carr, Aug. 10, 1787, *Papers* 12:16–17, quotation on 17–18.

123. Query 14, *Works* 4:60 ff.

124. To Thomas J. Randolph, Nov. 24, 1808, ibid., 11:79.

125. See Healey, *Jefferson on Religion,* 172, referring to letter to Thomas Law of June 13, 1814.

126. To John Adams, May 5, 1817, *Writings* 7:62.

127. Nathaniel F. Cabell, ed., *Early History of the University of Virginia as Contained in the Letters of Thomas Jefferson and Joseph C. Cabell* (Richmond, 1865), 435.

ent countries, under different circumstances, different habits and regimes, may have different utilities; the same act, therefore, may be useful, and consequently virtuous in one country which is injurious and vicious in another differently circumstanced."[128]

It has been said that for Jefferson, "democracy is a moral enterprise, that freedom must be exercised within the context of responsibility. . . . Each citizen must have, first, a sense of commitment, a sense of loyalty or final responsibility to a supreme value, principle, or source of law, to an ideal transcending himself, his nation, and any other particular local or temporal interest bidding for his support. This should be the motivation behind all his actions."[129] These words express that individual freedom must be restrained by morality. They also convey the thought that morality is a source of law. According to Jefferson, the freedom of the individual living in a society was to be restricted not only by morality, but also by the law.

Much as Jefferson believed that men were born with a moral faculty, he felt that they possessed that faculty to different degrees.[130] And while he believed that men were good enough to be trusted with self-government, he thought they could not be trusted absolutely. Men behaved badly enough to require restraints upon their behavior, going beyond those of morality which, after all, could not be enforced. He wanted to make sure that at least a moral minimum was enforceable through the law. If man is created a social being who for that reason was to behave morally, care had to be taken that he would be prevented from behaving like an asocial, antisocial animal. Jefferson hoped this could be achieved by the law.

Jefferson studied to be a lawyer and practiced law at the beginning of his professional career. His choice of a profession concerned with norms that by definition restrict the freedom of the individual indicates that from an early stage Jefferson felt the need for effective restraints upon the actions of individuals. As a politician, Jefferson recognized that "every political measure will forever have an intimate connection with the laws of the land."[131] Much as Jefferson cherished liberty, throughout his career he saw the need for legal restrictions upon freedom.

Comparing Jefferson's performance before a court with that of Patrick Henry, Edmund Randolph remarked, "Mr. Jefferson drew copiously from the depth of the law, Mr. Henry from the recesses of the human heart."[132] This indicates that Jefferson would not be easily tempted into unduly increasing liberty at the expense of the law. As a member of a committee of revisers to

128. To Thomas Law, June 13, 1814, *Writings* 6:351.

129. Healey, *Jefferson on Religion,* 271.

130. To Thomas Law, June 13, 1814, *Writings* 6:350.

131. To Thomas Mann Randolph, July 6, 1787, *Papers* 11:557.

132. Edmund Randolph, "Essay on the Revolutionary History of Virginia," *Virginia Magazine of History and Biography,* 43 (1935):123.

adapt the existing law to modern conditions and more humane principles, Jefferson did not favor writing a new code, which would have made liberalization easier. Rather, he proposed a revision and clarification of existing laws, at the expense of freedom.[133] Much as Jefferson was active in liberation through a revision of the laws, he recognized the value of legal restrictions of liberty. For instance, while the death penalty was abolished for twenty-seven felonies, these felonies remained punishable, and capital punishment continued for murder and treason. Jefferson was opposed to working criminals on public works, so they would no longer be humiliated by being a public spectacle. Still, he favored work in the prisons.[134] His legislative program, liberalizing as it generally was, always implied certain restrictions on the freedom of the individual.

Jefferson's recognition of a need for such restrictions is evident in national documents. His *Summary View of the Rights of British America,* while asserting these rights, does not maintain that they should be unlimited.[135] The enumeration of infringements of the rights of the colonists in the Declaration of Independence denounces excessive infringements, infringements going beyond those permitted by the laws and *ultra vires.* It does not question normal legal restrictions.

In the beginning of that enumeration, the king is denounced for having "refused his assent to laws the most wholesome and necessary for the public good," laws which restrict the freedom of the individual. At the end, the king is said to be a "tyrant . . . unfit to be the ruler of a free people." From this follows that Jefferson does not object to a nondespotic ruler who restricts freedom in a nonarbitrary manner. Many infringements of rights are denounced for being excessive or having occurred without the consent of the colonists. Otherwise, they would have been acceptable for Jefferson. The fact that, basically, restrictions of freedom are taken for granted also can be seen in the statement that the people's right to throw off their government and to provide new guards for their future security exists only when there is "a long train of abuses and usurpations," "all having in direct object the establishment of an absolute tyranny." While it would go too far to interpret this passage as meaning that Jefferson was sanctioning legal restraints upon individual freedom amounting to tyranny, there can be little doubt that the Declaration permits limitations upon freedom that follow from man's nature as a social being. The First Inaugural Address shows that Jefferson considered restrictions of the individual's freedom under law desirable.[136]

Jefferson was opposed to anarchy. In 1785 he blames London gazettes and

133. Patterson, *Constitutional Principles,* 18–19.

134. Ibid., 21–22.

135. Edward Channing, *A History of the United States* (New York, 1927), 4:248.

136. It speaks of the high authorities provided by the Constitution, of the rules of the Constitution, that all will arrange themselves under the will of the law. It expresses the hope that every man, at the call of the law, would fly to the standard of the law and would meet invasions of the public order, and promises to give firmness and effect to legal administration.

papers discussing America for leading people "to suppose that all there is anarchy, discontent and civil war."[137] Two years later he denounces persistent British "lies about our being in anarchy, that the world has at length believed them."[138] In 1790 he writes that "much has been gained by the new constitution; for the former one was terminating in anarchy, as necessarily consequent to inefficiency."[139] Later on he states: "Let this then be the distinctive mark of an American that, in cases of commotion, he enlists himself under no man's banner, inquires for no man's name, but repairs to the standard of the laws. Do this and you need never fear anarchy or tyranny. Your government will be perpetual."[140] He fears that "our falling into anarchy would decide forever the destinies of mankind, and seal the political heresy that man is incapable of self-government."[141]

Jefferson's denunciations of anarchy are matched by exhortations to obey the laws. In 1781 he remarks: "Laws made by common consent must not be trampled on by Individuals."[142] Twenty years later he praises that "love of order and obedience to the laws, which so remarkably characterize the citizens of the United States, are sure pledges of internal tranquility."[143] In 1809 he opposes protests against the laws: "While the principles of our Constitution give just latitude to inquiry, every citizen faithful to it will deem embodied expressions of discontent, and open outrages of law and patriotism, as dishonorable as they are injurious."[144]

Law as a moral minimum is part of, and derives from, morality. Since man is endowed with a moral faculty, he will discover certain moral principles transmuted into law. Law is discovered, made to serve social ends, and positive laws are supposed to be merely declaratory of universal moral principles.[145] While law as a moral minimum derives from morality, it is in turn conducive to the preservation of moral standards because of its sanction. Jefferson speaks of "our wish, to preserve the morals of our citizens from being vitiated by courses of lawless plunder and murder."[146] And whereas the moral sense is "the first excellence of well-organized man,"[147] it would be good to promote that excellence by that well-organized moral minimum, the law, which was to be clear.[148]

137. To Geismar, Sept. 6, 1785, *Papers* 8:499.

138. To William Stephens Smith, Nov. 13, 1787, ibid., 12:356.

139. To George Mason, June 13, 1790, ibid., 16:493.

140. From manuscripts, probably for the First Inaugural Address. *Ford I* 8:1.

141. To John Hollins, May 5, 1811, *Writings* 5:597.

142. To Col. Vanmeter, Apr. 27, 1781, *Ford I* 3:24.

143. To Benjamin Waring, Mar. 23, 1801, *Writings* 4:378.

144. To the Republican Mechanics of the Town of Leesburg and its Vicinity, Assembled on the 27th of February last, Mar. 29, 1809, ibid., 8:161.

145. Wiltse, *Jeffersonian Tradition,* 157.

146. To George Hammond, May 15, 1793, *Works* 7:327.

147. To John Adams, Feb. 25, 1823, *Writings* 7:275.

148. To George Wythe, Nov. 1, 1778, *Papers* 2:230; to Judge William Johnson, June 12, 1823, *Writings* 7:297.

Like morality, law must be useful. It will vary as societies do, much as it may furnish principles of justice that are valid everywhere and at all times. These principles must be adjusted to the needs of a given society at a given time and take into consideration various ways of life and circumstances. For instance, in America horses were easy to steal. Consequently, horse-stealing was severely punished. In Europe, it was lightly punished because the crime was difficult and rare. On the other hand, in parts of Europe it was a serious offense to steal fruit from trees, whereas in America it was not.[149] To be useful, laws must go with the times. Jefferson is glad that "commerce has taught the world more humanity" by prompting a change of a law under which a Jew, as an alien, could not sue.[150] For him, it is "self evident, '*that the earth belongs in usufruct to the living*': that the dead have neither powers nor rights over it."[151] Still, he is not in favor of too rapid a change in the laws, believing that people must have faith in the laws and that it is better for the law to be certain than to be just.[152] Living at the beginning of the age of legislation, Jefferson recognizes the danger of an undue multiplication of the laws. "The instability of our laws is really an immense evil. I think it would be well to provide in our constitutions that there shall always be a twelvemonth between the ingrossing a bill and passing it: that it should then be offered to it's passage without changing a word: and that if circumstances should be thought to require a speedier passage, it should take two-thirds of both Houses instead of a bare majority."[153] Jefferson's ideas on the modernization of the laws are perhaps best reflected in the statement that, slightly altered from its original, is engraved in the Jefferson Memorial in Washington, D.C.: "I am certainly not an advocate for frequent and untried changes in laws and constitutions. . . . But I know also, that laws and institutions must go hand in hand with the progress of the human mind. As that becomes more developed, more enlightened, as new discoveries are made, new truths disclosed, and manners and opinions change with the change of circumstances, institutions must advance also, and keep pace with the times."[154]

It has been stated that the "Jeffersonian state is essentially a legal state, and the equality of men is in the end an equality before the law. The principle is laid down in the Declaration of Independence in the same sense in which it appears in the Roman law: men are equal, not in wealth, or talent, or intelligence, but in the eyes of the law. The law is the common factor in the state which affects all

149. Wiltse, *Jeffersonian Tradition,* 159–60.

150. Ibid., 160, quoting from Jefferson's Commonplace Book, 320.

151. To Madison, Sept. 6, 1789, *Papers* 15:392. Cf. letters to John Adams, Apr. 25, 1794, *Works* 8:145; John Cartwright, June 5, 1824, *Writings* 7:355 ff.

152. As to change of laws and constitutions, Jefferson writes: "I think moderate imperfections had better be borne with; because, when once known, we accommodate ourselves to them, and find practical means of correcting their ill effects." To Samuel Kercheval, July 12, 1816, *Works* 12:11–12.

153. To Madison, Dec. 20, 1787, *Papers* 12:442.

154. To Samuel Kercheval, July 12, 1816, *Works* 12:11–12.

the same way. In the legal state, natural rights become the civil rights of citizenship: the rights guaranteed to men under the law."[155] Now rights under law are not absolute. They exist according to laws characterized by sanctions curtailing the freedom of the individual for the sake of society and its peace. "Natural rights may be abridged or regulated in their exercise by law" we read in an official opinion of 1790.[156] The reason is obvious: "While the laws shall be obeyed all will be safe," Jefferson writes in 1801.[157] In 1816 he adds: "No man has a natural right to commit aggression on the equal rights of another; and this is all from which the laws ought to restrain him."[158]

The individual's obedience to the laws for the sake of the safety of all should not be too difficult to achieve. After all, Jefferson's legal state is a representative republic based upon self-government. Under popular sovereignty, restrictions of freedom are self-imposed. According to the principle *volenti non fit iniuria,* they hardly will be considered unduly restrictive, especially in view of Jefferson's opinion expressed early in his political career, that "the law of the *majority* is the natural law of every society"[159] and that, as he said later on, "Laws . . . abridging the natural right of the citizen, should be restrained by rigorous construction, within their narrowest limits."[160] Furthermore, in a representative republic an oppression through laws is improbable because the people as the sovereign lawmaker usually will see to it that the laws are conceived to also limit the government.

Law as a Limitation upon Government

The preceding pages have shown that Jefferson, in spite of his adamant advocacy of the spreading of liberty, wanted the freedom of individuals curtailed for the sake of society and its component parts. He proposed restrictions through morality. However, realizing that such restrictions amounted to mere autolimitation and thus might be ineffective, he felt the need for limiting human behavior effectively through enforceable positive laws.

What laws can limit those in power? It can be argued that a government, being the supreme creator, adjudicator, and executor of positive laws, cannot well be limited by these laws, that a limitation of a sovereign is a contradiction in terms. This is the basic attitude of absolutist philosophers from Bodin to Kelsen and his Pure Theory of Law. However, constitutional government, traces of which can be found even in Bodin's assertion that the sovereign king is under the laws of the land, has demonstrated that it is possible to subject the

155. Wiltse, *Jeffersonian Tradition,* 158.
156. Opinion on the Constitutionality of the Residence Bill (July 15?), *Papers* 17:197.
157. From what was taken to be a paragraph for Inaugural of 1801, *Works* 8:1.
158. To Francis W. Gilmer, June 7, 1816, ibid., 11:534.
159. Opinion on the Constitutionality of the Residence Bill (July 15?), *Papers* 17:195.
160. To Isaac McPherson, Aug. 13, 1813, *Writings* 6:176.

government to positive law even if made by the ordinary legislature. This applies to Jefferson's favorite, the representative republic, often referred to as free government in America's formative period.

However, free government, a popular government where the ruling majority is required by law to respect the rights of minorities, is a sophisticated, tender fabric. It can degenerate into the tyranny "of the many, the few, or the one." Jefferson, who, like Montesquieu, had studied the various governments throughout history, was aware that tyrannies could not well be limited by positive law which, after all, was controlled by the tyrant. Aside from favoring a limitation of government by positive law, he, therefore, thought of restrictions by natural law, justified by the belief that the "freedom and happiness of man . . . are the sole objects of legitimate government."[161]

Restrictions of the government by natural law appear to be natural to Jefferson, given his emphasis upon morality and the fact that natural law seems to be morality's alter ego. If individuals must behave morally, there is no reason why members of the government should not. Otherwise they would act against their innate, moral faculty, against nature. They would infringe upon natural law and subject themselves to criticism based upon that law.

Jefferson indicates as early as 1770 that governments are bound by natural law. His assertion that under the law of nature all men are born free suggests that governments should not infringe upon the freedom provided by that law. *A Summary View of the Rights of British America* is full of exhortations that the English government not infringe upon these rights because they are natural and protected by the law of nature. It denounces "many unwarrantable encroachments and usurpations, attempted to be made by the legislature of one part of the empire, upon the rights which God, and the laws have given equally and independently to all." It mentions the right of emigration, made use of by the Saxons settling in England and by the English going to America, as "a right, which nature has given to all men," a "universal law." It calls the right of "free trade with all parts of the world" a "natural right" that was "the object of unjust encroachment" by the British. It denounces acts of Parliament as "a phenomenon unknown in nature," continuing that "the common feelings of human nature must be surrendered up, before his Majesty's subjects here, can be persuaded to believe that they hold their political existence at the will of a British Parliament." It denounces royal impositions and prohibitions as being incompatible with "the rights of human nature." It says that the colonists are a "free people, claiming their rights as derived from the laws of nature, and not as the gift of their Chief Magistrate," who are "asserting the rights of human nature." It makes clear "that kings are the servants, not the proprietors of the people," urging the king: "Open your breast, Sire, to liberal and expanded thought."[162]

161. To General Kosciusko, Feb. 26, 1810, *Writings* 5:509.

162. Quoted from the reprinting in John P. Foley, ed., with an introduction by Julian P. Boyd, *The Jeffersonian Cyclopedia* (Reissued New York, 1967), 2:963 ff.

The restriction of governments by natural law for the sake of the rights of the individual is evident in Jefferson's draft of the Declaration of Independence, accepted by Congress with slight changes. As a matter of fact, that restriction can be considered the *leitmotif* of that draft. Its very first paragraph, setting the tone for what is to follow, states that under "the laws of nature and of nature's God" the bonds with Great Britain were being dissolved, obviously because Britain did not respect those laws. Certainly the following paragraph makes clear that governments are bound by those laws. It speaks of the "self-evident" truths "that all men are created equal; that they are endowed by their creator with inherent and inalienable rights. . . . that to secure these rights, governments are instituted among men. . . . that whenever any form of government becomes destructive of these ends, it is the right of the people to alter or to abolish it, and to institute new government." Later on the king is accused of having "waged cruel war against human nature itself, violating its most sacred rights of life and liberty in the persons of a distant people who never offended him, captivating and carrying them into slavery in another hemisphere, or to incur miserable death in their transportation thither."[163] According to the Declaration of Independence, then, any form of government is limited by natural law protecting the rights of the individual.[164]

Jefferson does not change his opinion later on. *Notes on Virginia* states that "our rulers can have authority over such natural rights only as we have submitted to them."[165] In a letter of 1797 defending the freedom of correspondence, we read that the purpose of government is the enforcement of man's natural rights.[166] The First Inaugural Address expresses the hope that "that infinite power which rules the destinies of the universe lead our councils to what is best."[167] In the same year Jefferson gives the assurance to "see with sincere satisfaction the progress of those sentiments which tend to restore to man all his natural rights."[168] Ten years later he writes: "If there be a god, & he is just His day will come. He will never abandon the whole race of man to be eaten up by the leviathans and mammoths of a day."[169] In 1822 he tells Lafayette that the "general insurrection of the world against it's tyrants will ultimately prevail by pointing the object of government to the happiness of the people, and not merely to that of their self-constituted governors."[170] Since insurrection usually

163. Quoted from the reprinting of the Declaration, ibid., 2:969 ff.

164. Cf. Carl L. Becker, *The Declaration of Independence* (New York, 1922, 1940), esp. 24 ff.

165. Query 17, *Works* 4:77–78.

166. "A right of free correspondence between citizen & citizen, . . . is a natural right, it is not the gift of any municipal law, either of England, or of Virginia, or of Congress; but in common with all our other natural rights, is one of the objects for the protection of which society is formed, & municipal laws established." To James Monroe, Sept. 7, 1797, ibid., 8:339.

167. Ibid., 9:200.

168. To a Committee of the Danbury Baptist Association, Jan. 1, 1802, *Writings* 8:113.

169. To Lafayette, Jan. 20, 1811, *Works* 11:177.

170. To Lafayette, Oct. 28, 1822, ibid., 12:258–59.

is not provided for by positive laws, the insurrection mentioned will be based upon natural law. The next year Jefferson considers God a "fabricator of all things from matter and motion, their preserver and regulator while permitted to exist in their present forms, and their regeneration into new and other forms." He sees "evident proofs of the necessity of a superintending power, to maintain the universe in its course and order."[171] All things come from matter and motion, including government which is constantly under the eyes of the Preserver and Regulator and must act accordingly.

It was stated that along with his colleagues of the American Philosophical Society, "Jefferson agreed that society was a divinely ordered community based on motives implanted in man by the Creator." That community was, for the sake of natural rights, divinely ordered by the bounds of natural law. "The best government was therefore the least government, the absolute minimum necessary to protect man from certain unhappy but essential qualities of the human species."[172] For Jefferson the limitations of natural law play an important part in restricting ruling members of that species. The doctrine that natural law curtailed government came to America primarily through the writings of John Locke, James Harrington, and William Blackstone. Locke's influence on Jefferson, who wrote that "Locke's little book on government is perfect as far as it goes,"[173] is well known.[174] While Jefferson had reservations about Blackstone, there are no indications that he disagreed with the latter's statement that the "law of nature, being coeval with mankind and dictated by God himself, is of course superior in obligation to any other. It is binding over all the globe, in all countries, and at all times: no human laws are of any validity, if contrary to this; and such of them as are valid derive all their force, and all their authority, mediately and immediately, from this original." Neither did Jefferson contest Blackstone's opinion that liberty is "a right strictly natural."[175]

Aside from believing in restrictions of governments by natural law for the sake of the freedom of the individual, Jefferson believed in such restrictions through the common law. This is not surprising in view of the fact that customary law, having been accepted by people for generations, appears to be natural and sanctioned by God. It has been said that Jefferson's debt to the English law is great.[176] Having read Blackstone he was familiar with the other two great commentators, Bracton and Coke, men known for their subjection of the government to traditional law.

In their struggle with the mother country, the colonists emphasized the rights they had under the English law, that is, their rights as Englishmen. From

171. To John Adams, Apr. 11, 1823, *Writings* 7:282.

172. Healey, *Jefferson on Religion,* 67–68, with references.

173. To Thomas Mann Randolph, May 30, 1790, *Papers* 16:449.

174. Cf. Carl Becker, *Declaration of Independence,* 27, 29, 35–36, 63 ff., 75, 108.

175. *Commentaries on the Laws of England,* ed. Thomas M. Cooley (Chicago, 1899), 41, 135.

176. Wiltse, *Jeffersonian Tradition,* 161. Cf. Patterson, *Constitutional Principles,* 6 ff., 16, 18, 20.

the Declaration of Independence on, emphasis shifted to the rights of man, in a large measure because once independence had been declared, one could not well assert English rights any longer. Still, during the revolutionary period, the rights individuals possessed under the positive laws of the English constitution would not be ignored. This is evident in Jefferson's writings.

A Summary View of the Rights of British America contains many references to rights English subjects have always enjoyed because their traditional law curtailed governmental power. It starts out by making a reference to the "rights which God, and the laws have given equally and independently to all." It thus mentions laws next to God without indicating that these laws are God's. The king is considered "no more than the chief officer of the people, appointed by the laws, and circumscribed with definite powers, to assist in working the great machine of government, erected for their use." Again, there is no mention of natural law. The reference to the definite powers and the working of the machine of government makes clear that the laws Jefferson speaks of are positive. Furthermore, after enumerating infringements upon rights that traditionally have been protected under English law, there are complaints, without reference to natural law or the law of God, of "acts of power, assumed by a body of men foreign to our constitutions, and unacknowledged by our laws." The king is accused of "deviations from the line of duty" under "the Constitution of Great Britain." Under that constitution, as well as under the constitutions of "the several American States," he has the power to exercise a veto on oppressive acts of Parliament, a veto he should use to protect the colonists' rights under English law.[177] There are examples that demonstrate the idea that positive law restricts the government in *A Summary View of the Rights of British America.* The document reminds one of the Magna Carta's enumeration of infringements and their denunciation on grounds of common law.

The same can be said about Jefferson's draft of the Declaration of Independence. While it heralds "the laws of nature and of nature's God" as limitations upon governments and thus puts, on the face ot it, greater emphasis upon natural law than *A Summary View,* it denounces infringements upon a great many rights that for a long time had been considered rights of Englishmen. The king is accused of having refused his assent to good laws, an assent Englishmen had taken for granted since the Glorious Revolution. He is blamed for having unduly dissolved legislative bodies, made judges dependent upon his will, kept standing armies in time of peace, rendered the military independent of, and superior to, the civil power, for imposing taxes without consent, depriving the colonists of the benefits of trial by jury, "abolishing the free system of English laws in a neighboring province, establishing therein an arbitrary government," for "taking away our charters, abolishing our most valuable laws, and altering fundamentally the forms of our governments," for "suspending our own legis-

177. *Jeffersonian Cyclopedia* 2:963 ff.

latures."[178] Clearly the Declaration is a document that, with all its emphasis upon natural law as a limitation upon government, does not deny that traditional positive law constitutes such a limitation. For that reason the American Revolution can be called an eighteenth-century version of the *diffidatio* of Runnymede, a continuation of the English Whig Revolution during the preceding century.

A letter to John Cartwright, written in 1824, shows that Jefferson credited the English constitution with Whig values, implying limitations upon the government. That constitution is traced back to the Anglo-Saxons. From early times it stood for limited government, for "right." "And although this constitution was violated and set at naught by Norman force, yet force cannot change right. A perpetual claim was kept up by the nation, by their perpetual demand of a restoration of their Saxon laws; which shows they were never relinquished by the will of the nation. In the pullings and haulings for these ancient rights, between the nation, and its kings of the races of Plantagenets, Tudors and Stuarts, there was sometimes gain, and sometimes loss, until the final re-conquest of their rights from the Stuarts. The destitution and expulsion of this race broke the thread of pretended inheritance, extinguished all regal usurpations, and the nation entered into all its rights; and although in their bill of rights they specifically reclaimed some only, yet the omission of the others was no renunciation of the right to assume their exercise also, whenever occasion should occur. The new King received no rights or powers, but those expressly granted to him." Jefferson regrets that the English debated whether sovereignty was vested in the majority, the minority, or one man. America was more fortunate: "Our Revolution commenced on more favorable ground. It presented us an album on which we were free to write what we pleased. We had no occasion to search into musty records, to hunt up royal parchments, or to investigate the laws and institutions of a semi-barbarous ancestry. We appealed to those of nature, and found them engraved on our hearts."[179] This letter is telling. After discussing the importance of English traditional laws as a limitation upon the government for the sake of the rights of the individual, Jefferson refers to the law of nature as such a limitation, just as in his draft to the Declaration of Independence he mentions traditional English rights following his confession to the law of nature and of nature's God. Natural and English laws as limitations upon the power of government thus seem to be inseparable. But the comparison of America and England makes us turn to Jefferson's thought on American laws limiting government.

When the American Constitution was framed in Philadelphia, Jefferson wrote John Adams from Paris that the English Constitution is "acknowledged to be better than all which have preceded it," as it has approached nearer to the

178. Ibid., 2:969 ff.
179. June 5, 1824, *Writings* 7:355–56.

"first principle of a good government . . . a distribution of it's powers into executive, judiciary and legislative, and a subdivision of the latter into two or three branches." He adds that by that criterion, American constitutions are much more perfect than the British constitution.[180] This confirms a statement earlier in the year, that "the worst of the American constitutions is better than the best which ever existed before in any other country, and that they are wonderfully perfect for a first essay, yet every human essay must have defects."[181]

His praise of American state constitutions was due to their principle of the separation of powers and their bills of rights to make doubly sure that the people "are . . . guarded against State governments."[182] Since "it is to secure our just rights that we resort to government at all,"[183] it is not surprising that Jefferson would dislike the absence of a bill of rights in the federal constitution. That absence appears to be his main criticism of the new constitution. He refers to it more often than to any other criticism. After he received a copy of the federal Constitution in Paris the year it was framed, he writes James Madison: "First the omission of a bill of rights providing clearly and without the aid of sophisms for freedom of religion, freedom of the press, protection against standing armies, restriction against monopolies, the eternal and unremitting force of the habeas corpus laws, and trials by jury in all matters of fact triable by the laws of the land." He adds "that a bill of rights is what the people are entitled to against every government on earth, general or particular, and what no just government should refuse, or rest on inference."[184] Considering the rights protected by "a declaration of rights, . . . fetters against doing evil which no honest government should decline,"[185] Jefferson confirms the priority of his criticism in the year the Constitution was ratified: "I disapproved from the first moment . . . the want of a bill of rights to guard against the legislative as well as the executive branches of the government."[186] In between the framing and ratification of the Constitution, Jefferson again and again expresses the need for a bill of rights.[187] Happy to see some states had ratified the Constitution, he hopes that others would make ratification conditional on the adding of a bill of rights: "Were I in America, I would advocate it warmly till nine [states] should have adopted, and then as warmly take the other side to convince the remaining four that they ought not to come into it till the declaration of rights is annexed to it. By this means we should secure all the good of it,

180. Sept. 28, 1787, *Papers* 12:189.

181. To Thomas Mann Randolph, Jr., July 6, 1787, ibid., 11:557.

182. To Madison, July 31, 1788, ibid., 13:443.

183. To M. d'Ivernois, Feb. 6, 1795, *Works* 8:165.

184. To Madison, Dec. 20, 1787, *Papers* 12:440.

185. To Alexander Donald, Feb. 7, 1788, ibid., 12:571.

186. To Francis Hopkinson, Mar. 13, 1789, ibid., 14:650.

187. To Alexander Donald, Feb. 7, 1788; to James Madison, July 31, 1788; to General Washington, Dec. 4, 1788. Ibid., 12:571; 13:443; 14:328.

and procure so respectable an opposition as would induce the accepting states to offer a bill of rights. This would be the happiest turn the thing could take."[188]

Jefferson's standards on the contents of bills of rights are high. Upon receipt of a declaration from Madison, he writes: "I like it as far as it goes; but I should have been for going further." He suggests at length how certain proposed provisions could be improved in order "to hinder evil." He adds that "if we do not have them now, I have so much confidence in my countrymen as to be satisfied that we shall have them as soon as the degeneracy of our government shall render them necessary."[189] Shortly before his election to the presidency, Jefferson, more than a decade after the ratification of the Constitution, continues to be wary about rights. Hoping that his party would win in elections and have a solid majority, he states, "we must have 'A Declaration of the principles of the constitution,' in nature of a Declaration of rights, in all the points in which it has been violated."[190]

The rights of the individual would not be secured only through a national bill of rights. Among the principles of the United States Constitution securing freedom there was federalism. "But the true barriers of our liberty in this country are our State governments," Jefferson writes in 1811, "and the wisest conservative power every contrived by man, is that of which our Revolution and present government found us possessed. Seventeen distinct States, amalgamated into one as to their foreign concerns, but single and independent as to their internal administration, regularly organized with legislature and governor resting on the choice of the people, and enlightened by a free press, can never be so fascinated by the arts of one man, as to submit voluntarily to his usurpation. Nor can they be constrained to it by any force he can possess."[191]

The states can be barriers of liberty because under the federal system established by the Constitution they have retained the bulk of governmental power. Jefferson considers "the foundation of the Constitution as laid on this ground that 'all powers not delegated to the U.S. by the Constitution, not prohibited by it to the states, are reserved to the states or to the people.' [XIIth Amendmt.] To take a single step beyond the boundaries thus specially drawn around the powers of Congress, is to take possession of the boundless feild of power, no longer susceptible to any definition."[192] A few years later, the author of the Kentucky Resolutions[193] expresses fear of power even more emphatically: "The true theory of our constitution is surely the wisest & best, that the states are independent as to everything within themselves, & united as to

188. To William Stephens Smith, Feb. 2, 1788, ibid., 12:558.

189. To Madison, Aug. 28, 1789, ibid., 15:367, 368.

190. To Philip Norborne Nicholas, Apr. 7, 1800, *Works* 9:128–29.

191. To A. C. V. C. Destutt de Tracy, Jan. 26, 1811, ibid., 11:187.

192. Opinion on the Constitutionality of a Bill for Establishing a National Bank, Feb. 15, 1791, *Papers* 19:276.

193. Cf. Peterson, *Jefferson Image,* 56–58.

everything respecting foreign nations. Let the general government be reduced to foreign concerns only, and let our affairs be disentangled from those of all other nations, except as to commerce, which the merchants will manage the better, the more they are left free to manage for themselves, and our general government may be reduced to a very simple organization, & a very unexpensive one; a few plain duties can be performed by a few servants."[194] The First Inaugural speech again favors the "support of the State governments in all their rights, as . . . the surest bulwarks against antirepublican tendencies." It considers that support one of the essential principles of his government "which ought to shape it's administration."[195]

For Jefferson, then, the essential principles of free government in the United States, implying legal limitations upon the government for the sake of the protection of the rights of the individual, are the separation of the legislative, executive, and judicial branches of the government, complemented by a spatial separation of powers through federalism. While these institutions divide governmental power and thus are conducive to the rights of the individual, Jefferson, the apostle of freedom, wants additional guarantees in the form of specific limitations of divided governmental power through bills of rights.

Since the national Constitution embodies all these principles, especially after the addition of a bill of rights, Jefferson, who felt that its good aspects outweighed its shortcomings even before the bill of rights had been added, has praise for it. As early as 1789 "the constitution . . . is unquestionably the wisest ever yet presented to men."[196] Two years later Jefferson writes that the preservation of the Federal Constitution "is all we need contend for."[197] In 1800 the Constitution is considered "the ark of our safety, and grand palladium of our peace and happiness."[198] In 1813 Jefferson tells John Adams that the Constitution, while not perfect, is "competent to render our fellow citizens the happiest and the securest on whom the sun has ever shone."[199] A few years before his death he speaks of "the adored principles of our constitution."[200]

The Constitution, being a document dividing and restricting government for the sake of the individual's rights, must be strictly construed. During his first administration, Jefferson states: "Our peculiar security is in the possession of a written Constitution. Let us not make it a blank paper by construction." If a grant of power is considered "boundless," "then we have no Constitution."[201] He often repeats his advice that the Constitution must be strictly

194. To Gideon Granger, Aug. 13, 1800, *Works* 9:140.
195. Ibid., 9:197–98.
196. To David Humphreys, Mar. 13, 1789, *Papers* 14:678.
197. To Archibald Stuart, Dec. 23, 1791, *Works* 6:351.
198. To Stephen Cross, Mar. 28, 1800, *Writings* 8:160.
199. Oct. 28, 1813, *Works* 11:350.
200. To Jedediah Morse, Mar. 6, 1822, ibid., 12:224.
201. To Wilson C. Nicholas, Sept. 7, 1803, *Writings* 4:506.

construed.[202] Shortly before his death he criticizes judges who "are practising on the constitution by inferences, analogies, and sophisms, as they would on an ordinary law. They do not seem aware that it is not even a *constitution,* formed by a single authority, and subject to a single superintendence and control; but that it is a compact of many independent powers, every single one of which claims an equal right to understand it, and to require its observance."[203]

Jefferson's opposition to a liberal interpretation of the Constitution does not imply that he favored a rigid constitution. Like morals, laws were to be useful to the people.[204] Since the people were the best and only legitimate guardians of their interest and rights,[205] and laws were to be useful to the living, and the living only could have rights; they could amend their constitutions. Jefferson leaves no doubt that the federal Constitution should be amended, seeing the need for amendment even after a bill of rights had been added. He writes in 1790 "tho' I approve of the mass, yet I would wish to see some amendments, further than those which have been proposed, and fixing it more surely on a republican basis."[206] In 1803 he adds: "Let us go on then perfecting it by adding, by way of amendment to the Constitution, those powers which time and trial show are still wanting."[207] Twenty years later he fears the Constitution might not be amended anymore because "the states are now so numerous that I despair of ever seeing another amndmt to the constn, although the innovns of time will certainly call for some." Shortly before his

202. See his letters to George Ticknor, (May?), 1817; Spencer Roane, Sept. 6, 1819. *Works* 12:59, 137–38.

203. To Edward Livingston, Mar. 25, 1825, *Writings* 7:403–4.

204. "The study of the law is useful in a variety of points of view. It qualifies a man to be useful to himself, to his neighbors, & to the public. It is the most certain stepping stone to preferment in the political line." To Thomas Mann Randolph, May 30, 1790, *Works* 6:62. To Edmund Randolph, Jefferson writes on Aug. 18, 1799: "The law being law because it is the will of the nation . . . the will of the nation, the law." Ibid., 9:74, 76. See also the letter to Kercheval of July 12, 1816, ibid., 12:11–12; Wiltse, *Jeffersonian Tradition,* 158, 160, 171 ff., 175 ff.

205. The people "are the ultimate, guardians of their own liberty." *Notes on Virginia* in *Works* 4:64; they are "the only safeguard of the public liberty." To Edward Carrington, Jan. 16, 1787, *Papers* 11:49. To Madison, Jefferson writes that on the people's "good sense we may rely with the most security for the preservation of a due degree of liberty." Dec. 20, 1787, ibid., 12:442. The will of the people "is the only legitimate foundation of any government." To Benjamin Waring and others, Mar. 23, 1801, *Writings* 4:379. "The people of every country are the only safe guardians of their own rights." To John Wyche, May 19, 1809, ibid., 5:448. The people are "the only safe depository of power." To Walter Jones, Jan. 2, 1814, *Works* 11:374. To Samuel Kercheval, Jefferson writes on July 12, 1816: "I am not among those who fear the people. They, and not the rich, are our dependence for continued freedom," ibid., 12:10. See also his letter of Sept. 5, 1816, *Writings,* 7:36. "I know no safe depository of the ultimate powers of the society but the people themselves." To William C. Jarvis, Sept. 28, 1820, *Works* 12:163. To M. Coray, Jefferson writes on Oct. 31, 1823, that "the people . . . are the only safe . . . depositories of the public rights," *Writings* 7:319.

206. To George Mason, June 13, 1790, *Papers* 16:493.

207. To Wilson C, Nicholas, Sept. 7, 1803, *Writings* 4:506.

death, he writes that he had read with pleasure and satisfaction a speech on an amendment to the Constitution, and concurs with much of its contents.[208]

Jefferson's emphasis on limiting the government through morals, natural and positive laws reflects his fear of tyranny and governmental power.

Jefferson's hatred of tyranny was the opposite side of his love of liberty, a lifelong companion. "Rebellion to tyrants is obedience to God" was the motto on his seal, and through all of his life his remarks are studded with condemnations of despotism. *A Summary View of the Rights of British America* is a polemic against English despotism and tyranny. It denounces "the designs of despotism," warns "that bodies of men as well as individuals, are susceptible of the spirit of tyranny," and speaks of "a deliberate, systematical plan of reducing us to slavery." Were it admitted that the colonies would be run by those who elect Parliament, "instead of being a free people, as we have hitherto supposed, and mean to continue ourselves, we should suddenly be found the slaves, not of one, but of one hundred and sixty thousand tyrants; . . . removed from the reach of fear, the only restraining motive which may hold the hand of a tyrant." It fears "the measure of despotism be filled up," speaks of "Parliamentary tyranny," of "arbitrary measures."[209] The *Declaration of Taking up Arms* blames the English for erecting "a despotism of unlimited extent."[210] Jefferson's draft of the Declaration of Independence complains of a British design to reduce the colonies "under absolute despotism," of the king's attempting "the establishment of an absolute tyranny," of completing "the works of death, desolation and tyranny," of laying "a foundation so broad and undisguised for tyranny over a people fostered and fixed in principles of freedom."[211] The *Notes on Virginia* states: "The time to guard against corruption and tyranny, is before they shall have gotten hold of us. It is better to keep the wolf out of the fold, than to trust to drawing his teeth and talons after he shall have entered."[212] In 1811 Jefferson expresses the hope that God would protect man from tyrants.[213] Eleven years later he is glad that "this general insurrection of the world against it's tyrants will ultimately prevail by pointing the object of government to the happiness of the people, and not merely to that of their self-constituted governors."[214]

Jefferson emphasizes his negative feelings toward governmental power throughout his lfe. The *Diffusion of Knowledge Bill* of 1779 states that "under the best forms" of government "those entrusted with power have . . . per-

208. To George Hay, Aug. 17, 1823, *Works* 12:303; to Edward Everett, Apr. 8, 1826, ibid., 12:469.

209. *Papers* 1:121 ff.

210. Fair Copy for the Committee, 1775, *Papers* 1:200–201.

211. *Jeffersonian Cyclopedia,* 2:969.

212. Query 13, *Works* 4:22.

213. To Lafayette, Jan. 20, 1811, ibid., 11:177.

214. To Lafayette, Oct. 28, 1822, ibid., 12:258–59.

verted it into tyranny."[215] Even "in a free country . . . every power is dangerous which is not bound up by general rules."[216] Jefferson is glad that "the true principles of our constitution . . . are wisely opposed to all perpetuations of power, and to every practice which may lead to hereditary establishments."[217] The possession of power will lead to the desire for more: "The functionaries of public power rarely strengthen in their dispositions to abridge it."[218] He concurs particularly with one sentiment of a speech made by Edward Livingston: "If we have a doubt relative to any power, we ought not to exercise it."[219]

Given the dubious character of power Jefferson writes: "I have never been so well pleased, as when I could shift power from my own, on the shoulders of others; nor have I ever been able to conceive how any rational being could propose happiness to himself from the exercise of power over others."[220] Two years later he adds: "An honest man can feel no pleasure in the exercise of power over his fellow citizens. And considering as the only offices of power those conferred by the people directly, that is to say, the executive and legislative functions of the General and State Governments, the common refusal of these and multiplied resignations, are proofs sufficient that power is not alluring to pure minds, and is not, with them, the primary principle of contest. This is my belief of it; it is that on which I have acted; and had it been a mere contest who should be permitted to administer the government according to its genuine republican principles, there has never been a moment in my life in which I should have relinquished for it the enjoyments of my family, my farm, my friends and books."[221]

The best depositories of power are the people. "No other despositories of power have ever yet been found, which did not end in converting to their own profit the earnings of those submitted to their charge."[222] In 1819 Jefferson writes of "an axiom of eternal truth in politics, that whatever power in any government is independent, is absolute also; in theory only, at first, while the spirit of the people is up, but in practice, as fast as that relaxes. Independence can be trusted nowhere but with the people in mass. They are inherently independent of all but moral law."[223] A year later Jefferson knows "no safe depository of the ultimate powers of the society but the people themselves; and if we think them not enlightened enough to exercise their control with a

215. A Bill for the More General Diffusion of Knowledge, *Papers* 2:526.
216. To Philip Mazzei, Nov. 1785, *Works* 4:480.
217. To Messrs. Bloodgood and Hammond, Sept. 30, 1809, *Writings* 5:473.
218. To John Taylor, May 28, 1816, *Works* 11:532.
219. To Edward Livingston, Apr. 4, 1824, ibid., 12:350.
220. To A. C. V. D. Destutt de Tracy, Jan. 26, 1811, ibid., 11:186.
221. To John Melish, Jan. 13, 1813, ibid., 11:278–79.
222. To Samuel Kercheval, Sept. 5, 1816, *Writings* 7:36.
223. To Judge Spencer Roane, Sept. 6, 1819, *Works* 12:137.

wholesome discretion, the remedy is not to take it from them, but to inform their discretion by education."[224] Two years before his death Jefferson considers the people the origin of all power.[225]

The Necessity of State Law

In spite of his skepticism toward governmental power and his belief that the government is best which governs least,[226] Jefferson concedes important functions to the state. They fall into two major categories: the regulation of various aspects of societal life and the enforcement of the laws.

It has been said that "according to all American historians," free enterprise "was a major issue in the American Revolution and, in the opinion of many, the most important issue."[227] Perhaps it is symbolic that the very year independence was declared with a denunciation of mercantilism, Smith's *Wealth of Nations* was published, a work Jefferson considered "the best book extant" in political economy.[228] He shared its ideas, believing in the principle of private enterprise yet making certain concessions to governmental activities.

Expressing himself for free trade among the nations,[229] Jefferson basically favors unhindered private enterprise within the United States. His First Inaugural shows faith in a republican government that "shall restrain men from injuring one another," but "shall leave them otherwise free to regulate their own pursuits of industry & improvement," and "shall not take from the mouth of labor the bread it has earned."[230] His First Annual Message to Congress states: "Agriculture, manufactures, commerce, and navigation, the four pillars of our prosperity, are the most thriving when left most free to individual enterprise."[231] His Second Annual Message continues in a similar vein, attributing the great prosperity of the country to "the skill, industry and order of our citizens, managing their own affairs in their own way and for their own use,

224. To William C. Jarvis, Sept. 28, 1820, ibid., 12:163.

225. To Johns Cartwright, June 5, 1824, *Writings* 7:356.

226. Patterson, *Constitutional Principles,* 111.

227. Ibid., 103.

228. To Thomas Mann Randolph, Jr., May 30, 1790, *Papers* 16:449.

229. "I think all the *world would gain* by *setting commerce* at perfect *liberty.*" To John Adams, July 31, 1785, ibid., 8:332. "[Congress] had in the year 1784, made up their minds as to the system of commercial principles they wished to pursue. These were very free. They proposed them to all the powers of Europe. All declined except Prussia. To this general opposition they may now find it necessary to present a very different general system to which their treaties will form cases of exception." To C. W. F. Dumas, Dec. 9, 1787, ibid., 12:407. "I am for free commerce with all nations." To Elbridge Gerry, Jan. 26, 1799, *Works* 9:18. "The permitting an exchange of industries with other nations is a direct encouragement of your own, which without that, would bring you nothing for your comfort, and would of course cease to be produced." To Samuel Smith, May 3, 1823, ibid., 12:286.

230. *Works* 9:197.

231. Ibid., 9:339.

unembarrassed by too much regulation, unoppressed by fiscal exactions."[232] In conformity with the principle of free enterprise, Jefferson turned down an offer to convey an iron mine to the government, stating that he "always observed that public works are much less advantageously managed" by the government "than the same are by private hands."[233] He refused government assistance to operating the New Orleans Canal Company, considering such assistance "too much out of our policy of not embarking the public in enterprises better managed by individuals."[234] These statements show that even as president, in spite of all the temptations of his office to use and enlarge executive power, Jefferson continued to favor private enterprise. He was against bounties or drawbacks that enrich a few at the expense of others.[235] He opposed a subsidized merchant marine or too many ships of war merely "to feed the avidity of a few millionary merchants" and to protect "their commercial speculations."[236] His *Autobiography* states his belief in plain, down-to-earth words: "Were we directed from Washington when to sow, & when to reap, we should soon want bread."[237] Free enterprise promotes national wealth and is fair and just.[238] It is conducive to frugal government and reduces a bureaucracy tending to big government, a government wasteful and dangerous to the freedom of the individual.[239]

However, wherever there is a principle, there are exceptions. Jefferson was not opposed to all government interference in the private sector. The First Inaugural mentions the "Encouragement of Agriculture, & of Commerce as it's handmaid."[240] The First Annual Message, while stating that agriculture, manufactures, commerce, and navigation, are the most thriving when left to individual enterprise, adds: "Protection from casual embarrassments, however, may sometimes be seasonably interposed."[241] In the Second Annual Message we read of a presidential policy "to foster our fisheries and nurseries of navigation and for the nurture of man, and protect the manufactures adapted to our circumstance."[242] The Second Inaugural Address states that after payment of the national debt, "the revenue thereby liberated may, by a just repartition among the states, and a corresponding amendment of the constitution, be applied, *in time of peace,* to rivers, canals, roads, arts, manufactures, education, and other great objects within each state."[243] "The fondest wish of my heart," Jefferson stated in 1813, "ever was that the surplus portion of these taxes, destined for the payment of that [Revolutionary War] debt, should, when that object was accomplished, be . . . applied, in time of peace, to the improvement of our country by canals, roads and useful institutions, literary or others; and in

232. Ibid., 9:407.
233. To Bibb, July 28, 1808, *Writings* 5:326.
234. To W. C. C. Claiborne, July 17, 1808, ibid., 5:319.
235. To Benjamin Stoddert, Feb. 18, 1809, *Works* 11:98.
236. To William H. Crawford, June 20, 1816, ibid., 11:539.
237. *Ford I* 1:113.
238. See Patterson, *Constitutional Principles,* 113.
239. Ibid., 112.
240. *Works* 9:198.
241. Ibid., 9:339.
242. Ibid., 9:414–15.
243. Ibid., 10:130.

time of war to the maintenance of the war."[244] To Alexander von Humboldt, he writes: "We consider the employment [in public works] of the contributions which our citizens spare, after feeding, and clothing, and lodging themselves comfortably, as more useful, more moral, and even more splendid, than that preferred by Europe, of destroying human life, labor and happiness."[245] Jefferson inaugurated internal improvements at government expense, including a coast survey, river and harbor installations, the construction of roads and canals. When Ohio was admitted to the Union in 1803, it was with the provision that one-twentieth of the net proceeds from the sale of land within that state would be used for building roads from the east coast to the Ohio valley. In 1806 Congress appropriated money for the Cumberland Pike. "Public works, the benefit of which would be felt by large numbers of citizens, were within the scope of governmental activity as Jefferson conceived it."[246] Commerce could be restricted for the sake of peace with other nations and for winning a war.[247]

Jefferson is in favor of taxation. While he opposed the arbitrary taxes raised by the English, he denounced those who, after the Constitution had been framed would "wish to take from Congress the power of internal taxation. Calculation has convinced me this would be very mischievous."[248] While the rich should not be taxed in order to give to the poor, "it may be the interest and the duty of all . . . to pay for a time an impost on the importation of certain articles, in order to encourage their manufacture at home, or an excise on others injurious to the morals or health of the citizens."[249] He remarks that "the government which steps out of the ranks of the ordinary articles of consumption to select and lay under disproportionate burdens a particular one, because it is a comfort, pleasing to the taste, or necessary to health, and will therefore be bought, is, in that particular, a tyranny. Taxes on consumption like those on capital or income, to be just, must be uniform." Yet he immediately adds: "I do not mean to say that it may not be for the general interest to foster for awhile certain infant manufactures, until they are strong enough to stand against foreign rivals."[250]

Jefferson in principle objects to the government's borrowing of money. However, he concedes that sometimes it may be necessary and that it may be the duty of the citizens to lend what they can. He warns: "It is a wise rule, and should be fundamental in a government disposed to cherish its credit, and at the same time to restrain the use of it within the limits of its faculties, 'never to borrow a dollar without laying a tax in the same instant for paying the interest

244. To John W. Eppes, Sept. 11, 1813, *Writings* 6:195.

245. June 13, 1817, *Works* 12:69.

246. Wiltse, *Jeffersonian Tradition,* 147.

247. To William Crawford, June 20, 1816, *Works* 11:538–39. Cf. to James Monroe, June 17, 1785, and to John Adams, July 7, 1785, *Papers* 8:227 ff., 265 ff.

248. To William Carmichael, Dec. 25, 1788, *Papers* 14:385.

249. To Joseph Milligan, Apr. 6, 1816, *Writings* 6:574.

250. To General Samuel Smith, May 3, 1823, *Memorial ed.* 15:432–33.

annually, and the principle within a given term; and to consider that tax as pledged to the creditors on the public faith.' " Yet he qualifies: "On such a pledge as this, sacredly observed, a government may always command, on a *reasonable interest,* all the lendable money of its citizens."[251]

Jefferson favored public support for education. This is not surprising in view of the importance he attributed to it for the working of republican government: "No other sure foundation can be devised for the preservation of freedom, and happiness."[252] Education also is conducive to peace and order. "And say, finally," he asks Madison, "whether peace is best preserved by giving energy to the government, or information to the people. This last is the most certain, and the most legitimate engine of government. Educate and inform the whole mass of the people. Enable them to see that it is their interest to preserve peace and order, and they will preserve them. And it requires no very high degree of education to convince them of this. They are the only sure reliance for the preservation of our liberty."[253] A few years later, as president, he writes that "to open the doors of truth, and to fortify the habit of testing everything by reason, are the most effectual manacles we can rivet on the hands of our successors to prevent their manacling the people with their own consent."[254]

In his Sixth Annual Message Jefferson proposed to Congress that education should be an object of public care and that a public endowment be established for that purpose.[255] Later, in 1817, he prepared an Act for Establishing Elementary Schools, relating specifically to the state of Virginia, but written in hopes that it would be applied in other states. It proposes universal public education, including colleges teaching the "Greek, Latin, French, Spanish, Italian and German languages, English grammar, geography, ancient and modern, the higher branches of numerical arithmetic, the mensuration of land, the use of the globes, and the ordinary elements of navigation." At the top of the system there would be a university offering courses in "history and geography, ancient and modern; natural philosophy, agriculture, chemistry and the theories of medicine; anatomy, zoology, botany, mineralogy and geology; mathematics, pure and mixed; military and naval science; ideology, ethics, the law of nature and of nations; law, municipal and foreign; the science of civil government and political economy; languages, rhetoric, belles lettres, and the fine arts generally."[256] Jefferson's great love was the publicly supported University of Virginia, "the last of my mortal cares, and the last service I can render my country."[257] The year before his death he writes: "I am closing the last scenes

251. To John W. Eppes, June 24, 1813, *Writings* 6:136.

252. To George Wythe, Aug. 13, 1786, *Papers* 10:244.

253. To James Madison, Dec. 20, 1787. *Memorial ed.* 6:392. (I could not find these words in *Papers* 12:442).

254. To Judge Tyler, June 28, 1804, *Writings* 4:549.

255. *Works* 10:318–19.

256. *Memorial ed.* 17:430–31, 436–37. See Wiltse, *Jeffersonian Tradition,* 140–41.

257. To J. Correa de Serra, Oct. 24, 1820, *Works* 12:167.

of my life by fashioning and fostering an establishment for the instruction of those who are to come after us. I hope its influence on their virtue, freedom, fame and happiness will be salutary and permanent."[258]

For Jefferson public education was not limited to the operation of a school system. The circulation of books and papers was equally important. During his first administration, he favored the abolition of postage on newspapers to facilitate the progress of information. In 1809 he proposed the establishment of a circulating library in each county.[259]

For the lawyer Jefferson an important activity of the government was the enforcement of the laws. "The execution of the laws is more important than the making of them."[260] The execution of the laws must be strict, available to all, and impartially applied to all cases. "The slightest deviation in one circumstance becomes a precedent for another, that for a third and so on without bounds." This is detrimental to public security.[261] Jefferson is of the opinion that "an equal application of law to every condition of man is fundamental."[262]

For the sake of law enforcement, the judiciary should be independent. The Declaration of Independence denounces George III for making judges dependent on his will as to the tenure of their offices and the amount and payment of their salaries. According to Jefferson, American judges "should not be *dependent upon any man, or body of men.*"[263] He is glad to note: "The courts of justice exercise the sovereignty of this country, in judiciary matters, are supreme in these, and liable neither to control nor opposition from any other branch of the government."[264] Jefferson favors judicial review, even though he became bitter against the Supreme Court when, in his opinion, it abused its power by loosely constructing the Constitution for the sake of nationalism.[265]

Law must be enforced against all, high and low. Jefferson complains that the intended trial of Warren Hastings before a special court means that "he may be judged, not according to the law of the land, but by the discretion of his judges," that he would be "disfranchised of his most precious right, the benefit of the laws of his country."[266] Jefferson wants to "deal out justice without partiality or favoritism."[267] His First Inaugural states that "equal and exact justice to all men, of whatever state or persuasion, religious, or political," is an essential principle of government and ought to shape its administration.[268]

258. To Judge Augustus B. Woodward, Apr. 3, 1825, ibid., 12:408.
259. See Wiltse, *Jeffersonian Tradition,* 144.
260. To Abbé Arnoux, July 19, 1789, *Papers* 15:283.
261. To George Joy, Mar. 31, 1790, ibid., 16:284.
262. To George Hay, Aug. 20, 1807, *Writings* 5:175.
263. To George Wythe, (June?) 1776, *Papers* 1:410.
264. To Edmond C. Genet, Sept. 9, 1793, *Works* 8:36.
265. See Patterson, *Constitutional Principles,* 73 ff.
266. To John Rutledge, Feb. 2, 1788, *Papers* 12:556–57.
267. To Hugh Williamson, Apr. 1, 1792, *Works* 6:458–59.
268. Ibid., 9:197.

Two years later he writes that "when one undertakes to administer justice, it must be with an even hand, & by rule; what is done for one, must be done for every one in equal degree."[269] Years after he had left the presidency he states that the most sacred of the duties of a government is to do equal justice to all its citizens.[270] To him, "justice is the fundamental law of society."[271]

Since law enforcement is a means of securing justice, laws must be carried out so as to comply with justice. Jefferson favors obedience to the letter of the law. "Constructions, which do not result from the words of the legislator, but lie hidden in his breast, till called forth, *ex post facto,* by subsequent occasions, are dangerous, and not to be justified by ordinary emergencies,"[272] and "constructions must not be favored which go to defeat instead of furthering the principal object of the law, and to sacrifice the end to the means."[273] Nevertheless, "where the words of a statute admit of two constructions, the one just and the other unjust, the former is to be given them."[274] Parties, even though they had the letter of the law on their side, ought not to take advantage of it, for it "is not honorable to take a mere legal advantage when it happens to be contrary to justice."[275] As an attorney, he "practiced a little art in a case where honesty was really on our side, and nothing against us but the rigorous letter of the law."[276]

As governor of Virginia he clearly indicated that the enforcement of the law was basically a pragmatic process and that the law as a means to an end had to be enforced so as to best accomplish that purpose.[277] While Jefferson entertained doubts about constructions of the laws in case of ordinary emergencies, he permitted such constructions in severe emergencies. "A strict observance of the written laws is doubtless *one* of the high duties of a good citizen, but it is not *the highest.* The laws of necessity, of self-preservation, of saving our country when in danger, are of higher obligation. To lose our country by a scrupulous adherence to written law, would be to lose the law itself, with life, liberty, property and all those who are enjoying them with us; thus absurdly sacrificing the end to the means." After citing cases in which the "unwritten laws of necessity, of self-preservation, and of the public safety, control the written laws of *meum* and *tuum,*" he adds that these examples "do not go to the case of persons charged with petty duties, where consequences are trifling, and time allowed for a legal course." Petty officers are not permitted to

269. To Benjamin Rush, Oct. 4, 1803, ibid., 10:31.

270. To Joseph Milligan, Apr. 6, 1816, *Writings* 6:574.

271. To M. Dupont de Nemours, Apr. 24, 1816, ibid., 6:591.

272. Second Report of Conference Committee, Jan. 9, 1778, *Works* 2:314.

273. To W. H. Cabell, Aug. 11, 1807, *Writings* 5:159.

274. To Isaac McPherson, Aug. 13, 1813, ibid., 6:175.

275. Opinion in Favor of the Resolutions of May 21st, 1790 . . . , June 3, 1790, *Memorial ed.* 3:25.

276. To John Taylor, June 4, 1798, ibid., 18:205.

277. To Gov. Thomas Sim Lee, Feb. 1, 1781, *Papers* 4:494.

take cases out of the written law because "the example of overleaping the law is of greater evil than a strict adherence to its imperfect provisions." On the other hand, those holding important office can do so: "It is incumbent on those only who accept great charges, to risk themselves on great occasions, when the safety of the nation, or some of its very high interests are at stake. . . . The line of discrimination between cases may be difficult; but the good officer is bound to draw it at his own peril, and throw himself on the justice of his country and the rectitude of his motives."[278] In a word, for the preservation of the body politic and its system of law, those on top of the government can transgress written laws, can go *ultra vires* by exercising self-assumed dictatorial powers. In great emergencies, the legal order can be secured by extralegal means.

Conclusion

Jefferson's statements on freedom, law, and order reveal him as a man of measure.

Jefferson played an active role in the American Revolution. He was ambassador to France at the beginning of the French Revolution. His writings influenced Bolívar and other Spanish American revolutionaries. He envisaged the independence of Spanish America. He lived through a half-century that saw successful revolutions for the sake of liberty. Was he a revolutionary? It is perhaps proper to say that Jefferson was a revolutionary with measure. In a Lockean vein he proposed revolutionary action. Yet, again like Locke, Jefferson made plain that a revolution was justified only by a long chain of serious oppressions and vain petitions for redress. In 1775, when he saw Lord Chatham's bill, he "entertained high hope that a reconciliation could have been brought about" with the mother country.[279] A few months later he looked "with fondness towards a reconciliation with Great Britain."[280] Unlike Burke, Jefferson never condemned the French Revolution; yet he regretted its bloodshed.[281]

While he emphasized that laws and constitutions must go with the times, he wrote that he was not an advocate for frequent and untried changes. While he felt that "man should be bound down by the chains of the Constitution," he stated: "The real friends of the constitution in its federal form . . . should be attentive, by amendments, to make it keep pace with the advance of the age in science and experience."[282] Yet again, "Jefferson never felt . . . that the Con-

278. To John B. Colvin, Sept. 20, 1810, *Works* 11:146, 147, 149. Cf.: "On great occasions every good officer must be ready to risk himself in going beyond the strict line of law, when the public preservation requires it." To Gov. Claiborne, Feb. 3, 1807, *Writings* 5:40.

279. To William Small, May 7, 1775, *Papers* 1:166.

280. To John Randolph, Aug. 25, 1775, ibid., 1:241.

281. See George H. McKee, *Thomas Jefferson, Ami de la Révolution Française* (Lorient, 1928).

282. To Robert J. Garnet, Feb. 14, 1824, *Works* 12:342.

stitution was merely 'a restricted railroad ticket good for this day and train only,' and that therefore it should be changed every Monday by a life-time constituent convention determined upon converting a limited constitutional federal system of government into a unitary authoritarian state as the agent of liberalism."[283]

The preceding pages reveal Jefferson as a liberal, in line with Montesquieu, Smith, and Kant. His liberalism was one of measure. The "Apostle of Liberty" opposed anarchy and wanted freedom to be restricted by morality, natural, and positive law. Opposing despotism, he also wanted governments to be restricted by these values. His concept of the rule of law implied restrictions of the government for the sake of the protection of the rights of the individual as well as sufficient governmental authority to guarantee the safety of the citizen from his fellow men in peace and order.

The government best suited to his concept of the rule of law was a limited popular government, usually referred to by Jefferson as republican government. It was known to the founding fathers as free government, under which the ruling majority was restricted for the sake of the freedom of the individual and the minority, a minority that could become a majority through elections. It was a government of tolerance, as expressed in the First Inaugural which, after the election campaign, states: "Let us, then, fellow-citizens, unite with one heart & one mind; let us restore to social intercourse that harmony & affection, without which Liberty & even Life itself, are but dreary things. . . . every difference of opinion, is not a difference of principle. We have called, by different names, brethren of the same principle. We are all republicans: we are all federalists. If there be any among us who wish to dissolve this union, or to change its republican form, let them stand undisturbed, as monuments of the safety with which error of opinion may be tolerated where reason is left free to combat it."[284]

The ideal republican constitution for the America Jefferson knew—for to him no particular constitution was permanent because it was supposed to be suited to given conditions—is one providing for divisions of governmental power and a good balance between its various branches, a constitution "which defined the various divisions of government and delineated their functions, powers, duties, and interrelationships."[285] The division of powers was to exist on institutional and territorial levels. Jefferson, who strongly believed in a genuine institutional separation of powers, also emphasized a genuine division of the powers of the states and the national government.[286] A few years before he was elected president he praised "that beautiful equilibrium on which our Constitution is founded, and which I believe it will exhibit to the world in a

283. Patterson, *Constitutional Principles,* 79–80.
284. *Works* 9:195–96. (Abbreviations in the last sentence have been spelled out.)
285. Healey, *Jefferson on Religion,* 76.
286. Ibid., 84–85. See Jefferson's letter to James Madison, Dec. 20, 1787, *Papers* 12:439–40.

degree of perfection, unexampled but in the planetary system itself. The enlightened statesman, therefore, will endeavor to preserve the weight and influence of every part, as too much given to any member of it would destroy the general equilibrium."[287] His opinion did not change. After pointing out the need for an institutional separation of powers on the national level in 1820,[288] he writes in 1821: "It is a fatal heresy to suppose that either our State governments are superior to the federal, or the federal to the States. The people, to whom all authority belongs, have divided the powers of government into two distinct departments, the leading characters of which are *foreign* and domestic, and they have appointed for each a distinct set of functionaries. These they have made co-ordinate, checking and balancing each other, like the three cardinal departments in the individual States: each equally supreme as to the powers delegated to itself, and neither authorized ultimately to decide what belongs to itself, or to its coparcenor in government. . . . a spirit of forbearance and compromise, therefore, and not encroachment and usurpation, is the healing balm of such a constitution."[289] For the sake of the individual's protection by the government, the division of powers between the legislature, the executive, the judiciary and between the state and national governments was not supposed to destroy governmental authority. Jefferson was glad America possessed "the combined blessing of liberty and order," wishing "the same to other countries."[290]

Jefferson's ideas on freedom and government reflect his measureful view of the people who institute government and for whom governments are instituted. Enlightened as he was, he did not share the optimism of the typical Enlightenment *philosophe* who tended to see just good qualities in people.[291] He felt that people were good enough to be trusted with self-government, but not so perfect that they could be trusted absolutely. He did not share "the heedless optimism of Condorect" and "was not, for the most part, overly sanguine and unduly optimistic about the possibility of progress."[292] Yet he hoped for some

287. To Peregrine Fitzhugh, Feb. 23, 1798, *Works* 8:377.

288. To William C. Jarvis, Sept. 28, 1820, ibid., 12:163.

289. To Spencer Roane, June 27, 1821, *Writings* 7:213–14.

290. To M. Coray, Oct. 31, 1823, ibid., 7:318.

291. Cf. Carl L. Becker, *The Heavenly City of the Eighteenth-Century Philosophers,* 103; Healey, *Jefferson on Religion,* 54.

292. Healey, *Jefferson on Religion,* 54. Here are some of Jefferson's comments on man and mankind: "I do not recollect in all the animal kingdom a single species but man which is eternally & systematically engaged in the destruction of its own species. What is called civilization seems to have no other effect on him than to teach him to pursue the principle of *bellum omnium in omnia* on a larger scale, & in place of the little contests of tribe against tribe, to engage all the quarters of the earth in the same work of destruction. . . . the lions & tigers are mere lambs compared with man as a destroyer." To James Madison, Jan. 1, 1797, *Works* 8:264. To Volney he writes that "man . . . is in all his shapes a curious animal." Jan. 8, 1797, *Writings* 4:159. "The greatest honor of a man is in doing good to his fellow men, not in destroying them." To the Chiefs of the Shawanee Nation, Feb. 19, 1807, ibid., 8:208 (Address to Indians). "The Great Spirit did not make men that

improvements: "Whether the succeeding generation is to be more virtuous than their predecessors, I cannot say; but I am sure they will have more worldly wisdom, and enough, I hope, to know that honesty is the first chapter in the book of wisdom."[293] "I look to the diffusion of light and education as the resource most to be relied on for ameliorating the condition, promoting the virtue, and advancing the happiness of man. That every man shall be made virtuous, by any process whatever, is, indeed, no more to be expected, than that every tree shall be made to bear fruit, and every plant nourishment. The brier and bramble can never become the vine and olive; but their asperities may be softened by culture, and their properties improved to usefulness in the order and economy of the world. And I do hope that, in the present spirit of extending to the great mass of mankind the blessings of instruction, I see a prospect of great advancement in the happiness of the human race; and that this may proceed to an indefinite, although not to an infinite degree."[294]

---

they might destroy one another, but doing to each other all the good in their power, and thus filling the land with happiness instead of misery and murder." To Kitchao Geboway, 1809, ibid., 8:228 (Indian Address). "men are disposed to live honestly, if the means of doing so are open to them." To M. de Marbois, June 14, 1817, ibid., 7:77. "What a Bedlamite is man?" To John Adams, Jan. 22, 1821, *Works* 12:199. "We believed . . . that man was . . . a rational animal, endowed by nature with rights, and with an innate sense of justice; and that he could be restrained from wrong and protected in right, by moderate powers, confided to persons of his own choice, and held to their duties by dependence on his own will. . . . We believed that men, enjoying in ease and security the full fruits of their own industry, enlisted by all their interests on the side of law and order, habituated to think for themselves, and to follow their reason as their guide, would be more easily and safely governed, than with minds nourished in error, and vitiated and debased, as in Europe, by ignorance, indigence and oppression." To William Johnson, June 12, 1823, *Writings* 7:291–92. "In truth, man is not made to be trusted for life, if secured against all liability to account." To M. Coray, Oct. 31, 1823, ibid., 7:322.

293. To Nathaniel Macon, Jan. 12, 1819, *Works* 7:112.

294. To Cornelius Camden Blatchly, Oct. 21, 1822, *Writings* 7:263.

CHAPTER VI

LIBERALISM AND DEMOCRACY

The Liberalism of Montesquieu, Smith, Kant, and Jefferson

Montesquieu lived from 1689 to 1755, Smith from 1723 to 1790, Kant from 1724 to 1804, and Jefferson from 1743 to 1826. The lives of these men span the period from the Glorious Revolution to the Restoration in continental Europe and Jacksonian democracy in the United States, a period that witnessed the rule of Louis XIV, the Lisbon earthquake, the French Revolution, Napoleon I, and the independence of English and Spanish colonies in the New World. It saw enthusiasm and doubts about human reason, the replacement of royal absolutism by Jacobin terror, democracy, and constitutional government. It saw the substitution of the contractual theory of the state by the organic one. It was the period in which Rousseau lived, a period of change, the kind Burckhardt found fascinating because of its transitions.[1] The work considered here ranges from the publication of the *Persian Letters* in 1721 to remarks by Jefferson in the year of his death, from the third decade of the eighteenth century to that of the nineteenth. It came forth at about the time that initiated the modern movement known as liberalism.

Montesquieu, Smith, Kant, and Jefferson lived in different nations and cultural environments. Montesquieu grew up in the France of Louis XIV, the

1. Jacob Burckhardt, *Reflections on History,* trans. M. D. Hottinger (Indianapolis, 1979), 213 ff., esp. 248 ff.

Sun King, said to have stated *L'Etat c'est moi.* He published under that king's absolutist successors in the land in which the concept of the nation was coined. Kant spent his childhood under Frederick William I, the Soldier King. He lived throughout the rule of Frederick the Great, who as crown prince wrote an anti-Machiavellian treatise and considered the king the first servant of the state, and that king's successors. Smith and Jefferson knew a freer environment, under British parliamentarism where the monarch could do no wrong because he had no power to do so, under popular and constitutional government. These authors thus lived under despotism, enlightened despotism, democracy and constitutionalism—a great variety of regimes.

The four men came from different backgrounds. Baron Louis de Secondat de Montesquieu was the scion of an old aristocratic family with substantial holdings, belonging to what Jefferson called the artificial aristocracy by birth. Jefferson was a member of the Virginian gentry; his possessions were small compared to those of the Frenchman. Smith and Kant were of humble origin: Smith was the son of a corset-maker; Kant's father was a poor saddle-maker.

Differences due to birth were complemented by the ways in which they lived. Montesquieu and Jefferson were gentlemen farmers, active in public life. Smith and Kant were professors. The Frenchman and the American travelled widely. Smith went from his native Scotland to England and made a short journey across the Channel. Kant remained in and around his birthplace all his life.

In spite of these differences our authors have been considered liberals who share certain basic values, among which human freedom plays an important role. To them, freedom is something men are born with, something natural, innate to human beings, of which in principle they cannot and ought not, be deprived. Liberty is the prerequisite for the wealth of nations in a most comprehensive sense: for the wealth of the individual, of his society, of all societies. It is a prerequisite for the progress of the human race. As a source of progress and wealth, freedom appears to be inexhaustible.

The authors conceive of liberty as an abstract concept that they cannot define. As Kant put it: "The *inscrutability* of the idea of freedom precludes any positive demonstration."[2] However, much as freedom as a general idea may have been considered undefinable, they distinguish various classes of freedom. There is an inner and an outer freedom. The former cannot be restricted and is beyond the control of external forces. The latter is divided into two major types, namely, the freedom of the individual from outside interference and that of participating in public affairs. Popular participation in government is a means for the protection of the rights of the individual, among which those of contract and property have a high standing.

2. "Denn die *Unerforschlichkeit der Idee der Freiheit* schneidet aller positiven Darstellung gänzlich den Weg ab: das moralische Gesetz aber ist an sich selbst in uns hinreichend und ursprünglich bestimmend, so daß es nicht einmal erlaubt, uns nach einem Bestimmungsgrunde außerhalb desselben umzusehen." *Krit. d. U.,* 5:275.

The designation of freedom from external regulation as the end of government does not mean that unlimited freedom is desirable. To Montesquieu, Smith, Kant, and Jefferson unlimited liberty was an idea, not an ideal. Freedom is a principle permitting exceptional restrictions, be they self-imposed or imposed by the government. The authors did not advocate all rights found in modern bills of rights. For instance, we look in vain for a defense of freedom of association. Furthermore, they did not want an unlimited exercise of some of the rights they favor. For example, they admitted curtailments of free speech and of laissez-faire. To preclude anarchy and license, they wanted freedom restricted. To prevent such restrictions from being arbitrary, they wanted them according to the law.

Their concept of law was a wide one. Law is not just the equivalent of positive law, a law that can be enforced by the public authority. It comprises unenforceable metapositive law as well. This opinion is logical: Montesquieu, Smith, Kant, and Jefferson wanted curtailments upon internal as well as external freedom and the former cannot well be restricted by positive laws.

All four emphasized a restriction of liberty through morals, a concept that nowadays is no longer connected with, but juxtaposed to, the law. Their attitude is not surprising in view of the fact that the eighteenth century has been considered one of morality. Montesquieu, Smith, Kant, and Jefferson agreed that a moral faculty is innate in human beings, who should act in accordance with it. They found that man's conscience puts his mind at ease when he acts morally and prompts suffering if he does not.

Aside from morality, the liberty of individuals is restricted by imperatives usually connected with the concept of law, even though these norms cannot be enforced by the government. They are the imperatives of so-called higher law, such as divine law, natural law, and the law of nations.

Human actions also are restricted by enforceable positive laws. These laws, usually customary laws, legislative enactments, executive rules and regulations, and judicial decisions, should conform to morality and higher law. However, they often do not and are bad and unethical. Still, they must be obeyed.

The hardship resulting from the requirement of obeying laws, even bad ones, is attenuated by the fact that Montesquieu, Smith, Kant, and Jefferson emphasized the limitation of governments through the law. Again, they conceived of law in a wide sense, comprising morals, higher law, and positive law. Because governments often will be the makers and masters of positive law and a master can hardly be restricted by what he masters, our authors in a large measure based their restrictions of governmental power upon morals, divine, natural, and customary law. In view of the fact that these kinds of law are not really binding upon those in power, Montesquieu, Smith, Kant, and Jefferson favored the limitation of rulers by constitutions. These constitutions would transmute morals and higher law into positive law, be they unwritten, as in England, or written, as in the United States and continental Europe.

Concentration of power being conducive to tyranny, a constitution is to provide for divisions of governmental power and, in order to prevent one or a combination of the branches of government from getting too strong, for checks and balances. With these arrangements, the rights of the individuals are protected. Life, liberty and property are safe, trade flourishes. The individual enjoys a great deal of freedom for the pursuit of his natural inclinations.

While Montesquieu, Smith, Kant, and Jefferson wanted individuals and governments restricted by the same types of law, they realized that only individuals, not governments, can be made to obey positive law, i.e., administrative rules and regulations, legislative enactments, judicial decisions, and custom. Therefore the authors wanted government to be bound by the positive laws of constitutions which they hoped would reflect morals, higher law, and custom, from which all other positive laws emanate and to which they conform. Constitutionalism implies a government of law which, while curtailing the liberty of the individual in order to prevent anarchy, is restricted for his sake in order to avoid tyranny.

The decrease of governmental power through the laws does not mean that Montesquieu, Smith, Kant, and Jefferson were opposed to state activities. While they were cautious about that power, they favored its rightful authority. They believed in the principle that the government is best that governs least, but were well aware that such a government is still a government and that divisions of its power are not supposed to result in an absence of authority. Governments have important functions. The authors favored public order and the good citizenship that goes with it, a citizenship that would not jeopardize but sustain society. Their fear of anarchy was complemented by a rejection of too much egoism on the side of individuals and a certain wariness about unlimited laissez-faire. In a good society, there is room for charity, but helpfulness must not induce laziness. There is room for social programs, although such endeavors are preferred on a temporary rather than permanent basis.

The state can play an active role in public life. It has the right to taxation to finance public necessities such as defense, the construction of roads and canals, health, and education. It may encourage the arts, commerce, and industry. Probably its most important function is the maintenance of justice through the strict execution of positive laws, for the sake of peace and security within the realm. Whereas individuals must be protected from undue interference by public officials, the government must protect the rights of all from infringements by fellow-citizens. This protection must be guaranteed by penalties, including capital punishment.

Throughout the writings of Montesquieu, Smith, Kant, and Jefferson there are passages that show that all four shied away from extremes. The same is true of their philosophies of liberalism. The great liberals were advocates, not apostles, of freedom. They were men of measure. Fearing the extremes of anarchy and tyranny, they favored the liberty of the individual, but not on an absolute scale. They wanted freedom restricted by the law. Much as they desired autolimitation in accordance with higher law, they realized that restrictions of freedom must be secured through positive laws. Yet they saw the dangers of such restrictions and prefer enforceable laws that are in conformity with higher laws and are good, just, and well-balanced. For the sake of a measureful restriction of the individual's liberty, the great liberals, fearing big government and a concentration of power, wanted rulers limited by a constitution that reflects morals, divine law, natural and customary law, and divides governmental power. To prevent too much power in any one of the divisions or combinations thereof, checks and balances are advocated. The latter, however, must not jeopardize government. Skepticism of power is thus matched by fear of a loss of authority. Government is considered necessary for the execution of the laws so that the society and the individuals composing it may prosper and survive. While that government is best that governs least, the state has to fulfill important functions beyond those of making and executing the laws. Whereas the safety of the rights of the individual is the end of society and its government, there must be government for the sake of a society in which the individual can safely enjoy a maximum of rights. Liberalism, conceived as a remedy against despotism, is free government, not the absence of government.

These are the principles which Montesquieu, Smith, Kant, and Jefferson agreed constitute a proper liberalism.

A general agreement on the principles of a proper way of life does not preclude differences of opinion. And while an evaluation of the great liberals here discussed must bear in mind Jefferson's statement that every difference of opinion is not a difference of principle, it cannot be denied that differences of opinion among our authors do exist. Whereas the love of free government, as that of any ideal, can unite the human race, a meeting of the minds often will be difficult to achieve due to the diversity of people caused by biology, environment, and interest.

The writings of Montesquieu, Smith, Kant, and Jefferson demonstrate that the struggle for the official recognition of human rights is a gradual one. One step leads to another. Without doubt, Montesquieu and Smith favored many aspects of the freedom of the individual and resented royal absolutism. Yet Montesquieu, while disliking Colbertism, was less specifically concerned with economic freedom than was Smith. Smith, while liking divisions of governmental power, emphasized free enterprise. Montesquieu is primarily known as the advocate of certain forms of government which are conducive to freedom, such as institutional and spatial separations of power and checks and balances. Smith usually is mentioned in connection with his doctrines of economic freedom. In Montesquieu one sees mainly a liberator from the bonds of absolutist institutions, and in Smith, one from mercantilism.

Kant has been called "The Liberator" without any specification and qualification. While he favored divisions of governmental power as well as many human rights, including economic ones, his reputation as a liberator in a large measure rests upon his *Critique of Pure Reason.* In the preface to its second edition, we read: "Until now it was assumed that all our knowledge must conform or be adjusted toward objects. But upon this assumption all attempts to figure out *a priori* by concepts anything regarding such objects, that is, anything which would enlarge our knowledge, were failures. Therefore let us try to see whether we can get ahead better with the tasks of metaphysics, if we assume that the objects should conform or be adjusted to our knowledge. This [approach] would harmonize better with the desired possibility of *a priori* knowledge of objects which shall determine something regarding objects prior to their being given to us. It is like the first thought of Copernicus who, when he could not get ahead with explaining the motions of the heavenly bodies as long as he assumed that the stars revolved around the observer, tried whether he might not be more successful if he let the observer revolve and allowed the stars to remain stationary."[3] Whereas Copernicus humbly let man in his smallness move around the mighty fixed stars, Kant freed the mind from the object and adjusted the object to human knowledge. Clearly, he took a giant step toward the liberation of the mind from matter, toward the subordination of matter to mind, toward subjective thinking. Aware of the enormous and possibly dangerous potential of his liberation, he let the *Critique of Pure Reason* be followed by his *Critique of Practical Reason,* prescribing autolimitation by categorical imperatives and going out of his way to urge people to fulfill their duty at the cost of happiness.

We miss exhortations of such strength in the writings of Jefferson. True, the Virginian's words emphasize moral behavior, but basically they find no fault with a highly materialistic pursuit of happiness. The man who drafted the Declaration of Independence in 1776 was influenced by the *Wealth of Nations,* rather than by the wealth of wisdom in the works of the sage of Königsberg. Jefferson refrained from emphasizing that the pursuit of happiness is incompatible with one's duty and thus immoral. What Jefferson has in common with Kant is that he did not stress any one particular aspect of freedom, but favored freedom quite generally. This may be the reason why Jefferson was called "The Apostle of Liberty," just as Kant was referred to as "The Liberator."[4] Yet the word *apostle* is perhaps indicative of demagoguery. It implies that Jefferson did not have all of Kant's moral inhibitions. Perhaps it is significant that the very year the *Wealth of Nations* urged a basically egoistic and utilitarian free enterprise, Jefferson coined the basically egoistic and utilitarian phrase "pursuit of happiness." There are other differences between the Prussian and the American, the most eastern and the most western of the authors here discussed, which may be symbolic of the differences between their respective nations. Much as he accepted the French Revolution as an accomplished fact, Kant was

3. Translation by Carl J. Friedrich in *The Philosophy of Kant* (New York, 1949, 1977), xxvi–xxvii.

4. Cf. C. Randolph Benson, *Thomas Jefferson as Social Scientist* (Cranbury, N.J., 1971), 271; Heinz Zimmermann, *Der Befreier* (München, 1930).

strongly opposed to resistance to government, to uprisings, and to revolutions. Jefferson, active in the American Revolution and favorably inclined toward the French Revolution, stated that the tree of liberty must be refreshed from time to time with the blood of patriots and tyrants. Jefferson may have rejected an elective despotism. Basically, he was not opposed to democratic government. Kant, his republican leanings notwithstanding, was.

Whatever the differences between Montesquieu, Smith, Kant, and Jefferson may be, there can be found a basic agreement on the need for free government as a means for the good of society and the individuals composing it. They saw an important aspect of freedom in the protection of property rights. This is not surprising in an age of morality and propriety, an age in which the word *property* was interchangeably used with the word *propriety*. In their opinion, then, a proper liberalism exists under a free government in which the people participate for the protection of the rights of the individual, among which those of property rank highly.

At the time the authors wrote, popular participation in government was restricted. Even Rousseau, who is often considered the father of modern democracy, wanted a participation by reasonable people only; so did Montesquieu, Smith, Kant, and Jefferson. In their time, ownership was considered an important criterion for the ability to make rational decisions. Most qualifications for the suffrage were property qualifications. This raises the question as to whether such decisions could be expected once property qualifications were abolished. Kant, to whom the French Revolution was an event with far-reaching consequences, saw the coming march of democracy; so did Jefferson. This does not necessarily mean that they despaired of the future of proper liberalism. Both Kant and Jefferson believed that the common man was as much able to behave morally as the man of standing, that the ability to act morally was innate in man irrespective of intelligence, education, and position. On the other hand, Kant was more skeptical than Jefferson about the prospects of proper liberalism in a democratic age. Schiller seems to have shared that pessimism when he wrote that the rich fruits of Kant's teaching would often be poor and pitiful. Kant's categorical imperatives, opposed as they are to the pursuit of happiness, constitute much stronger exhortations to dutiful behavior than do Jefferson's moral laws, which suggest such a pursuit. Kant, when stating that his day would arrive only in about a hundred years, perhaps meant that the significance of his categorical imperatives would be much greater later on, when the masses had a say in the formulation of public policy and in the definition of freedom.

This makes us ask whether after the expansion of the suffrage, due in a large measure to an abolition of property qualifications, democratic rule will be as proper as the free government desired by Montesquieu, Smith, Kant, and Jefferson. We must inquire whether democracy is conducive, or a challenge, to liberalism. This takes us to a discussion of democracy proper and proper democracy.

Democracy Proper and Proper Democracy

Since Montesquieu, Smith, Kant, and Jefferson, democracy has been on a victorious march. The men who framed and ratified the American constitution were skeptical of democracy. A generation later Chancellor Kent feared the march of democracy but did not succeed in preventing an extension of the suffrage in New York.[5] During the following decade de Tocqueville described his observations under the title *Of Democracy in America* and made plain that the world would become more and more democratic. In the middle of the nineteenth century Guizot wrote of the power of the word *democracy* which stood on the banners of all governments and parties.[6] Whereas Disraeli considered democracy an evil,[7] Winston Churchill in 1947 remarked in the House of Commons, that democracy was the best form of government.[8] Bismarck fought democracy. The Weimar Republic was quite democratic. When in 1949 UNESCO questioned more than a hundred scholars on their attitude toward democracy, not one unfavorable reply was returned. Its report stated that probably for the first time in history democracy had been classified as the proper ideal of all political and social organizations.[9] In the year in which I outlined my study on America's development from limited to unlimited democracy, Galbraith, as lightly as a nightingale, stated that, like the family, the truth, sunshine, and Florence Nightingale, democracy was beyond reproach.[10]

Although there can be little doubt concerning the general recognition of

5. *Reports of the Proceedings and Debates of the Convention of 1821, Assembled for the Purpose of Amending the Constitution of the State of New York* (Albany, N.Y., 1821), 222.

6. F. P. G. Guizot, *Democracy in France* (New York, 1849, 1974): "The Monarchists say, 'Our Monarchy is a Democratic Monarchy' . . . The Republicans say, 'The Republic is Democracy governing itself.' . . . Socialists, Communists, and Montagnards require that the republic should be a pure and absolute democracy. . . . Such is the power of the word Democracy, that no government or party dares to raise its head, or believes its own existence possible, if it does not bear that word inscribed on its banner; and those who carry that banner aloft with the greatest ostentation and to the extremest limits, believe themselves to be stronger than all the rest of the world. . . . The word *Democracy* is not new, and in all ages it has signified what it signifies now. But what is new and proper to our times is this: the word *Democracy* is now pronounced every day, every hour, and in every place; and at every time and place it is heard by all men . . . the empire of the word *Democracy* is not to be regarded as a transitory or local accident. It is the development—others would say the explosion—of all the elements of human nature throughout all the ranks and all the depths of society" (2, 3, 5, 6).

7. Dorothy Pickles, *Democracy* (London, 1970), 11, without giving the source. Other opinions of Disraeli which recognize democracy as the government of the future in Jens A. Christophersen, *The Meaning of 'Democracy'* (Oslo, 1966), 56–60. Wilhelm Hasbach, *Die moderne Demokratie* (Jena, 1912), is critical of democracy.

8. He actually said it was the worst form of government with the exception of all other forms which had been tried from time to time. Quoted by Pickles, *Democracy,* 9.

9. UNESCO, *Democracy in a World of Tensions* (Paris, 1951), 527.

10. John Kenneth Galbraith, Reith Lecturers, 1966/67. *The Listener,* Dec. 15, 1966, 882.

democracy, questions about it have remained. As to the possibility of a definition of democracy, are we to be as pessimistic as with respect to liberty? This indeed seems to be the case, given the many things which today pose as democracies and hide under democratic concepts. Similar, different, even incompatible forms of government are called democratic. One need only think of western, eastern, liberal, social, socialist, and communist democracies as well as of scholarly classifications.[11] Pickles starts a discussion of what democracy is with a quotation from MacPherson, according to which democracy was something bad until about a hundred years ago, something good during the following fifty years, and something ambiguous in the past fifty years, and Sartori's statement that democracy is more complex and complicated than any other political form.[12] It is hardly surprising that she does not arrive at a satisfactory answer and is content with describing various democracies and their problems.

However, the fact that democracy is a form of government indicates that its definition is easier than that of freedom. Forms are concrete and thus defina-

11. One often has distinguished between liberal, despotic, plebiscitary, parliamentary, representative, direct, western, eastern democracy. More recently, one has spoken of "Proporzdemokratie" (Gerhard Lehmbruch, *Proporzdemokratie* [Tübingen, 1967]); "concordant democracy" (Lehmbruch, "Segmented Pluralism and Political Strategies in Continental Europe: Internal and External Conditions of 'Concordant Democracy'," Paper at the Round Table of the International Political Science Association, Turin [September 1969]); "consociational democracy" (Arend Lijphart, *Democracy in Plural Societies* [New Haven, 1977], 1); of depoliticized, centripetal, centrifugal democracy (ibid., 106). Gerhard Winterberger spoke of "Konkordanzdemokratie," "Konkurrenzdemokratie," "Gefälligkeitsdemokratie," in *Politik und Wirtschaft* (Bern, 1980), 39, 43, 151, Christopherson, *Meaning of 'Democracy',* gives hundreds of interpretations of democracy in Europe from the French Revolution to the Russian Revolution.

12. Pickles, *Democracy,* 9. The opinion of C. B. MacPherson can be found in *The Real World of Democracy* (Oxford, 1966), 1–2. This book starts with the sentence: "There is a good deal of muddle about democracy" (1). Cf. Giovanni Sartori, *Democrazia e definitione,* 3rd ed. (n.p., n.d.), 8. The translation, *Democratic Theory* (Detroit, 1962), v, brings as a motto de Tocqueville's statement: "It is our way of using the words 'democracy' and 'democratic government' that brings about the greatest confusion. Unless these words are clearly defined and their definitions agreed upon, people will live in an inextricable confusion of ideas, much to the advantage of demagogues and despots." Cf. George Orwell, *The Machiavellians, Defenders of Freedom* (New York, 1943), 243: "In the case of a word like *democracy* not only is there no agreed definition but the attempt to make one is resisted from all sides. . . . The defenders of any kind of regime claim that it is a democracy, and fear that they might have to stop using the word if it were tied down to any one meaning." Sartori, *Democratic Theory,* writes on page 6, "Omnis definitio est pericolosa" and on page 7 uses the subtitle "The Age of Democratic Confusion." On page 8 he quotes T. S. Eliot, *The Ideal of a Christian Society* (London, 1939), 11–12: "When a term has become so universally sanctified, as 'democracy' now is, I begin to wonder whether it means anything, in meaning too many things." On page 9 Sartori quotes Bertrand de Jouvenel, *Du pouvoir* (Geneva, 1947), 338: "Discussions about democracy, arguments for and against it, are intellectually worthless because we do not know what we are talking about." Cf. Alfredo C. Rossetti, *El problema de la democracía* (Córdoba, Argentina, 1966), 9–11. Manoel Gonçalves Ferreira Filho, *A democracia possível,* 3rd ed. (São Paulo, 1976), 1, speaks of the 'democratic paradox" and in chapter 1 of "Democracy and Democracies." Lijphart, *Democracy,* 4, writes: "*Democracy* is a concept that virtually defies definition."

ble. On the other hand, they often are empty. Different positions will lead to filling different substances into these forms, i.e., to different concepts of democracy.[13] Furthermore, since forms long to be filled and tempt people to fill them, they can bring about a veritable deluge of democratic concepts making it difficult and frustrating to try to define democracy.

The following is restricted to examining the plain meaning of democracy (democracy proper) and what, from the point of view of the liberalism considered proper by Montesquieu, Smith, Kant, and Jefferson, democracy should be (proper democracy). Present inundations with democratic concepts call for an emphasis upon the essential, even though such an emphasis may not result in a complete definition of democracy. The great variety of these concepts requires an attempt to see what is basic and simple, even though it may not be noble. We shall first examine popular government as a mere form and, later on, what, in the opinion of our authors, could constitute proper democracy. In the end, the chances of democracy proper to be a proper democracy will be dealt with.

Fashionable throughout today's world, the word *democracy* is generally understood to be the rule by the people. Its global popularity is matched by that of a broad conception of the democratic principle to participate in government. This was not always the case. In the Greek city state, democracy was seen as a rule of the lowest strata of society or as one in which the mob played a significant part.[14] This belief still prevailed at the time the American constitution was adopted. De Tocqueville connected democracy with the growing involvement of all strata of society. When Lincoln spoke at Gettysburg of the government of the people, by the people, for the people, he referred to all the people and did not indicate contempt for any of them. Democracy had lost its bad connotation. Two generations later Woodrow Wilson, perhaps in a polemic against the Prussian three-class electoral system, entered the war in order to make the world safe for democracy. The idea that democracy was the rule by all the people became generally accepted.

This modern concept corresponds to the plain linguistic meaning of the word democracy. Since the component part *demos* is not restricted, one can conclude that all the people were to rule and think less and less of qualifications made by Aristotle and others. The liquidation of upper strata of society and the emancipation of lower ones, resulted in equalization and promoted, especially after the French Revolution, inclinations toward simplification. After historicism, this trend was not just expressed in turning away from studying antiquity. Increasingly, expressions were taken at their face value, especially if this was flattering. One overlooked the unpleasant connotations that had been

13. Similar, with respect to the *Rechtsstaat,* Carl Schmitt, "Was bedeutet der Streit um den 'Rechtsstaat'?" *Zeitschrift für die gesamte Staatswissenschaft* 95 (1935):193–94.

14. Zevedei Barbu, *Democracy and Dictatorship* (New York, 1956), 12, with reference to Aristotle's *Politics.* Cf. also 102 ff., and Pickles, *Democracy,* 29–41.

attached to the populace for a long time and are still attributed to it by authors who agree with Schopenhauer that he who does not understand Latin belongs to the people.[15] As a rule by all the people, democracy accommodates all men who can pride themselves for presumably carrying some weight without having the feeling of being looked down upon. Also, as in the case of law,[16] the concept of democracy became something abstract that was severed from its originators and considered wiser than those who in antiquity had created it and whose ideas were either ignored or considered out of date. Democracy developed from a demigod to a God. All this was in tune with modern trends toward abstraction and deification. Thus democracy, originally feared as the rule of the mob, attained by virtue of a change of meaning a legitimacy the clarity of which was beyond doubt. With the egalitarian march of democracy, the mob had elevated itself to the position of the people. Its proletarian aspects, absorbed by the people as a whole, either evaporated or were assimilated. A clear democratic truth had come about. In its clarity it became the new idol. Guizot might condemn it, but he could not doubt its existence.[17]

This broad democratic principle so far has not been realized in practice. Never was democracy a rule by all the people. In modern states more people participate in the governmental process than ever before. Nevertheless, later generations will look down upon our time for not having had a sufficiently broad popular participation in government, just as we criticize previous generations on that account. Aside from these quantitative limitations of democracy, there are limitations connected with the possibility and the ensuant effectiveness of government, as well as with its rationality.

A rule depends upon the possibility to rule. To govern always implies activity. No matter how passive a government may be, its passivity always is some kind of governing, of being active. Laissez faire, *laissez passer,* originally directed against mercantilism, was directed against too much government, not against government itself. Great advocates of liberalism and a free economy, such as Montesquieu, Smith, Kant, and Jefferson, left no doubt about this.[18] Even the nightwatchman state is a state that watches and governs. Should laissez faire increase beyond its original dubious meaning[19] and go beyond free trade—the present decline of law and order shows that this is occurring in democracies—the rule of law would still be a rule no matter how much it may protect the individual from the state, and the *Rechtsstaat* would still be a state with proper authority.[20]

15. Arthur Schopenhauer, "Über Sprache und Worte," Sec. 299, in Arthur Hübscher, ed., *Sämtliche Werke,* 2d ed. (Wiesbaden, 1947), 2:606.

16. Gustav Radbruch, *Rechtsphilosophie,* 6th ed. (Stuttgart, 1963), 201–2.

17. François Pierre Guillaume Guizot, *Democracy in France* (1849; New York, 1974), v.

18. Cf. Wilhelm Röpke, *A Humane Economy* (Chicago, 1960).

19. See Hayek, *Constitution of Liberty,* 60, and "Grundsätze einer liberalen Gesellschaftsordnung" in *Freiburger Studien* (Tübingen, 1969), 113.

20. Cf. Dietze, *Two Concepts of the Rule of Law* (Indianapolis, 1973).

Democracy is a specific form of government. The first syllable of the word merely indicates, like an adjective, the kind of rule and is thus subordinated to the following substantive—government.[21] Since government implies the possibility to govern, it is necessary that in a democracy there must be not merely exceptions to the principle of popular participation. Care must be taken that those governing can govern effectively. The opposition may influence, but not prevent, government. Therefore, the question arises whether the majority or the minority shall govern. It is obvious that minority rule corresponds less to the democratic principle than majority rule. In spite of his defense of the rights of the individual and the minority, Locke favored majority rule,[22] which has become tantamount to democracy. The equation "democracy=majority rule" is, of course, justified when the minority is reduced to zero and does not oppose the majority. Since this seldom will be the case, however, one is satisfied with the rule of a simple or qualified majority, depending upon one's appreciation of minority rights. Calhoun, who certainly cared about the minority, realized that the effectiveness of government might be curtailed too much by a unanimity rule and was satisfied with that of the concurrent majority.[23] In the League of Nations the undesirability of the unanimity rule of Article 5 of the Covenant was obvious.[24] Just as the governments of a loose league of states and a federal state are made ineffective by that rule, the same situation will exist in simpler communities. Therefore, the unanimity rule has been tried rarely, as for instance in Poland, to the detriment of that nation. Today, majority rule is no longer questioned in democracies. In view of the fact that majority rule implies the rule over—and against—the minority and that democracy means the government of all the people, majority rule amounts to a necessary restriction of democracy.

In an age of enlightenment, an age that did not come to an end with Kant,[25] every government will want to appear reasonable.[26] This applies especially to democratic governments because the common people often have been accused of a lack of reason and education. Perhaps on account of this one has interpreted the slogan *vox populi vox dei* to mean that the voice of the people is that of a rational God, or reason, in tune with the conversion of Notre Dame de Paris into a temple of reason. Thus there exists in democracy, aside from the requirements of possibility and effectiveness, that of rationality. It implies restrictions of democracy. However, because it is not a *sine qua non* for

21. Sartori, *Democratic Theory,* 26, is of a different opinion when he writes that "democracy implies that society takes precedence over the State, that *demos* precedes *cracy.*"

22. Edwin Mims, Jr., *The Majority of the People* (New York, 1941).

23. John C. Calhoun, *A Disquisition on Government, and a Discourse on the Constitution of the United States* (Charleston, 1851).

24. Margaret E. Burton, *The Assembly of the League of Nations* (Chicago, 1941), 175 ff.; Edward Hallett Carr, *The Twenty Years' Crisis, 1919–1939,* 2d ed. (London, 1946).

25. Immanuel Kant, "Beantwortung der Frage: Was ist Aufklärung?" (1784).

26. Cf. Barbu, *Democracy,* 75.

democratic rule, it is merely advisable. Its two main aspects are suffrage and representation.

Suffrage is a right of codetermination. It is considered essential to democracy. In the Greek city-state it consisted, above all, of the right to choose what laws should be passed and what measures be taken. In large communities it entitles those who are supposed to rule, to vote, to propose and accept laws by means of initiative and referendum, and to recall officials. For reasons of rationality, it always has been restricted. A Roman emperor is said to have confessed that the most powerful man in Rome was his little son because the empress did everything he wanted and he, the emperor, fulfilled all the wishes of the empress. Actually, the young and women were excluded from the right to vote for a long time.

Young people were denied suffrage not only since the time of *Sturm und Drang*. They are, so it was argued, too emotional, too irresponsible, too irrational, too immature. They were to do military service for their country in order to become more mature and more reasonable and thus more worthy of full citizenship. On the other hand, they were denied the right to codetermine the necessity and type of that service. It was argued that those who had to qualify themselves for something could not well determine the conditions of that qualification. Young people were even denied the right to vote after they had come of age. It was felt that their ability to act in matters of private law could be detrimental to a relatively small circle of people, whereas voting could be dangerous to the whole society. It was maintained that the voting age must be raised with that of public responsibility. As a result, the age for the right to run for public office was set higher than that for the right to vote, and was determined, furthermore, by the importance of the office.[27] Thus the qualifications for public responsibility grew with getting away from the age of youth and its emotionalism, which was feared to endanger order. Raising the age for the right to vote above that of the right to act in private matters was quite compatible with the fact that the age of liability for crimes was still lower. Just as a dubious youthful behavior and its dangerous influence upon the public will could be prevented by raising the age of voting and of running for office, such behavior could be punished, at an earlier age, if in the form of crime it hurt the public weal.

For a long time women did not have the right to vote either. Until the end of the nineteenth century it was taken for granted that they would not enjoy the rights men did. As late as 1892 Gladstone remarked that he feared an extension of the suffrage might result in the loss of "the delicacy, the purity, the refinement" of women. Gladstone's stand cannot only be defended by saying that politics is a dirty business in which men had to decide whether women

27. For instance, the minimum age for serving in the U.S. House of Representatives is 25, in the Senate, 30. The President must be at least 35. Members of the West German *Bundestag* must be 25, the Bundespräsident must be 40.

were too pure to be permitted to engage in it.[28] It probably was not just prompted by a desire to appear as a gentleman. Furthermore, the often heard argument, a woman's place was in the house and kitchen, does not account for the denial of woman's suffrage. A more relevant reason for that denial probably is that women were considered too emotional and irrational. This argument is still heard today because, for instance, American women in 1945 prevailed upon the government to withdraw troops from large stretches of land which were turned over to the communists and elect candidates for good looks rather than abilities.[29] In spite of the absence of women suffrage in Great Britain, Switzerland, and the United States, these nations were considered exemplary democracies.

For reasons of rationality the suffrage for a long time was restricted to property owners. The great liberal revolutions in England, America, and France in a large measure were prompted by the considerations that a liberal and moral order as well as the wealth of nations would be promoted by free trade and free property.[30] Therefore, it seemed only natural that property rights, asserted against absolutism, would also be protected from the new popular governments. Restrictions of the suffrage to property owners appeared to be proper. It was asserted that those who have something to lose would act more rationally and responsibly than poor firebrands; that those who acquire property are more reasonable than the have-nots. Even though there are property owners who have more luck than brains, the property owner is, on the whole, a man with *Vernunft* and *Verstand.* It takes brains to make money. The *homo economicus* thinks rationally.

Similarly, limitations of the suffrage through educational qualifications appeared to be reasonable. The more people are participating in the governmental process, the more difficult governing becomes. This was even seen by authors who wanted to secure the freedom of the individual by his participation in government. For Kant, the powerful *Autokrator* or *Selbstherrscher* (self-ruler) was, as far as the substance of liberal law itself is concerned, the most dangerous despotic government. That type of government, however, through its simplicity was probably the best with respect to the administration of the law.[31] In order to make a "bourgeois constitution" possible, Kant recommended enlightenment. On the other side of the Atlantic, Jefferson, known in his country not only as the father of the Democratic party but more generally as the father of American democracy, left no doubt about the value of education for the democratic community.[32] Elected twice to the presidency of the United

28. Quoted by Pickles, *Democracy,* 10.

29. My critical evaluation of John F. Kennedy can be seen in *In Defense of Property,* 194 ff., 206, and in *America's Political Dilemma,* 234–241, 268–69, 271–72.

30. Cf. Dietze, *In Defense of Property,* 22–34.

31. Kant, *Metaphysische Anfangsgründe der Rechtslehre* (1797), in *Werke,* 6:339.

32. To John Adams on Oct. 28, 1813, *Memorial ed.* 13:394 ff.

States, he considerably enlarged its territory with the Louisiana Purchase. Yet on his tombstone he only wanted it stated that he drafted the Declaration of Independence, favored a law for religious freedom, and founded the University of Virginia, facts that show him as a man of the age of reason.[33]

It was considered reasonable to deprive the feeble-minded of the right to vote. One did not follow the opinion of the late vice-president of the United States, Hubert H. Humphrey, who answered to the complaints that there are fools in Congress that this was quite all right: After all, there are fools in the electorate and there was no reason not to represent them by their kind.[34]

Aside from restrictions of the suffrage, representation was recommended for reasons of rationality. Rousseau, known as the father of the French Revolution, considered representation a restriction of popular government. Born and raised in Geneva, he only recognized direct democracy as a genuine democracy and saw in representation an adulteration of the will of the people.[35] On the other hand, James Madison, father of the American Constitution, recommended representation because it refined and rationalized popular government. He denounced the direct democracies of the Greek city-states for their demagoguerie and tumults and asserted that representative government alone, enobling popular government, was in tune with the interest of the *res publica*.[36]

The described restrictions of the people, prompted by the quest for rationality, were considerably reduced by the march of democracy under the principle of equality. They had been adopted when the people appeared to be clumsier to many than the proletariat did to Marx. Later on, when democracy became so acceptable that even monarchists paid tribute to it,[37] there was less and less room for excluding people from participating in the democratic process, even if this appeared to be unreasonable. Already Montesquieu had considered the love of equality the outstanding feature of democracy. Later on, Volney spoke of the holy dogma of equality.[38] After Jefferson had opened the Declaration of Independence with the remark that all men are created equal and endowed by their Creator with certain unalienable rights, the opinion spread that different rights to participation in the democratic process ought no

33. Cf. Jefferson's First Inaugural Address: "If there be any among us who would wish to dissolve this Union or to change its republican form, let them stand undisturbed as monuments of the safety with which error of opinion may be tolerated where reason is left free to combat it." Ibid., 3:319.

34. Speech of Jan. 17, 1964, at the Johns Hopkins University.

35. *Contrat Social,* book 3, chap. 15. See Claes G. Ryn, *Democracy and the Ethical Life* (Baton Rouge, 1978), 120 ff.

36. *The Federalist,* essay 10. Similar Carl Schmitt, *Verfassungslehre* (München and Leipzig, 1928), 315, with references to Burke and Bluntschli. On the whole problem, compare Gerhard Leibholz, *Die Repräsentation in der Demokratie* (Berlin, 1973).

37. Guizot, *Democracy in France,* 2.

38. Montesquieu, *De l'esprit des lois* book 5, chap. 3. Volney is quoted by Georges Ripert, *Le régime démocratique et le droit civil moderne,* 2d ed. (Paris, 1948), 83.

longer to exist. In 1864 Gladstone, living in conservative England, looked upon suffrage as a privilege. Still he realized that it had to be extended.[39] Later on, fewer and fewer people felt it was a privilege.

Even before de Tocqueville visited America, property qualifications for the right to vote were abolished in the United States. Prussia followed suit toward the end of World War I. In between, similar emancipations took place in other nations. Women suffrage was established in Germany in 1919, in the United States in 1920, in Great Britain in 1929, in France in 1945, in Switzerland in 1972. In many countries the voting age was lowered. Whereas previously it had been above the age to do business under private law, it later was lowered to that age and today often is under that age. Educational qualifications that had existed into the 1960s, especially in the United States, are now for the most part abolished.

Representation also came under attack. Madison's ideas were increasingly replaced by those of Rousseau. This is not surprising. It simply runs parallel to the abolition of qualifications for suffrage. Wherever these qualifications, favoring an elite believed to be rational, were reduced there was hardly room for the elite of representatives. The realization of the democratic participation principle is uncompromising in its egalitarian demands. Equalization does not suffer exceptions, especially not those that appear incompatible with the broadening of democracy. Representatives are considered more of an elite than those they represent. They stand out more prominently because their number is smaller and because they constitute the government. Therefore, when the influence of adult, male, property-owning, and educated voters was reduced by an extension of the suffrage, it was to be expected that a lessening of the influence of representatives would follow. After all, the latter, the government in the narrow sense, were suspected of falsifying the will of the government in the broad sense—the sovereign people. This low opinion of representatives was nourished by the fact that they increasingly lost their elitist image, coming as they did as a result of the broadening of the suffrage from ever wider strata of society. Often, they behaved in a way that raised questions as to whether they really were an elite that could be entrusted with the formulation of public policy. Modern aspects of direct democracy, such as initiative, referendum, and recall, were introduced. The plebiscite became popular.

The reduction of restrictions which were supposed to make democracy more reasonable raises the question as to whether popular government has become irrational. A negative reply will be supported by the argument that the complaint that women are less rational than men rested on prejudices.[40] Irène

39. Speech of the Chancellor of the Exchequer on the Bill for the Extension of the Suffrage in Towns, May 11, 1864 (London, 1864), 20: "What are the qualities which fit a man for the exercise of a privilege such as the franchise? Self-command, self-control, respect for order, patience under suffering, confidence in the law, regard for superiors?"

40. Pickles, *Democracy,* 9–10.

Joliot-Curie, it will be said, received a Noble prize in chemistry on account of scientific achievements just as her husband did; Lise Meitner was an outstanding physicist; Marianne Weber in her field of interest was about as significant as Max Weber. It will be added that it was due to century-old discriminations that women could prove their intellectual worth only after women's emancipation. Furthermore, it will be pointed out that a more general education bore the fruits Jefferson had expected. It enabled the young, the poor, the women to make rational choices, the more so since they were increasingly educated. To this was answered that education for all is no education at all; that the extension of education to more and more people led to lower educational standards, to half-education, proving the truth of Alexander Pope's words, "a little learning is a dangerous thing." Given the decline of education one has asked whether education has aided the masses to make reasonable political decisions or whether, aided by tabloids, films, and television, it has made the citizens victims of a propaganda that stands in stark contrast to the kind of popular enlightenment Kant had desired.[41]

It will be argued that the abolition of restrictions supposedly making democracy more rational is not only compatible with democracy proper, but even required by it because the realization of the democratic principle grows with the broadening of direct participation in the process of government. People will quote Hegel who said that what is, is reasonable.[42] They will maintain that a democracy proper is rational by definition. From this follows that the more people participate in the democratic process more directly, the more rational a rule based upon the principle of popular participation in government must be. This kind of thinking corresponds to ideas of Rousseau and Hichborn. According to the former, who said of himself that he was the best of all men,[43] the desire of the general will always is moral and proper, impulsive as it may be. Hichborn, who shortly after the American Declaration of Independence, wrote for democracy full of enthusiasm and perhaps without expecting a moral exercise of the spontaneous will, felt that civil liberty implied not "a government of laws, made agreeable to charters, bills of rights or compacts, but a power existing in the people at large, at any time, for any cause, or for no cause, but their own sovereign pleasure, to alter or annihilate both the mode and essence of any former government, and to adopt a new one in its stead."[44]

What is reasonable, is not necessarily proper. Even less so is of necessity

41. Kant, *Streit* 7:89.

42. G. F. W. Hegel, *Grundlinien der Philosophie des Rechts oder Naturrecht und Staatswissenschaft im Grundrisse,* Edvard Gans, ed. (Berlin, 1833), 17.

43. Rousseau, *Confessions,* book 10; to Malherbes on Jan. 4, 1762, in Charles W. Hendel, *Citizen of Geneva: Selections from the Letters of Jean-Jacques Rousseau* (New York, 1937), 206.

44. Benjamin Hichborn, Speech in Boston, 1777, in Hezekiah Niles, ed., *Principles and Acts of the Revolution* (Baltimore, 1822), 27, 30.

proper in an ethical sense what is reasonable or proper merely from the democratic point of view. This is obvious in case of its incompatibility with the laws, which have been said to constitute at least an ethical minimum and to be rational. Having examined the main features of democracy as a form and organization of the principle of popular participation in government, we shall now attempt to find the kind of democracy that could be compatible with what Montesquieu, Smith, Kant, and Jefferson considered to be a proper liberalism. In the following we refer to this type as "proper democracy" as distinguished from democracy proper.

The question of proper democracy concentrates on substantive restrictions of democracy proper. So far an attempt has been made to show what popular government must be formally in order to qualify as a democracy proper. Now we ask how a democracy proper—probably the most powerful form of government because as a majority rule it need not, like aristocracies and monarchies, live in fear of the majority—must act to be a proper democracy. Thinking of Burckhardt's statement that power is evil, of the opinions of the authors of the *Federalist* and the aged Kant on human viciousness,[45] we look for necessary limitations of democratic power.

Democracy proper is merely oriented toward what is democratic. Only what is democratic, and everything that is democratic, is conducive to democracy proper: the more people participate in the democratic process, the more democratic everything is. By contrast, proper democracy in addition must orient itself toward what is proper from an ethical and moral point of view while, of course, it also corresponds to the democratic principle of participation and is a democracy proper. This is not easy, for what has been said about freedom can be said about propriety. We do not know all its dimensions. We think that God only can be absolutely proper, nothing here on earth: not man, irrespective of how much he may obey God and the moral law (Montesquieu), the great demigod and judge in the breast (Smith), categorical imperatives (Kant) or Jeffersonian concepts of morals; not the Pope as the deputy of God; not the king ruling according to divine law; not democracy under the principle *vox populi vox dei.*

Guizot's comments on France can be applied to the world today. There is a general trend to consider democracy as something proper from an ethical point of view and to call one's government a proper democracy. Capitalist and communist nations alike claim to be proper democracies. Given the fact that communism fights capitalism as its opposite and vice versa, the question arises as to what can be considered a proper democracy. People wonder why communists call their states "people's democracies," letting the word *demos* be pre-

45. See Benjamin F. Wright, "The Federalist on the Nature of Political Man," *Ethics* 59, No. 2, part 2 (1949):1 ff.

ceded by the word *people,* mentioning the same thing twice in a row and thus overemphasizing it. It looks as if they suspect that others do not trust their type of democracy, just as Marxists doubted the socialism of Hitler because the name of his party did not only state that it was socialist, but on top of it, that it was a workers' party.[46] However, the communist double emphasis does not necessarily indicate an inferiority complex toward western democracies. It may well symbolize the opinion that western democracies are not real democracies because the will of the people is monitored by checks and balances. Capitalists counter that without these checks the minority will be oppressed, that it is democratic to check the majority by institutions such as the separation of powers, federalism, and judicial review. Both capitalists and communists say they enjoy proper democracy. According to the literature, both are right;[47] *Dieu et mon droit: honi soit qui mal y pense.*

Under different circumstances, different things may appear as proper. Aron wrote that since Hobbes and Montesquieu, the best regime is whatever is considered best.[48] As long as a world state has not yet existed for some time and created a world consensus as to what is proper, there will be different positive laws, natural laws with changing contents, and a great variety of opinions as to what is proper. Following Holmes, who emphasized that there was no common law for all of America, the United States Supreme Court stated that local communities had their own ideas as to what is moral and that there was no common moral standard for the whole nation.[49] Dangerous as such opinions may be for the coherence of a republic, certainly over the whole earth where different nations have not yet formed a world state, propriety is interpreted differently in different places. It is open to doubt whether nations who disagree on propriety like the words of the humanist Goethe in *Westöstlicher Divan,* which can be understood as a warning to some nations to leave others alone and to stop trying to impose their standard of propriety on them:

46. NSDAP is the abbreviation for National Socialist German Labor Party.

47. Bertrand Russell, *What is Democracy?* (London, 1946), 14, writes that our definition of democracy "is that it consists in the *rule* of the majority, the Russian view is that it consists in the *interests* of the majority." Georges Vedel, *Manuel élémentaire de droit constitutionnel* (Paris, 1949) esp. 240–53, defends the Soviet theory as a second concept of democracy and bases his opinion upon Rousseau. Maurice Cranston, *Freedom: A New Analysis* (London, 1953), writes: "I see nothing to be gained from insisting that they [the communists] ought not to call their totalitarian republics 'democracies'." MacPherson, *The Real World,* distinguishes between new and old dimensions of democracy and between the non-liberal democracies in communist nations and the non-liberal democracies in the developing nations, and deals with them next to liberal democracies. See esp. 36.

48. Raymond Aron, *Democracy and Totalitarianism* (London, 1968), 17–19.

49. Holmes in *Southern Pacific Co.* v. *Jensen,* 244 U.S. 205, 222 (1917); cf. the opinion of Louis D. Brandeis in *Erie Railroad Company* v. *Tomkins,* 304 U.S. 64 (1938). See also *Roth* v. *U.S.,* 354 U.S. 476 (1957); *Ginsberg* v. *New York,* 390 U.S. 629 (1968); William B. Lockhart, Robert C. McClure, "Censorship of Obscenity," *Minnesota Law Review* 45 (1960):5 ff.

Gottes ist der Orient!
Gottes ist der Okzident!
Nord- und südliches Gelände
Ruht im Frieden Seiner Hände.

It is more probable that today's East-West debate as to what constitutes a proper democracy will deteriorate into a quarrel that will show only a thin dividing line between democracy and demagoguery.

We restrict ourselves to an examination of what liberals, followers of Montesquieu, Smith, Kant, and Jefferson might consider a proper democracy. The modern trend toward liberalism preceded that toward democracy.[50] Democracy was seen as a means to serve freedom and for that reason lost the evil connotation it had since antiquity, a connotation still obvious in Kant.[51] It follows that from the point of view of seniority as well as purpose, liberalism, as the older goal, is entitled to a higher ranking than democracy as the more recent means for achieving that goal. Proper democracy thus serves the protection of human rights from the government. This was seen by Montesquieu when he favored a division of governmental power and suggested checks and balances for the security of the individual. A similar thought was expressed by the French Declaration of the Rights of Man and Citizen of August 26, 1789, which was motivated by the idea of protecting the individual by means of popular government. Article 16 states that a society in which rights are not secured and the separation of powers is not recognized has no constitution. Constitutionalism is identified with the limitation of governmental power for the sake of human rights. Constitutionalism means free government. This is, basically, the liberalism considered proper by Montesquieu, Smith, Kant, and Jefferson. According to these authors, proper liberals cannot follow Rousseau and Hichborn because democracy must be a mere means for the protection of human rights, and limited by the imperative of protecting these rights.

For proper liberals, a democracy is proper to the degree it protects human rights. The safer the individual, the more proper a democracy. That safety must exist vis-à-vis the government as well as fellowmen, be promoted by law and organization (bills of rights, separations of power, criminal law), and preserved by a strict execution of the laws. Democratic majority rule and its effectiveness must not be compromised by a lax execution of the laws.

As to the protection of human rights, it must not be overlooked that the rights we are aware of only are aspects of freedom in general and traditionally have been considered as such. Therefore, none of these aspects must be treated as inferior to others. Consequently, property rights must enjoy full protection. In the West, where liberalism originated and where we find several liberal

50. MacPherson, *The Real World,* 6–11, 57.
51. Kant, *Frieden,* 8:352–53.

democracies today, property rights traditionally have been connected with propriety. The connection between property and propriety is evident in words and proverbs.[52]

In view of this connection it could be argued that property, as a right recognized as proper since antiquity—for longer than any other right—deserves a special, privileged protection. Montesquieu, who did not care so much about how many people ruled but rather about how well they ruled, to what degree they acted conformably to *vertu,* and how properly they acted,[53] did not emphasize property rights before other rights even though as a Frenchman he knew that *propriété* stood for both property and propriety. Perhaps this was because in his time other aspects of freedom were not yet as clearly delineated by the laws as was property, which in private law was defined early and protected by law before modern bills of rights mentioned other aspects of freedom.[54] Perhaps Montesquieu also thought that property rights were not curtailed more than other rights, and therefore felt that a special emphasis upon these rights was not necessary. By contrast, today, when property rights are no longer considered as important as other rights, it appears natural for proper liberals in the sense of Montesquieu, Smith, Kant, and Jefferson to emphasize the necessity for their protection. This corresponds to the thesis that the oppression of a specific aspect of freedom led to the fight for, and an emphasis upon, that aspect until it was guaranteed by the government.[55] These liberals will be of the opinion that everything that could be demanded during the age of absolutism from royal minority governments must be demanded now from democratic majorities, which potentially and often actually are more powerful. Just as Montesquieu, Smith, Kant, and Jefferson emphasized property rights in the age of absolutism vis-à-vis conservative rulers, proper liberals following them will do so today vis-à-vis socialist, national-socialist, and communist rulers, the "socialists of all parties."[56] Their emphasis on property rights does not necessarily imply a preferred status for these rights. It merely demands that property rights be rehabilitated and given the same protection as other rights in order to secure proper democracy.

From the preceding pages it follows that for those believing in the principles of Montesquieu, Smith, Kant, and Jefferson, democracy proper could well be a proper democracy.

52. See Dietze, *In Defense of Property,* 9–12.

53. Aron, *Democracy,* 17. On Montesquieu's concept of "virtu," see Merry, *Montesquieu's System of Natural Government,* 10 ff., 69, 171–72, 174–75, 187–88, 197 ff., 245, 280, 376. According to Pangle, *Montesquieu's Philosophy of Liberalism,* 107 ff., Montesquieu subordinates "virtu" to liberty.

54. For instance, in the Magna Carta (1215), the Petition of Right (1628), the English Bill of Rights (1689).

55. Georg Jellinek, *Die Erklärung der Menschen-und Bürgerrechte.*

56. F. A. Hayek addressed *The Road to Serfdom* (Chicago, 1944) to them.

This is borne out by ample evidence. Whenever people in Western nations today speak of democracy, they usually have in mind a proper democracy, as here described. Gone are the days when the American founding fathers denounced democracy as some kind of despotism,[57] when Lincoln shied away from using the word, and when late in the nineteenth century it was argued that democracy was tantamount to communism.[58] Certainly ever since Woodrow Wilson set out to make the world safe for democracy, the word democracy has been used in the sense of a popular government in which the majority, while ruling, is bound by law to respect the rights of the ruled.

Even though the name democracy was shunned for generations, the United States was, in today's meaning of the term, a democracy all along. So were other nations during the liberal era. This is not surprising. The revolutions in England, America, France, Latin America as well as those in Europe around 1848, were liberal revolutions, made to curtail the power of rulers, to protect the rights of the individual. Popular participation in government was considered the appropriate guarantee for achieving that end. It stands to reason that as soon as people saw in democracy a means for the protection of the individual, democracy proper was likely to be a proper democracy. Ideologies push their realization. When the ideology of liberalism was predominant, it was natural that new democratic governments would be limited by the liberal principle of the protection of the rights of the individual, including economic rights, to be proper democracies.

Many examples can be supplied. Where absolute monarchy was fought on the basis of a legal tradition like that of the common law, as in England, it was emphasized that the laws provided for the protection of human rights. Magna Carta, the Petition of Right, the Bill of Rights, and the Act of Settlement embody this attitude. In America, written state constitutions established popular government for the sake of human rights, designing government so as to secure those rights and limiting governmental power by bills of rights.[59] So did the federal Constitution which, although providing for divisions of power and checks and balances for the sake of human rights, was ratified under the condition that a bill of rights be added to make doubly sure that these rights were protected.[60] The French Declaration of the Rights of Man and Citizen of 1789 has enjoyed such general esteem that it has been considered an ingredient of French constitutions. The idea of proper democracy was evident in French constitutions made during the Revolution and thereafter.[61] The newly indepen-

57. See Dietze, *Freiheit und Eigentum in der amerikanischen Überlieferung* (Tübingen, 1976).

58. See *Pollock* v. *Farmers' Loan and Trust Company,* 157 U.S. 429 (1894), esp. the arguments of Joseph H. Choate. Cf. Carl B. Swisher, *American Constitutional Development,* 2d ed. (Boston, 1954), 447.

59. See Jellinek, *Erklärung der Menschen-und Bürgerrechte.* For the position of property rights in these bills of rights, see Dietze, *In Defense of Property,* 217n92.

60. Cf. *The Federalist,* essay 84.

61. Cf. Eric Cahm, *Politics and Society in Contemporary France 1789–1971* (London,

dent states in Spanish America adopted democratic constitutions patterned after those made in the United States and France and thus provided for proper democracy.[62]

The situation is similar with respect to the Belgian constitution of 1831[63] and constitutions that were adopted from 1848 on. For instance, the draft by the National Assembly at Frankfurt, incorporating a bill of rights, left little doubt about the desire to give the liberal principle of the protection of the individual as the end priority before the democratic principle of popular participation as the means.[64] King Albert of Piedmont-Sardinia gave to his people a supreme law which upon unification became the constitution of Italy. This *Statuto* expressed the idea of a democracy that would protect the citizens.[65] In the cases mentioned, concessions to democracy proper were made with the stipulation that it be a proper democracy, a fact which Alain kept hammering into the minds of the French prior to World War I.[66] Across the Rhine, Bismarck considered the liberal *Rechtsstaat* something artificial.[67] However, he had also warned of "majorization," of unduly being forced by the majority.[68] Under the Empire, the *Rechtsstaat,* although increasingly challenged by nationalism and socialism, basically remained liberal.[69] Germany enjoyed proper democracy.

Given the fact that the largest and most powerful of the German states,

---

1972). On the *Chartre Constitutionelle* of 1814, see Friedrich, *Constitutional Government and Democracy,* 179–80.

62. See Dietze, "Government of the People," *Américas,* May 1981, 10 ff.

63. That constitution brings a bill of rights (art. 4 ff.) in title II. Title III, "Concerning Powers," starts with art. 25, stating: "All powers emanate from the people. They are to be exercised in the manner established by the constitution." See John Martin Vincent, *Constitution of Belgium* (Philadelphia, 1896), in *Annals,* vol. 7.

64. Even though, unlike in the Belgian constitution, human rights are not enumerated in the beginning, but in sections 25 ff.

65. See esp. the preamble, arts. 2, 24 ff., 33 ff., 39 ff., 48 ff. This constitution was preceded by the liberal constitutions of Tuscany (1848), Sicily (1848) and by Albert's declaration of Mar. 4, 1848, which outlined the principles of the *Statuto.* See S. M. Lindsay and Leo S. Rowe, *Constitution of the Kingdom of Italy* (Philadelphia, 1894). *Annals* 5.

66. Notably in Alain (Émile Chartier), *Éléments d'une doctrine radicale* (Paris, 1925); *Le citoyen contre les pouvoirs* (Paris, 1926). See La Nouvelle Revue Française, *Hommage à Alain,* Sept. 1952, esp. the contributions by G. Bénézé, Simone Petrement, Enzo Paci, Takeo Kuwabara, 7 ff., 138 ff., 259 ff., 274 ff.; David Thomson, *Democracy in France since 1870,* 4th ed. (New York, 1964), esp. 52; John A. Scott, *Republican Ideas and the Liberal Tradition in France 1870–1914* (New York, 1951).

67. To Gosler on Nov. 25, 1881. Quoted in Johannes Heckel, "Die Beilegung des Kulturkampfes in Preussen," *Zeitschrift der Savigny-Stiftung für Rechtsgeschichte,* 50 (1930):269.

68. Horst Kohl, ed., *Die politischen Reden des Fürsten Bismarck* 1 (Stuttgart, 1892), 127–28, 143, 182, 284; 3 (Stuttgart, 1922): 223–24. The Prussian constitution of 1850 did not provide for equal suffrage, but, with its *Dreiklassenwahlrecht,* for popular participation in legislation. At its beginning (arts. 3 ff.), it contained a long bill of rights. See James Harvey Robinson, *Constitution of the Kingdom of Prussia* (Philadelphia, 1894). *Annals* 5.

69. See Dietze, *Two Concepts of the Rule of Law,* 29 ff.

Prussia, did not have universal suffrage until 1917, the reader will wonder whether Germany could be called a democracy. While Germany was not as democratic as other nations, this question can also be asked, from today's vantage point, about those nations. The growth of popular participation in government has been gradual everywhere. It does not change the fact that the constitutions here mentioned do reflect that growth, which was officially recognized at the time of their validity. Also, in view of the reputation Prussia has had in some quarters,[70] it will be argued that civil rights were not safe in Germany. However, these rights were also restricted in other nations; we need think only of freedom of the press and of association.[71] Human rights were on the march everywhere enjoying increasing recognition by governments.

The constitutions mentioned were characterized by acknowledgements of the rights of the people, who were well aware that theirs was a liberal era and that the democratic form of government was to secure their freedom. In pointing out that these constitutions provided for proper democracies, my desire was, above all, to demonstrate that whatever democracy existed, it was supposed to secure human rights. I was not so much interested in showing how many people participated in government and to what degree these rights were protected. I tried to emphasize that these constitutions, insofar as they were democratic from the point of view of the liberalism of Montesquieu, Smith, Kant, and Jefferson, were properly democratic.

Proper democracy continued after World War I, when, especially due to the extension of the right to vote to women, there was an enormous increase of popular participation in government. However, democracies remained proper democracies. To stay with Germany, the Weimar constitution of 1919 has been regarded as the most democratic constitution of its time. Yet the majority of commentators considered the government it set up as a liberal democracy,[72] a popular government for the protection of the rights of the individual which were explicitly enumerated throughout the constitution. Schmitt, who urged that the government in order to secure its own survival fully use its power to quell abuses of civil rights, was a lonely figure.[73] In spite of emergency mea-

70. Cf. Hayek, *Constitution of Liberty,* 196. However, Hayek at once points out that the beginning of the German movement for a government of law is to be found in Prussia. He quotes A. L. Lowell, *Government and Parties in Continental Europe* (New York, 1896), 2:86: "In Prussia, the bureaucracy was so ordered as to furnish a better protection of individual rights and a firmer maintenance of law. But this broke down with the spread of French ideas after 1848, when the antagonistic interests in the state, taking advantage of the parliamentary system, abused the administrative power and introduced a veritable party tyranny." *Constitution of Liberty,* 481.

71. See the chapter on civil rights in Eugene N. Anderson and Pauline R. Anderson, *Political Institutions and Social Change in Continental Europe in the Nineteenth Century* (Berkeley, 1967), 238 ff.

72. See Schmitt, *Verfassungslehre,* 30 ff. The excessive liberalism of the Weimar constitution has been blamed for Hitler's access to power and resulted in certain restrictions of liberal excesses in the Bonn Basic Law.

73. Schmitt consistently voiced doubts about the possibility of reducing the essentials of the

sures under Article 48, the Weimar Republic remained a proper democracy in the opinion of most authors until it was superseded by Hitler's dictatorship.[74] Other constitutions adopted after World War I also established proper democracies.[75]

The same can be said of constitutions made after the Second World War. The French, Italian, and West German constitutions were reactions not only to the regimes of Pétain, Mussolini, and Hitler, but also to the liberal regimes that preceded these heads of state. It was asked whether the defeat of France in 1940 and the arrival of the Vichy government was perhaps caused not only by the German invasion, but also by shortcomings of the Third Republic which had been denounced before the war by Pétain, his admirer de Gaulle, and the French Right. One asked whether the rise of Mussolini was perhaps due to the liberalism of the Albertian Statute, and the coming of Hitler to the permissiveness of the Weimar Constitution. While defeats need not, and never must, result in defeatism, there should be in the wake of defeat, soul-searching about one's own faults and mistakes that made defeats possible. No matter how formidable the external forces of a regime may be, its decline and destruction usually will be hastened by internal ills. Therefore, the defeated should blame themselves as well as the victor. Self-criticism must precede criticism of others. After World War II, investigations took place concerning the imperfections of the Third Republic, the *Statuto,* and the Weimar constitution which could have been responsible for the fall of these governments. They probably were the least evident in France, where the end of the Third Republic was blamed on the German invasion rather than its internal weaknesses. Soul-searching was more evident in Italy, where the advent of fascism could not be attributed to an invading army. It was still greater in West Germany because Hitler's assumption of power was more recent than Mussolini's, and his rule more cruel.

Weimar constitution according to Art. 76, an article more often referred to in his *Verfassungslehre* than any other article. See esp. 16–20, 24–26, 98, 102–104, 108–109, 163, 177, 391 (the last page of that work, as if its author wanted to give his doubts a final emphasis). See also "Zehn Jahre Reichsverfassung," *Juristische Wochenschrift* 58 (1929):2313; *Der Hüter der Verfassung* (Tübingen, 1931), 113; *Legalität und Legitimität* (München und Leipzig, 1932), reprinted in *Verfassungsrechtliche Aufsätze* (Berlin, 1958), esp. 293–312, 312–19, 344–45; "Inhalt und Bedeutung des zweiten Hauptteils der Reichsverfassung," in Gerhard Anschütz/Richard Thoma, eds., *Handbuch des deutschen Staatsrechts* (Tübingen, 1932), 2:572, reprinted as "Grundrechte und Grundpflichten" in *Verfassungsrechtliche Aufsätze,* 186, 192, 201–203, 220–22. On the national-socialist threat, see *Der Hüter der Verfassung,* 113; *Legalität und Legitimität,* 286, 302–303, 344–45.

74. Cf., however, Hayek, *The Road to Serfdom.*

75. As to Austria, see the constitution of Oct. 1, 1920, Articles 1, 2, 149. Cf. Hans Kelsen, *Österreichisches Staatsrecht* (Tübingen, 1923), 74 ff.; Mary Macdonald, *The Republic of Austria, 1918–1934* (London, 1946), esp. 42 ff. In the constitution of Czechoslovakia of 1920, see esp. sections 1, 2, 106 ff., 128 ff.; see Jirí Hoetzl, "The Definite Constitution of the Czecho-Slovak Republic," *International Conciliation,* No. 179 (1922), esp. 379–80, 388 ff.

Furthermore, the destruction of Germany was more complete than that of Italy.[76] The question of "how could it happen" usually is intensified by the degree of the undesirability of what happened. Yet in spite of the criticism of their liberal predecessors, the new constitutions of France, Italy, and West Germany adopted in the late forties make it evident that democracy is a means for the protection of the individual.[77] The governments they establish are liberal, proper democracies. Their "negative" character, implying emphasis upon the freedom to be left alone rather than upon individual activity, has been pointed out.[78] While they guarantee popular participation in government, they leave no doubt that the end of democracy is the protection of the individuals living in it, and they protect human rights generously.[79]

From its beginning, the Fourth Republic was attacked as a revival of the Third Republic and its liberal disadvantages.[80] Yet the constitution of the Fifth Republic, framed by the very man who, next to de Gaulle, had been the most outspoken in finding fault with the Fourth Republic, again establishes, while strengthening the presidency, a parliamentary democracy protecting human rights and qualifying as a proper democracy.[81]

The preceding pages show that democracy proper may well be a proper democracy. It need not be. Irrespective of how much proper democracy may correspond to democracy proper, it is not necessarily as purely democratic as democracy proper is. As here defined, proper democracy is a democracy

76. See Dietze, *Deutschland—Wo Bist Du?* (München, 1980), 47 f.

77. See Dietze, "Natural Law in the Modern European Constitutions," *Natural Law Forum* 1 (1956): 73 ff.

78. Carl J. Friedrich, "The Political Theory of the New Democratic Constitutions," *Review of Politics* 12 (1950):215 ff.

79. The preamble of the constitution of the Fourth Republic reads: "Au lendemain de la victoire remportée par les peuples libres sur les régimes qui ont tenté d'asservir et de dégrader la personne humaine, le peuple français proclame à nouveau que tout être humain, sans distinction de race, de religion ni de croyance, possède des droits inalienables et sacrés. Il réaffirme solennellement les droits et les libertés de l'homme et du citoyen consacrés par la Déclaration des Droits de 1789 et les principes fondamentaux reconnus par les lois de la République." The preamble of the constitution of the Fifth Republic reads: "Le peuple français proclame solennellement son attachement aux Droits de l'homme at aux principes de la souveraineté nationale tels qu'ils ont été définis par la Déclaration de 1789, confirmée et complétée par la préambule de la Constitution de 1946." Cf. Gordon Wright, *The Reshaping of French Democracy* (New York, 1948); Alfred Cobban, *A History of Modern France, Volume 3, 1871–1962* (Penguin Books, 1965), to give only two examples of an abundant literature. A similarly abundant literature exists on the liberalism of the Italian constitution of 1947 and the Bonn Basic Law, both of which contain long bills of rights.

80. The most outstanding critic was de Gaulle, who resigned from the provisional presidency of France because the framers of the constitution of the Fourth Republic did not comply with his wishes. See Michel Debré, *La mort de la République* (Paris, 1947), *La République et ses problèmes* (Paris, 1952). Cf. Alain Peyrefitte, *Le mal français* (Paris, 1976).

81. See Carl J. Friedrich, "The New French Constitution in Political and Historical Perspective," *Harvard Law Review* 72 (1959):801 ff.

qualified by the liberalism expressed by Montesquieu, Smith, Kant, and Jefferson. Since what qualified restricts what is being qualified, proper democracy may well compete with democracy proper.

Democracy proper is democracy in the literal meaning of the word *democracy*—government by the people. It need not be, to use Lincoln's language, a government for the people or of the people, although it may be both. As long as the people rule, there exists democracy proper, or pure democracy, or, more simply expressed, democracy. The forms of popular participation are irrelevant. It can be direct, as in ancient Greece or in some Swiss cantons, or indirect, as in most modern states. It can be by acclamation or by secret vote. Democracy can imply representation in the sense of Hobbes or in that of pluralistic societies with free elections. The only qualification that seems to disturb the purity of democracy as a government by the people seems to be one born out of the necessity to be able to govern, namely, majority rule. However, upon closer inspection, this qualification turns out not to be a real qualification. The word *democracy* contains the syllable *cracy*. The ability to rule thus is of the very essence of democracy. Since unanimity can hardly be expected and minority rule would be a more serious qualification of democracy than majority rule, the latter is of the essence, and thus can hardly be considered a qualification, of democracy.

While the word *democracy* says something about the form of government, it is silent as to what that type of government can do: democracy can do good and bad things. Since what is good and bad has been open to dispute, depending upon values, we shall confine ourselves to stating that democracy can do good and harm from the point of view of the liberalism agreed upon by Montesquieu, Smith, Kant, and Jefferson. Democracy is good, proper, if it acts in accord with that kind of liberalism, bad, improper, if it does not. Since the liberalism of these four men is one of measure and proposes a golden mean between anarchy and tyranny, it shows that that golden mean, as it is reflected in proper democracy, will be jeopardized by anarchy and tyranny and trends approaching these extremes.

In a democratic age, threats of anarchy and tyranny usually will exist in democracies, whatever their forms and window dressings may be. For few governments, fascist and communist ones included, will admit today that they are undemocratic. Democracy can have all kinds of forms and demonstrate all kinds of ideologies. Democracy can be dictatorial as well as liberal to the degree of verging on anarchy, it can exist in a highly centralized as well as under a decentralized system, in a uniform as well as a pluralistic society. Democracy can be a jack-of-all-trades as much as the jackass of intelligent traders, and so on. In view of this diversity, attacks against proper democracy can come about in, and be launched by, the most diverse types of democracy proper.

In our democratic age, proper democracy, while still recognized in many quarters, has come under attack throughout the world. This is not surprising because proper democracy implies liberalism as agreed upon by Montesquieu,

Smith, Kant, and Jefferson. This ideology has been the target of formidable forces, such as nationalism, various types of socialism ranging from communism to fascism, of despotism and anarchism. Given these attacks, usually made in the name of democracy, liberals will try to assert proper democracy whenever and wherever it is about to be established, reestablished, or jeopardized. They will do so with measure and, as was suggested especially by Montesquieu, by taking into account local traditions and conditions.

Just as proper democracy was attained slowly and under difficulties following struggles for the rule of law protecting freedom, a struggle that facilitated Rudolf von Jhering's *Kampf ums Recht,*[82] it appears difficult today in many places to defend and promote it. The followers of the great liberals of the eighteenth century here analyzed perhaps will not permit themselves to be handicapped by liberal inhibitions when they are engaged in the defense and promotion of proper democracy. Considering that proper democracy, for the sake of human rights, guards against anarchy and despotism, its defense and promotion will be directed against these two extremes.

In the face of anarchist threats, the defense of proper democracy will amount to upholding the laws. Liberals could abstain from liberalistic inhibitions which might induce them to be too lenient toward those who challenge proper democracy through a permissiveness that goes beyond that allowed by the laws and moves toward license. We think of all positive laws, not just of criminal law. Although sanction for a legal order is largely provided by the latter, with penalties ranging from the imposition of a fine to the death penalty, sanctions for fulfilling private contracts and protecting private property are just as important. Infringements upon any kind of law or legal obligation challenge the legal order. Influenced by Rousseau's idea that men and women are spoiled by their environment, an idea that delinquents, especially those who have not read Rousseau carefully, like to emphasize, people have given generous pardon to criminals and overlooked Goethe's lines from the beginning of *Faust,*

> Ein guter Mensch in seinem dunkeln Drange
> ist sich des rechten Weges wohl bewusst.

These people have forgotten that a constitution is not a suicide pact and that a popular government has the right to properly defend its order.[83] An effective defense will seem to be especially appropriate in the case of a proper democracy. For that defense will be, in the opinion of liberals who share the thoughts Montesquieu, Smith, Kant, and Jefferson agree upon, not just one of any kind of a way of life, but of the proper way of life.

The means for the defense of proper democracy against anarchy will vary

82. Rudolf von Jhering, *Der Kampf ums Recht,* 4th ed. (Wien, 1874).
83. Robert H. Jackson, dissent in *Terminiello* v. *Chicago,* 337 U.S. 1, 37 (1948).

according to circumstances and conditions. As a general principle, they will be determined by the respective government. Those judging threats to a specific society must come from that particular society because only they are likely to possess the familiarity with existing conditions which enables them to correctly assess behavior against the well-being of that society and its laws.

Different societies will have different laws which will make different provisions as to when proper democracy is threatened by behavior tending toward anarchy.[84] For instance, in nations with artificial borders, there usually is a greater need for defense than in those having protective natural borders. Therefore, attempts to shirk military service will be judged more severely. Terrorism can be fought in various ways, depending upon the specific conditions. Doubts have been raised about Chancellor Schmidt's policy during the Schleyer crisis of 1977 of going "to the limits of the *Rechtsstaat*" in the treatment of terrorists.[85] It was felt that the terrorists were treated too leniently, that a group that claimed the status of belligerents ought to be dealt with according to the sentence *inter arma silent leges.* Others feared that giving terrorists the rights of belligerents would unduly entitle them to the protection of the Hague and Geneva conventions.[86] For a long time, Uruguay was praised as the proper democracy in Latin America. When the Tupamarus threatened it to the point of collapse, the military took over in 1973 and restored law and order.[87] Later on, similar events came to pass in Turkey, where under a proper democratic government terrorism claimed several lives each week.[88] In both nations, military dictatorships replaced proper democracy. While the police methods of those regimes ought not to be overlooked, it should be kept in mind that without the anarchist threats preceding them, dictatorships would probably not have come about. The fact that the military takeover was considered an emergency action indicates that it was seen as a necessary step toward the restoration of proper democracy, something borne out by the planning of elections in 1984 in Uruguay and, later on, in Turkey, where in 1983 a referendum gave overwhelming support to the constitution proposed by the military.

84. See Ernst Fraenkel, ed., *Der Staatsnotstand* (Berlin, 1965).

85. Speech before the Bundestag, Sept. 15, 1977, in Bundespresseamt, ed., *Politische Zeittafel* (Bonn, 1981), 247.

86. See L. Oppenheim, *International Law,* 6th ed., rev. by H. Lauterpacht, 2:269–306.

87. See Omar Costa, comp., *Los Tupamaros* (Mexico, 1971); Maria Ester Gilio, *The Tupamaro Guerillas,* trans. Anne Edmondson (New York, 1972), with an introduction by Robert J. Alexander; Cahiers libres 226–27, *Nous les tupamaros, suivi de apprendre d'eux par Régis Debray* (Paris, 1972); Martin Weinstein, *Uruguay: The Politics of Failure* (Westport, Conn., 1975); Comando General del Ejercito, ed., *La subversión* (Montevideo, 1977), and *Testimonio de una nación agredida* (Montevideo, 1978); Edy Kaufman, *Uruguay in Transition* (New Brunswick, N.J., 1979).

88. See Feroz Ahmad, *The Turkish Experiment in Democracy, 1950–1975* (Boulder, Colo., 1977); Clement Henry Dodd, *Democracy and Development in Turkey* (1979); Walter F. Weiker, *The Modernization of Turkey* (New York, 1981); Paul Henze, "The Long Effort to Destabilize Turkey," *Wall Street Journal,* Oct. 7, 1981; General Secretariat of the National Security Council, *12 September in Turkey: Before and After* (Ankara, 1982).

In both nations the protection of the individual's rights from attacks by fellow-citizens was put above popular participation in government with a view to restoring proper democracy. One may have doubts about this procedure. It is one thing, it can be argued, for the government of West Germany to go to the limits of the democratic *Rechtsstaat,* but quite another to replace democracy by a military dictatorship, much as such a replacement may be depicted as a means for the restoration of proper democracy. On the other hand, it cannot be denied that the Schleyer crisis did not endanger proper democracy as much as did Tupamarus and Turkish terrorists. Therefore, it can be argued that if Schmidt was willing to go the limits of the *Rechtsstaat,* the governments of Uruguay and Turkey could go beyond those limits.

What applies to terrorism, applies to riots, insurrections, and civil war, although not necessarily *a fortiori.* For these more or less anarchist challenges to proper democracy are not of necessity more dangerous than terrorism. While they may have more participants and thus appear quantitatively bigger, they need not be larger qualitatively: in the eyes of Marx the whole proletariat was not more dangerous to the existing order than a small selected elite recruited from it. Moreover, rioters, insurrectionists, and those engaged in civil war fight more openly and can more easily be spotted and resisted than terrorists who act clandestinely.

During the American Civil War, President Lincoln acted against a constitution embodying free government. He suspended human rights in order to win the war.[89] While the dangers of such behavior to proper democracy have been pointed out, it also has been stressed that Lincoln's actions were prompted by a desire to save the Union and the Constitution and the proper democracy they embodied.[90] No doubt, free government under him was less free and proper than it had been. However, it probably still qualified as a proper democracy. Lincoln was considered a Whig in the White House in spite of his war measures.[91] He never questioned democratic government, to which he confessed at Gettysburg. This cannot be said of the military dictatorships in Uruguay and Turkey. Yet since it was asserted that these dictatorships were backed by popular majorities, the question arises as to whether in their case one could speak of a commissary democratic rule. Given the fact that in Uruguay and Turkey the protection of economic rights and of private property has been favored by the military, some people would perhaps go so far as to classify the governments of these nations as proper democracies even in the absence of popular participation in government.

When Chancellor Schmidt said he would go to the limits of the *Rechtsstaat,*

89. See Kenneth A. Bernard, "Lincoln and Civil Liberties," *Abraham Lincoln Quarterly* 6 (1951):375; Thomas F. Carroll, "Freedom of Speech and of the Press during the Civil War," *Virginia Law Review* 9 (1923):516.

90. See Dietze, *America's Political Dilemma,* 44 ff.

91. Ibid., 29.

he had in mind curtailments of the rights of terrorists up to the barrier set by the Bonn Basic Law. He acted within the constitutional order that permits restrictions of human rights for the sake of the survival of that order.[92] Schmidt did not attack democracy proper in any way. His attitude toward the terrorists had the backing of all parties represented in the legislature, showing a rare unanimity indicative of the seriousness of the terrorist threat. There was no competition between democracy proper and proper democracy. The situation was different in Uruguay and Turkey. Even if the military acted for, and was backed by, the majority of the people, it was formally not authorized by that majority to establish a dictatorship and to exclude formal popular participation in public affairs. Given the confessed desire of the military rulers to restore the safety of individuals from their fellow-citizens, it could be said that in Uruguay as well as Turkey a competition between the principles of the protection of the individual—at least from attacks by fellow citizens—and his participation in government was evident. If we disregard the opinion that the military acts as a commissariat for the people, that competition ended with a victory for the liberal principle of the protection of the individual, a victory of sorts because the protection from fellow-citizens was perhaps neutralized by the absence of a protection of the individuals from the government, which has been considered a *sine qua non* of proper democracy.

The seizure of power by the military in Uruguay and Turkey has been criticized for having been *ultra vires.* It would have been more acceptable, it has been said, had the respective constitutions permitted it in case of emergency. On the other hand, the protection of human rights in a proper democracy presupposes a government. It can be argued that proper democracy protects the rights of the individual merely as a matter of principle, that a principle implies exceptions and that the citizens must reckon with a suspension of their rights in the case of anarchical threats.

A suspension of human rights in emergencies can also be provided for *expressis verbis,* as, for example, in Article 48 of the Weimar Constitution and Article 16 of the constitution of the Fifth Republic. These provisions give the presidents of Germany and France the right to restrict human rights in emergencies. One has spoken of "constitutional dictatorship."[93] That kind of dictatorship is compatible with the principle of the protection of human rights from the state authorities because these rights are suspended just in exceptional cases in order to save the system that regularly protects them. It is in accor-

92. Art. 18 Basic Law reads: "Whoever abuses the freedom of expression of opinion, in particular the freedom of the press . . . of teaching . . . of assembly . . . of association . . . the secrecy of the mail, post and telecommunications . . . property . . . or the right of asylum . . . in order to attack the free, democratic basic order, shall forfeit these basic rights."

93. See Clinton Rossiter, *Constitutional Dictatorship* (Princeton, 1948). Rossiter deals both with Lincoln and art. 48.

dance with the principle of popular participation in government, for the chief executive is an elected official, the people's commissar.[94]

A constitution also can simply provide that individuals and organizations who plan to overthrow proper democracy shall not have the benefit of the constitution's bill of rights. This means quite clearly and generally that only those who support the system protecting rights deserve the protection of those rights, that it should not be possible for those who want to destroy proper democracy to do so by taking advantage of its protection of human rights. After the experience of the Weimar Republic, this method was adopted by Article 9 of the Bonn Basic Law.

The parties outlawed, the Socialist Reich's party (SRP) and the Communist party of Germany (KPD), were highly centralized. Open enemies of liberalism, their platforms favored authoritarianism, not anarchy. Nevertheless, they can be mentioned in connection with anarchist threats to proper democracy. Although there is a despotism of anarchy, the *bellum omnium contra omnes,*[95] despotism, as the word is generally used, is the despotism of government, the very opposite of anarchy. Because even the best organized opposition is not yet a government, it may well have an anarchist effect. An opposition to a government that goes beyond what is permitted by the laws is illegal, and every illegal act challenges the legal order and is more or less anarchist, whether or not its perpetrators are aware of it. While professed anarchist movements are anarchist by definition, even authoritarian movements, internally well organized and standing for order, have an anarchist effect during their fight against established orders.

On the face of it, anarchist threats to proper democracy do not seem to reflect a challenge of proper democracy by democracy proper. After all, democracy proper, meaning government by the people, is a government and government is the very opposite of anarchy. However, it must not be overlooked that the governmental effectiveness of democracy proper is largely due to the fact that the government of all people is reduced to that of the majority because it is realized that unanimity can hardly exist, certainly not in a pluralistic society. Therefore, those posing anarchist threats to proper democracy may well assert that they consider themselves oppressed by its ruling majority and attack that majority for being undemocratic because it does not represent all the people. They will claim that their attack is sanctioned by the idea that democracy proper means the government of all the people, not just of the majority.

94. Cf. Carl Schmitt, *Die Diktatur* (München, 1921). On 136, Lincoln is called a *kommissarischer Diktator* who suspended the constitution in order to save it.

95. On that idea, as well as on that of *homo homini lupus,* see M. M. Goldsmith, *Hobbes's Science of Politics* (New York, 1966).

While there is a good possibility that a belief in democracy proper will spark anarchist attacks upon proper democracy, there is little doubt that democracy proper, be it the rule of all or that of the majority, can constitute despotic threats to proper democracy. The sentences outlawing the two extremist German parties mentioned above state that these parties planned to replace the liberal democracy under the Bonn Basic Law by despotic governments.[96]

Indeed, proper democracy has been challenged, threatened, and replaced by antiliberals, by communists and fascists. Irrespective of how the latter may differ, they both denounce liberalism, the ideology of proper democracy. Occupying a center position, proper democracy is surrounded by communism on the left and fascism on the right, and both meet in designs to destroy liberalism,[97] which to them is a thing of the past. This explains why the animosity between communists and fasicsts is more vehement than that between them and liberals, who are believed to stand for a lost cause. Liberalism is not considered a competitive enemy, whereas communist and fascist socialisms compete for the future. History already has taken care of liberalism, the fight against which no longer has priority. Now socialist movements must fight, and eliminate, each other until there is just one kind of socialism left to bring about paradise. This century being democratic, communists and fascists have attacked liberal democracy by denouncing its liberalism for being a falsification and unwarranted qualification of democracy. In a word, communists and fascists have attacked proper democracy on the grounds that it is a liberal perversion of democracy proper. Both have denounced liberal democracy for being undemocratic, hypocritical and oppressive.[98]

The communist and fascist challenges of liberal democracy have been quite successful. In a democratic age, their success in a large measure has been due to the fact that they attacked proper democracy with confessions to democracy proper. Needless to say, proper democracy was not attacked qua proper democracy. The proper democracy praised by liberals was considered to be an improper democracy. In addition, communists and fascists posed as liberators from the serfdom of capitalism and liberalism and made their dictatorial programs appear as effective means of such liberation. For in politics, it is as suicidal not to emphasize that one favors liberty as it is to attack something for

96. See Bernhard Wolff, "Die Rechtsprechung des Bundesverfassungsgerichts von 1954–1957." *Jahrbuch des öffentlichen Rechts* (N.F.), 7:127–28.

97. Cf. Arthur M. Schlesinger, Jr., *The Vital Center* (Boston, 1949).

98. Communists often assert that Western democracies, in which the legislature as the most democratic of the branches of government is checked by Montesquieu's ideas on the separation of powers, are less democratic than communist regimes, where the legislature, or soviet, is absolute. They claim to be more in conformity with Rousseau than Western democracies. The *Fasces* symbolize the unity of the people, irrespective of classes, and it was always emphasized in the Third Reich that national socialism stood for the unity of white and blue collar workers, *des Arbeiters der Stirn und der Faust.*

being proper. In a democratic age, the enemies of liberal democracy will advance paying tribute to democracy proper, an undiluted and unrestricted type of democracy, and asserting that this kind of democracy, being the purest, is preferable to all other types and the only truly proper democracy.

Whatever the specific circumstances in any particular situation may have been, attacks upon liberal democracy by communists and fascists usually were defended along the lines just stated. There were, of course, differences between these two major groups. While both communists and fascists are in the socialist camp, they resent being considered identical. According to official programs—and programs are more luring and appealing than their administration which usually is less pure[99]—communists are more opposed to private property and free enterprise than fascists, which accounts for the accusation that Mussolini and Hitler betrayed socialism.[100] Furthermore, fascists emphasized that they wanted to come to power legally, not by revolution.[101] These concessions to liberalism attracted voters, notably among the middle and upper strata of society. They tipped the balance in favor of Mussolini and Hitler.[102] Another difference between communists and fascists has been that the former, advertising that theirs is a grass-roots democracy, have claimed to cherish the ideas of Rousseau, whereas the fascists, believing in the leadership principle, have tended toward a Hobbesian outlook and considered their regime an enobled type of democracy.[103]

There are, of course, not only differences between communists and fascists, but among the members of each group. Fascism being a national socialism, these differences can be expected to be greater among fascists than among communists. The spirit of liberty is everywhere. Even dogmatists out to

99. In his last days, Hitler is reputed to have said that his orders are good only for the generals and the further they trickle down in the military hierarchy, the less they are enforced. When told by an old member of the party that the party program had not been quite realized, he expressed doubts about the collaboration of the German bureaucracy.

100. This is, of course, the accusation made by Marxists. Although it can hardly be denied that there is some truth in it, one should also not overlook that communist regimes have as often as state capitalism betrayed labor, as is evident and emphasized in the case of Poland today.

101. In accord with the Italian constitution, Mussolini was appointed prime minister by the king on Oct. 30, 1922 and obtained a vote of confidence of 306 to 116 votes on Nov. 18. A week later, the Chamber of Deputies granted him plenary powers by a vote of 275 to 90. In accord with the Weimar Constitution, Hitler was appointed chancellor by President Hindenburg on Jan. 30, 1933, and received a comfortable majority of 441 to 94 for the Enabling Act of Mar. 24, 1933, no votes being cast by 81 communists and 26 socialists who were imprisoned or in hiding.

102. It is often overlooked that in Italy and Germany the governing center parties lost votes, whereas the strength of communists, fascists, and national-socialists, increased. To many observers, both nations seemed to be faced with the alternative between the extreme left and right. Another concession of fascists and national-socialists to liberalism was their rejection of the Marxist principle that religion is opium for the people.

103. Mussolini called fascism "the purest form of democracy," an "organized, centralized, authoritarian democracy." *The Doctrine of Fascism,* (1932), in Carl Cohen, ed., *Communism, Fascism and Democracy* (New York, 1962), 352, 359.

destroy freedom cannot escape its spell and feel free to respond to the requirements of specific situations. Italian fascism, German National Socialism, Spanish Falangism, Argentine Peronism: they all were, in accordance with Mussolini's statement that fascism is not for export,[104] influenced by national conditions when they were programmatically conceived and underwent changes and adjustments.[105]

Although communism has claimed to be an international socialist movement, a fact that increased its appeal throughout the world, it made concessions to nationalism. At the outbreak of World War I, Marxist parties left no doubt that their allegiances were to the fatherland rather than to Marx and his call for the solidarity of the proletarians of all countries. Following the establishment of the communist regime in Russia, a split occurred between the internationalist Trotsky and the nationalist Stalin. The latter, with his idea of communism in one country, was victorious. After World War II, Soviet communism officially was challenged by China and, later on, by the Eurocommunists, who emphasized the national features of their respective parties.[106] Needless to say, just as fascists were not divided merely along national lines, neither were the communists. From the debates between orthodox and revisionist Marxists following the failure of the Paris Commune,[107] there have been discussions within the various communist nations and schools as to the proper interpretations and administrations of communist doctrines.[108]

The diversity within groups challenging liberalism shows that freedom cannot be barred even from authoritarian movements, that there is a bit of liberalism everywhere. This does not mean that these movements did not fight what in this study is called proper democracy. Their fight has been formidable indeed.

Despotic threats to proper democracy in the name of democracy proper have issued from authoritarian movements. These challenges usually came from outside of proper democracy, even though fascists have worked within the constitutional framework of free government as did, notwithstanding Lenin's advice, communists as partners of Popular Front coalitions or as Eurocommunists.[109] However, such threats also can come from within liberal democracy by those who pay tribute to proper democracy. Here we enter a twilight zone. Communist and fascist threats to proper democracy are clear-cut. In the

104. Cf. Cohen, *Communism,* 356.

105. See ibid., 349: Fascism "has a form correlative to the contingencies of place and time."

106. See Alexander Dallin, ed., *Diversity in International Communism: A Documentary Record, 1961–1963* (New York, 1963); Dan N. Jacobs, ed., *From Marx to Mao and Marchais* (New York, 1979); *The New Communisms* (New York, 1969).

107. See Leopold Labedz, ed., *Revisionism* (New York, 1962).

108. See Carl Landauer et al., *European Socialism* (Berkeley and Los Angeles, 1959); G. R. Urban, *Communist Reformation* (New York, 1979). These are only two examples from a rich literature.

109. See Franz Borkenau, *European Communism* (London, n.d.).

name of the majority, communists (in Russia originally their majority, the bolsheviks) and fascists openly turn against liberalism and offer authoritarian solutions to what they conceive to be the ills of free government. By contrast, those believing in free elections at regular periods of time accept liberal democracy and often emphasize its values.

Still, a majoritarian challenge of proper democracy by the latter is possible. It may come about if the ruling majority decides not to respect the rights or any particular right of an individual. Since according to Madison, the most common source of faction is the unequal distribution of property,[110] and communist and fascist attacks against liberal democracy in a large measure turn against property rights, a majoritarian challenge of proper democracy from the inside in all likelihood will be directed against these rights, if only to deflate the causes of communism and fascism. The egalitarian twentieth century has been a century of socialism; thus even those who believe in the principle of liberalism will challenge proper democracy by attacking the right that semantically is connected the most with propriety, namely, the right of private property.

We mentioned Madison, the father of the American Constitution. Lincoln, who considered himself the savior of that constitution, took upon himself dictatorial powers to master the emergency of the Civil War. His dictatorship has been criticized and considered the beginning of a steady increase of presidential power which ended in what has been called "the imperial presidency."[111] Lincoln was aware that his actions were commissary. In spite of his Emancipation Declaration which in the opinion of many authors constituted a flagrant attack on property rights,[112] he, the Whig, never doubted that these rights were and ought to be protected and that the United States was a proper democracy. This attitude remained prevalent for some time. Human rights, including those of free enterprise and property, remained protected by the government because they were cherished by the American people. In the rare cases in which state legislators or Congress passed laws interfering with economic rights, these laws were carefully scrutinized by the Supreme Court and usually declared null and void because of their conflict with the Constitution.[113] As pointed out, proper democracy was firmly entrenched in America for a long time.

But what would happen if the imperial presidency was backed by an imperial majority represented in Congress and if both were interested in curtailing the individual's economic rights, if the combined power of the two were so enormous that due to the pressure of public opinion the Supreme Court

110. Hayek, *Constitution of Liberty,* 409.

111. Arthur M. Schlesinger, *The Imperial Presidency* (Boston, 1973).

112. David Donald, "Abraham Lincoln: Whig in the White House," in Norman A. Graebner, ed., *The Enduring Lincoln* (Urbana, Ill., 1959), 50, mentions that the declaration was considered "the most stupendous act of sequestration in the history of Anglo-Saxon jurisprudence."

113. See Dietze, *In Defense of Property,* 78 ff.

would capitulate? The New Deal, arriving in 1933, was a democratic program of the Democratic party in favor of an increasing regulation of free enterprise and property rights. The Supreme Court, recognizing that this program constituted a majoritarian challenge to a liberal democracy protecting property, during the first years of the Roosevelt administration found laws passed under this program to be in violation of the constitution and struck them down. The president of the American Liberty League referred to the New Deal as a democratic despotism, comparing it with Kemalism, communism, and fascism.[114] The Supreme Court, under pressure of being packed, capitulated and admitted New Deal legislation in 1937.[115] Soon therafter, it announced a doctrine of preferred freedoms, emphasizing that rights necessary for the democratic process are more important than economic rights.[116] Rights to participate in government were elevated above rights to be protected by the government. Democracy proper, for a long time considered a mere means for the protection of the individual's rights, among which those of property and free enterprise figured prominently and certainly were not discriminated, was now valued as an end in itself. Was proper democracy subordinated to democracy proper?

Some people will answer that question in the negative. They will argue that a democracy with free elections at regular periods is proper by definition. Even if human rights or a particular right are destroyed by the ruling majority, this would be exceptional because it would happen only for a limited time, until the rulers are voted out of office. It will be answered that the time limit on despotism may not be so limited if the majority is reelected; that even in a short time much harm can be done to the individual citizen and that certainly proper democracy can fall victim to democracy proper. Those denying that under the New Deal liberal democracy was replaced by a democratic despotism will claim that infringements upon private property and free enterprise were slight as compared with communist and fascist curtailments of a whole range of rights. They will say that actions taken under Roosevelt were an exception to the rule of leaving human rights intact and that proper democracy continued to exist. The reply will be that the protection of property and free enterprise has been so essential an aspect of American constitutionalism that its violation amounts to an abolition of proper democracy. Support for this contention will be marshalled by a reference to Herbert Hoover's idea on the Fifth Freedom.[117]

114. Raoul E. Desvernine, *Democratic Despotism.*

115. *West Coast Hotel Company* v. *Parrish,* 300 U.S. 379 (1937).

116. See Chief Justice Stone in *U.S.* v. *Carolene Products Co.,* 304 U.S. 144, 152 (1938); *West Virginia School Board* v. *Barnette,* 319 U.S. 624 (1943); *Thomas* v. *Collins,* 323 U.S. 516 (1944). For a critical review of the doctrine of preferred freedoms, see Justice Frankfurter in *Kovacs* v. *Cooper,* 336 U.S. 77, 89–97 (1949).

117. Herbert Hoover stated that "there is a Fifth Freedom—economic freedom—without which none of the other four freedoms will be realized." *Addresses upon the American Road: World War II, 1941–45* (New York, 1946), 222.

Mindful of John Adams's statement on the need for a protection of property, it will be added that even if such a protection was not central to the American development, it is still essential to proper democracy by definition and that as soon as property rights are subordinated to democratic rights, proper democracy is made inferior to democracy proper.

Similar arguments have been heard in the evaluation of other democracies. For instance, while the Weimar Republic has been considered the most democratic nation of its time, the question was raised as to whether under its constitution proper democracy was replaced by democracy proper because of curtailments of property rights.[118] The majority of commentators maintained that it established a liberal democracy. Yet it also was indicated that this constitution, the creation of which was influenced by the Social Democrats, provided for social features to a degree that these features put Germany on the road to serfdom and paved the way for Hitler's dictatorship.[119] The question as to whether there have been despotic challenges of proper democracy by democracy proper on account of social legislation has been raised with respect to England under Labor governments.[120] In has been discussed in connection with the *soziale Rechtsstaat* under the Bonn Basic Law.[121] It has been raised during the Fourth Republic and, in the Fifth Republic, under the presidency of Mitterand.[122]

However this question may be answered, the replacement of proper democracy by democracy proper has become a general problem. Liberal democracy has been threatened not only by confessedly dictatorial movements that deny free elections and resent pluralism. It also has become endangered by majorities that derive from free elections in pluralistic societies. Whatever the differences between all these types of government may be—and each one of them would resent being identified with the other—in all cases threats to proper democracy seem to derive mainly from an unequal distribution of property and to be motivated by egalitarian, socialist thinking. This bears out Madison's statement that "the most common and durable source of factions has been the various and unequal distribution of property."[123] What Madison, looking back into history and at existing conditions in the New World of America, considered the most common and durable source of political conten-

118. See Dietze, *In Defense of Property,* 122–23.

119. See Hayek, *The Road to Serfdom.*

120. See John Jewkes, *Ordeal by Planning* (New York, 1948); *The New Ordeal by Planning,* 2d ed. (New York, 1968).

121. See Fritz Werner, "Sozialistische Tendenzen in der Rechtsprechung," *Archiv des öffentlichen Rechts* 81 (1956):84 ff.; Werner Thieme, "Liberalismus und Grundgesetz," *Zeitschrift für die gesamte Staatswissenschaft* 113 (1957):285 ff.; Dietze, *Two Concepts of the Rule of Law,* 37 ff., and the sources cited there.

122. The election of Mitterand resulted in enormous transfers of French money to other nations believed to have a more stable currency.

123. *The Federalist,* essay 10.

tion nearly two hundred years ago, can still be so considered today, when the major despotic threats to proper democracy and its protection of human rights derive from the movements favoring social legislation.

Madison presided over the convention that framed the American Constitution. He was a major contributor to the *Federalist,* a classic on free government, written for the adoption of that constitution. Both as president of the Philadelphia Convention and as commentator on its work Madison showed himself to be a man of measure. The "father of the Constitution" is known as the great compromiser who helped bring about that "bundle of compromises," the Constitution.[124]

The American Constitution is a bundle of compromises which, designed as it was to fight the evil of factions, was made to counter despotic and anarchist trends. In good measure, it combines liberty and authority. Adopted at the time of Smith, Kant, and Jefferson and showing the ideas of Montesquieu, it reflects what these men considered a proper liberalism. America's constitution-makers left no doubt that monarchy and royal absolutism were things of the past, were un-American.[125] Yet after 1776, they saw how popular factions posed anarchist and despotic threats to free government, threats mainly directed against property rights,[126] and probably prompting John Adams's remark that violations of property lead to anarchy and tyranny.[127] As a result, America's founding fathers had a deep distrust of democracy. It is obvious in the debates at Philadelphia, in the *Federalist,* and in the ratifying state conventions.[128] The new Constitution was to create a free popular government under law, which con-

124. The latter term is used by Alpheus T. Mason, "The Nature of Our Federal Union Reconsidered," *Political Science Quarterly* 65 (1950):503. See Dietze, *The Federalist,* 256–57, 258 ff., 260 ff., 268 ff.

125. Hamilton's praise of the English constitution was based upon the republican substance of that constitution rather than upon its monarchical form. A student of the United States, Simon Bolívar made clear to San Martín, who wanted to invite Spanish *infantes* to become the monarchs of the newly independent Spanish American states, that this would be incompatible with the idea of America.

126. Charles A. Beard, *An Economic Interpretation of the Constitution* (New York, 1913), emphasizes the self-interest of the men who made and adopted the Constitution. There are strong indications that their desire to protect property in a large measure derived from their belief that such a protection is a prerequisite for freedom and order and conducive to justice, progress and the welfare of the individual and society. See Robert E. Brown, *Charles Beard and the Constitution* (Princeton, 1956); Forrest McDonald, *We, the People* (Chicago, 1958).

127. My comments on that statement can be found, in connection with Madison's comments on factions endangering property rights, in "Rights, Riots, Crimes," *Revue européenne des sciences sociales et Cahiers Vilfredo Pareto* 16 (1978):78 ff.

128. Cf. Edward S. Corwin, *The Doctrine of Judicial Review* (Princeton, 1914); "The Progress of Constitutional Theory between the Declaration of Independence and the Meeting of the Philadelphia Convention," *American Historical Review* 30 (1925):511 ff. See Max Farrand, ed., *The Records of the Federal Convention* (New Haven, 1911); Jonathan Elliot, ed., *The Debates, Resolutions and other Proceedings in Convention on the Adoption of the Federal Constitution* (Washington, 1827–30).

ceived the ruling majority as a means for the protection of the rights of the individual. In our parlance, America's founders, in accord with the liberalism Montesquieu, Smith, Kant, and Jefferson agreed upon, favored proper democracy over democracy proper. They recognized problems concerning the compatibility of liberalism and democracy, dealt with in the preceding pages. It remains to point out problems arising from disagreements among the four authors, notably those between Kant and Jefferson concerning democracy and liberalism.

Democracy and Liberalism

Governments derive from ideas. While governments can form beliefs, forms of government always result from beliefs. The very creation of government is due to the opinion that it is preferable to the absence of government. Fear of anarchy determines the quest for order: The specter of a *bellum omnium contra omnes* may well bring about the conviction that an absolute monarchy is necessary, as is evident with Hobbes. Absolute rulers can do much to make people believe that theirs is the best form of government. Nevertheless, subjects may doubt that this is so, and desire other forms of authority. Specific forms of government are sought as remedies for specific complaints and their causes.

Liberalism as a concrete historical movement came about as a reaction to big government in the age of absolutism. Originally reflecting mere discontent, liberalism turned into a desire to replace despotic government. Because in given situations despotism usually would be monarchical,[129] the remedies liberals thought of were popular governments. Modern democracy was conceived to be a means against infringements upon, and for the protection of, human rights. The replacement of absolute monarchy by democracy always was one of substance, sometimes also one of form. It took place by leaving the monarchy formally intact as in Great Britain in 1688, in France in 1789, in Piedmont-Sardinia in 1848, and in other continental nations where the absolute ruler gave his people a *constitution octroyée.* It did abolish monarchy also in form as in the United States in 1776 and in France with the execution of Louis XVI. These developments may have occurred in different nations and times, under a variety of conditions and details. In each case, however, liberalism created democracy. Democracy did not create liberalism, no matter how much the hope that democracy would promote liberalism may have been instrumental in the inception of liberalism.

The priority of liberalism before modern democracy suggests that under that form of government, liberalism will continue to have priority before de-

129. During the age of absolutism, republican governments were few and far between. They existed in the Hanseatic cities, in some of the states of Italy, in Swiss cantons.

mocracy, just as the existence of human rights before any form of government—assumed under various doctrines of natural law preponderant at the birth of the liberal movement—is said to continue once government has been established. It also can be argued that what creates is more important than what it creates, that democracy, established as a means for the realization of liberalism, must be less important than liberalism as its end.

These arguments can be countered. Means have power, ends do not. Whatever is established to achieve certain ends is a concrete institution with power, since without power nothing can be achieved. On the other hand, an end to be achieved cannot be something concrete, much as its realization may be desirable. It cannot have power. Consequently, democracy must be more powerful than liberalism, especially in view of the fact that it is, in contrast to liberalism, a government, and that government being sovereign is a strong power.

To assert that the creator is more powerful than his creation is a weak argument. Parents are not always more powerful than their children. An older generation is not necessarily more powerful than a younger one. Electors are not of necessity more powerful than the elected. The presidents in the Third and Fourth Republics, elected as they were by legislatures, were weak because of their personalities and legal restrictions, not because of the mode of election, much as that mode may have made the election of weak personalities probable. James Bryce stated that Americans refrain from putting strong personalities into the White House.[130] This does not mean that there would not have been strong presidents. It can be added that many an American president found out that men he appointed to the Supreme Court asserted a remarkable independence, to the point of turning against him. Newly sovereign nations conditionally established by colonial powers did not care about fulfilling these conditions once they were sovereign.

Although it is assumed that human rights under natural law doctrines have existed prior to governments, the rights of man were oppressed by absolute rulers. The fact that liberalism preceded modern democracy does not necessarily mean that it remains more powerful than democracy once the latter is established. The longer is not necessarily the stronger. Democracy is a form of government, liberalism is not, and governmental power ought not to be underestimated. The term *liberal democracy* seems to symbolize the priority of liberalism to democracy. On the other hand, it uses liberal as a mere adjective to the noun democracy, indicating that in a liberal democracy, democracy is stronger than liberalism.

These considerations suggest the gist of the problem of the relationship between liberalism and democracy. It basically is that between liberal or proper democracy and democracy proper. We indicated the compatibility of, and the

130. James Bryce, *The American Commonwealth,* 2d ed. (London, 1891), 1:73.

tensions between, the two. Will they get along or will one of them prove to be stronger than the other, perhaps to the point of eliminating the other?

After liberalism created democracy as an appropriate means for its realization, the relationship between the two was one of give and take. In the beginning the creator usually is stronger than his creation, just as parents initially are stronger than their children, so liberalism for a long time determined democracy. Originally, modern democracy meant the rule by a selected few who, although more numerous than the traditional aristocracy, did not constitute a majority of the population. Majority rule meant the rule by the majority of those who could vote. In time, those barred from voting complained according to the principle of "no taxation without representation." They could use the word "taxation" in a wider sense than the Americans did during the Revolution, asserting that the government was taxing all those excluded from participating in decision-making. The disenfranchised would assert that they were oppressed and under liberal banners would protest. As Goethe put it,

> Freiheit erwacht in jeder Brust
> Wir protestieren all mit Lust.[131]

Since democratic governments for some time remained under the wings of liberalism, they went by the liberal principle of "live and let live" and permitted broader and broader segments of the population to vote and to run for public office. Thus in the beginning of modern democracy, the growth of liberalism was matched by that of democracy: more and more people wanted the right to participate in government so that their freedom would be secure. As a result, democratic governments extended the suffrage to more and more people and became more and more representative of the entire population.

This remained so for generations. The molding of democracy by liberalism into forms of liberal democracy became an outstanding feature of the bourgeois era, an era praised by Thomas Mann.[132] It characterized a century which, as foreseen by de Tocqueville, was one of the march of democracy and was called the liberal century.[133] It has continued ever since. Montesquieu, Smith, Kant, and Jefferson are still with us. The shadows of the kind of liberalism they agreed upon are cast over democracies today. Yet the shadows have become longer.

131. Zahme Xenien IX. Cf. Thomas Mann, "Goethe und die Demokratie," *Schriften und Reden zur Literatur, Kunst und Philosophie* (Frankfurt, 1968), 3:225.

132. Thomas Mann, "Leiden und Grösse Richard Wagners" (1933), ibid., 2:121–22.

133. Mussolini uses the term "liberal century" in *Doctrine of Fascism,* 360. On the preceding page, we find the statement that "liberalism is the historical and logical beginning of anarchism." He distinguishes it from "organized, centralized, authoritarian democracy." For Hayek's distinction between liberalism and democracy, see *Constitution of Liberty,* 55, 103–104, 106, 442n2, 459n10.

Hayek's work, drawing on Montesquieu, Smith, Kant, and Jefferson, reminds us of, and tries to reinvigorate, the liberal ideas these men shared.[134] Its impressive documentation—there are more footnotes and references in *The Constitution of Liberty* alone than in all the works of the authors just mentioned—makes it a heroic attempt. It also indicates a need for a reassertion of these ideas, which are now on the defensive. Works against the tide[135] require a more careful documentation than those running with the fashions of the day. This is especially true if academicians cater to politicians, those questionable actors and fashion-designers of the day, and if a scholar, by attacking the former, also attacks the latter. When Hayek wrote, his type of liberalism was challenged from without and from within by communists, fascists, social democrats, and advocates of the welfare state. The author of *The Constitution of Liberty* and *Law, Legislation and Liberty* earlier had published *The Road to Serfdom,* a work that shows how liberal democracy became replaced by social democracy and how under the banner of democracy proper liberalism was discarded and the road to serfdom taken.[136] Hayek's warning did not reflect the opinion of most social scientists. He was denounced as a reactionary and became a lonely figure in the profession.[137] It is perhaps telling that in 1974 he shared the Nobel Prize in Economic Science with Gunnar Myrdal, a man of socialist inclinations, and that previous prizes had been awarded only to economists not exposing Keynes.[138] Furthermore, the award to Hayek was made only after the reputed enemy of socialism conceded that among totalitarian doctrines, that of socialism is "the noblest and most influential."[139]

The Road to Serfdom is addressed, not dedicated, "To the socialists of all parties." *The Constitution of Liberty* is addressed, not dedicated, "To the unknown civilization that is growing in America." *Law, Legislation and Liberty* is not dedicated to anyone, but can be considered as addressed to the unknown civilization that is growing in America because Hayek indicated that it is a continuation of *The Constitution of Liberty* and deserving the same title.[140] Addressing *The Road to Serfdom* to socialists was meant as a warning lest

134. The index of *The Constitution of Liberty* lists 11 references to Montesquieu, 16 to Smith, 4 to Kant, 12 to Jefferson. His work on *Law, Legislation and Liberty* quotes Montesquieu as a motto at the very beginning. It starts out on page 1 with the words: "When Montesquieu and the framers of the American Constitution articulated the conception of a limiting constitution that had grown up in England, they set a pattern which liberal constitutionalism has followed ever since."

135. *Against the Tide,* trans. Elizabeth Henderson (Chicago, 1969) is a work by Wilhelm Röpke. Röpke's work is less documented than Hayek's. This may well indicate that in Switzerland there existed at the time of his writing a more friendly intellectual attitude toward the free market than in England and the United States, where Hayek wrote.

136. Comp. William F. Buckley, Jr., "The Road to Serfdom: The Intellectuals and Socialism," in Fritz Machlup, ed., *Essays on Hayek* (New York, 1976), 95 ff.

137. Herman Finer, *Road to Reaction* (Boston, 1945), accuses Hayek of insanity.

138. One exception is Leontief (1973), who, however, was not as anti-Keynesian as Hayek.

139. *Law, Legislation and Liberty,* 1:6.

140. Ibid., 1:3.

socialism destroy the kind of liberalism Hayek believed in. The address in *The Constitution of Liberty* is another warning, obviously prompted by the consideration that the known civilization under which the United States prospered when the liberalism Montesquieu, Smith, Kant, and Jefferson believed in determined American democracy, has been fading away so that America now was facing an uncertain civilization.[141] Similar thoughts have been expressed by other authors.[142]

Among liberal democracies the United States enjoys a certain preeminence. The only nation starting out as a liberal democracy, free government was established there in an unqualified way. Popular government in substance was matched by one in form and restricted under law for the sake of the rights of the individual. As de Tocqueville had predicted, the United States today is the most powerful of all liberal democracies. John Locke, who influenced the American Revolution and the Declaration of Independence and who can be considered a forerunner of Montesquieu,[143] stated that "in the beginning all the world was *America*."[144] It can be added that the New World of the United States of America was liberal-democratic from the start and the origin of liberal democracy in the world. It was in the United States that popular government was first established in modern times without formal aristocratic or monarchical trimmings. It was here that from the beginning one was wary of democratic despotism and saw to it that democracy would be restrained according to the principles of liberalism. The first outstanding liberal-democratic constitution was that of the United States. The first great work in modern times on free government and problems of democracy in theory and practice, the *Federalist*, was written in America. The first well-known book on modern democracy, written by a liberal who weighed the pros and cons of popular government, was entitled *Of Democracy in America.*

The concern lest the traditional liberal-democratic civilization in America is on the way out is natural. De Gaulle was of the opinion that communism would soon fade away in Russia, where it was established first as a regime. Wouldn't liberal democracy fade away in the United States, where it was established first? In contrast to religions, political movements come and go like the ordinary human beings who conceive them. The old dies when ordinary. On the other hand, it can be argued that since liberal democracy has existed in America longer than elsewhere, it will be solidly established there so that we

141. I stated this on the last page of *America's Political Dilemma.* When I asked Hayek during his 1975 visit to the Johns Hopkins University whether my thoughts were correct, he answered that this idea might have crossed his mind.

142. Eric Voegelin, *The New Science of Politics* (Chicago, 1952), has the motto, "Posterity may know we have not loosely through silence permitted things to pass away as in a dream."

143. On the influence of Locke on the Declaration of Independence, see Becker, *The Declaration of Independence.* Like Montesquieu, Locke proposed a separation of powers, the aspect of government the Frenchman found characteristic of England.

144. John Locke, *Two Treatises of Government,* ed. Peter Laslett (Cambridge, 1960), 319.

need not worry over its survival. This corresponds to Madariaga's opinion that Christianity will disappear first from those parts of the world to which it was introduced last.[145] But then, a political ideology is not a religion. Be this as it may, a concern that the liberal-democratic civilization in America might be replaced ought not to be taken lightly. In view of the fact that the United States is the strongest of liberal democracies, the disappearance of free government there may herald its demise elsewhere.

The decline of a civilization may be due to foreign conquest or internal causes which may well facilitate such a conquest. Age may be one of these causes, but there are others. Civilizations have perished because they became corrupted, went into extremes and lost measure. Plato and Aristotle mentioned various good types of government, seeing them as law-abiding and existing for the public good. We found these purposes expressed in the liberalisms of Montesquieu, Smith, Kant, and Jefferson. Plato and Aristotle also distinguish their good types of government from their corrupted forms and contrasted moderate democracy from extreme democracy and mob-rule,[146] suggesting our distinction between proper democracy and democracy proper, between liberalism and democracy.

Hayek expressed fear concerning the survival of liberal democracy in the United States. Since he is a man of measure,[147] he may well have thought that the possibility of excesses is greater in the United States than elsewhere. Of all liberal democracies, which are often called Western democracies, the United States is geographically located the farthest to the west. Is the country of Jefferson also the most western in the sense of Western democracy, the most liberal and the most democratic of all? Have liberalism and democracy gotten dimensions there which in the land of unlimited opportunities verge on the colossal and in their extremity jeopardize liberal democracy?

The opposite geographic location of the land of Kant indicates that with respect to the realization of liberal democracy it contrasts sharply with the United States, being as close as it is to absolutist Russia. As a matter of fact, while at the time of Jefferson Prussia could boast of great liberals aside from Kant, and was the only nation in Europe which agreed to Jefferson's proposal of free trade[148] she later got a reputation for not being liberal and did not introduce universal suffrage until 1917.[149] Prussia's image of being militaristic

145. Salvador de Madariaga, *Portrait of Europe* (University, Ala., 1967), 183, with respect to the Scandinavians.

146. See Sabine, *A History of Political Theory,* 74 ff., 101.

147. See Dietze, "Hayek on the Rule of Law," Machlup, *Essays on Hayek,* 107 ff.

148. Wilhelm von Humboldt, a contemporary of Kant, and Eduard Lasker, a contemporary of Bismarck, come to mind. Cf. Federico Federici, ed., *Der deutsche Liberalismus* (Zürich, 1946).

149. When after World War I a new German constitution was framed, it was done in Weimar, where Goethe and Schiller had lived, and not in Berlin, the Prussian capital of Germany. This was in a large measure due to the desire to symbolize the deprussianization of the Weimer constitution, which was reflected in a weakening of the Prussian government in the Reichsrat. It is interesting

prompted the Allied Control Council after World War II to eliminate her. But the ideas of man do not die with death; neither do those of a nation. The spirit of Prussia is alive today, as is testified by exhibitions in 1981 in both East and West Berlin. If that spirit is alive in the liberal democracy under the Bonn Basic Law, which in its original version abolished compulsory military service, it certainly is not alive, as it is in West Point and in Swiss military schools, because of its advocacy of military discipline. It lives because, even at the height of liberalism, Prussians emphasized the need for frugality and order. Many citizens feel that West Germany stands in need of such emphasis because the order of her consumer-society is being jeopardized by consumptive excesses of liberalism which in a large measure are attributed to Americanization.

Certainly Kant, the philosopher of Königsberg, is not forgotten in his fatherland at a time when the bicentennial of the publication of the *Critique of Pure Reason* is remembered. This bicentennial coincides closely with that of American independence, suggesting a further look at Kant and Jefferson. We have seen that both basically were in agreement regarding liberalism. Yet there were also points of difference which may account for the fact that liberalism and democracy have swelled to greater dimensions in the United States. They ought not to be overlooked in a discussion of the prospects of liberal democracy.

The American and the Prussian were natural aristocrats in the sense of Jefferson, but with a difference. Jefferson's achievements were in public, Kant's in academic life. A political career implies seeking acclaim and recognition by others, the search for the truth does not.[150] Desiring acclaim means catering to those by whom one wants to be recognized, and someone entering a political profession wants that recognition immediately. The academic calling, or exploration of the truth, requires constant criticism of others and therefore seldom is popular. *Maiorum gloria posteris lumen est.*[151] The one seeks the voice of the people as the voice of God, the other seeks God irrespective of public opinion. Jefferson wanted to be, and was, the man who drafted the Declaration of Independence, an honor that was likely to result in praise by his fellowmen. He wanted to be, and was, ambassador to Paris, a position full of glamor and social prestige. He wanted to be, and was, twice elected president of the United States, the most cherished and powerful position of his country. Against the tide, the professor at the University of Königsberg wrote, among other things, three critiques. Most people hardly took notice of him. *Mehr sein als scheinen.*[152] Jefferson was more free and irregular in his daily routine and in his way

that later on, Prussia stood for more of a liberalism than the government of the Reich. See *Preussen contra Reich vor dem Staatsgerichtshof* (1932), with a foreword by Arnold Brecht.

150. See Dietze, *Youth, University and Democracy* (Baltimore, 1970).

151. This inscription can be found in the Greek Cafe, near the Spanish Steps in Rome.

152. These words are attributed to Moltke. When he was seen by the king of Prussia riding by in his first parade, the king remarked that Moltke was not a good acquisition (Aquisition), because

of life than Kant, who was regular and disciplined to the point of pedantry, with people setting their watches by the minute he was passing their home. While they were both concerned with politics, Kant was a political scientist rather than a politician, Jefferson was a politician rather than a political scientist.

These differences had an impact upon their concepts of liberalism and democracy. Politics implies conceding and giving. Political science insists on restricting and adhering to principles. While both authors valued morality highly, Jefferson, the "Apostle of Freedom," was more generous in this advocacy of liberty than Kant, the "Liberator." According to this classification, Jefferson was more of a preacher and Kant, more of a teacher. Although Jefferson stated that man has no natural rights in opposition to his social duties, he advocated the rights of the individual in a broader sense than Kant. The same applies to the concepts of happiness and *Glückseligkeit.* Jefferson favored a wide concept, whereas Kant's categorical imperatives put duty above happiness and decried materialism. In the Declaration of Independence, which shows a strong influence of Locke's *Second Treatise,* Jefferson replaced Locke's "life, liberty and property" by "life, liberty and the pursuit of happiness." Although he probably did not want to change the substance of the Lockean concept of the rights of man,[153] he replaced a word, and the word is a master that can bring about an enormous change of meaning, especially if abused.[154] Combined with Jefferson's statement that man has no natural rights in opposition to his social duties, which can be contrasted to Kant's opinion that only the moral individual can enjoy freedom, Jefferson's substitution of property through happiness could have important consequences. By virtue of references to Jefferson[155] the development of democracy could take directions that deviated from one Kant would have appreciated. For there are, in addition, differences between Kant and Jefferson with respect to democracy. Although Jefferson had opposed an elective despotism, he who was considered "the most powerful advocate democracy has ever had" in the United States by the greatest observer democracy in America ever had,[156] favored popular government more unequivocally than Kant, who denounced democracy proper and found popular government acceptable only as a proper democracy duly limited by his concepts of liberalism.

---

he did not cut a great figure. Later on, after the successful wars against Denmark, Austria, and France, the king, now also emperor of Germany, wrote Moltke that he probably would not have been able to celebrate his 90th birthday hadn't it been for Moltke's help throughout his life.

153. See Dietze, *In Defense of Property,* 31–32.

154. An example for a change with far-reaching consequences is the replacement of *ius* by *lex,* or the translation of the Greek *nomos* by the Latin *lex.* Cf. Dietze, *Deutschland—Wo bist Du?,* 82.

155. During the New Deal especially, the Democratic party in the United States emphasized that it believed in the ideas of Jefferson. In the 1960s Barry Goldwater, attacking the New Deal, often made references to Jefferson, asserting that the New Deal was incompatible with his ideas.

156. De Tocqueville, *Democracy in America,* 1:270.

Since the days of Jefferson, the characteristic feature of democracy in America has been the march of democracy. The first great broadening of the suffrage took place in various states during Jefferson's last years. It was complemented by national civil rights measures in the 1860s, by the extension of the right to vote to women after World War I, and by civil rights legislation after World War II. After lapses amounting to approximately half a century, Americans became aware that their democracy was unfinished. As a result, the assumed need for electoral reform found expression in the laws.

A confession to democracy proper through an extension of the right to vote need not conflict with proper democracy, or liberal democracy or, as Americans often put it, free government. As a matter of fact, it always was hoped that an extended suffrage would increase, not endanger, the protection of the individual. This hope resulted from the rationale for the establishment of modern democracy and can be expressed by the formula: the greater the number of participants in the political process, the greater the protection of human rights.

Observers of the Warren Court, which was characterized by an enormous expansion of civil rights in an expanding democracy,[157] will claim that the hope that greater participation will lead to more freedom is justified. Yet during that period, there occurred unusually many riots. It will be answered that the latter were prompted by desires to increase rights and thus in the best liberal tradition. On the other hand, the question has been raised as to whether an abundance of rights as a result of the march of democracy unjustifiably may have whetted an insatiable appetite for further rights and led to indefensible riots.[158] The latter argument can be buttressed by the fact that the period of the Warren Court also witnessed an enormous increase in ordinary crime. Democracy expanded to a degree that the right of participating in making the law by voting turned into people's assuming they could take the law into their own hands and turn against law and order.[159] This can be called the anarchist effect of the expansion of democracy proper.

There also is a despotic effect of that expansion. It is the oppression of the minority and the individual by the majority. The oppression need not be all-out, as, for instance, in the case of slavery, which denied a minority all human rights, treating them as chattel. It can be an oppression of certain rights, of the kind that, as has been asserted, took place under the New Deal, when social legislation affected property owners. It is perhaps telling that such legislation has been favored by Americans for Democratic Action, a name symbolic of governmental design, as distinguished from what Smith, von Mises, and Hayek

157. See Alpheus T. Mason, "Understanding the Warren Court: Judicial Self-Restraint and Judicial Duty," *Political Science Quarterly* 81 (1966):523 ff.

158. See Dietze, "From the Constitution of Liberty to Its Deconstitution by Liberalistic Dissipation, Disintegration, Disassociation, Disorder," *Ordo* 30 (1979):177 ff.

159. See Dietze, "Rights, Riots, Crimes."

called human action,[160] defended by Americans for Constitutional Action who, in order to prevent the discrimination of property rights, want democratic power restrained by constitutional limitations.[161] One group desires to enlarge democracy proper at the expense of proper democracy, whereas the other tries to maintain proper democracy. All this indicates that in the United States, democracy or free government is on the defensive from unlimited democracy,[162] something that was envisaged by de Tocqueville.

Recent American development is another dimension of America's experience at the time of the founding of the republic. Two hundred years ago the problem was to what degree the majority, while ruling, should be restricted under law for the sake of minority rights and to what degree democracy proper should be made into a free government. In our day, the problem has been how free government can defend itself from democratic attacks upon liberalism.

It is a problem for most liberal democracies. The growth of democracy proper endangers proper democracy. In view of the fact that equality is the first god of democracy, the despotic effect of the expansion of democracy is likely to be a government that considers the unequal distribution of property an anomaly and will regulate economic rights through social legislation. The anarchist effect probably will be an excess of liberality and license and problems of law and order. Both effects bear out Acton's statement that power tends to corrupt.[163] The greater the number of those having the right to vote, the greater the probability that this right, supposed to influence the making of laws, will entice people to take the law into their own hands and in turn to break it. The power to vote thus tends to corrupt into the assumption that it justifies the right to act illegally. Furthermore, the greater the number of persons with the right to vote, the more the government is representative of the whole people and the more the ruling majority will feel entitled to carry out its mandate at the expense of the minority.

The problems of liberal democracy are enhanced by another aspect of

160. Ludwig von Mises, *Human Action;* Hayek, *Constitution of Liberty,* 54 ff.

161. Cf. Thomas M. Cooley, *A Treatise on the Constitutional Limitations Which Rest upon the Legislative Power of the States of the American Union* (Boston, 1868). For Americans for Constitutional Action, such limitations exist *a fortiori* on the national government, given its enormous increase of power since the days of Cooley.

162. See Dietze, *America's Political Dilemma,* the subtitle of which is *From Limited to Unlimited Democracy.*

163. To Bishop Creighton, Apr. 5, 1887, John N. Figgis and Reginald V. Lawrence, eds., *Historical Essays and Studies* (London, 1907), 504. John Adams wrote that "power is always abused when unlimited and unbalanced, whether it be permanent or temporary," that "absolute power intoxicates alike despots, monarchs, aristocrats, and democrats, and jacobins, and *sans culottes.*" "Defence of the Constitutions of Government of the United States of America," *Works* 6:73, 477. According to James Madison, "All power in human hands is liable to be abused," and "Power wherever lodged is liable more or less to abuse." To Thomas Ritchie on Dec. 18, 1825, and to Thomas Lehre on Aug. 2, 1828. Gaillard Hunt, ed., *The Writings of James Madison* (New York, 1900–1910), 9:232, 315.

voting power, namely, direct, as contrasted to indirect, democracy. This is evident in, but by no means restricted to, the United States. American democracy today comes close to another version of unlimited democracy its founders tried to avoid, the kind of direct popular rule they denounced and sought to replace by representative government.[164] According to James Madison, the latter constitutes a refinement of the public views.[165] And while the human frailty, abuse of power, and instability of officials elected without an imperative mandate ought not to be underestimated,[166] the danger of direct democracy is likely to be greater. In an age of shifting public opinions and opinion polls, elected representatives, irrespective of the Burke's concept of representation,[167] think of their reelection rather than selfless service to those to whom they pledged and are supposed to serve. Governments in liberal democracies are opinion-makers, -sifters, -shifters, and opinion-shakers. They can spawn oppression and anarchy at any time. Is the principle of modern liberal democracy the absence of principle?

The absence of principles to act by jeopardizes liberal democracy from without as well as from within. It amounts to a denial of the rule of law and is a source of arbitrariness.[168] It makes society vulnerable to foreign attacks. If

164. See Madison in *The Federalist,* essays 10 and 14.

165. According to Madison, representative government refines and enlarges the public views "by passing them through the medium of a chosen body of citizens, whose wisdom may best discern the true interest of their country, and whose patriotism and love of justice will be least likely to sacrifice it to temporary or partial considerations." Ibid., essay 10.

166. Most constitutions today provide for an absence of the imperative mandate and state that representatives shall vote according to their conscience and for the good of society irrespective of the wishes of their particular constituency, a notable exception being the representatives in the federal chambers of Germany under the constitutions of the Second Empire, the Weimar Republic and the Federal Republic Germany, in which the delegates vote according to the instructions of their respective state governments.

167. In "Two Letters to Gentlemen of Bristol," Burke stated: "Certainly gentlemen, it ought to be the happiness and glory of a representative, to live in the strictest union, the closest correspondence, and the most unreserved communication with his constituents. Their wishes ought to have great weight with him; their opinion high respect; their business unremitting attention. . . . But his unbiased opinion, his mature judgment, his enlightened conscience, he ought not to sacrifice to you, to any man, or to any set of men living. These he does not derive from your pleasure; no, nor from the law and the constitution. They are a trust from Providence, for the abuse of which he is deeply answerable." *The Works of Edmund Burke* (London, 1899), 2:12–13. In a speech at Bristol on his parliamentary conduct, Burke stated in 1780: "I did not obey your instructions. No. I conformed to the instructions of truth and Nature, and maintained your interest, against your opinions, with a constancy that became me. A representative worthy of you ought to be a person of stability. I am to look, indeed, to your opinions—but to such opinions as you and I *must* have five years hence. I was not to look to the flash of the day. I knew that you chose me, in my place, along with others, to be a pillar of the state, and not a weather-cock on the top of an edifice, exalted for my levity and versatility, and of no use but to indicate the shiftings of every fashionable gale." *Works* 2:382. Cf. Hans Barth, *The Idea of Order* (Dordrecht, 1960); Russell Kirk, *The Conservative Mind, from Burke to Santayana* (Chicago, 1953).

168. Viewing the rule of the state legislatures under the Articles of Confederation, Alexander

Prinzipienlosigkeit results in anarchy, foreign ideologies and nations will take advantage of the weakness it produces. If it leads to despotism, they will be tempted to attack in order to liberate. Aggressors always find excuses for attacking others, but sometimes excuses are handed to them on a platter by their victims.

The *Prinzipienlosigkeit* of liberal democracies, much as it may result from the growth of democracy proper, also is due to an excess of liberalism. While it may be an aspect of democracy proper, the absence of principles is innate to liberalism proper, for pure liberalism knows no bounds to the promotion of liberty, which suffers no restraints, and by definition has no limits. What has no limits cannot have restraining principles. Just as democracy proper, liberalism proper may well destroy liberal democracy.

Our search for a proper liberalism, as distinguished from liberalism proper, made us turn to the ideas of Montesquieu, Smith, Kant, and Jefferson, men standing at the beginning of the historical movement known as liberalism. Theirs is a measureful balance between the freedom of the individual and the well-being of the community. They recognize that what counts is not only the individualistic utilitarian concept of the greatest good for the greatest number, but an awareness in the greatest number that they have an obligation to bring about the greatest good for all, not just in a material sense but in an ethical one. While they desire a maximum of rights for the individual, including those of free enterprise and private property, they reject an excess of freedom. They do not want rights to be protected absolutely, but along with certain ethical and moral principles, of which the laws constitute a minimum, a prerequisite for the existence of their measureful kind of freedom.

In the age of legislation, the beginning of which closely coincides with that of the historical movement called liberalism, law was likely to change, with legislation superseding custom. As students of liberalism emphasized, law became problematical.[169] It would change more and more, faster and faster. There would be a good possibility that it would less and less approach the ethical or moral maximum. Montesquieu, Smith, Kant, and Jefferson probably envisaged this development and for that reason emphasized higher law and ethics.

Hamilton complained of "those occasional ill-humors, or temporary prejudices and propensities, which . . . beget injustice and oppression of a part of the community," of "those practices . . . which have undermined the foundations of property and credit, have planted mutual distrust in the breasts of all classes of citizens, and have occasioned an almost universal prostration of morals." *The Federalist,* essays 27, 85. Madison, in essay 62, stated: "The internal effects of a mutable policy are . . . calamitous. It poisons the blessings of liberty itself. It will be of little avail to the people, that the laws are made by men of their own choice, if the laws be so voluminous that they cannot be read, or so incoherent that they cannot be understood; if they be repealed or revised before they are promulgated, or undergo such incessant changes that no man, who knows what the law is to-day, can guess what it will be to-morrow."

169. See Schmitt, *Die Lage der europäischen Rechtswissenschaft;* Hayek. *Law, Legislation and Liberty.*

The question as to whether or not liberal democracy can survive the challenges of democracy proper and liberalism proper in a large measure depends on the degree to which democratic lawmakers will consider themselves bound by, and honor, morality and propriety in the sense of the great liberals analyzed here. Democracy proper is pure democracy, liberalism proper is pure liberalism. Liberal democracy, being a qualified democracy, is an impure democracy, much as it may be considered proper, good, ethical, moral. Purity is a formidable power and its victory over impurity seems to be inevitable. If art could arrive at the recognition of the principle, *l'art pour l'art,* and science, at that of *la science pour la science,* there is no reason why the century of liberalism could not produce a liberalism for the sake of liberalism, and the democratic era, a democracy for the sake of democracy. On the other hand, purist concepts such as *l'art pour l'art* and science for the sake of science have seen their day. It may well be that pure liberalism and pure democracy can never be victorious. If they temporarily are, they might fade away and leave the field to liberal democracy. This may well depend on whether or not liberal and democratic purists make concessions to the kind of propriety cherished by Montesquieu, Smith, Kant, and Jefferson, a propriety implying a high evaluation of private property as propriety's *alter ego,* a thought that had been cherished by Locke.

Since property is connected with Jefferson's concept of happiness, the latter, whether interpreted in the sense of the protection or redistribution of property, has a materialistic overtone. It can be considered all too egoistic and, in view of Jefferson's advocacy of a broadening of popular government, dangerous. For that reason, people may turn to Kant in hopes that his skepticism of democracy proper, combined with idealist moral categorical imperatives, will be appropriate for the preservation of liberal democracy against democracy and liberalism. Whether Kantian autolimitation will work in an era symbolized by the automobile, in a time that is much more democratic, liberalistic, and materialistic than his own, is another question.

INDEX